50 YEARS
lonely planet
OF TRAVEL

BUDAPEST & HUNGARY

Kata Fári, Shaun Busuttil, Steve Fallon, Anthony Haywood, Andrea Schulte-Peevers, Barbara Woolsey

CONTENTS

Plan Your Trip

The Guide

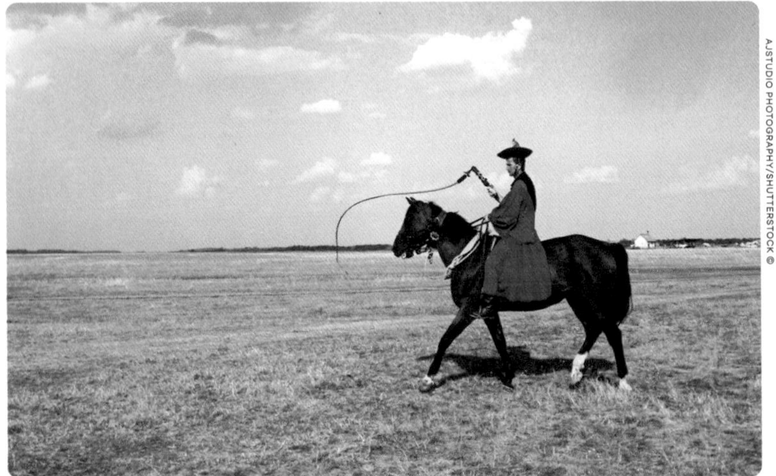

***Csikós* (cowboy), Hortobágy National Park (p214)**

Budapest Eye (p89)

Toolkit

Storybook

Traditional Matyó embroidery (p285)

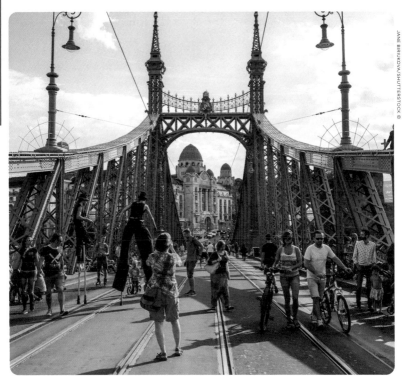

Liberty Bridge (p68)

BUDAPEST & HUNGARY

THE JOURNEY BEGINS HERE

Right in the heart of Europe, Hungary might be small, but it packs a big punch. The country is steeped in history and tradition, its bounty of Art Nouveau architecture is astonishing, its warm thermal waters are healing, and its cuisine is as delicious as it is hearty. When it comes to the most stunning capitals in Europe, Budapest lays serious claim to the crown, but it's so much more than a pretty face. Budapest and I go back a long way, and our story has involved leafy strolls around Margaret Island, long soaks at thermal baths, awe-inspiring sunsets savoured with a *fröccs* (wine spritzer) in hand and fun-filled nights lost in the Jewish District's buzzing bars. Carrying itself with such an effortless charm, Budapest makes you fall head over heels, and in cases like mine, it's a love that lasts forever.

My favourite experience is crossing Liberty Bridge. No matter how busy life gets, I always take time to look in awe at just how unbelievably beautiful Budapest is.

Kata Fári

@kata.fari

Kata is a writer and Budapest expert devoted to showing the Hungarian capital's beauty to all its visitors.

WHO GOES WHERE

Our writers and experts choose the places which, for them, define Hungary

LEFT: GEZA KURKA_HUNGARY/SHUTTERSTOCK ©
CENTER: KATARZYNA MAKSYMIUK/SHUTTERSTOCK ©

No matter what time of the day or night, the **Hungarian Parliament Building** is always a stunner. This mesmerising symbol of national sovereignty is the seat of the National Assembly of Hungary.

Shaun Busuttil

shaunbusuttil.com

Shaun is a writer and anthropologist working at the intersection of travel, culture and mobilities.

Hungary's capital, **Budapest**, has given me much since our first meeting decades ago, and there's no doubt that the 'Queen of the Danube' will offer you just as much.

Steve Fallon

steveslondon.com

Steve is a travel writer and a qualified London Blue Badge Tourist Guide. He's a prolific Lonely Planet contributor and has worked on every edition of this Budapest and Hungary guide.

The view from the hilltop **Pannonhalma Abbey** east of Sopron is stunning. But the rolling, stop-start journey by local train on a warm summer's day, the sweeping view from the curved walkway and hiking the forest trails are also what make this place so special.

Anthony Haywood

anthonyjhaywood.com

Anthony is a writer who has explored the Danube River from source to delta.

LEFT: ANDOCS/SHUTTERSTOCK ©
RIGHT: BERNI0004/SHUTTERSTOCK ©

Szeged has a captivating alchemy of setting, looks and experience, wrapping everything needed for a city trip into one neat package: stunning architecture, culture, lovely surroundings, a riverside location and fabulous food.

Andrea Schulte-Peevers

@aschulte-peevers

Andrea has written Lonely Planet guidebooks for 25 years.

I was drawn to **Pécs** by its ancient Roman origin story, grand baroque buildings and cultural touchstones from ceramics to contemporary art. But the hospitality of locals is what turned my crush on this city into a full-on love affair.

Barbara Woolsey

@xo_babxi

Barbara writes about the people behind food, travel and culture.

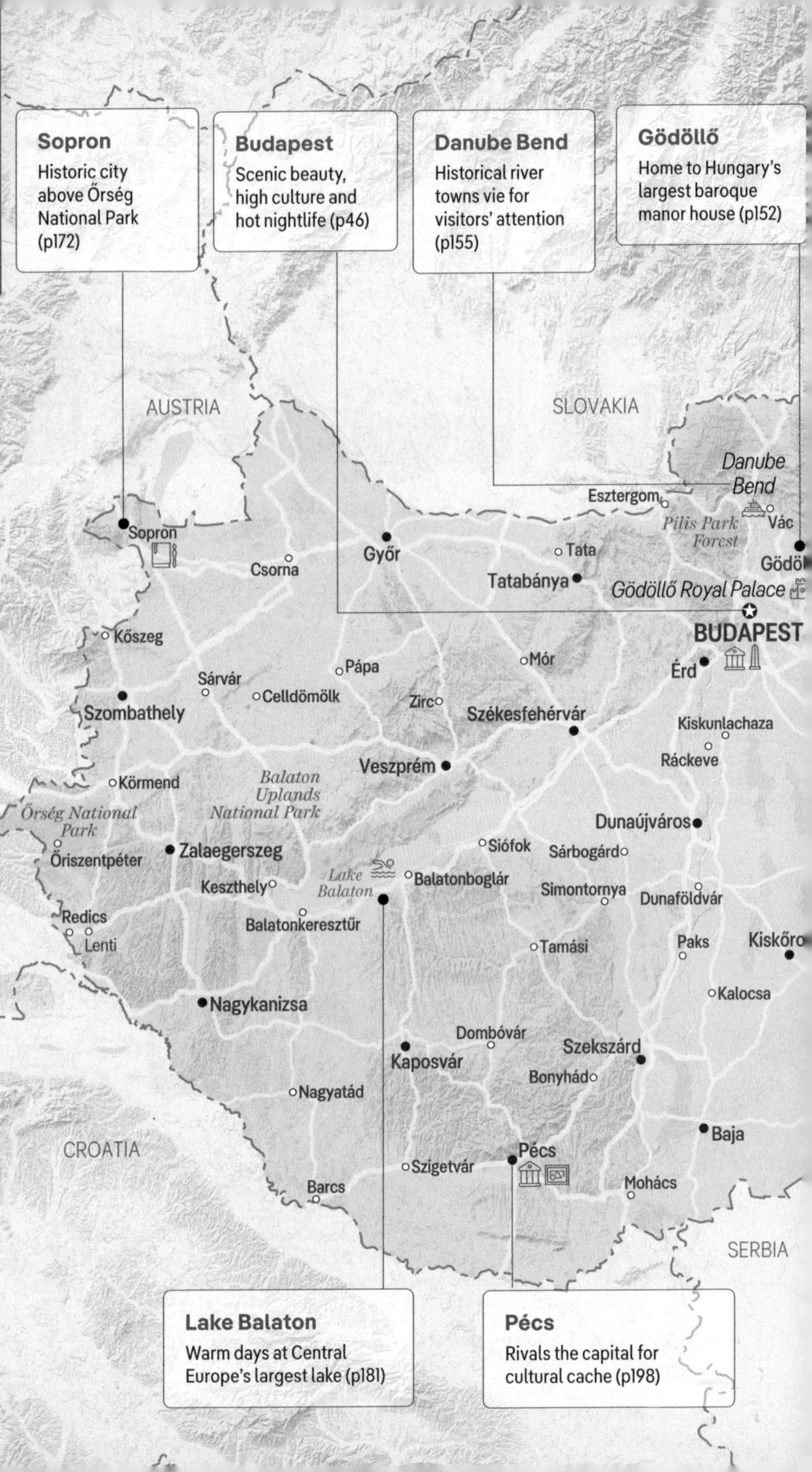
Sopron
Historic city above Őrség National Park (p172)
Budapest
Scenic beauty, high culture and hot nightlife (p46)
Danube Bend
Historical river towns vie for visitors' attention (p155)
Gödöllő
Home to Hungary's largest baroque manor house (p152)
AUSTRIA
SLOVAKIA
Danube Bend
Esztergom
Pilis Park Forest
Vác
Sopron
Csorna
Győr
Tata
Tatabánya
Gödöllő Royal Palace
BUDAPEST
Kőszeg
Pápa
Mór
Érd
Sárvár
Celldömölk
Zirc
Székesfehérvár
Szombathely
Kiskunlachaza
Ráckeve
Veszprém
Körmend
Balaton Uplands National Park
Őrség National Park
Dunaújváros
Őriszentpéter
Zalaegerszeg
Siófok
Sárbogárd
Keszthely
Lake Balaton
Balatonboglár
Simontornya
Dunaföldvár
Redics
Lenti
Balatonkeresztúr
Tamási
Paks
Kalocsa
Nagykanizsa
Dombóvár
Szekszárd
Kaposvár
Bonyhád
Nagyatád
Baja
CROATIA
Pécs
Szigetvár
Barcs
Mohács
SERBIA
Lake Balaton
Warm days at Central Europe's largest lake (p181)
Pécs
Rivals the capital for cultural cache (p198)

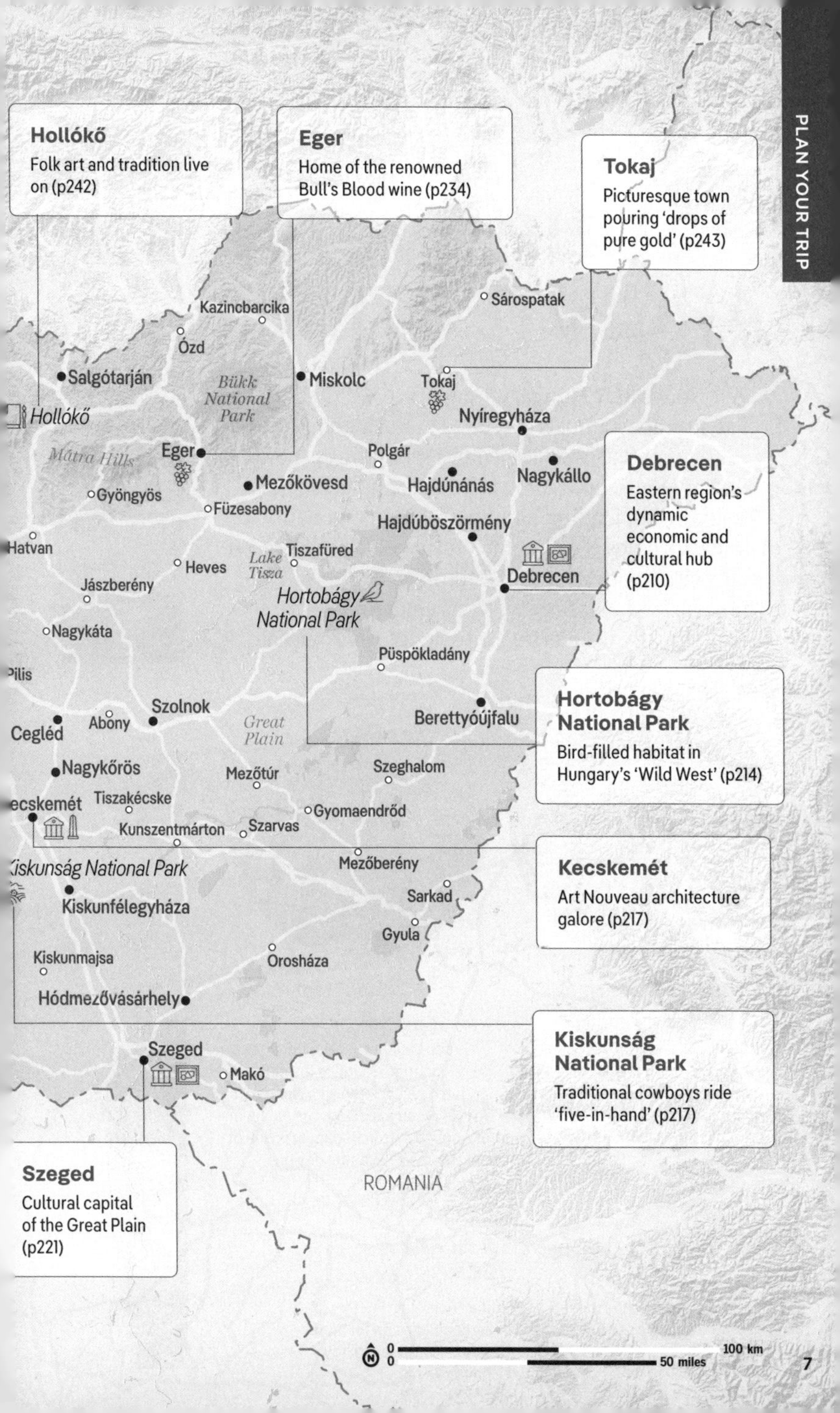
Hollókő
Folk art and tradition live on (p242)
Eger
Home of the renowned Bull's Blood wine (p234)
Tokaj
Picturesque town pouring 'drops of pure gold' (p243)
Sárospatak
Kazincbarcika
Ózd
Salgótarján
Bükk National Park
Miskolc
Tokaj
Hollókő
Nyíregyháza
Debrecen
Eastern region's dynamic economic and cultural hub (p210)
Mátra Hills
Eger
Polgár
Nagykállo
Hajdúnánás
Mezőkövesd
Gyöngyös
Füzesabony
Hajdúböszörmény
Hatvan
Lake Tisza
Tiszafüred
Heves
Debrecen
Jászberény
Hortobágy National Park
Nagykáta
Püspökladány
Pilis
Hortobágy National Park
Bird-filled habitat in Hungary's 'Wild West' (p214)
Szolnok
Berettyóújfalu
Cegléd
Abony
Great Plain
Nagykőrös
Mezőtúr
Szeghalom
ecskemét
Tiszakécske
Gyomaendrőd
Kunszentmárton
Szarvas
Mezőberény
Kecskemét
Art Nouveau architecture galore (p217)
iskunság National Park
Sarkad
Kiskunfélegyháza
Gyula
Kiskunmajsa
Orosháza
Hódmezővásárhely
Szeged
Makó
Kiskunság National Park
Traditional cowboys ride 'five-in-hand' (p217)
Szeged
Cultural capital of the Great Plain (p221)
ROMANIA
0
100 km
0
50 miles

ART NOUVEAU ARCHITECTURE

Art Nouveau is Hungary's signature architectural style, and examples can be seen throughout the capital and around the country. Buildings show off sinuous curves, flowing forms and colourful Zsolnay tiles, lending an unparalleled personality to Hungary's cities. This architectural golden age graced many cities with beautiful buildings: Budapest is the most blessed, but Szeged, Kecskemét and Debrecen have equally wonderful examples of Art Nouveau.

By Any Other Name

Art Nouveau is known as Szecesszió in Hungary, Sezessionstil in Austria, Jugendstil in Germany, Modern in Russia, Modernisme in Catalonia and Stile Liberty in Italy.

Architect Icon

Ödön Lechner, nicknamed the 'Hungarian Gaudí', is the main architect associated with Hungary's Art Nouveau buildings. The Museum of Applied Arts in Budapest is one of his most beautiful designs.

Famous Porcelain in Pécs

Established in 1853, the Zsolnay Porcelain Factory in Pécs was at the forefront of European design for more than 50 years. Many of its tiles decorate buildings around the country.

Cifrapalota (p219), Kecskemét

BEST ART NOUVEAU EXPERIENCES

Designed by Ödön Lechner in 1896, Budapest's **Museum of Applied Arts** ❶ is decorated with Zsolnay ceramic tiles inside and out. (p133)

Lindenbaum House ❷ was Budapest's first Art Nouveau block, and its entire front elevation is covered with suns, stars, peacocks, flowers and long-haired nudes. (p126)

Szeged's 1907 **Reök Palace** ❸ is a green-and-lilac Art Nouveau beauty that looks like a decoration at the bottom of an aquarium. (p222)

The 1902 **Cifrapalota** ❹ (Ornamental Palace) in Kecskemét features multicoloured majolica tiles decorating its 'waving' walls. (p219)

The facade of the 1912 County Hal in **Debrecen** ❺ has Zsolnay tiles and wonderful stained-glass windows of early Magyar chieftains. (p210)

Fisherman's Bastion (p55), Budapest

SCENIC VIEWS

The peak of Hungary's highest mountain is barely 1000m above sea level, but the country still boasts spectacular vistas across its rural and urban scenery. See history from a hilltop citadel along the Danube, enjoying the dramatic play of water, light and land, or get high at a viewpoint or rooftop bar in Budapest.

Take in Tihany

The 80m-high Tihany Peninsula is home to wild and vineyard-filled swaths of green and the most dramatic views across Lake Balaton.

Around the Bend

The wonderful panoramic view from the mighty fortress in Visegrád, completed in 1259, will convince you that the Danube River really does 'bend'.

BEST SCENIC EXPERIENCES

Cycle past peaceful meadows and through the hills of **Őrség National Park** ❶. (p178)

Climb the Cat's Stairs to **Esztergom Basilica** ❷ for a different angle on the Danube. (p168)

Enjoy views of the Danube, Gellért Hill and Pest from **Fisherman's Bastion** ❸ in Budapest. (p55)

Head for the hilltop **Pannonhalma Abbey** ❹ for all-encompassing views of the surrounding countryside. (p176)

See Budapest from above at a rooftop bar like **High Note Sky Bar** ❺ above the Aria Hotel. (p107)

FINE WINE

A century ago, Hungary was one of Europe's most important wine-making regions, but pests, war and Soviet-era mass production resulted in troubled times for Hungary's vineyards. Now a new generation is bringing passion and attention back to the tradition. The country's 22 wine regions boast diverse topographies and a lush range of reds and whites.

Wine Cellars

Various regions of Hungary are peppered with atmospheric wine cellars, where you can take a tour of the bottles or simply sample the fruits of their labour. The famed Tokaj wine region has some 3000 vineyards alone.

Gorgeous Scenery

Hungary has about 600 sq km of grape-growing ground. These verdant vineyards make for beautiful driving, hiking and cycling, as well as dinners with a picture-perfect panorama.

All in the Family

Many wineries are family-run businesses with only a few employees. Arrange your visit in advance by phone or email to ensure they are open and welcoming guests.

BEST WINE EXPERIENCES

More than two dozen wine cellars are carved into rock in the **Valley of the Beautiful Women** ❶. (p238)

Bolyki ❷ is set in a massive medieval stone quarry. It offers wine tastings and tours, but it's fine to just swing by for a glass. (p238)

Holdvölgy ❸, near Tokaj, sets up its wine tastings through its labyrinthine 600-year-old cellar network. (p246)

The brethren of **Pannonhalma Abbey** ❹ have resurrected the monastery's age-old tradition of winemaking. Taste their hard work on a terrace with views. (p176)

Pop a bottle at a regional wine festival, such as the summertime **Keszthely Wine Festival** ❺. (p194)

MUSIC FESTIVALS

This country knows how to put on a festival. Hungarians have a penchant for setting up wooden kiosks side by side, filling them with traditional fare, and eating, drinking and making merry for days on end. Hungary hosts increasingly popular music festivals where major headliners and up-and-coming acts hit the stage. To set the scene, many festivals take place near Lake Balaton or on an island in Budapest, so having a swim between sets is possible.

Beyond Music

Music rocks Hungary's festival stages from early afternoon until the break of dawn, but photo booths, arts and crafts, and film screenings entertain the crowds too.

Arrive in Style

Major music festivals often provide transfers from Budapest. Festival buses serve the countryside, while reaching Budapest's Sziget Festival is possible on a boat. Book ahead.

From Headliners to Rising Stars

At Hungary's major music festivals, you can enjoy multiple concerts a day by the hottest headliners, as well as by other popular local and international acts.

Sziget Festival (p85)

BEST MUSIC FESTIVAL EXPERIENCES

Hungary's most famous music festival, **Sziget Festival** 1, takes place on Óbuda Island and is Budapest's answer to Glastonbury. It attracts some 500,000 visitors every August. (p85)

Sopron's hugely popular **VOLT festival** 2 has 100,000 revellers rocking out to a diverse mix of musical genres.

Lake Balaton's **Strand Festival** 3 is smaller than the rest, but it stages big international names on the Balaton lakeside.

The open-air electronic **Balaton Sound** 4 creates a 24/7 party atmosphere for a hip crowd on its own beach at Lake Balaton. (p192)

The **Veszprém Street Music Festival** 5 just north of Lake Balaton features buskers from all over the world.

Balaton Cycling Route (p40)

BIKEPACKING

Boasting a mix of flat and hilly terrain, Hungary is ripe for a bikepacking adventure. Numerous cycling routes span the entire country, passing through a kaleidoscope of diverse landscapes from idyllic rural settings and forested horizons to rolling wine country and the dazzling Danube, and can be tackled at your own pace.

Overnight Accommodation

Wild camping is technically illegal in Hungary, but it is tolerated in rural areas. Hungary has more than 200 official campsites and even more hotels.

Road Conditions

From crunchy gravel roads to paved bike paths, road conditions in Hungary are generally good, and car traffic is respectful of cyclists.

BEST BIKEPACKING EXPERIENCES

Four EuroVelo routes (6, 11, 13 and 14) visit Hungary, including the Vienna-to-Budapest **Danube Cycle Path ❶**.

The 200km **Balaton Cycling Route ❷** goes around Central Europe's largest lake. (p40)

BUBA ❸, a 108km-long cycle path completed in 2022, links the capital to Lake Balaton.

Őrség National Park ❹ has campsites and routes through forests and villages. (p178)

The annual 1400km **Hungarian Divide ❺** is the longest unsupported cycling adventure in the country.

TRADITIONAL TÁNCHÁZ

Táncház (folk music and dance; literally 'dance house') is an excellent way to hear traditional Hungarian music and learn dances like the *karikázó* (circle dance) and *csárdas* (tavern dance). It's great fun and easy to find and attend, especially in Budapest, where the dance house revival began in 1972.

Seasonal Entertainment

The *táncház* season generally runs from September to June, but you'll likely find a meeting or performance in the capital year-round.

It's Everywhere

Budapest is the home of *táncház*, but you can find it across Hungary. In the capital, try the Aranytíz House of Culture or the Municipal Cultural House.

What's On

For upcoming events, check the Dance House Association website (Táncház Egyesület; tanchaz.hu).

BEST TÁNCHÁZ EXPERIENCES

Hungary's biggest *táncház* is the three-day **Táncháztalálkozó** ❶ (Dance House Festival) in early April at László Papp Budapest Sports Arena.

Fonó Buda Music House ❷ in Budapest has *táncház* programmes several times a week.

Keep an eye out for the Sültü band and the children's dance house hosted by the folk group Muzsikás at Budapest's **Municipal Cultural House** ❸.

Marczibányi tér Cultural Centre ❹ in Budapest has Hungarian, Moldovan and Csángó music and dance hosted regularly by the Guzsalyas band.

At the **Aranytíz House of Culture** ❺ in Budapest, you might catch a performance by Kalamajka Táncház, the major players behind the movement a half-century ago. (p107)

Szimpla Kert (p124), Budapest

RUIN BARS & GARDENS

No self-respecting partygoer clubs indoors in Hungary's warm summer months – that's what *kertek* (outdoor garden clubs) and *romkocsmák* (ruin bars) are for. These rough-and-ready venues began appearing in Budapest about 20 years ago when entrepreneurs turned empty spaces into pop-up bars. They're now found all over Hungary.

Year-Round Fun

Many ruin bars have transformed from ramshackle, temporary sites full of flea-market furniture to more slick, year-round fixtures with covered and heated areas.

What's On

Entertainment at ruin bars can include DJs, live music or jam sessions. Foosball, table tennis, pool and other pub games are common, and street food is often on the menu.

BEST RUIN BAR EXPERIENCES

Szimpla Kert ❶ is Budapest's first and most iconic ruin pub. It's filled with bric-a-brac, graffiti and art. (p124)

Szeged's **Maláta** ❷ is a hipster ruin bar with craft beer and a colourful cafe.

Roncsbár ❸ in Debrecen means 'wreck bar', but its covered courtyard with live music would do Budapest proud. (p210)

Cooltour Café ❹ in Pécs is a ruin pub with occasional live music and a rear garden. (p199)

Kaleidoszkóp Ház ❺ in Esztergom is a mix between a bistro, gallery, 'concert cave' and courtyard pub. (p168)

HUNGARIAN FOLK ART

Hungary has one of the richest folk traditions in Europe, and it occupies a sentimental spot in the nation's soul. Museums, villages, festivals and workshops around the country keep this artistic legacy alive. Differences in colours and styles identify the work's regional origin.

Festival of Folk Arts (p284), Budapest

Traditional Embroidery

Three groups stand out for their embroidery, the pinnacle of Hungarian folk art: the Palóc of the Northern Uplands, the Matyó from Mezőkövesd, and the women of Kalocsa.

Hungarian Heritage

The Museum of Applied Hungarian Folk Art in Budapest showcases collections of embroidery, carvings, leatherwork, pottery, metalwork and dolls dressed in traditional costume from around the country.

BEST FOLK ART EXPERIENCES

Explore the teensy village of **Hollókő** ❶, a living showcase of traditional folk art, architecture and the way of life for the Palóc people. (p242)

Admire wooden churches filled with naïve murals and the delicate needlework made by locals in the **Bereg region** ❷. (p246)

See the work of the finest artisans from all over Hungary at the mid-August **Festival of Folk Arts** ❸ in Budapest. (p284)

Immerse yourself in colourful floral Matyó embroidery by joining a tour or workshop at **Matyódesign** ❹ in Tard. (p241)

Visit Szentendre's **Margit Kovács Ceramic Collection** ❺, dedicated to the ceramicist who combined Hungarian folk, religious and modern themes. (p162)

REGIONS & CITIES

Find the places that tick all your boxes.

The Danube Bend & Western Transdanubia

PICTURESQUE TOWNS AND REMOTE FOREST

Lined with romantic riverside towns such as Szentendre, Esztergom and Visegrád, the Danube Bend makes a perfect getaway from Budapest. Visit this region for sprawling vistas and historic castles. Further west, the city of Sopron is ready to reveal its long history and colourful houses to curious travellers.

p155

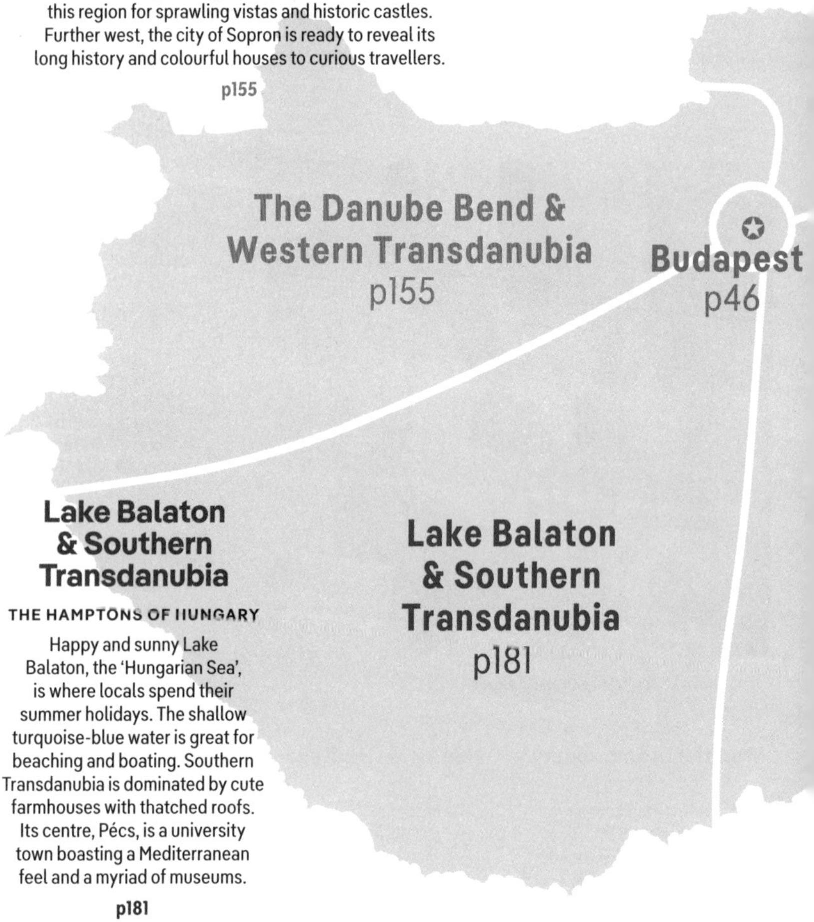

The Danube Bend & Western Transdanubia
p155

Budapest
p46

Lake Balaton & Southern Transdanubia
p181

Lake Balaton & Southern Transdanubia

THE HAMPTONS OF HUNGARY

Happy and sunny Lake Balaton, the 'Hungarian Sea', is where locals spend their summer holidays. The shallow turquoise-blue water is great for beaching and boating. Southern Transdanubia is dominated by cute farmhouses with thatched roofs. Its centre, Pécs, is a university town boasting a Mediterranean feel and a myriad of museums.

p181

Northern Hungary

WINE, FOLKLORE AND FORESTS

Northern Hungary is as hilly as the country gets. Hike on forested trails amid lovely rolling hills and scout castle ruins. Explore the gorgeous green Bükk National Park and the Mátra and the Zemplén Mountains before tasting delicious red wines from Eger and scrumptiously sweet whites from Tokaj.

p229

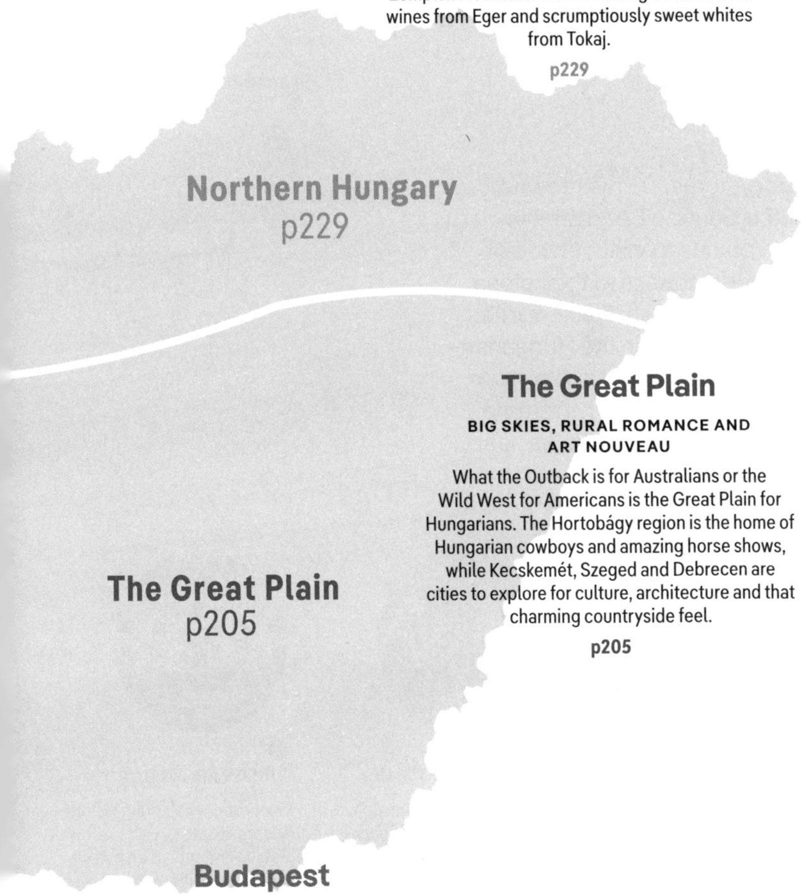

Northern Hungary
p229

The Great Plain
p205

The Great Plain

BIG SKIES, RURAL ROMANCE AND ART NOUVEAU

What the Outback is for Australians or the Wild West for Americans is the Great Plain for Hungarians. The Hortobágy region is the home of Hungarian cowboys and amazing horse shows, while Kecskemét, Szeged and Debrecen are cities to explore for culture, architecture and that charming countryside feel.

p205

Budapest

SCENIC BEAUTY, HIGH CULTURE AND PARTIES

Budapest, the grand dame on the Danube, is Central Europe's most beautiful city. It safeguards a fin-de-siècle splendour with baroque, neoclassical, Eclectic and Art Nouveau buildings galore; has countless historic landmarks; offers healing thermal waters to satisfy soakers; and entices cool crowds with its unparalleled nightlife.

p46

ITINERARIES

Budapest & the Bend

Allow: 6 Days
Distance: 275km

The picturesque river towns of the Danube Bend are the best places to visit outside of Budapest thanks to their close proximity to the capital. Further west in a crook in the Hungarian–Austrian border lies the historic city of Sopron and the remote forests and rustic villages near Őrség National Park.

❶

BUDAPEST ⏱ 2 DAYS

Start the journey in **Budapest** (p46). Pack in a dense concentration of heavyweight sights, such as the Castle Museum and the Hungarian National Gallery, on a visit to the compact Castle District. Don't miss the splendid view of the Pest skyline from Fisherman's Bastion. Wrap up your whirlwind days in the capital by hopping on the H5 suburban train to Szentendre.

❷

SZENTENDRE ⏱ 1 DAY

Soak up the artsy atmosphere of **Szentendre** (p160) by walking its cobblestone streets past colourful houses and visiting its intriguing churches, museums and galleries. Learn about the local way of life just outside town at the Hungarian Open-Air Ethnographic Museum, an ambitious *skanzen* (folk museum displaying village architecture). Buildings and even villages have been reconstructed, teleporting travellers to all corners of the country.

❸

VISEGRÁD ⏱ 1 DAY

Spend a day exploring historic **Visegrád** (p164). Visit the Royal Palace and set out on a short hike to the ruins of the Citadel, one of the most prominent and photographed spots in the Danube Bend.

Detour: *Head to Dömös to hike up to the Prédikálószék Lookout Tower, which provides the absolute best panorama of the Danube Bend.*

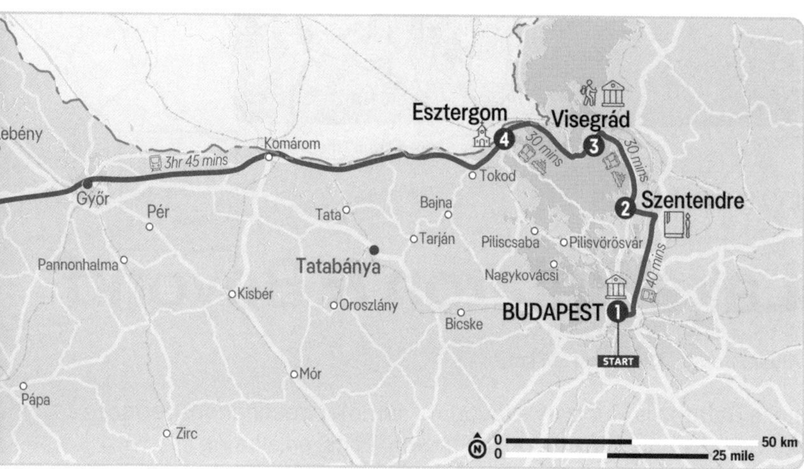

4
ESZTERGOM 1 DAY

Esztergom (p168) is home to the breathtaking basilica, Hungary's largest church. It's a 19th-century reconstruction of the cathedral where the country's first king, Stephen I, was crowned and was the seat of Roman Catholicism in Hungary for more than 1000 years. Esztergom is a small but picturesque town to walk around, and you can even cross the bridge to step foot in Slovakia.

5
SOPRON 1 DAY

Take in the many monuments of **Sopron** (p172). The iconic Fire Tower provides fabulous views, and on a clear day, you can see as far as Austria. After a day around the city, relax at a wine bar and try Kékfrankos, the region's characteristic red wine.

Detour: *For serene scenery and the chance to spot wildlife, visit nearby Lake Fertő or Őrség National Park.*

SHAUN BUSUTTIL/LONELY PLANET ©

Lake Balaton from Tihany (p190)

ITINERARIES

Lake Balaton & Beyond

Allow: 7 days **Distance:** 365km

Lake Balaton is Hungary's favourite summer destination, perfect for boating and relaxing on the beach. Pécs, an alluring city with museums galore, anchors the region of Southern Transdanubia, where whitewashed farmhouses with thatched roofs dot the landscape.

1 BUDAPEST 2 DAYS

Spend at least two days exploring the splendid sites, historic landmarks and lively nightlife of **Budapest** (p46). Cure any lingering hangover with a dip in the healing waters of the capital's gorgeous thermal baths, such as Gellért, Széchenyi or Rudas. Visit the Drinking Halls at the bathhouses to taste the water and bring your own bottle to take some with you on your trip.

2 BALATONFÜRED 1 DAY

Leave behind the buzz of Budapest to feel the tranquil atmosphere in **Balatonfüred** (p186), the oldest and most fashionable resort on Lake Balaton's northern shore. Stroll the lakeside Tagore Sétány promenade, savouring the picture-postcard marinas over a coffee or ice cream. Relax at a beach and then take a romantic sunset cruise to see off the day with a perfect pink sunset.

3 TIHANY 1 DAY

Set on a peninsula extending 5km into the lake, **Tihany** (p190) is the place on Lake Balaton with the most historical significance. Visit the Benedictine Abbey Church and have a meal at the panoramic Echo Restaurant. Spend the afternoon walking around the thatched-roof houses and trying lavender-infused treats, or hop on the cute mini train for a breezy sightseeing tour.

BOTOND HORVATH/SHUTTERSTOCK ©, ANDRAS_CSONTOS/SHUTTERSTOCK ©, KLAGYIVIK VIKTOR/ SHUTTERSTOCK ©

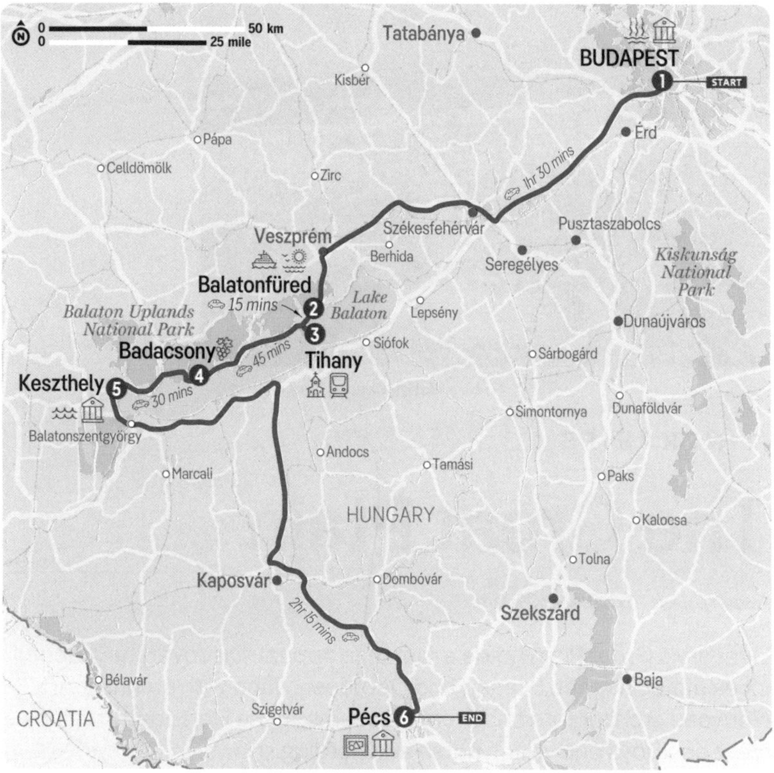

0 50 km
0 25 mile
Tatabánya
BUDAPEST
1 START
Kisbér
Érd
Pápa
Celldömölk
Zirc
1hr 30 mins
Székesfehérvár
Pusztaszabolcs
Veszprém
Berhida
Seregélyes
Kiskunság National Park
Balatonfüred
15 mins
2
Lake Balaton
Lepsény
Balaton Uplands National Park
3
Dunaújváros
Badacsony
Siófok
4
45 mins
Tihany
Sárbogárd
Keszthely
5
30 mins
Simontornya
Dunaföldvár
Balatonszentgyörgy
Andocs
Marcali
Tamási
Paks
HUNGARY
Kalocsa
Tolna
Kaposvár
Dombóvár
2hr 15 mins
Szekszárd
Bélavár
Baja
CROATIA
Szigetvár
Pécs
6 END

❹ **BADACSONY** ⏱1 DAY

The rolling hills around **Badacsony** (p188) provide the fertile grounds for grapes that make Hungary's exceptional wines. Hike or bike between wineries to sample the local bottles and enjoy top-notch food.

Detour: *Nearby Szigliget, crowned by a castle, is one of the most atmospheric villages of Lake Balaton's north shore. To the north, Szent-György Hill is an excellent viewpoint for sunset.*

❺ **KESZTHELY** ⏱1 DAY

At the western tip of Lake Balaton, **Keszthely** (p194) offers smaller crowds and more relaxation than other lakeside towns closer to Budapest. The main site to visit is the glimmering white 18th-century Festetics Palace. The palace's greatest treasure is the Helikon Library, with 90,000 volumes and splendid carved furniture. Nearby **Hévíz** (p197) is home to Europe's largest thermal lake.

❻ **PÉCS** ⏱1 DAY

Many travellers rank **Pécs** (p198) second only to Budapest, and it's one of the most interesting cities to visit in Hungary for its cool university-town vibe and interesting museums. The sprawling Zsolnay Cultural Quarter is built on the grounds of the original 1853 Zsolnay porcelain factory, which was at the forefront of European art and design for more than half a century.

ZGPHOTOGRAPHY/SHUTTERSTOCK ©

Votive Church, Szeged (p221)

ITINERARIES

The Great Plain

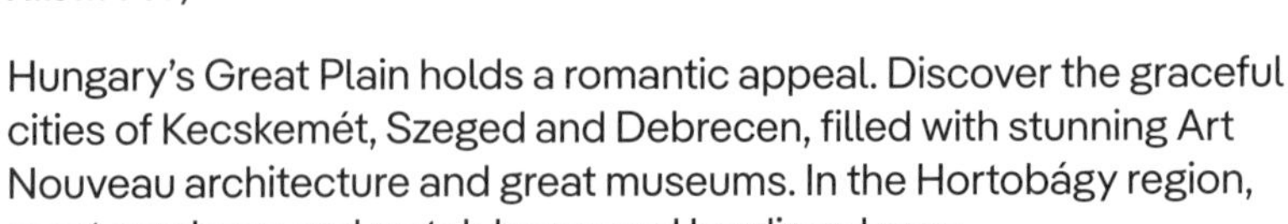

Allow: 6 days **Distance:** 390km

Hungary's Great Plain holds a romantic appeal. Discover the graceful cities of Kecskemét, Szeged and Debrecen, filled with stunning Art Nouveau architecture and great museums. In the Hortobágy region, meet cowboys and watch horse and herding shows.

1

BUDAPEST 2 DAYS

Immerse yourself in culture – and a thermal bath – in **Budapest** (p46). Visit the Ethnographic Museum in City Park to see ceramics from around the globe and a huge model of how Budapest looked in 1910. Melt away tense muscles at Széchenyi Baths, which has 15 indoor thermal pools and three outdoor pools, before listening to live folk music at an authentic *táncház* ('dance house').

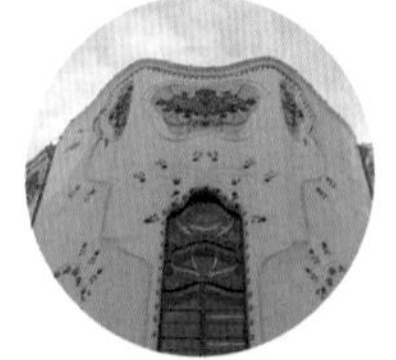

2

KECSKEMÉT 1 DAY

Drool over architecture in **Kecskemét** (p217). Cifra Palace is one of the best examples of Hungarian Art Nouveau, and City Hall is adorned with colourful Zsolnay tiles. Its bells play every hour to honour Kecskemét-born composer Zoltán Kodály. Kecskemét is the gateway to **Kiskunság National Park** (p217) – a fabulous place for birdwatching – and is famous for its apricot *pálinka* (fruit brandy).

3

SZEGED 1 DAY

Straddling the Tisza River, **Szeged** (p221) is the Great Plain's cultural capital. This lovely university town has a charming pedestrian area, the gorgeous Votive Church, green spaces and year-round cultural events. The Szeged Open-Air Festival in summer brings folk dancing, music and opera to the city's main square. Sample Szeged's foods, including Pick, Hungary's finest salami.

ATTILA KISBENEDEK/GETTY IMAGES ©, SKOVALSKY/SHUTTERSTOCK ©, SERGII KORSHUN/ SHUTTERSTOCK ©

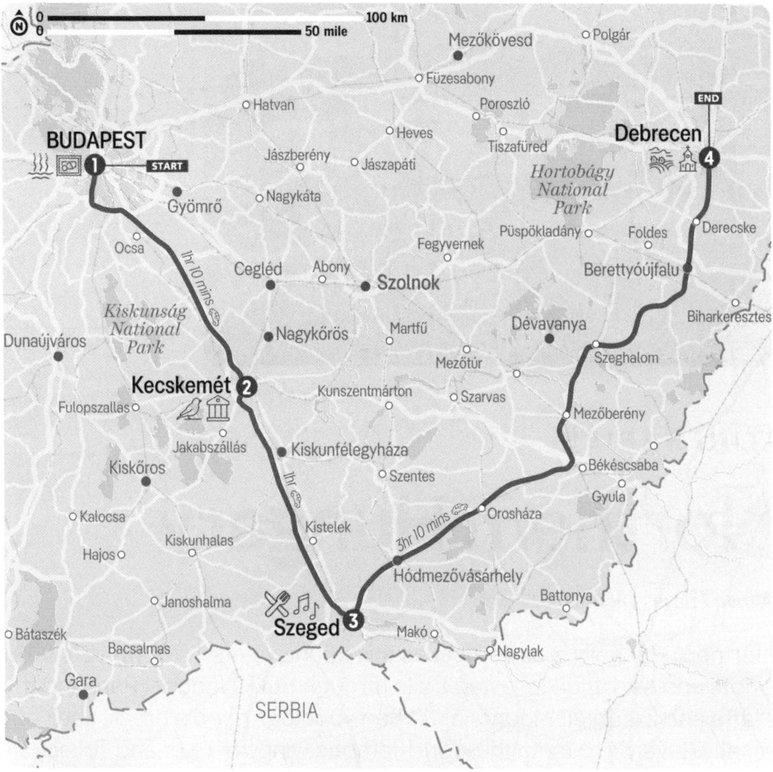

0 100 km
0 50 mile
BUDAPEST 1 START
Kecskemét 2
Szeged 3
Debrecen 4 END
1hr 10 mins
1hr
3hr 10 mins
Mezőkövesd
Polgár
Füzesabony
Hatvan
Poroszló
Heves
Tiszafüred
Jászberény
Jászapáti
Hortobágy National Park
Gyömrő
Nagykáta
Püspökladány
Foldes
Derecske
Ocsa
Fegyvernek
Cegléd
Abony
Szolnok
Berettyóújfalu
Kiskunság National Park
Biharkeresztes
Nagykőrös
Martfű
Dévavanya
Dunaújváros
Mezőtúr
Szeghalom
Kunszentmárton
Szarvas
Fulopszallas
Mezőberény
Jakabszállás
Kiskunfélegyháza
Kiskőrös
Békéscsaba
Szentes
Gyula
Kalocsa
Orosháza
Kistelek
Kiskunhalas
Hajos
Hódmezővásárhely
Battonya
Janoshalma
Bátaszék
Makó
Bacsalmas
Nagylak
Gara
SERBIA

4

DEBRECEN 2 DAYS

In **Debrecen** (p210), marvel at the grandeur of the city's iconic Great Church and visit the main square, where street festivals take place in summer. Try the namesake meat-filled pancake. From Debrecen, you can visit Hungary's first national park, the unspoiled **Hortobágy National Park** (p214), to witness Hungarian cowboys pulling off impressive stunts and showing off their skills with horses.

Great Church, Debrecen (p210)

EVRYKA/SHUTTERSTOCK ©

Lillafüred

ITINERARIES

Northern Hungary

Allow: 7 days **Distance:** 250km

Northern Hungary is as vertical as this country gets. Lace up your hiking boots and set off on forested trails through Bükk National Park and the Mátra and Zemplén Mountains. When your legs need a break, seek out local vineyards to taste the world-famous wines of Eger and Tokaj.

1 BUDAPEST 2 DAYS

Even in the capital of **Budapest** (p46), it's easy to get outdoors to prepare for the rest of this trip. The Buda Hills offer great walking and the loftiest views of the city. The Elisabeth Lookout Tower sits atop the highest point in Budapest, and the 360-degree panorama – or the 100-step spiral staircase to the top – will take your breath away.

2 EGER 2 DAYS

Relaxed **Eger** (p234) is flanked by two ranges of inviting hills. Some of Hungary's best wines come from this region, including the renowned Bull's Blood (Egri Bikavér). You can try Eger's wines at many places around town, but in the Valley of Beautiful Women, wine cellars are carved into the hillside, and you can walk from one to the next tasting local bottles.

3 BÜKK NATIONAL PARK 1 DAY

Bükk (p239) is an easily accessible natural escape, and its plateaus and pine forests hide wildlife, hiking trails and serene waterfalls. An old-timey narrow-gauge train chugs through Szalajka Valley, and a forest-fringed lake with Renaissance castle hotel makes the romantic village of **Lillafüred** a perfect place to stop on the way to Tokaj.

GEZA KURKA_HUNGARY/SHUTTERSTOCK ©, ALIZADA STUDIOS/SHUTTERSTOCK ©, MGY/ SHUTTERSTOCK ©

Aggtelek
Rimavská Sobota
Hantianske Nemce
Encs
Putnok
Kazincbarcika
Ózd
Sajószentpéter
END
Szerencs
Lillafüred
Miskolc
1hr 20 mins
4 Tokaj
Balassagyarmat
Szécsény
Salgótarján
1hr
3 Bükk National Park
Bátonyterenye
Nyékládháza
Tiszavasvári
Pásztó
Recsk
Szirák
Kékestető (1014m)
2 Eger
Polgár
Hajdúnánás
Vác
Mezőkövesd
Gyöngyös
1h 30 mins
Füzesabony
Kartal
Kat
Hajdúböszörmény
Fót
Hatvan
START
Godöllő
Jaszarokszallas
Heves
Tiszafüred
Hortobágy
1 BUDAPEST
Jászberény
Hajdúszoboszló
Gyömrő
Nagykáta
Kunmadaras
Kunhegyes
Püspökladány
Berettyóújfalu
Szolnok
Cegléd
Törökszentmiklós
Mezőtúr
Dévavanya
0 50 km
0 25 mile

4

TOKAJ ⏱ 2 DAYS

At the confluence of the Bodrog and Tisza Rivers, **Tokaj** (p243) has produced world-renowned sweet wines since the 15th century. It's just one of 28 towns and villages of Tokaj-Hegyalja, a 70-sq-km vine-growing region. Grapes growing on the lush hills make wonderful dry whites, but it's the Tokaji Aszú dessert wines that are the 'drops of pure gold' referenced in the Hungarian national anthem.

Vineyards around Tokaj (p243)

WHEN TO GO

Hungary is at its busiest in summer and during the winter holidays, but it's best to visit in spring or autumn.

Hungary's shoulder seasons of spring and autumn welcome travellers with pleasant weather, reasonable prices and smaller crowds at museums and historic sites. From March to June, Hungary is in full bloom, with wildflowers covering the hillsides. Summer continues into September, which means the weather is still balmy, but prices start to drop. In October and November, the country prepares for a quiet, dormant season, and the landscapes explode in gorgeous autumnal colours of red, brown and yellow. Winter settles in with cold and dreary weather. Because Hungary doesn't have many evergreens, this season is especially bare, and the sun sets at 4pm. But in December, the country often covers itself with a blanket of snow and turns on lovely fairy lights everywhere.

On a Budget

You can get the best deals on accommodation in November, January and February, but attractions and museums sometimes close or have limited opening hours.

I LIVE HERE

CASTLES & WINE

Kecskemét local and multisport paratriathlete Péter Boronkay shares his favourite place to visit. @peterbotonkay

I've travelled to many places, but the Zemplén Mountains hold a special place in my heart. The Füzér, Regéc, Boldogkő, Sárospatak and Szerencs castles and the Amadé castle ruin are all around here, and wine cellars serving amazing Tokaj wines abound. This area is a perfect place for hikes and cycling any time of year because it shows a different face in every season.

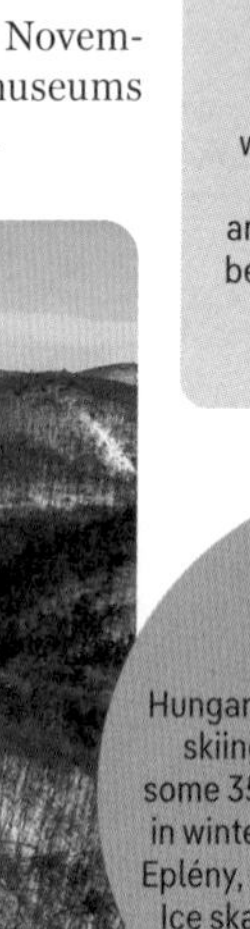

Füzér Castle

SNOWY SCENES

Hungary might not be a well-known skiing destination, but it offers some 35km of snow-covered slopes in winter. The largest ski resort is in Eplény, and the highest in Kékestető. Ice skating is sometimes possible on Lake Balaton.

Weather Through the Year

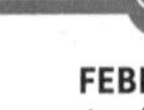

JANUARY	FEBRUARY	MARCH	APRIL	MAY	JUNE
Av. daytime max: **3°C**	Av. daytime max: **5°C**	Av. daytime max: **11°C**	Av. daytime max: **17°C**	Av. daytime max: **22°C**	Av. daytime max: **25°C**
Days of rainfall: 9	Days of rainfall: 7	Days of rainfall: 6	Days of rainfall: 7	Days of rainfall: 6	Days of rainfall: 6

CONTINENTAL CLIMATE

Hungary has a continental climate with four distinct seasons: winter (December to February), spring (March to May), summer (June to August) and autumn (September to November). January is the coldest month – sometimes blocks of ice float down the Danube – and July is the warmest.

Must-Visit Festivals & Events

Hungary's biggest carnival *(farsang)* is the Unesco-recognised **Busójárás** (p202) in Mohács. Men don scary masks and woolly outfits to scare away winter. The finale is a huge bonfire. **Late February/early March**

See **Easter** traditions, such as men reciting poems to women and drenching them in perfume or water to get painted eggs and homemade treats in return, in the World Heritage village of Hollókő (p242). **April**

Budapest's answer to Glastonbury is **Sziget Festival** (p85), which hosts big-name headliners and smaller acts, as well as other attractions from a funfair to bungee jumping. **August**

Santa Claus comes to Hungary on 6 December, so the country is in a holiday mood for the whole month. All major towns set up **Christmas markets**; the biggest and best is on Budapest's Vörösmarty tér. **December**

I LIVE HERE

SWEET SUMMER EVENINGS

Artist and longtime Budapest resident Marcus Goldson shares his favourite place to visit. @marcusgoldson

I always like going to Római-part, especially in early summer when the weather is not boiling yet. The Danube flows south behind a tree-lined path dotted with cafes, bars and restaurants on the beach and a little further inland. I love having a drink at Fellini's, overseen by the relaxing flow of the river.

Local Art, Wine & Culture Festivals

To see *la vie en rosé,* head to Budapest's City Park during the family-friendly **Rosalia Rosé and Champagne Festival**, when it fills with kiosks offering refreshing rosé wines and fizzy champagnes. **May**

The annual all-arts **Valley of Arts Festival** turns streets, buildings and institutions in three picturesque Balaton villages into concert halls, galleries and theatres, filling them with hundreds of events over 10 days. **July**

For great wine, good food and all that jazz, visit the **Paloznak Jazz Picnic**, which serenades a hillside Balaton village with live performances accompanied by tasty wine. **August**

When lavender is in full bloom, the town of Tihany becomes a purple paradise for the **Tihany Lavender Festival** (p190). Try lavender-infused drinks and desserts, buy crafts, tour the lavender fields and join the harvest. **Mid-June/early July**

SPLASHING INTO SUMMER

Lake Balaton, 'the Hungarian Sea', is the country's favourite summer destination, and locals love paddling and playing in the shallow water and going out on boats. The water temperature is 20°C to 28°C in summer, while outside temperatures generally nudge towards 35°C.

JULY	AUGUST	SEPTEMBER	OCTOBER	NOVEMBER	DECEMBER
Av. daytime max: **27°C**	Av. daytime max: **26°C**	Av. daytime max: **22°C**	Av. daytime max: **18°C**	Av. daytime max: **8°C**	Av. daytime max: **4°C**
Days of rainfall: 5	Days of rainfall: 5	Days of rainfall: 5	Days of rainfall: 6	Days of rainfall: 9	Days of rainfall: 7

Gellért Baths (p67), Budapest.

GET PREPARED FOR HUNGARY

Useful things to load in your bag, your ears and your brain

Clothes

Style Hungarians generally dress casually in jeans and a t-shirt, so no need to bring anything too fancy.

Shoes Plan to do a great deal of walking, including on cobblestone streets, so wear comfortable shoes. Bring trainers or hiking boots for trips into caves, up into the hills and in the countryside.

Swimsuits No matter the season, pack your swimsuit for Hungary, which has thermal spas, bathhouses and lakes to enjoy year-round.

Layers Winters get cold. Snow can be expected from December to February, so bring enough warm clothes.

Flip-flops Whether you're heading to Lake Balaton, Lake Hévíz or any of Hungary's thermal baths, bring flip-flops because the floors can be slippery.

Hats Pack a warm hat for winter, and in summer, protect yourself from the strong sun.

Manners

Punctuality is important to Hungarians. Arrive on time if you're invited somewhere or book a restaurant table.

Some Hungarians refuse to **clink glasses of beer** because this was how the Austrians celebrated the quell of the 1848 Revolution.

If you're invited to someone's home, **bring a small gift**, such as a bouquet of flowers or a bottle of good local wine.

READ

The Door (Magda Szabó; 1987) This deep novel examines the relationship between a writer and her housekeeper.

The Paul Street Boys (Ferenc Molnár; 1906) The story of a war between boys living in 1900s Budapest.

Fatelessness (Imre Kertész; 1975) Harrowing tale of the Holocaust by Hungary's only Nobel Prize–winning author.

Embers (Sándor Márai; 1942) A friendly dinner begins to resemble a trial for a man who disappeared for 41 years.

Words

'Szia/sziasztok' (see ya/ see ya-stoke) is a friendly way to say 'hi' to one or more people. It also means 'goodbye'.

To greet people more formally at different times of the day, say **'Jó reggelt/ napot/estét'** (yoh reg-gelt/ nah-poht/esh-tet), meaning 'good morning/afternoon/ evening'.

'Viszontlátásra' (vee-saunt-lah-tash-ra) is a polite way to say 'goodbye'.

'Köszönöm' (kew-sew-newm) means 'thank you'.

A less formal and more friendly way is to say **'köszi'** (kew-see).

Open with **'elnézést'** (el-ney-zeysht; 'excuse me') if you want to approach someone on the street with a question or if someone is in your way.

'Bocsánat' (boh-cha-not) is a way to say 'sorry'. The shorter informal word is **'bocsi'** (bo-chi).

'Szívesen' (see-ve-shen) means 'you're welcome'.

'Semmi baj' (shem-me-boy) is how to say 'no problem' or 'no worries'.

Say **'egészségedre'** (ag-eh-sheg-ad-reh), meaning 'cheers', when you clink glasses, and don't forget to look into the other person's eyes. Hungarians use the same word to say 'bless you' when someone sneezes. Among friends, you can say **'egs'** (eggsh).

'Puszi' (poo-see) doesn't mean what it sounds like in English. It means 'kiss' (on the cheek), and Hungarians use it to say 'goodbye'. Sometimes you'll hear words like this get repeated to show more affection: 'puszi-puszi', 'szia-szia'.

WATCH

Sunshine (István Szabó; 1999) Epic film about three generations of a Hungarian Jewish family.

Kontroll (Nimród Antal; 2003) Quirky comic thriller about a Budapest ticket inspector.

Son of Saul (László Nemes; 2015; pictured above) Unflinching story of an Auschwitz prisoner's quest to bury his son.

Bad Poems (Gábor Reisz; 2018) An ironic look at Hungarian society through the story of Tamás, who's coping with a breakup.

Spy (Paul Feig; 2015) Action comedy starring Melissa McCarthy and the beautiful buildings of Budapest and Lake Balaton.

LISTEN

Levél Nővéremnek 2 (Tamás Cseh; 1994) Poetry mingled with music. *Forró a Város* is the best soundtrack for a Budapest walk.

X (Szabó Balázs Bandája; 2019) This band brings folk music back into fashion with funk, pop and modern beats.

Csavargó (Bohemian Betyars; 2017) Folk, Roma and Balkan sounds with a ska-like upbeat tempo to make your body groove.

Egyszer Volt (Margaret Island; 2015) Combining folk elements with indie pop, this band makes music that moves the soul.

SLAWOMIR FAJER/SHUTTERSTOCK ©

Beef stew with egg dumplings

THE FOOD SCENE

Dig into dining in Hungary, where the portions are hearty, the dishes are meaty and the service is friendly.

'You can't have been here that long – you haven't got a pot belly', Prince Philip, Duke of Edinburgh, said to a British person in Budapest in 1993. Touché. Traditional Hungarian fare is rich, hearty and spicy, and Hungarians are enthusiastic eaters and friendly hosts. The country's cuisine is a reflection of its agricultural abundance and the influence of neighbouring and invading nations like Austria and Turkey, as well as minority communities like Hungary's significant Jewish population. Different types of alcohol are made around the country, including wine – like the renowned red Bull's Blood from Eger and the honey-sweet Tokaji Aszú – the fiery spirit of *pálinka* (fruit brandy) and beer. Hungary's national dishes are characteristically meaty, but more vegetarian options are appearing on restaurant menus. While Hungarians relish their famous *pörkölt* (meat stew) and paprika and sour cream are superstar ingredients that go into nearly every recipe, Hungary has many other gastronomic delights that will make you fall in love at first bite.

Soup

A traditional Hungarian meal always consists of three courses: soup, the main course and dessert. Soup always comes first. If the soup is hearty and meaty, it is followed by a lighter and sweet main course, such as pancakes or *túróscsusza* (sweet pasta with creamy cottage cheese and bacon). If the soup is simple and vegetable-based, a meaty dish comes next. Favourite local soups

Best Hungarian Dishes

GULYÁSLEVES
Soup made of beef cubes, vegetables and plenty of paprika.

HALÁSZLÉ
Fish soup with paprika. Best tasted in riverside cities like Szeged.

ÚJHÁZI TYÚKHÚSLEVES
Chicken broth served with angel hair pasta.

MARHAPÖRKÖLT
A stew of beef cubes and vegetables spiced with paprika.

include meat-based goulash; a chicken broth or bean soup; vegetable-based mushroom, pea or green bean soup; or fisherman's soup made of carp or catfish. Hungarians also consume a fruit soup served cold in summer, most commonly made of cherries, strawberries, plums or cinnamon-spiced apples.

Main Course

Hungarians eat lots of meat. A staple dish is schnitzel made from chicken, turkey or pork chop served with potatoes or rice. The country's characteristic stews are made with beef, lamb, veal, chicken or game and dished up with quintessentially Hungarian *nokedli* (egg dumplings). Vegetarians who don't want to miss out on a hearty Hungarian stew can try it made of mushrooms instead of meat. One of the healthy choices on the list of classic Hungarian dishes is *főzelék*, a thick vegetable roux most commonly made of potatoes, peas or lentils, and served with sausages, meatballs, or fried or boiled eggs. Freshwater fish are plentiful, and the Hungarian take on fish and chips is especially popular in summer.

Dessert

Hungarians have a sweet tooth. Desserts eaten at the end of a meal include *somlói galuska* sponge cake made with chocolate sauce, rum and raisins; *palacsinta* (pancakes) filled with jam, cocoa or cinnamon; chestnut purée with whipped cream; or sweet cottage cheese dumplings served with a sweet sour cream sauce. Slices of cake or strudel are usually consumed mid-afternoon with a coffee. Classic options include *Dobos torta* (layered sponge cake with chocolate buttercream and caramel), *Eszterházy torta* (vanilla-walnut buttercream between layers of meringue) and *krémes* (vanilla custard cake).

Eszterházy torta

FOOD & WINE FESTIVALS

Etyeki Piknik *(etyekipiknik.hu; four times a year)* The bijou village of Etyek hosts picnics every three months, presenting the wines and gastronomic delights typical of each season.

Gourmet Festival *(gourmetfesztival.hu; Jun)* The crème de la crème of Hungarian cuisine takes the stage at this annual festival in Budapest.

St Martin's Day Goose Feast *(p159)* Feasts of goose dishes take place at restaurants countrywide around St Martin's Day in November.

Sweet Days Budapest *(edesnapok.hu; Sep)* This chocolate and dessert festival sweetens a weekend in front of the basilica in Budapest.

International Tisza Fish Festival *(p209; pictured)* Every September, a fish soup-cooking contest takes place in Szeged.

RAKOTT KRUMPLI
Rings of hard-boiled eggs, potatoes and sausages baked with sour cream.

RÁNTOTT HÚS
Schnitzel: breaded and deep-fried meat; a superstar of Sunday lunches.

TÖLTÖTT KÁPOSZTA
Meat stuffed into sauerkraut leaves and topped with sour cream.

LECSÓ
Hungarian ratatouille made of peppers, tomatoes and onions.

Local Specialities

Try the unique tastes of Hungary.

Meats & Stews

Mangalica Hungary's own breed of pig, often called the 'Kobe beef of pork'.
Chicken paprikash Chicken stew served with *nokedli*.
Gombapaprikás Vegetarian mushroom stew.

Street Food

Lángos Round deep-fried dough that comes with a variety of toppings.
Kürtőskalács Dough wrapped around a spit, held above an open fire and rolled in cinnamon, sugar and other sweet toppings.
Hekk Hungary's version of fish and chips.
Rántott húsos szendvics A slice of schnitzel in a sandwich.

Sweet Treats

Rétes Flaky pastry strudel filled with poppy seeds, cherries or sweet cottage cheese.
Bejgli Spiral strudel filled with poppy seeds or walnuts; eaten at Christmas.
Somlói galuska Trifle-like cake made of several layers of sponge, custard, rum and raisins.

Lángos

Túró Rudi Packaged sweet cottage cheese covered in chocolate; found in every supermarket.
Szaloncukor Christmas sweets covered in chocolate and filled with marzipan, flavoured jelly or sweet cream.

Dare to Try

Hurka and kolbász Sausages cased in intestines. *Hurka* is usually boiled and flavoured with liver *(májas hurka)* or blood *(véres hurka)*, while *kolbász* is smoked and seasoned.
Kakastöke pörkölt Stew made of a rooster's family jewels.
Velős pirítós Toast with bone marrow and brain matter that could also include kidney marrow and spinal marrow.

MEALS OF A LIFETIME

Balkán Bistro (balkanbisztro.hu) Balkan dishes are in the spotlight at this fuss-free, cosy restaurant in Pécs.
Csalánosi Csárda (csalanosi-csarda.hu) Hearty home-style cooking and countryside hospitality in Kecskemét.
IKON (p213) An inventive countryside restaurant in Debrecen with unforgettable goulash.
Macok Bistro (p235) Top-notch menu and wine list at the foot of Eger Castle.
Prímás Pince (p170) Tasty Hungarian dishes served in a high-ceilinged cellar beneath Esztergom Basilica.
Stand25 (p63) Hungarian favourites with a modern twist in the capital city.

HAPPY_CONTRIBUTORS/SHUTTERSTOCK ©

THE YEAR IN FOOD

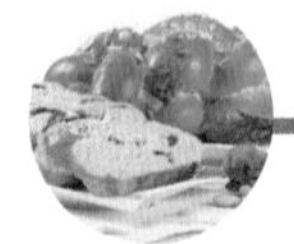

SPRING

Spring means lighter meals made of fresh vegetables like asparagus, spinach or sorrel. Soft fruits abound. For Easter, Hungary cooks ham, boiled eggs and braided bread (*fonott kalács*).

SUMMER

Hungary gets out its cauldrons to cook goulash and stews on an open fire. Freshwater fish, especially hake, is popular by the water. *Lecsó* is best in summer when the vegetables are freshest.

AUTUMN

Autumn is the season for eating jams that were put away at the end of summer and taste great in *palacsinta* or on toast. Wine festivals take place after the early September harvest countrywide.

WINTER

The lack of fresh produce is balanced by meat from the hunting season. Hearty dishes like fisherman's soup and stuffed cabbage are winter favourites, as are sweet *kürtőskalács* fresh off the fire.

VIKTORI/SHUTTERSTOCK ©, ARKADIUSZ FAJER/SHUTTERSTOCK ©, MARIAN CURKO/SHUTTERSTOCK ©, CAT US/SHUTTERSTOCK ©

Winery, Lake Balaton (p189)

HOW TO... Visit a Winery

Hungary is one of the world's oldest winemaking regions – but also one of the least known. Despite a wine history stretching back to the ancient Romans, phylloxera in the 1880s, two world wars and years under communism saw production falter. Thankfully, Hungarian wines are receiving newfound recognition, and Hungary is a fabulous place to become acquainted with high-quality, well-priced wines.

1. Pick a season

Harvest season runs from September to November. While you can visit the vineyards nearly year-round, tastings and some experiences are seasonal, especially at small winemakers.

2. Choose your region

Hungary has 22 wine regions, each with unique terroir and local traditions. Eger, Tokaj, Villány and Somló are considered the best known.

3. Know your grapes

Because of Hungary's history, many of its grape varieties are unknown even to frequent wine sippers. Hungarian Wines (hungarianwines.eu) is a useful pre-drinking resource.

4. Select a winery

In Hungary, ask bartenders at hotels or staff at wine bars for recommendations. Visit wineries that also have a B&B or restaurant.

5. Get in touch

Tastings in Hungary are still very formal. Call or write ahead, and you may find yourself sitting with the winemaker themselves. For no-cost tastings, it's polite to buy a bottle.

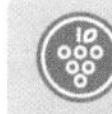

BACK TO THE VINES

Hungary's wine regions are known for their annual wine festivals where folk music, dance and the odd medieval castle or horse and buggy come together with the wares of local winemakers. Wineries also host concerts and cultural performances.

Széchenyi Baths (p141), Budapest

THERMAL BATHS & SPAS

Hungary might not have a dramatic coastline, but it has heaps of healing water gushing skywards from underground.

Hungary is a landlocked country, but taking the waters is a way of life. When visiting, it's a must to get rid of your clothes, don your swimsuit – no matter the season – and melt your muscles in the healing hot waters at one of the many thermal baths the country has to offer. It's a treat that's not only good for your body but also for your soul.

But where does all this aqua come from? Hungary is teeming with thermal water springs. The country has more than 1000 of them, mostly in the Great Plain. More than 100 are in Budapest, spurting some 40,000 cu metres of warm, mineral-rich water each day. This is what makes Budapest the world's spa capital.

What Bubbles Below Ground

Some 2000 years ago, the ancient Romans had already taken advantage of Hungary's thermal springs, evidenced by several ruins of baths found within the country's borders. The most notable such ruin is Thermae Maiores (Great Bath) near Flórián tér in Aquincum in Óbuda, which was equipped

Choose Your Bath

GELLÉRT BATHS This Art Nouveau wonderland in Budapest is the most beautiful bathhouse of all.

LUKÁCS BATHS One of Budapest's longest-standing spas, a true haven of health.

RUDAS BATHS Original Turkish bath in Budapest, renovated with a contemporary touch.

VELI BEJ BATHS Tranquil time in a traditional Turkish bath.

with luxuries like hot and cold water and underfloor heating. However, bathing only became an integral part of life in Hungary during the Ottoman occupation in the 16th and 17th centuries. The Ottomans built several hammam-style baths with similar structures: an octagon-shaped pool topped by a high-domed ceiling dotted with glass inlays that let rays of light shine through and pierce the water. Smaller pools surround the main pool. Some Ottoman-era bathhouses, such as Rudas Bath and Veli Bej Bath, are still in use. Most of Budapest's other historic spas – real architectural delights – were built in the 19th and 20th centuries.

The warm waters that bubble up from a network of underground caves are rich in dissolved minerals like calcium, hydrogen carbonate, magnesium, sodium, sulphate chloride and metaboric acid, and they are not just luxuriously calming but also curative. They relieve a number of health problems ranging from arthritis and muscle pains to slipped discs, circulatory disorders, nerve pain and respiratory illnesses. They're also a quick fix for hangovers – we tried and tested this for you. Bathing in these waters is not a luxury but part of a balanced life in Hungary, and it benefits more than bones and muscles. Drinking the therapeutic waters is said to boost your health from within. To give this liquid treatment a go, find the drinking hall *(ivócsarnok)* at Széchenyi, Lukács and Rudas Baths in Budapest. Bring an empty bottle to take some to go for a small price (around 100Ft for 1L).

Cave pool, Miskolctapolca

WHAT TO EXPECT AT HUNGARY'S THERMAL BATHS

In Budapest, you'll generally find a series of indoor thermal pools ranging in temperature from warm to hot, as well as colder pools for swimming laps. Other amenities include saunas, steam rooms, ice-cold plunge pools and medical massages. Except for Veli Bej, all baths have an outdoor section with water fountains, wave machines or whirlpools. Those who want to turn it up a notch can opt for private bathing sessions or soaking in a special beer bath.

Budapest is not the only place where you can immerse yourself in Hungary's healing waters. The countryside has many spas, especially in the Great Plain, but these are usually more modern facilities with adventure pools and slides.

Széchenyi Baths (p141), Budapest

SZÉCHENYI BATHS
Sunflower-yellow walls in a wedding cake-like building at one of Europe's largest spa complexes.

CAVE BATHS
Bathe in thermal water flowing through a natural cave in Miskolctapolca.

LAKE HÉVÍZ
The world's largest swimmable natural thermal lake.

HAGYMATIKUM
An architecturally pleasing, onion-shaped compound in Makó.

LEFT: IMAGE PROFESSIONALS GMBH/ALAMY STOCK PHOTO © RIGHT: POSZTOS/SHUTTERSTOCK ©

Rudas Baths (p69), Budapest

HOW TO... Visit Thermal Baths in Hungary

Find out the naked truth – here's everything you need to know to soak to your heart's content in Hungary's balmy baths.

SINGLE-SEX DAYS

The Turkish bath section at Rudas (p36) is the only one that still has single-sex sessions on weekdays (men only on Mondays, Wednesdays and Thursdays until 12.45pm and Fridays until 10.45am; Tuesdays are women only). On these days, men are given drawstring loincloths, and women wear apron-like garments, but most people prefer swimsuits. Nudity is not permitted in public areas at any thermal baths.

What to Bring

Pack swimwear, a towel and a pair of flip-flops as the floor can be slippery. Swimming caps are required in the lap pools. Bathing accessories are available to rent or purchase at most baths, but it's easier – and of course cheaper – to bring your own. Showers and hair dryers are available, so don't forget soap, shampoo and other shower products. Most baths have a cafeteria or a restaurant, making them ideal for a whole-day stay. Slip a book or anything you'd take to the beach in your bag for even more relaxation time.

When to Go

Baths operate year-round, but the warm water in the outdoor pools is best enjoyed on dreary days during the colder months. Hours vary by bathhouse, so check before you visit (spasbudapest.com). On weekends during the winter holiday season, the baths are busy and people are packed in like sardines. For a more peaceful experience, visit on a weekday. Rudas Baths offers late-night bathing on Fridays and Saturdays, while Széchenyi Baths throws a 'sparty' on Saturdays.

Ready, Steady, Splash!

Upon entering the baths, you'll receive a watch-shaped electronic bracelet that serves as the key for your locker or cabin where you can store your belongings. Some have an allocated number, but generally you just take any that are available. Széchenyi offers smaller lockers by the outdoor pools in case you want to take your phone or other valuables outside. If you need help, attendants are always around. Ticket prices vary based on what services you choose, so specify what you want when buying your ticket.

Rules of (Pruney) Thumb

Take a shower before plunging into the warm waters. In the pools, tie your hair back to avoid a gentle nudge from an elderly local. As most people are at the baths to relax or heal, keep noise to a minimum. Baths are not the same as lidos and waterparks, and usually anything more than quietly chatting is frowned upon – outdoor pools with waves and whirlpools are of course different. Avoid soaking in the hot water for too long because you might become light-headed. Signs at the baths specify the temperature of each pool and sometimes advise on how much time to spend inside, generally 20 minutes at a time. Children must be 14 years or older to use the thermal pools as their cardiovascular systems are affected by the higher temperatures – some baths like Rudas won't even let kids enter. Bathing is not recommended for people who are pregnant.

Gellért Baths (p67), Budapest

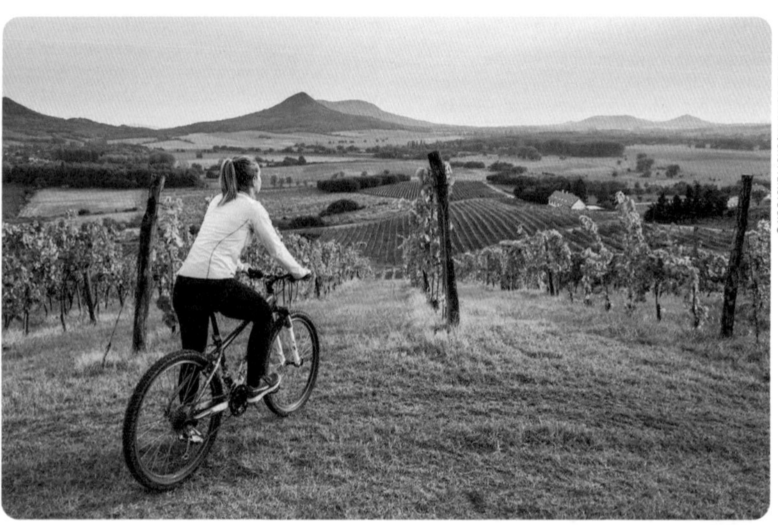
OPHOTOGRAPHY/SHUTTERSTOCK ©

Cycling near Badacsony (p188)

THE OUTDOORS

Hungary's topographical and climatic diversity offers fresh-air adventures for active travellers and adrenaline junkies all year long.

Adventure lies around every corner in Hungary, and those daring enough to venture beyond the charming cities and explore its rural landscapes, forested mountains and placid waterways are rewarded in spades. Hikers, cyclists and paddlers find their bliss in the country's seemingly unending network of trails, bike paths and navigable waterways, while rock climbers, paragliders and windsurfers won't be disappointed when they get to know Hungary's accommodating adventurous side.

Cycling

Fairly flat and blessed with more than 2200km of cycling paths, Hungary is a delight to explore by bike. Keen cyclists love tackling the 200km Balaton Cycling Route that encircles Lake Balaton. This breathtakingly beautiful cycle path along dedicated and quiet country roads passes through historic towns, including Keszthely (close to Hévíz, famous for its thermal lake) and Tihany (known for its thatched-roof dwellings, lavender and ceramics). For a longer two-wheeled adventure, the popular Danube Cycle Path from Vienna to Budapest via Györ and Esztergom is part of the EuroVelo 6 Atlantic–Black Sea route. The entire journey is relatively flat, well marked and generally in excellent condition, making it ideal for cyclists of all fitness levels. In far west-

Adventure Sports

WINDSURFING
Thanks to its steady winds, Lake Balaton is a popular windsurfing spot that promises plenty of freeride fun.

VIA FERRATA
Several via ferrata trails of varying difficulty levels can be tackled in the village of Csesznek.

PARAGLIDING
Surrounding the capital, the Buda Hills offer launch points for paragliders.

FAMILY ADVENTURES

Take the kids hiking in Normafa (p82) near Budapest on the short and easy 5km-long János Hill Loop.

The narrow-gauge Children's Railway (p80) chugs through the rolling Buda Hills from Széchenyihegy to Hűvösvölgy.

Trot through the gorgeous village of Szilvásvárad (p240) on horseback.

Put skates on and hit the ice if Lake Balaton (p181) freezes over in winter.

Go spelunking inside Szemlőhegy Cave (p84) in Budapest for a fairy-tale family adventure.

ern Hungary, along the Slovenian–Austrian border, Őrség National Park promises an enjoyable day in the saddle, with clearly numbered bike routes on both paved and unpaved surfaces through ancient wooded forests, sleepy rural villages and undulating verdant vistas.

Paddling

For a landlocked country, Hungary offers a surprising amount of water-based adventures and boasts more than 4000km of waterways navigable by kayak and canoe. The best launching points for exploring the Danube Bend by kayak or canoe are Nagymaros and Visegrád. Near Győr, the village of Dunasziget is the perfect base for paddlers keen to see the lush tributaries of the Danube and its islets, inner lakes, and rich flora and fauna. Not far from Pécs, Danube-Dráva National Park, with its dotted island and canal topography, is an alluvial plain flaunting a wealth of biodiversity, including red deer, boar and protected bird species such as black stork and white-tailed eagle. Paddlers keen on multiday trips can tackle the 386km-long Rajka-to-Mohacs route on the Danube.

Boats on Lake Balaton (p181)

Hiking

Hikers of all fitness levels are in for a treat in Hungary. With basalt rocks, pine forests and geyser cones, the geological wonderland of Tihany on Lake Balaton's northern shore is especially gorgeous trekking territory. Near Eger, Bükk National Park is Hungary's largest protected reserve, bursting with caves, forested trails, waterfalls and incredible lookout points. Closer to the capital, trails around the Danube Bend at Nagymaros and Visegrád offer exceptional hiking, as does Normafa in the Buda Hills, a popular spot with Budapest-based trail runners. Serious hikers can take on the 1130km-long National Blue Trail (Kéktúra), the oldest long-distance hiking trail in Europe, which snakes its way through the Mátra and Bükk Mountains in northern Hungary. The entire trek can be done in around two months, but those shorter on time can tick off one (or more) of its 27 parts, collecting stamps after every completed section.

ROCK CLIMBING
The Gerecse Mountains in northwestern Hungary are a big draw for rock climbers.

MOUNTAIN BIKING
Explore some of the 350km of MTB trails in the Bükk Mountains.

SKYDIVING
Fly above the clouds on a tandem skydive over Budapest.

SAILING
Don your captain's hat and hire a boat on Lake Balaton.

ACTION AREAS

Where to find Hungary's best outdoor activities.

Kayaking

1. Nagymaros (p167)
2. Visegrád (p167)
3. Dunasziget (p177)
4. Danube-Dráva National Park
5. Lake Tisza (p244)
6. Szentendre (p160)
7. Rajka to Mohacs (p41)

Walking/Hiking

1. National Blue Trail (p164)
2. Normafa (p82)
3. Hollókő (p242)
4. Hortobágy National Park (p216)

0 100 km
0 50 miles

Sárospatak
Kazincbarcika
Ózd
Salgótarján
Bükk National Park
Miskolc
Tokaj
Hollókő
Nyíregyháza
Eger
Mátra Hills
Polgár
Mezőkövesd
Hajdúnánás
Nagykállo
Füzesabony
Hajdúböszörmény
Hatvan
Heves
Lake Tisza
Tiszafüred
Hortobágy National Park
Debrecen
Jászberény
Püspökladány
Cegléd
Szolnok
Great Plain
Berettyóújfalu
Nagykőrös
Szeghalom
Tiszakécske
Gyomaendrőd
ecskemét
Kiskunfélegyháza
skunság
ational
Park
Gyula
Orosháza
ROMANIA
Hódmezővásárhely
Szeged

National Parks

1. Őrség National Park (p178)
2. Bükk National Park (p239)
3. Hortobágy National Park (p214)
4. Kiskunság National Park (p217)

Cycling

1. Balaton Cycling Route (p40)
2. Danube Cycle Path (p40)
3. EuroVelo 6 (p40)
4. EuroVelo 11 (p40)
5. EuroVelo 13 (p40)
6. EuroVelo 14 (p40)
7. BUBA Cucle Path

BUDAPEST & HUNGARY

THE GUIDE

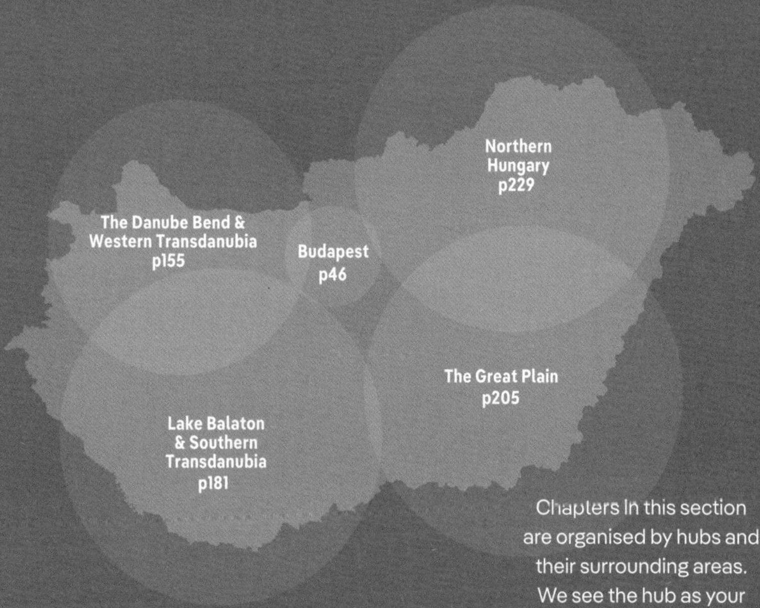

Chapters in this section are organised by hubs and their surrounding areas. We see the hub as your base in the destination, where you'll find unique experiences, local insights, insider tips and expert recommendations. It's also your gateway to the surrounding area, where you'll see what and how much you can do from there.

Great Synagogue (p116)

BUDAPEST

SCENIC BEAUTY, HIGH CULTURE AND PARTIES

Straddling the romantic Danube River, with the Buda Hills on one side and the start of the Great Plain on the other, Budapest is central Europe's most beautiful city.

Budapest's beauty is not all God given; humankind has played a role in shaping this pretty face too. The city is an architectural gem, with enough baroque, neoclassical, Eclectic and Art Nouveau buildings to satisfy anyone's appetite. Overall, Budapest has a fin-de-siècle feel to it, for it was then, during the capital's golden age, that most of what you see today was built. And nearly every building has some interesting detail, from Art Nouveau glazed tiles and neoclassical bas-reliefs to bullet holes and shrapnel scorings left over from WWII and the 1956 Uprising.

With parks brimming with attractions, museums filled with treasures, pleasure boats sailing down the Danube and Turkish-era thermal baths belching steam, the Hungarian capital is a delight both by day and night. The food and wine are excellent, abundant and reasonably priced, and the nightlife carries on into the wee hours. Indeed, in recent years, Budapest has taken on the role of the region's party town, especially in the warmer months when outdoor entertainment areas called *kertek* (garden clubs) heave with merrymakers.

Just when the city was beginning to find its feet again in the post-pandemic world, Russia's invasion of Ukraine triggered a new set of challenges: namely, soaring inflation and energy prices. How smaller businesses will fare in the face of spiking utility costs remains to be seen. And that's in addition to the more entrenched problems: organised crime, pollution, globalisation and mindless graffiti defacing much of that gorgeous architecture.

Still, while Hungarians may 'take their pleasure sadly', a bizarre arrangement for which there's even a phrase *(sírva vigadni),* they continue to embrace life with gusto. The clubs heave at the weekend, there's often a queue at the Széchenyi thermal baths and you won't get a seat at the Ruszwurm cafe on Castle Hill in an entire month of Sundays. Stroll along the Duna korzó, Pest's riverside embankment, or across any of the Danube bridges, and you'll pass young couples embracing passionately. It's then that you'll feel the romance of a place that, despite all the attempts from both within and without to destroy it, has never died.

THE MAIN AREAS

CASTLE DISTRICT Historic nerve centre. p52

GELLÉRT HILL & TABÁN Leafy riverside spas. p65

ÓBUDA & THE BUDA HILLS Lost-in-the-past feel. 76

BELVÁROS Well-heeled city centre. p86

PARLIAMENT & AROUND Signature sights and squares. p96

Left: Gellért Baths (p67). Above: Funicular (p57)

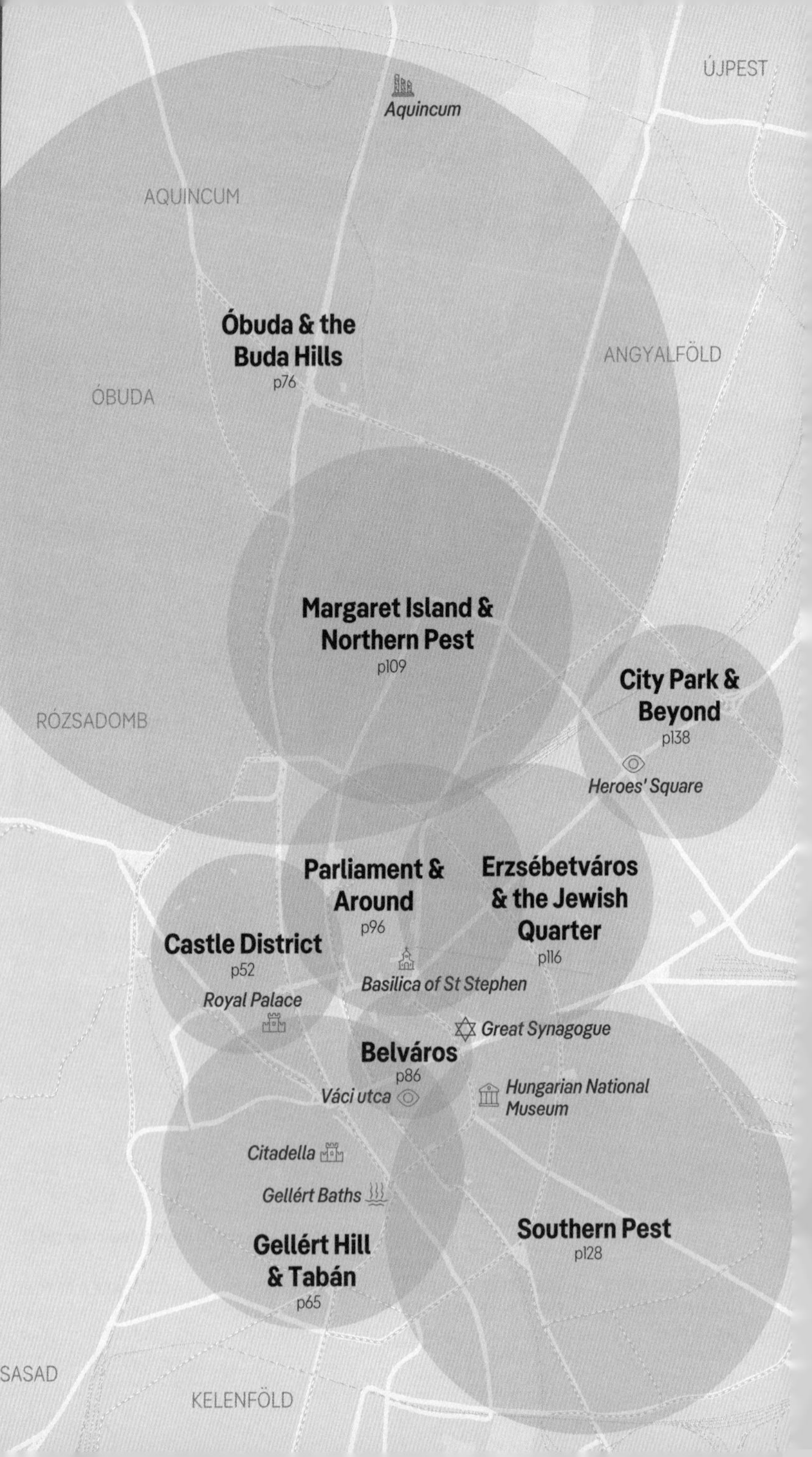

Aquincum

ÚJPEST

AQUINCUM

Óbuda & the Buda Hills
p76

ÓBUDA

ANGYALFÖLD

Margaret Island & Northern Pest
p109

RÓZSADOMB

City Park & Beyond
p138

Heroes' Square

Parliament & Around
p96

Erzsébetváros & the Jewish Quarter
p116

Castle District
p52

Basilica of St Stephen

Royal Palace

Great Synagogue

Belváros
p86

Váci utca

Hungarian National Museum

Citadella

Gellért Baths

Gellért Hill & Tabán
p65

Southern Pest
p128

SASAD

KELENFÖLD

Find Your Way

Budapest is an easy city to navigate. The Danube clearly defines east and west and Pest and Buda, and the public transport system is safe, efficient and inexpensive. You can also get around under your own steam by bicycle or on foot.

FROM THE AIRPORT

Shuttle buses to/from central Pest (stop: Deák Ferenc tér) run daily round the clock but can get very crowded at key travel times. Public buses are cheaper, but slower and less direct. Taxis, still reasonably inexpensive, are the fastest way to get to/from the airport.

METRO & TRAIN

Budapest has four colour-coded underground metro lines, three of which converge at central hub Deák Ferenc tér. Lines run from 4.30am and begin their last journey at around 11.30pm. The HÉV suburban trains run on five lines and are useful for destinations outside the city.

ZUGLÓ

BUS & TRAM

An extensive system of buses running on more than 270 lines day and night serves greater Budapest. An 'E' after the number means it makes limited stops; night buses begin with 9. Trams (33 lines) are faster and more pleasant for sightseeing than buses.

WALK & CYCLE

One of the best ways of getting around Budapest is on foot. More and more cyclists can be seen on the city's growing network of bike paths. Use the public bicycle-sharing scheme, Bubi Bikes, with more than 1800 bicycles at docking stations around Budapest.

N 0 — 2 km
0 — 1 mile

Plan Your Days

Do as the Hungarians do and start your day with a black coffee *(fekete kávé)* or coffee with milk *(tejes kávé)* before hitting the streets in search of treasures and adventure.

ROBALITO/SHUTTERSTOCK ©

Széchenyi Baths (p141)

Day 1

Morning

● Head up to the Castle District, taking in the views from the **Royal Palace** (p54). Several museums are up here; choose either the **Hungarian National Gallery** for fine art or the **Castle Museum**.

Afternoon

● After lunch at the **Royal Guard Restaurant**, take the **funicular** (p57) down to **Clark Ádám tér** (p59) and jump on tram 19 or 41 to the **Rudas Baths** (p69) for a soak.

Evening

● Depending on your mood, enjoy a glass of wine at the **Palack Borbár** (p74) or head further south to the **A38** (p72) for an evening of music and dancing.

YOU'LL ALSO WANT TO...

After all the must-see sights, turn your attention to Budapest's neighbourhoods: head for the hills, join a *táncház* evening of folk music and dance, and travel back to Roman times.

CRUISE THE RIVER

Jump aboard a **RedJet** for a high-speed trip of a lifetime along the Danube.

MEET ERSTWHILE HEROES

Meet Lenin, Engels and Marx as well as superhuman workers, in the socialist Disneyland of **Memento Park**.

DIG FOR TREASURE

Head for **Ecseri Piac**, one of Europe's largest flea markets, to search for diamonds in the rust.

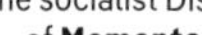

YAKIV KOROL/SHUTTERSTOCK ©, IRENA IRIS SZEWCZYK/SHUTTERSTOCK ©, SZB/SHUTTERSTOCK ©

Day 2

Morning

- Cross the Danube and see Pest at its finest by walking up leafy **Andrássy út** (p116) to **Heroes' Square** (p138), past the delightful **Hungarian State Opera House** (p105) and wonderful **Művész Kávéház** (p118).

Afternoon

- As you approach **City Park** (p138), decide whether you want an educational or leisurely afternoon. For the former, stop at the **House of Terror** (p118) and **Museum of Fine Arts** (p140). For the latter, visit the **Budapest Zoo** (p151) and the **Széchenyi Baths** (p141).

Evening

- Make your way back down Andrássy út to the Erzsébetváros neighbourhood for dinner and drinks at lively **Havana** (p124).

Day 3

Morning

- Concentrate on the two icons of Hungarian nationhood: the Crown of St Stephen in the **Parliament** (p96) and the saint-king's mortal remains in the **Basilica of St Stephen** (p98).

Afternoon

- After lunch at **Dobrumba** (p106), visit the Jewish Quarter, taking in the **Orthodox Synagogue** (p119) and the original **ghetto wall** (p122). Leave ample time for a look inside the **Great Synagogue** (p116) and its **Hungarian Jewish Museum & Archives** (p119).

Evening

- Move on to the nearby *kertek* (garden clubs) along Kazinczy utca, including the original one, **Szimpla Kert** (p124). Or there might be *klezmer* (Jewish folk music) at **Spinoza Café** (p124).

TAKE UP THE SWORD

Step back in time with a trip to Roman **Aquincum** and play gladiator with the kids.

KICK UP YOUR HEELS

Learn all the *táncház* moves at **Aranytíz House of Culture**.

ENJOY SKATING

Go ice-skating at Europe's largest outdoor rink in **City Park**, with dramatic Vajdahunyad Castle as your backdrop.

TASTE THE DIFFERENCE

Grab a table at **Gettó Gulyás** and learn to distinguish ***gulyás*** (beef soup) from ***pörkölt*** (goulash).

CASTLE DISTRICT

HISTORIC NERVE CENTRE

With a gasp-worthy monument on practically every corner, the Castle District is unparalleled for sightseeing. There's hardly another neighbourhood in the city with so many heavyweight sights crammed into such a compact space: the Royal Palace, Fisherman's Bastion and Matthias Church are all steps away from each other.

The Castle District encompasses World Heritage site Castle Hill (Várhegy) and ground-level Víziváros (Water town). Castle Hill is the nerve centre of historic Budapest, characterised by winding cobbled streets, splendid staircases and some of the best museums in town. Víziváros offers less when it comes to sights, but compensates with great restaurants and pubs, especially around Széll Kálmán tér, the centre of urban Buda.

At the time of writing, the district was undergoing major renovations as part of the Hauszmann Alajos Program. The Hungarian National Gallery is set to move to City Park in the next few years.

TOP TIP

You can reach Castle Hill from Pest via bus 16 from Deák Ferenc tér. It's more fun to take the funicular *(sikló)* from Clark Ádám tér, and easier via an escalator, steps or a lift from Castle Garden Bazaar (Várkert Bazár). Alternatively, you can walk up from Clark Ádám tér.

Habsburg Gate

Habsburg Gate

ELEGANT ENTRANCE TO THE ROYAL PALACE

The Habsburg Gate provides a magnificent entrance to the Royal Palace's front terrace. The dual stairways are symmetrical, and the eastern flight is the perfect place to snap a photo of the Pest skyline. You can't miss the bronze *turul* – a falcon-like totem of the ancient Magyars and a national symbol – perched atop a column, its wings outstretched and a sword in its talons. Hungary's historic coat of arms can be seen on its pedestal. The sculpture dates from 1905.

Sándor Palace

HUNGARY'S PRESIDENTIAL PALACE

The austere Sándor Palace is the official office and residence of Hungary's president, and stands in the shadow of the much grander Royal Palace on Szent György tér. Built in 1806 in a neoclassical style, the building is only occasionally open to the public; the main attraction here is the **Changing of the Guard ceremony** that takes place every hour on the hour from 9am to 5pm – with a special show at midday – in front of the main entrance.

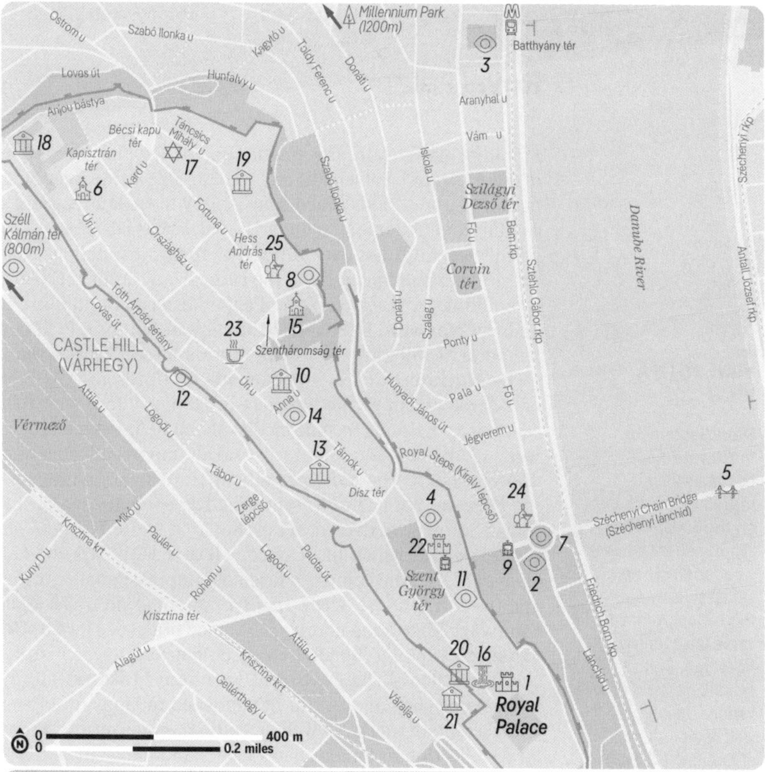

HIGHLIGHTS
1 Royal Palace

SIGHTS
2 0km Stone
3 Batthyány tér
4 Carmelite Monastery
5 Chain Bridge
6 Church of Mary Magdalene
7 Clark Ádám tér
8 Fishermen's Bastion
9 Funicular
10 Golden Eagle Pharmacy
11 Habsburg Gate
12 Hospital in the Rock
13 House of Houdini
14 Labyrinth
15 Matthias Church
16 Matthias Fountain
17 Medieval Jewish Prayer House
18 Museum of Military History
19 Museum of Music History
20 Royal Guardhouse
21 Royal Riding Hall
22 Sándor Palace

EATING
23 Ruszwurm

DRINKING & NIGHTLIFE
24 Leo Budapest
25 White Raven

Carmelite Monastery

THE PRIME MINISTER'S OFFICE

Adjacent to Sándor Palace stands a former Carmelite monastery, originally built in a late baroque style in 1734 at the end of the Turkish occupation, on the site of the former pasha's palace. In 1784, King Joseph II dissolved the Carmelite order and gave the building to the state. Three years later, Buda's first theatre opened here, welcoming Beethoven for a grandiose concert in 1800. Over the course of the 19th century the building was rebuilt many times, and after World War II, several cultural institutions moved in. Since 2019, the Carmelite Monastery has been home to the office of Hungary's prime minister. The building's event hall is open to visitors when concerts take place.

Royal Palace

THE CROWN JEWEL OF CASTLE HILL

Standing majestically atop Castle Hill, the Royal Palace is one of the city's most emblematic and recognisable attractions. First built in the mid-1200s, when King Béla IV moved the country's capital from Esztergom to Buda, the palace has been razed and rebuilt several times over 700 years. Today, it functions as a cultural destination, housing the Hungarian National Gallery in buildings A through D, the Castle Museum in building E and the **National Széchényi Library** in building F. Major temporary exhibitions also draw crowds several times a year.

The **National Gallery** documents and presents the rise and development of the fine arts in Hungary from the 11th century on. Exhibits include medieval and Renaissance stonework, Gothic wooden sculptures and an important collection of paintings by the most prominent Hungarian painters of the 19th and 20th centuries. See the *Yawning Apprentice* by Mihály Munkácsy, the painter of the Great Plain; *The Balloon* (the subject of which has cameos all over City Park) by Pál Szinyei Merse, the country's foremost impressionist painter; and the *Ruins of the Greek Theatre at Taormina* by Tivadar Csontváry Kosztka, whom Picasso once praised. The **Castle Museum** explores Budapest's turbulent 2000-year history over three floors. The **National Széchényi Library** stores at least one copy of everything published in Hungary or the Hungarian language, as well as codices, manuscripts and a large collection of foreign newspapers and magazines.

WINE WITH A VIEW

Every September, the Royal Palace becomes the magnificent backdrop for the Budapest Wine Festival, when wooden kiosks are set up side-by-side at this historic venue to serve the country's finest red, white and sparkling wines from various regions, as well as a plethora of foreign bottles. A wide range of gastronomic delights is also available, while events, wine-focused workshops and concerts also take place in the gorgeous setting. This is one of the most elegant wine festivals in the country.

Royal Palace

Matthias Church

SACRED CHURCH WITH LACE-LIKE FACADE

Perched high and mighty above Szentháromság tér, Matthias Church is a neo-Gothic confection. Even while walking towards it, you'll be struck by the rich ornamentation, sculptures, reliefs and colourful Zsolnay tiles adorning its facade and roof; stepping inside, a unique combination of wooden statuary, colourful frescos and gold-leaf detail dominates the walls.

History records that a house of worship has stood here since 1015, but the church was refounded in the 13th century, when King Béla IV replaced the older, smaller structure with a towering three-nave basilica. Matthias Church has changed many times over the course of the past millennium. What you see today is something akin to the Gothic landmark that stood here in the 13th century, thanks to Frigyes Schulek, who went back to the original medieval plans when redesigning the church in the late 19th century.

One of the best ways to see the cathedral's interior is to attend one of the many classical concerts held here. The star, of course, is the organ.

TOP: PHOTOSTAR72/SHUTTERSTOCK ©, BOTTOM: ZGPHOTOGRAPHY/SHUTTERSTOCK ©

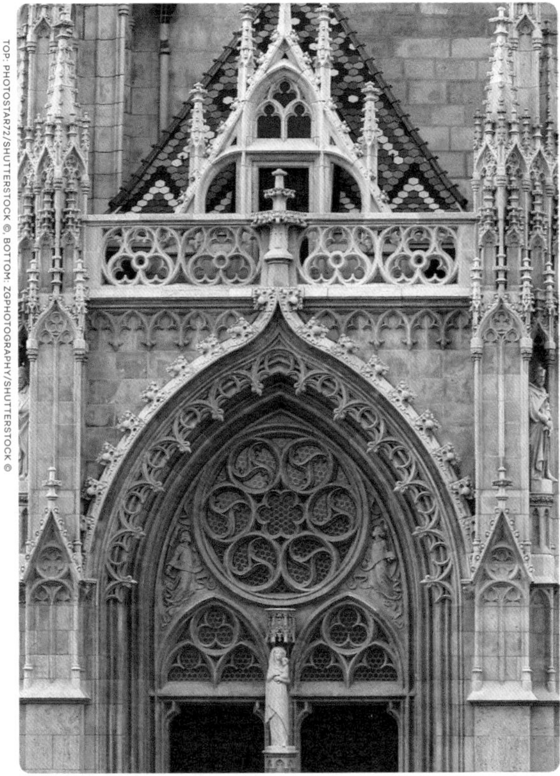

Matthias Church

Fisherman's Bastion

THE DISTRICT'S BEST VIEWS

This bone white, 140m-long neo-Gothic masquerade offers one of the best views of the Pest skyline. The Fisherman's Bastion is a faux-historic monument – Frigyes Schulek built it as a viewing platform in 1905 to offset nearby Matthias Church. Its name was taken from the medieval guild of fishermen responsible for defending this stretch of the old castle wall. The seven cone-topped turrets represent the seven Magyar chieftains who settled in this part of the Carpathian Basin in the late 800s. Be sure to have your camera ready, because this is the best photo-op in the Castle District.

Fisherman's bastion

Royal Riding Hall

Royal Riding Hall

AN ELEGANT EVENT VENUE

Behind the Royal Guardhouse, the Stöckl Steps, a renovated neo-Renaissance staircase, connects the Castle Garden with the Royal Riding Hall and Csikós Garden. The Riding Hall is the pretty building with green stained-glass windows and today serves as a multifunctional event space. Originally built in 1901, the hall was used by the royal household up through 1938, after which the Spanish Riding School started holding practices here. The windows and intricate wooden ceiling are a delight.

Royal Guardhouse

SAFEGUARDING THE PAST

Steps away from the Royal Palace is the Royal Guardhouse (Főőrség Palace), featuring huge Ionic columns and a facade adorned with intriguing statues, military symbols and weaponry. The lower level houses a lovely cafe-cum-restaurant, where you can sip tea beneath the gaze of lionhearted guards with well-groomed moustaches, who are peering down from the dozens of archive photos that cover the walls and ceiling. Upstairs, an exhibition presents the 260-year history of the Castle Guards, beginning with the founding of the Hungarian Royal and Noble Guards in 1760. Don't miss the archival photos and uniforms.

Matthias Fountain

Matthias Fountain

THE HUNGARIAN TREVI

Matthias Fountain stands in the Hunyadi Courtyard next to the Hungarian National Gallery. Famed fin-de-siècle sculptor Alajos Stróbl designed the fountain in 1904; in 2020, it was completely rebuilt with the help of his grandson, Mátyás Stróbl. The central figure portrays one of the most popular Hungarian monarchs, King Matthias the Just, in hunting attire. To his right is Szép Ilonka (Beautiful Helena), who in author Mihály Vörösmarty's famous poem falls in love with a dashing young hunter – the king in disguise – and upon learning his identity and feeling unworthy of his love, dies of a broken heart. Below the fountain lies the family crypt of the Habsburgs, accessible from the Hungarian National Gallery through guided tours.

Funicular

A FUN WAY TO REACH CASTLE HILL

The funicular *(sikló)* is a World Heritage site and one of Budapest's most popular attractions. Its steep 95m-long track offers a quick, convenient way up to the Royal Palace from the banks of the Danube, climbing at a speed of 1.5m per second and providing splendid views en route. It was opened in 1870 as only the second funicular in the world – eight years after the first in Lyon, France – and was originally powered by a steam engine.

In 1944, the structure was severely damaged during the war. Although there were several propositions to carry out renovations, it wasn't until 1986 that it finally reopened to the public. To mark its 150th anniversary in 2020, all of the rails along the track were replaced and the two little carriages, named Margit and Gellért, were overhauled with new vintage-looking wooden fittings. Since 1986, Gellért and Margit have carried between 500,000 and one million passengers each year up and down Castle Hill.

Passengers arriving at the upper station on Szent György tér can enter the Royal Palace via the Habsburg Gate, which is topped by a distinctive bronze statue of a *turul* (a mythical bird).

Funicular carriages

LEGEND OF THE TURUL

The mythic falcon-like *turul* is the national symbol of Hungary and first appeared in 'Emese's Dream', a legend dating back to the 9th century. In the story, the pregnant Emese saw the *turul* in a dream, during which the bird revealed to her that she would give birth to a line of mighty rulers. Her son, Álmos, became one of the seven chieftains who led their people to the Carpathian Basin, and his son, Árpád, was sovereign of all the Magyar tribes and founder of the ruling dynasty.

Ruszwurm

Medieval Jewish Prayer House

REMNANT OF THE PAST

Hidden until its discovery in 1964, the Medieval Jewish Prayer House regained its original function in 2018, and is now operating again as a house of worship, in addition to serving as an exhibition hall honouring the history of the Castle District's Jewish population. Inside, you can spot two fragments of frescos: one depicts the Star of David; the other shows a bow and arrow, inscribed with a line from 'Hannah's Prayer' from the Book of Samuel. It's closed on Mondays and Saturdays.

Medieval Jewish Prayer House

Ruszwurm

TIME-WARP CONFECTIONERY

In the Castle District, family-run Ruszwurm is the place to go for coffee and cake. Situated in a green townhouse and dating back to 1827, this is the longest-standing pastry shop in Budapest. Stepping inside the bite-sized, cosy confectionery feels like travelling back to the days of 19th-century Buda. Browse the lineup of delicious cakes, displayed on the landmark-protected cherrywood counter with mahogany inlays. While you'll be competing for a seat here, it's worth trying to snag a table. And don't miss one of the city's best *krémes* – a kind of vanilla custard cake. Delicious!

Mary Magdalene Tower

HISTORIC LOOKOUT TOWER

During the Ottoman occupation of Hungary, the 13th-century **Church of Mary Magdalene** on Kapisztrán tér was the only functioning Christian church in Budapest, and was used by both Catholics and Protestants until its later transformation into a mosque. Fighting during World War II severely damaged the structure, and the communist regime then proceeded to destroy everything but its steeple. After thorough renovations, this Gothic-style spire now functions as a lookout tower, with 170 steps to climb for a wonderful view. A big attraction is the hourly music played on the tower's 24 bronze bells, which were unfortunately seriously damaged by lightning in 2020. At the time of writing, funds were still being collected for their renovation.

Buda Castle Tunnel

Clark Ádám tér & Buda Castle Tunnel

GET YOUR BEARINGS

The flower-strewn roundabout on Clark Ádám tér is where the funicular's lower station is located and where the Víziváros neighbourhood begins. It was named after Adam Clark, a 19th-century Scottish engineer who supervised the building of the Széchenyi Chain Bridge. Clark also designed the large tunnel next to the funicular, which took just eight months to carve out of the limestone hill in 1853. Local lore has it that when it rains, Chain Bridge is pulled into the tunnel to protect its revered stone lions. The windows on the facade used to belong to an actual apartment, where the caretaker of the Chain Bridge lived for decades. While you should avoid walking through the tunnel (unless you enjoy inhaling heavy quantities of smog), climbing on top of it presents a great photo opportunity.

From Clark Ádám tér, you can take the funicular or walk up the Király Steps to Castle Hill, or venture into Víziváros and reach Batthyány tér or Széll Kálmán tér within minutes.

0km Stone

ALL ROADS LEAD TO BUDAPEST

Tucked away on Clark Ádám tér, the 0km Stone is an important monument. Erected in 1975 with a fool-proof design and name, this 3m-high statue marks the spot from where Hungary's single-digit main roads leading out of the capital are measured (except for Road 1, but including Roads 10, 11, 31 and 50). The next time you're driving around Hungary and see a sign that states Budapest is a certain number of kilometres away, you'll know it refers to this very spot. A handful of sample distances on the ground will help you plan your next trip.

0km Stone

Chain Bridge

AN ICONIC LANDMARK

The Chain Bridge is one of Budapest's most striking spans and the star of many a photograph. It was the first permanent bridge between Buda and Pest, built between 1840 and 1849. The name honours its initiator, the great Hungarian statesman Count István Széchenyi, who dreamt up the idea of the bridge in the winter of 1820, when blocks of ice floating down the Danube prevented him from crossing from Pest to Buda and caused him to miss his father's funeral.

The bridge was designed by William Tierney Clark – also responsible for the similar-looking suspension bridge at Marlow, near London – but the construction was overseen by Scottish engineer Adam Clark. As the bridge was built at a time when Budapest had begun to step out of Vienna's shadow and establish itself as its own metropolis, it stands as a symbol of the city's development and the connection between East and West. When crossing the bridge, get the world's smallest violin out for all the noblemen, who, though previously exempt from taxation, had to pay a toll just like everyone else in order to cross. Luckily for them, the toll was lifted in 1918.

WHO'S GOT THE CATS' TONGUES?

The dearly loved lion sculptures on Chain Bridge are the protagonists of many an urban legend. According to one, when a young apprentice pointed out that the lions all lacked tongues, the sculptor, proud of his creations, jumped off the bridge into the Danube. While the story's credibility is highly questionable, the lions have divided people for decades – some see tongues, others don't – and watchful eyes will spot many a curious soul peeking into their mouths. So, do they have tongues? We recommend you take a look yourself.

Chain Bridge

DZIEWUL/SHUTTERSTOCK ©

Millennium Park

ENORMOUS EVENT SPACE

Millennium Park is a lovely cultural complex comprising fountains, ponds, bridges, a playground and a gallery. Whenever a major event or festival takes place in the Castle District, it's either held near the Royal Palace or here. Big events like the Art Market Budapest (an international contemporary art fair), the International Book Festival and Chinese new year celebrations take place here regularly. Millennium Park is also home to the National Dance Theatre, which hosts impressive performances, while the Mammut shopping mall is steps away.

Millennium Park

Batthyány tér

THE BEST VIEWS OF PARLIAMENT

This square is the centre of Víziváros and the best place to take pictures of the majestic Parliament building across the Danube. Batthyány tér is an important transport hub, as you can catch the M2 metro to Pest or Széll Kálmán tér, as well as the H5 HÉV suburban train line to splendid Szentendre from here – Budapest's Óbuda district is on the way. The square is home to an imposing market hall full of fresh, colourful produce, as well as one of the prettiest baroque churches in Budapest, the twin-towered 18th-century Church of St Anne.

Parliament

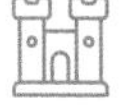

Széll Kálmán tér

THE CENTRE OF URBAN BUDA

This busy square is the centre of Buda and a major transport hub, in addition to serving as the unofficial entrance to the Buda Hills. You can catch the extremely useful 4 and 6 tram lines here, which follow the entire length of the Big Ring Road in Pest and return to south Buda; the M2 metro to Pest; and several buses that run to both Castle Hill and the Buda Hills. Although this area doesn't have much to offer when it comes to sightseeing, there are numerous restaurants, street-food spots, bars and shops to browse. If the weather is nice and you're up for a stroll, follow Várfok utca to reach the Castle District in about 20 minutes on foot.

BEST STATUES IN THE CASTLE DISTRICT

Eugene of Savoy (Savoy Terrace) The finest equestrian statue in Budapest depicts the commander who drove the Turks from Hungary.

Saint Stephen (Szentháromság tér) The enormous statue of Hungary's first king displays scenes like crowning and lawmaking.

Habsburg Count Hadik Among Hungarian students, it's a tradition to touch the stallion's crown jewels for exam success. It's at the intersection of Úri and Szentháromság utcas.

Szentháromság Monument (Szentháromság tér) Erected after two plagues, this monument depicts King David's supplication to end the pandemic.

House of Houdini

MORE IN THE CASTLE DISTRICT

Venturing Below the Castle

EXPLORE EERIE WORLDS UNDERGROUND

Take two spine-tingling trips below the Castle District to discover places frozen in time.

A stone's throw away from Matthias Church, the **Hospital in the Rock** (Sziklakórház) is a real underground hospital that was turned into a nuclear bunker kept secret for decades – the government only declassified its existence in 2002. Used to treat the wounded during World War II and the 1956 Uprising, the cave today presents a maze of hospital wards full of mysteries and untold stories, as well as some 200 lifelike wax figures, original furniture and medical equipment from the 1940s and 1950s. You can visit through a one-hour guided tour that departs hourly between 10am and 6pm.

Steps away you'll find the **Labyrinth** (Labirintus), where you can learn about the legends and ghost stories that continue to haunt the castle caves. Expect centuries-old rocks and ruins dating back to the Middle Ages, cave paintings (reproductions), coffins, mannequins dressed up as characters from

WHERE TO STAY IN THE CASTLE DISTRICT

Baltazár Boutique Hotel Family-owned boutique hotel offering individually decorated rooms with vintage furniture. **€€**

Lánchíd 19 Design Hotel Floor-to-ceiling windows provide a perfect panorama over the Danube and the Royal Palace. **€€**

Hilton Hotel While the building itself is architecturally controversial, nothing beats the views. **€€€**

famous operas, the history of Dracula and a stretch where you'll experience complete darkness, with only your other senses and mysterious music to guide you. If you want to turn up the spooky factor, you can take a guided tour (every evening at 6pm), when the curving passages of the cave are illuminated solely by the flickering oil lamps that visitors carry.

A Day at the Museums

DISCOVER THE DISTRICT'S QUIRKIEST SIGHTS

Besides the main museums, this history-packed district has other hidden gems to discover. Sandwiched between the Royal Palace and Fisherman's Bastion is the **House of Houdini**, which honours one of history's greatest illusionists, who was born in Budapest. Enter the museum after solving a playful puzzle, then admire a vast collection of original items from Houdini's life, such as personal letters and century-old handcuffs. At the end of your visit, you'll be treated to a short live magic performance.

Steps away in the direction of Fisherman's Bastion, the **Golden Eagle Pharmacy** displays a mock-up of an alchemist's laboratory, with creepy stuffed creatures and a rack of herbs. It's located on the site of Budapest's first pharmacy, which was in operation until World War I. The **Museum of Music History**, past Fisherman's Bastion on Táncsics Mihály utca, might be small, but it has a lot to offer. Peruse the instruments, piano rolls and music-themed works of art to learn about the development of music in Hungary from the 18th century up through the present day.

The exhibits at the **Museum of Military History** on Kapisztrán tér begin outside the cannon-guarded entrance, where the walls still hold original cannonballs from the 1848–49 Revolution. Inside, the museum displays collections relating to Hungary's military history from medieval times to the present day.

Toast the High Life

COCKTAILS WITH JAW-DROPPING VIEWS

There's nothing quite like a bird's-eye view of the city's must-sees with a drink in hand. **Leo Budapest** honours the much-loved lion sculptures that adorn the Chain Bridge. It's located atop Hotel Clark on Clark Ádám tér and offers a close-up view of the bridge, the winding river and the Royal Palace. Complete the experience with a fun concoction and delectable nibbles amid the urban jungle atmosphere. All in all, it's a great place to sit back and relax after exploring the

BEST RESTAURANTS IN THE CASTLE DISTRICT

21 Magyar Vendéglő
Homestyle Hungarian dishes with a modern twist and an impressive assortment of local wines. €€

Arany Kaviár
Luxury, prestige, Russian food, lots of caviar and Hungarian fish dishes. €€€

Jamie's Italian
A laid-back but professional atmosphere, with guaranteed quality and *perfetto* Italian dishes. €€

Pavillon de Paris
Imaginative French cuisine and excellent service. In summer, enjoy your meal in the lovely garden. €€

Stand25
Traditional Hungarian dishes such as goulash and potato casserole by Bocuse d'Or winner Tamás Széll. €€

Hotel Clark
Come to adults-only Hotel Clark for relaxation right by the foot of the Chain Bridge. €€€

Hotel Victoria
This small boutique hotel has a great view of Parliament; a historic concert hall is next door. €€

Pest Buda Hotel
Charming boutique hotel where retro and modern design mingle and the service excels. €€

WHERE TIME STANDS STILL

Walking around the historic Castle District, you may wonder what all those residential houses looked like in the old days. Well, thanks to the **De La Motte Beer Palace**, you can take a peek. Although its bright yellow facade next to the Korona Café on Dísz tér is hardly suggestive of an exceptional interior, this 18th-century home of a Hungarian family still retains its baroque splendour. It showcases a lovely courtyard with an arcade loggia, a baroque doorway and a living space adorned with chandeliers and vintage furniture. Its most precious attraction, however, is the nearly 250 sq metres of painted walls dating from the 18th century, which emerged from beneath 15 other coats of paint in 1962.

ZGPHOTOGRAPHY/SHUTTERSTOCK ©

Castle District

Castle District, though you may have to compete for a seat when the sun's out. If you're interested in the lions' tongues debate (p60), try to peek into their mouths from here.

After taking the lift to **White Raven** at the top of the Hilton, you'll be welcomed with a view that's so special that your jaw might hit the floor. You can see pretty much all of Budapest from here, including the intricate and colourful Zsolnay tiles on the roof of Matthias Church – you won't be able to get this perspective anywhere else. The bar's name and signature cocktails are inspired by the ravens of King Matthias, the 'Raven King', and the legends about the bird's tail feathers. Finger food, mostly made of fresh local ingredients, also feature on the menu.

WHERE TO SHOP IN THE CASTLE DISTRICT

Bortársaság
For Hungarian wine, head to the biggest shop near the Chain Bridge. Great staff recommendations.

Fény Utca Market
Shopping for fresh local produce and organic goods? Head to this huge market hall, full of quality stalls.

Herend Shop
Delicate, handcrafted Herend porcelain pieces are world famous – Arnold Schwarzenegger is a fan.

GELLÉRT HILL & TABÁN

LEAFY RIVERSIDE SPAS

Tree-dotted Gellért Hill, surmounted by the Liberty Monument, is one of Budapest's signature landmarks. From the top, the views of Buda, the Pest skyline and the gently curving river are unbeatable. Below, Szent Gellért tér is an important transport hub.

Tabán is the hilly neighbourhood that stretches between Gellért Hill and Castle Hill. What used to be Budapest's Montmartre at the turn of the century – a bohemian district full of pubs and winding streets lined with one-storey houses – is today no more than a green park. In the 1930s, the city razed it all, and while there were many grandiose plans to replace Tabán with a newer, more modern district, none ever came to light. Today, Tabán has more picnic spots and playgrounds than sights, safeguarding its village-like atmosphere in legends and memories only. On the other side of Gellért Hill, hip Bartók Béla út brings some buzz to sleepy Buda.

TOP TIP

The Szent Gellért tér station on the M4 line is one of Budapest's prettiest. Taking the escalator down from street level, you'll first pass crisscross concrete work before descending even deeper into colourful spiral mosaics and white geometric chairs, which provide a perfect photo opportunity.

View from Gellért Hill

Gellért Hill

STRENUOUS CLIMB FOR SPLENDID VIEWS

Gellért Hill is visible from almost everywhere in the city. While it is touristy, you'll also spot many locals here at the weekends spicing up their post-lunch walk. Yet even with all the traffic, the top never gets too crowded. Climb it at the crack of dawn for a delightful sunrise.

To hike up to the top, start at the foot of Elisabeth Bridge and head towards the statue of St Gellért. Alternatively, choose a less steep but slightly longer journey from Liberty Bridge. There are rest and photo stops on the way, as well as playgrounds and a slide park for families.

HIGHLIGHTS
1 Citadella
2 Gellért Baths

SIGHTS
3 Bartók Béla Blvd
4 Bottomless Lake
5 Castle Garden Bazaar
6 Cave Church
7 Elisabeth Bridge
8 Garden of Philosophers
9 Gellért Hill
10 Liberty Bridge
11 Semmelweis Museum of Medical History
12 St Gellért Monument

ACTIVITIES
13 Rudas Baths

EATING
14 Czakó Kert

Gellért Baths

A CURATIVE SOAK

A true masterpiece of Art Nouveau architecture, Gellért Baths at the foot of Gellért Hill is unquestionably one of the most stunning historic spas in Budapest. Inside, shades of blue and turquoise overlap and intermingle – not only in the pools of water, but also on the walls, which are adorned with stained-glass windows, colourful mosaics, Zsolnay porcelain tiles and elegant sculptures. This richly embellished interior makes bathing in the hot waters, which emanate from deep within Gellért Hill, feel like a royal ritual. The thermal pools range in temperature from 35°C to 40°C, and there's also a cooler swimming pool for doing laps. Outside, a fun wave pool entertains crowds of all ages in summer.

Other amenities include medical massages, a sauna, a steam cabin and drinking fountains. The healing properties of the water – rich in sodium, calcium and magnesium among other minerals – are fortifying against ailments ranging from circulation-related disorders and spine and vertebrae injuries to degenerative illnesses and joint problems. Gellért Baths is co-ed all week and accessible for visitors with disabilities.

Gellért Baths

Citadella & the Liberty Monument

SYMBOL OF FREEDOM

The Citadella and the Liberty Monument atop Gellért Hill are emblematic symbols of Budapest. What makes the Citadella special is that while such fortresses were generally built for defence, Budapest's was created with a different idea in mind. It was erected after the 1848–49 Revolution – when Hungary wanted to break away from Habsburg rule – to discourage further insurrections by the Hungarian populace. The loopholes that dot the outside walls were for the big guns, which were aimed at the city itself. Today, however, Hungarians think of the Citadella not as a symbol of repression, but one of freedom. This sentiment is further reinforced by the statue that tops the fortress: a proud lady watching over Budapest with the symbol of peace, a palm branch, in her hands. Inaugurated in 1947, the statue commemorates those who sacrificed their lives for the freedom of Hungary. At the time of writing, the Citadella was closed for renovations. It is set to reopen as a public park in 2024.

Garden of Philosophers

Garden of Philosophers

A PLACE FOR PEACE AND MEDITATION

Most people who come to Gellért Hill head straight up to the Citadel for those postcard panoramas. However, if you're the type who prefers quiet rumination to the buzz of the crowds, consider a detour to the Garden of Philosophers, which is on the hillside closer to Elisabeth Bridge. This green space is filled with bronze statues of famous thinkers and prophets including Jesus Christ, Buddha and Mahatma Gandhi. The lovely sculpture depicting the union of Prince Buda and Princess Pest is a delight.

Liberty Bridge

THE LOCALS' FAVOURITE BRIDGE

Sage-green Liberty Bridge is one of Budapest's most stunning spans thanks to its striking colour and ornamental crisscross metalwork. Mythical *turul* birds top each of its towers, the red-and-white national coat of arms hanging in between. The bridge was originally opened in 1896 as Franz Josef Bridge, and the Habsburg emperor hammered the last silver rivet into the structure himself. Like all the other bridges across the Danube, Liberty Bridge was blown up during World War II. It was the first span to be rebuilt in the same style, and was renamed upon its opening.

Liberty Bridge

Cave Church

WORSHIP INSIDE A HILL

A functioning church set inside a cave in the middle of a big city? Now that's a sight to behold. This naturally formed grotto was turned into a church in 1931 and expanded outward into a neo-Romanesque monastery three years later. The church served as the seat of Hungary's Pauline order – the only male religious order founded in the country – until 1951, when the communists imprisoned the priests and the cave was sealed off with a thick concrete wall, part of which is still visible today as a reminder. The Pauline monks eventually returned after the fall of communism. The church can be visited anytime except during mass; the interior remains 20 degrees year-round, with no heating required.

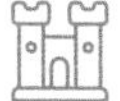

Elisabeth Bridge

THE CITY'S FIRST MODERN SPAN

This slender and elegant gleaming-white bridge is named after the Hungarians' favourite queen, Habsburg Empress Elisabeth (1837–98), affectionately known as Sissi. The bridge connects the city centre with Gellért Hill and offers great views to the Liberty Bridge, the Chain Bridge and the two sides of the city. Destroyed during World War II, Elisabeth Bridge wasn't rebuilt until 20 years later in 1964. The new modern bridge, designed by Pál Sávoly, is wider than the original, and suspension technology has replaced the earlier chains.

Elisabeth Bridge

TOP: PAUL HORIA MALAIANU/SHUTTERSTOCK ©, BOTTOM: MIKHAIL MARKOVSKIY/SHUTTERSTOCK ©

St Gellért Monument

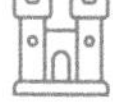

St Gellért Monument

MAJESTIC MONUMENT OF A MARTYR

You'll probably notice that the name Gellért is everywhere. Not only does he have a hill named after him, but there's also a bath, hotel, city square and metro station. So who was this guy? St Gellért was an Italian missionary who ended up in Hungary around 1020, after a storm disrupted his pilgrimage. King Stephen convinced him to stay, tutor his son and convert the masses to Christianity. After being named a bishop, he went on to live the life of a hermit. Unfortunately, legend has it that after the king died in 1038, the pagan Magyars hurled the bishop to his death in a spiked barrel. His statue now stands on the spot of his martyrdom, gazing peacefully down on Elisabeth Bridge.

Rudas Baths

WHERE HISTORY MEETS MODERN TRENDS

At this central spa, contemporary design elements mix with centuries-old bathhouse features. While the usual swimming pool, heated tubs, and a sauna and steam room await, Rudas has much more in store than a traditional Turkish bath. The star attraction is the rooftop hot tub, providing a grand view of the entire Pest skyline. Rudas also has an ornate drinking hall, where visitors can sample some of the mineral-rich liquid. The Turkish bath area is the only one that still holds same-sex bathing days. Men are welcome on Monday, Wednesday, Thursday (till 12.45pm) and Friday (till 10.45am), while Tuesday is women only.

Memento Park

A PEEK BEHIND THE IRON CURTAIN

While Memento Park is not, strictly speaking, part of this district (it's a way outside the city centre), it's an important south Buda site and worth a visit if you'd like to take a peek behind the Iron Curtain. Gigantic statues of Lenin, Marx, Engels, and homegrown red-star heroes, as well as other types of communist propaganda, fill this huge open-air park. These reminders were all removed from the streets of Budapest after the Berlin Wall fell in 1989. At Memento Park, you can sit inside an old Trabant – a classic East German car that was a dream for many Hungarian families during communism – and eavesdrop on the communist hotline to hear the voices of Joseph Stalin, Mao Zedong and even Che Guevara. Two intriguing exhibitions are also worth a look. One presents statues and busts of Lenin, while the other showcases the events of the 1956 Revolution and 1989 regime change, as well as fascinating footage of Hungary's secret police in training, which shares handy tips on how to spy on 'enemies of the state'.

WHEN STALIN GOT THE BOOT

Memento Park's main attraction is a pair of gigantic boots opposite the main entrance. It's a replica of the original 8m-high bronze statue of Stalin that was pulled down from its plinth in City Park during the 1956 Uprising and sawed apart until only the boots remained. Climb the stairs behind the monument to reach a balcony, where you can stand at the same spot from which communist leaders once waved to the crowds below.

Stalin's boots, Memento Park

Castle Garden Bazaar

FLOWERS, SCULPTURES AND VIEWS

History meets the present day at this stunning neo-Renaissance complex, which overlooks the Buda riverfront at the foot of the Royal Palace. Today, the garden and bazaar serve as a cultural hub with ample space for a variety of events: concerts, open-air film screenings and exhibitions. From here, stairs, lifts and an escalator make getting up to the Royal Palace easy. Opposite, the elegant restaurant Felix is housed inside a beautiful building that once pumped water to the Royal Palace.

Castle Garden Bazaar

Bottomless Lake

BUDA'S BELOVED PARK

Bottomless Lake (Feneketlen tó) and its surroundings make for one of Buda's favourite parks. Stretching along Bartók Béla út, it's the perfect place for either a quick picnic or some more active recreation: there's a running track, a tennis court and workout facilities. While the name suggests that the lake plunges deep into the Earth's crust, in fact, it's only four to five metres deep. Don't miss the statue of the bear, standing strong since 1961. He always has something in his paws – the neighbourhood children ensure that he is never without a gift or two.

Bottomless Lake

Semmelweis Museum of Medical History

WASH YOUR HANDS

How many people are familiar with the name Ignác Semmelweis (1818–65)? No? What about the practice of washing hands? The so-called 'saviour of mothers' was born and buried in this house on Apród utca, which now serves as a medical museum. Semmelweis' major discovery was that puerperal (childbed) fever could be eliminated if doctors – some of whom had just carried out autopsies – would simply wash their hands before delivering babies. While we now know this common practice greatly reduces the chance of passing on germs, the medical community actually rejected Semmelweis' findings during his lifetime. In addition to a section dedicated to his life and work, this quirky museum also presents the history of medicine, beginning with ancient Egypt.

NEAPOLITAN PIZZA IN GELLÉRT HILL & TABÁN

Amore di Napoli
The blue-and-white interior – including a blue mosaic wood-fired oven – honours the SSC Napoli football team, with one pizza dedicated to superstar Diego Maradona.

Moto Pizza
Try traditional Naples-style pizzas that are nice and thin in the middle all the while admiring the green Austin Cooper (a nod to *The Italian Job*) in the shop window.

Tasty Pizza
This local favourite makes pizzas from original Italian ingredients, but with a lot more toppings than just tomato and mozzarella.

POSZTOS/SHUTTERSTOCK ©

A38

MORE IN GELLÉRT HILL & TABÁN

Rock Out at a South Buda Concert

GO WILD AT THE RIVERSIDE

South from the Gellért Hill district lies one of the city's coolest concert spaces. Moored by the foot of Petőfi Bridge, **A38** is a major live-music venue housed on a decommissioned 1968 Ukrainian cargo ship. This is the city's go-to concert venue, where international and local acts across all genres – including pop, rock, alternative, jazz and electro – hit the stage pretty much every night of the week. When the weather is nice, the terraces open and provide a view to Pest's buildings, which look fabulous illuminated at night. Punters can also grab a bite to eat at the bistro before a gig. This concert venue is so cool that Lonely Planet readers once voted it the best bar in the world.

Past another bridge further south is **Dürer Garden**. Dürer has long been an iconic underground concert venue in Buda-

WHERE TO STAY IN GELLÉRT HILL & TABÁN

Engel View
Two apartments with a great view by the gleaming Elisabeth Bridge. Clean, quiet and cosy. **€€**

Hotel Gellért
Slated to become a top-notch five-star hotel, this is the district's iconic residence. **€€€**

Hotel Orion
Thirty tidy rooms walking distance from the Castle Garden Bazaar; sauna on-site. **€€**

pest, but in 2022 it had to relocate from City Park to south Buda. Now it's bigger and greener, boasting music festival vibes but still relatively close to downtown. Table tennis and colourful chairs, bean bags and hammocks by the riverside entertain hip crowds, and if you find yourself in a nostalgic mood, seek out a charming little spot underneath a staircase furnished with armchairs, rugs and lamps, reminiscent of a living room from the belle époque.

Break Bread on a Bridge

ROMANTIC RENDEZVOUS

Budapest's central span, the **Liberty Bridge** (p68), has always been a popular hangout for the city's residents. For as long as anyone can remember, lovebirds and friends have climbed up on the lower parts of the bridge with a drink in hand to watch the sun sink behind the Royal Palace and the boats float lazily below. But a few years ago, Budapesters took it one step further when a new phenomenon began: bridge picnics.

It all started in the summer of 2016, when Liberty Bridge was closed to cars for almost three months because of construction. It didn't take long for locals to take over the bridge: yoga classes, amateur musicians, street performers and groups of friends all gathered here for spontaneous summer picnics. Kids played hopscotch between the tram tracks during the day, couples canoodled in hammocks under the open sky come nightfall and there was even a wedding that took place right above the Danube.

As no harm was done, the city now tries to keep this new tradition alive by officially closing the bridge to traffic on summer weekends and letting people roam free. If you'd like to enjoy a picnic with locals on the bridge, look out for summer events in July and August which are named 'Szabihíd'.

Farm to Table

A TOUCH OF COUNTRYSIDE NOSTALGIA

Hidden amid the leafy streets of Tabán is a homey, rustic cottage, safeguarding a little slice of countryside right in the heart of the capital. The cottage, **Czakó Kert**, is the district's oldest house. The former vineyard home is today a bistro, dessert shop, bakery and deli, in addition to hiding a 250-year-old wine cellar. What connects these shops – besides their shared roof – is the fresh local ingredients they use.

Every weekend, a farmer's market sets up in the garden, offering colourful, garden-fresh goods and special local

BEST CAFES IN GELLÉRT HILL & TABÁN

Kelet
Rich coffee, Asian-inspired dishes, Czech beers and a book exchange with thousands of titles – take one, leave another behind.

Füge Bolt és Kávézó
This little pantry on Gellért Hill operates primarily as a shop, but also offers nibbles to snack on.

Hadik
One of Budapest's classic coffeehouses, this haunt favoured by local artists serves delicious drinks and Hungarian dishes.

Mitzi
This bohemian cafe focuses on breakfast, preparing everything from fruit-topped bowls of granola to a full English.

Jewel in Buda Apartments
Home away from home in a traditional building, with four bedrooms and two bathrooms. €€

Minilux Apartment
This top-floor, self-catering private apartment can accommodate just two guests. €€

Shantee House
Share a yurt with your friends or that special someone in the Zen-like garden. €

WHERE TO EAT IN TABÁN

Born and bred in Tabán, historian **Noémi Saly** shares her favourite places to eat in the neighbourhood.

Arany Szarvas
Iconic Arany Szarvas has a charming ambiance and a lovely terrace. It may not be the cheapest, but you get your money's worth, especially with the hearty meat dishes.

Gösser Tabán
Despite the name (it's a famous Austrian beer), this is not a pub but a restaurant serving huge portions of flavour-filled Hungarian favourites. This one's for hungry carnivores.

Tabáni Kakas
The interior design is nothing special, but the dishes at this time-honoured spot excel. Try the traditional duck and goose, and finish your meal off with a Hungarian pancake.

Liberty Bridge (p68)

products like chilies, honey and truffle paste from around the country. Some of the market produce also makes its way to the kitchen, where mouthwatering breakfasts and lunches are whipped up in the bistro. If you'd like a little taste of the countryside in a charmingly old-fashioned ambience, Czakó Kert is the perfect place to stop after a hike on Gellért Hill or a walk in the Tabán.

WHERE TO DRINK IN GELLÉRT HILL & TABÁN

Béla
Great selection of wine, Hungarian craft beers and meals from breakfast to tapas.

Palack Borbár
An impressive selection of wines, mostly from smaller cellars. Ask the sommelier for recommendations.

Szatyor bár
Adjacent to Hadik, Szatyor Bár is Buda's take on the ruin bar theme.

Starry Nights at Rudas Baths

SOAKING AFTER DARK

After a busy day of sightseeing, nothing beats the feeling of easing into a rooftop hot tub filled with muscle-melting hot water, a drink in hand and the night sky twinkling overhead. Live the dream at **Rudas Baths** (p69), where the doors reopen every Friday and Saturday between 10pm and 3am to welcome the city's night owls. Book your tickets online.

Pump up the Adrenaline

ENJOY SPEEDY STUNTS ON THE DANUBE

For a hair-raising ride, book yourself a seat on **RedJet** and buckle up. This 12-seat speedboat zooms by Budapest's most splendid sights on 30-minute trips, its 440-horsepower engine propelling it along at 80km/h. RedJet performs extreme stunts on the way: stopping, restarting and spinning around in front of and under historic landmarks like the Parliament or Chain Bridge. It's heaps of fun, but remember that the braver you are, the wetter you'll get. Catch RedJet at BudaPart, a car- and dog-free sandy riverside recreational zone full of restaurants, ice-cream parlours, cafes and bars.

Mingle with the Locals

BUDA'S BOHEMIAN SIDE

When it comes to eating, drinking and nights out on the town, sleepy Buda has got nothing on bustling Pest. But in recent years, bohemian cafes, bars and galleries have started springing up on one street in particular: **Bartók Béla Blvd (BBB)**, especially between Szent Gellért tér and Móricz Zsigmond körtér. Named after one of Hungary's most famous composers, BBB has now become the trendiest stretch in the district, if not in all of Buda, and is a haunt for hipsters, artists and students alike. Whether you crave coffee, cake, breakfast, lunch, brunch, ice cream or something a bit stronger, you'll find it on this street. Look for super-sleek repurposed spaces, like a bar set up in a former bus depot or at an open-air theatre.

BEST PLACES TO DANCE IN GELLÉRT HILL & TABÁN

Barba Negra
Everyone from unknown alternative bands to more popular names rock the stage at this partially open-air music venue all year long.

Fonó Ház
Don't miss this haven of Hungarian folk music, where you can learn how to folk dance – as well as make the iconic call outs – and watch concerts and performances.

Romkert
Romkert is a great summer only riverside outdoor club with amazing views. Show off your moves at hip-hop, R&B, house and back-to-the-'90s parties between Tuesday and Saturday.

WHERE TO SHOP IN GELLÉRT HILL & TABÁN

Fiók
More than just a stationery store, Fiók also carries a wide assortment of local designer goods.

Repertory
This cool concept store is the collaboration of two Hungarian design brands: Daige and Mama Kin.

Szia+
Stocks an eclectic assortment of colourful sunglasses, funky socks, jewellery, bags, clothes and more.

ÓBUDA & THE BUDA HILLS

LOST-IN-THE-PAST VILLAGE AND GREENERY

Óbuda is Budapest's oldest district: nearly 2000 years ago it was the site of Aquincum, the capital of the Roman province Pannonia Inferior. Today, the ruins of Aquincum are the main reason why people leave central Budapest to venture to this otherwise quiet neighbourhood. Óbuda's quaint, village-like layout and narrow streets are also home to a number of interesting museums that introduce the city's unique history and art.

Also here are the Buda Hills: many a local's favourite hiking destination with lofty views, a variety of walking trails and fun forms of transport. While Óbuda's primary attraction is cultural, a day spent exploring the serene Buda Hills is definitely worth it if you have the time. Easily accessible from Széll Kálmán tér, the hills are the perfect place to leave the city's buzz behind for some peace, greenery and fresh air.

TOP TIP

To reach Óbuda, hop on trams 17, 19 or 41 or the H5 HÉV suburban railway on Batthyány tér. The journey from downtown will take roughly 30 minutes. To reach the Buda Hills, head to Széll Kálmán tér and take bus 21A to Normafa, which is a great entry point.

Elisabeth Lookout Tower (p82)

BOTOND HORVATH/SHUTTERSTOCK ©

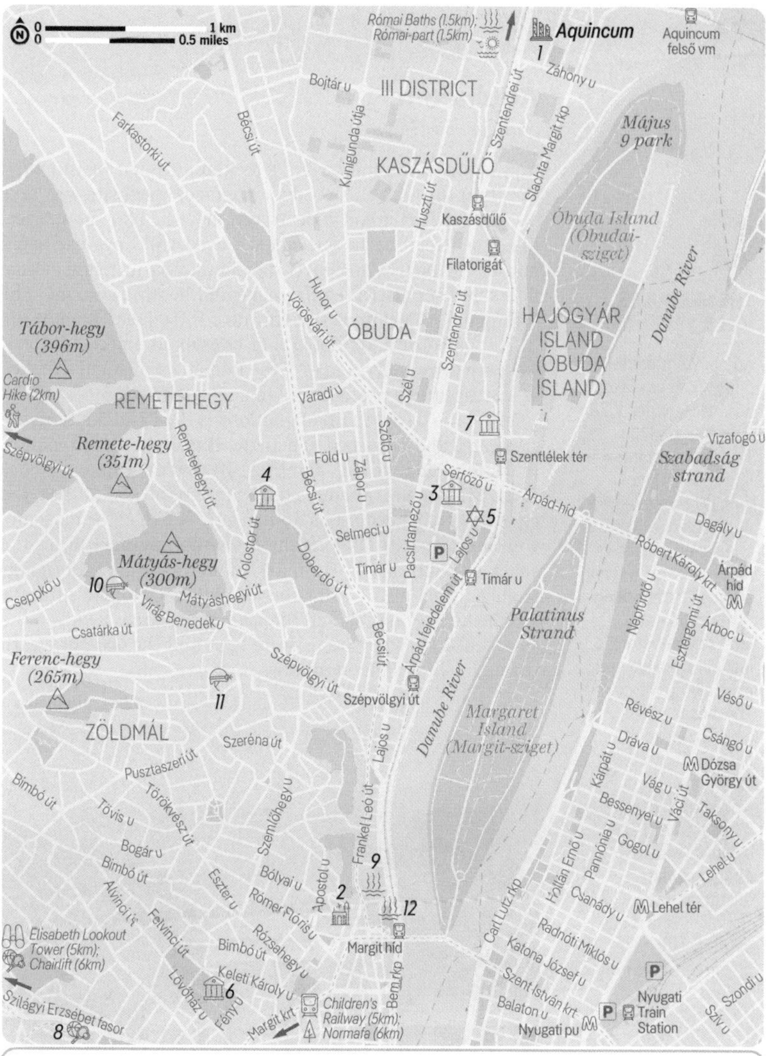

HIGHLIGHTS
1 Aquincum

SIGHTS
2 Gül Baba's Tomb
3 Hungarian Museum of Trade & Hospitality
4 Kiscelli Museum
5 Óbuda Synagogue
6 Palace of Wonders
7 Zichy Mansion

ACTIVITIES, COURSES & TOURS
8 Cogwheel Railway
9 Lukács Baths
10 Pálvölgy Cave
11 Szemlőhegy Cave
12 Veli Bej

Aquincum

HUNGARY'S POMPEII

Aquincum is the most complete Roman town in Hungary. Strolling through this outdoor archaeological site will take visitors back to the end of the 1st century, when Roman subjects filled the streets of the settlement. Paved walkways lead to old houses complete with courtyards, fountains, intricate mosaic floors and sophisticated drainage and heating systems. The Aquincum Museum at the entrance introduces Roman life in Hungary through displays of household objects, pottery, weaponry, jewellery, a map of the Roman empire and a replica of a 3rd-century portable organ called a hydra.

One of the park's main attractions is the Painter's House, a re-created and furnished Roman dwelling from the 3rd century that's adorned with wall paintings. Behind the Painter's House is the Mithraeum, a temple dedicated to the god Mithra, the chief deity of a mysterious Roman cult. North of the museum, you can take a stroll along the main thoroughfare to see the spacious public baths, the market and the forum. Not too far from Aquincum are the ruins of both the Roman military amphitheatre and the civilian amphitheatre; look for the small cubicles where lions were kept and the Gate of Death through which slain gladiators were carried.

THE HERCULES VILLA

Across Szentendrei út under 21 Meggyfa utca lies the Hercules Villa, unearthed in 1958. This lavish complex had luxuries like running water, heated floors, a sewer system and varied chambers for private use, as well as mosaics depicting many intricately crafted characters, including boxers and even a tipsy Hercules. The mosaic of the hero is believed to have been created in an Alexandrian workshop. Once the mansion of an unknown member of Aquincum's aristocracy, the Hercules Villa is one of Hungary's best-preserved ruins from the era.

Ruins, Aquincum

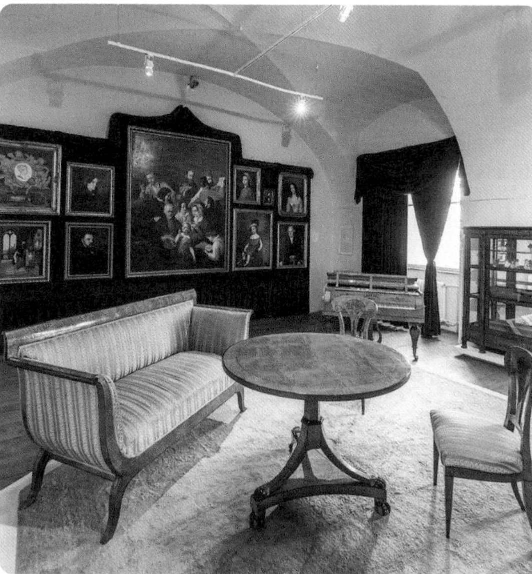

Kiscelli Museum

Kiscelli Museum

SAFEGUARDING BUDAPEST'S HISTORY

The Kiscelli Museum, housed in an 18th-century daffodil-yellow baroque monastery and church, manages a vast collection of objects related to the urban history of Budapest, as well as artwork from the 19th through 21st centuries. Visit a 19th-century pharmacy and admire an impressive display of trade signs, silver artefacts and rooms equipped with empire, Biedermeier and Art Nouveau furniture. Upstairs is an impressive collection of works by important 20th-century Hungarian artists like József Rippl-Rónai, Lajos Tihanyi and Béla Czóbel. The stark Gothic church used for temporary multimedia and art exhibits is striking.

Óbuda Synagogue

A TESTAMENT TO HUNGARIAN CLASSICISM

Built in 1821, at a time when the Jewish community in Óbuda was one of the largest in the country, this is Budapest's oldest synagogue. For many years the building housed Hungarian TV sound studios because the much-reduced post-WWII Jewish population couldn't afford the upkeep, but it is once again functioning as a *súl* (Jewish prayer house) with daily workshops and services. The synagogue is a superb example of the classical architectural style in Hungary. Call ahead for a tour.

Óbuda Synagogue

Zichy Mansion

THREE MUSEUMS IN ONE MANSION

This beautiful 18th-century baby-pink baroque mansion is home to three interesting museums. The **Victor Vasarely Museum** displays some 150 works by the 'grandfather of op-art', born as Győző Vásárhelyi in 1906 in Pécs. His visually arresting pieces trick the mind with illusions of depth and motion. A separate entrance leads to the **Óbuda Museum**, where you can discover the district's intriguing past from medieval times to the present day. The interactive exhibits test four of your senses – sight, hearing, smell and touch – and encourage visitors to get creative. The third site within the villa's walls is the **Kassák Museum**, which presents the intellectual legacy of Lajos Kassák, the celebrated writer, poet and editor of the 1920s Hungarian avant-garde.

All Aboard the Cutest Ride

A RAILWAY RUN BY CHILDREN

Chugging past some of the most superb hiking spots in the Buda Hills is the **Children's Railway**, operated almost entirely by kids. The staff, aged 10 to 14 and dressed in smart blue, white and red uniforms, hold all the positions on the railway, from conductors to signalmen, while a little adult supervision keeps the train on track (the engineers, thankfully, are grown-ups). Taking a trip on the Children's Railway is a time-transcending journey, as this special attraction is a living memorial of the communist era. Opened in 1948, the railway was originally operated by Soviet pioneer scouts. The goal was to give children the chance to learn about teamwork and responsibility. Today, a job on the railway is a prestigious position – only the top students are considered, and those who have been selected have to participate in training and take exams.

This is the longest narrow-gauge children's railway line in the world, and is now listed in the Guinness World Records. The line runs from Hűvösvölgy to Széchenyi Hill, taking in forested Normafa on the way. Even without the railway's retro charm, it's worth hopping on to see a side of Budapest that will make you forget you're in a busy European capital. Get your tickets ready for Hungary's cutest conductors!

GOOD TO KNOW

Bear in mind that tickets for the Children's Railway can only be purchased at the stations or on the train from conductors, so payment is cash only (Hungarian forints). Euros and credit cards are not accepted as children are in charge. If you'd like to learn more about the past and present of the Children's Railway, you can check out a short and sweet interactive exhibit and museum shop at Hűvösvölgy station, showcasing archival photos, documents, relics and games.

Children's Railway

VIENNASLIDE/ALAMY STOCK PHOTO ©

Hungarian Museum of Trade & Hospitality

QUIRKY AND COOL

Don't let the uninspired name fool you – this is a fun little place. It traces Hungary's catering and hospitality trades through the ages, displaying restaurant items, tableware, advertising posters, original shop signs, furniture and photographs. Sneak a peek into the early 20th-century through a variety of interiors: a hotel room, a cafe, a restaurant, a confectionery and a middle-class family home. You can also play interactive games, test your wine knowledge as a sommelier and learn the stories of the most famous Hungarian dishes. You can even take some original recipes home and impress your friends with your Hungarian cooking skills.

Gül Baba's Tomb

Gül Baba's Tomb

FORGET YOU'RE IN BUDAPEST

As you walk up the cobbled Gül Baba utca, you won't just feel like you're in another country, you might even wonder if you've travelled back in time. At the top of the street is the octagonal Gül Baba's Tomb, a popular pilgrimage site for Muslims, especially from Turkey. Gül Baba was a 16th-century dervish poet who took part in the capture of Buda in 1541 and is known in Hungary as the 'Father of Roses'.

The picturesque rose and lavender gardens surrounding his tomb are the perfect place to escape the buzz of Budapest and admire the panorama. Surrounding the gravesite is the Cultural Centre & Exhibition Hall. Don't forget to remove your shoes before entering the tomb.

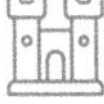

Palace of Wonders

HEAPS OF FUN FOR THE LITTLE ONES

A great family destination, the Palace of Wonders (CsoPa) invites curious kids to dive into science through hundreds of playful and interactive attractions, exhibitions, optical illusions, themed escape rooms, educational games and a 9D cinema. In total, it covers about 5000 sq metres within the Buda Entertainment and Gastro Centre. Visit Newton's apple garden, enjoy a fascinating physics show and repair an alien spaceship using fun logic games. While the centre is geared towards children of all ages, there's plenty to keep adults occupied too.

Normafa

LEAVE BEHIND THE BUZZ OF DOWNTOWN

Normafa, in the Buda Hills, is a favourite year-round hiking destination. This massive forested hill is within city limits and easily accessible via public transport. At the top are huge green spaces, hiking trails, a playground, food stalls, gorgeous views, picnic spots and even designated BBQ pits, all providing ample opportunity for quiet relaxation while busy Budapest stretches out below. If you visit the food stalls, be sure to buy yourself a Hungarian strudel – a delicious flaky pastry flavoured with cherries, poppy seeds or sweet cottage cheese.

An ancient birch tree used to stand at Normafa; legend has it that it sprouted in the year of King Matthias' birth (1443). The tree was a popular meeting spot for artists of the National Theatre, and singer Róza Schodelné Klein famously sung an aria from the opera *Norma* here, hence the name Normafa (the Norma tree). Unfortunately, the tree was destroyed by lightning in 1927. To reach Normafa, take bus 21 or 21A from Széll Kálmán tér, the Children's Railway (p80) from Hűvösvölgy or the Cogwheel Railway (p84) from Városmajor.

Normafa

Elisabeth Lookout Tower

THE HIGHEST POINT IN BUDAPEST

Topping 528m-tall János Hill, the highest point in Budapest, the neo-Roman Elisabeth Lookout Tower (Erzsébet kilátó) resembles a three-tier wedding cake – thanks to Frigyes Schulek's dazzling design (he also conceived Fisherman's Bastion). The lookout is named after Hungary's beloved Queen Elisabeth, affectionately nicknamed Sissi. To get to the top, you'll need to wind your way up a 100-step spiral staircase, but the stunning 360-degree panorama will make up for this calf-crunching exercise. From the top on a clear day, you can see as far as the High Tatra Mountains, as well as the city stretching out below.

Elisabeth Lookout Tower

Lukács Baths

MORE IN ÓBUDA & BUDA HILLS

Splash Around in Óbuda's Spas

A BATH FOR EVERYONE

Located in a lovely 19th-century building, **Lukács Baths** is one of the city's longest-standing spas. This enormous complex offers medical, leisure, plunge and swimming pools, as well as massage services, an outdoor fitness park and sunbathing terrace, a sauna, a steam room, private bath facilities and a cosy chamber lined with Himalayan salt. The thermal waters here are said to be of the highest quality among all the city's baths. Lukács also features a glass-covered drinking hall.

Less bombastic than the city's other baths, **Veli Bej** is perfect for those who want to avoid rowdy crowds. The interior is a mixture of old and new: the 16th-century Turkish baths' original walls and water pipes are still on display, though much of the interior has been renovated with modern touches. The centrepiece is a traditional octagonal Turkish pool surrounded by four small plunge pools of differing temperatures. A sauna with fresh ice, a steam room, leisure showers, Jacuzzi, small swimming pool and Kneipp basin are also on site.

Family-friendly **Római Baths** is a summer-only pool complex, equipped with winding water slides, a kids' pool and a playground. The thermal spring that fills this lido was a known water source in Roman times, when the grounds were regarded as a holy site – archaeologists found the ruins of a sanctuary here.

TAKE A TRIP TO RÓMAI-PART

Riverside Római-part (Római Shore) is at the northern tip of Buda. It's a popular weekend destination for those who enjoy kayaking, canoeing and stand-up paddleboarding – all available to rent – or just sitting by the river in a colourful deck chair with some Hungarian hake (Hungary's version of fish and chips) or *lángos* (deep-fried dough and the country's favourite street food), just like a local. It's easily accessible by bike or public transport. Római-part is a serene locale where you're able to get really close to the river – you can even dip your toes – and where it feels like you've left Budapest behind, even though you're only a comfortable 20 minutes away.

WHERE TO EAT IN ÓBUDA & THE BUDA HILLS

Csalánosi Csárda
Homestyle cooking, traditional recipes, authentic flavours and hearty portions are at this rustic restaurant. €€

Kéhli
This popular spot is known for traditional Hungarian dishes and a 19th-century atmosphere. €€

Hummus Bar
Fresh Middle Eastern delights like shakshuka and falafel bring in the crowds on Kolosy tér. €

WHERE TO EXERCISE IN ÓBUDA

Budapest Garden
A fun riverfront space with a cool skate park (rentals available), bubble football, beach volleyball, table tennis, trampolines and more.

Monkey Boulder
More than 100 different routes await at this enormous bouldering gym, where you can train for the Alps – or maybe just have fun – without a rope or harness.

Paddle Around
Check out Garden Placc on Római-part (p83) for SUPs, kayaks and canoes. You can even try SUP yoga at events organised by SUP Budapest.

The Journey, Not the Destination

TRAVEL IN STYLE

The Buda Hills are a great destination for some top-of-the-city relaxation, and you can make the journey there even more enjoyable if you take one of the district's quirky means of transport.

Start from Széll Kálmán tér station on the M2 and walk along Szilágyi Erzsébet fasor for about 10 minutes (or take tram 61 for two stops). You'll soon spot a towering circular-shaped building, the Körszálló, an iconic example of Brutalist architecture. Opposite is the terminus of the **Cogwheel Railway** (Fogaskerekű; also known as tram line 60). The historic red-and-white carriages are a nostalgic sight for many, and will take you the 4km to Széchenyi Hill in style. All you need is a regular public transport ticket.

Cross the park to Hegyhát út, where you can change to the **Children's Railway** (p80), staffed almost entirely by kids. Ride it all the way to János Hill (the fourth stop). Topped by the Elisabeth Lookout Tower (p82), this is the highest point in Budapest. You can spend the afternoon here or at nearby Normafa, enjoying leisurely walks, ice cream cones and the views. Afterward, make your way to the **chairlift** (about 500m from the Elisabeth Lookout Tower), which will take you down to Zugligeti út in 15 minutes while providing wonderful panoramas of the Buda surroundings en route. It's best at sunset.

Go Spelunking

TWO CAVES, ONE BIG ADVENTURE

While Budapest is widely known as the spa capital of the world, what's often overlooked is the massive cave system that the thermal waters have carved out below ground. Combine the two for an unforgettable experience.

Rich in unique dripstone and stalagmite formations, **Pálvölgy Cave** is the country's longest cave system with subterranean passages extending over 30 kilometres. Hourly 60-minute tours depart between 10.15am and 4.15pm every day except Monday, and take in some truly amazing stalagmite and stalactite formations. Those who want the full spelunking experience can leave the well-trodden paths behind for a more exciting three-hour-long tour (lots of crawling and scrambling) in protective coveralls and headgear. No experience is needed, but participants must be at least 14. Take bus 65 from Óbuda's Kolosy tér to the fifth stop, and don't forget to book ahead.

Nearby **Szemlőhegy Cave** has a completely different experience. Instead of towering stalactites, it provides sparkle – and lots of it. The cave's walls are lined with crystals and miner-

WHERE TO DRINK IN ÓBUDA & THE BUDA HILLS

Fellini Rómain
Lounge about in striped riverfront deck chairs while your feet touch the Danube at Római-part.

Két Rombusz
Sit inside (or atop) two old buses or enjoy a hammock in the shade, the river in arm's reach.

Kobuci Kert
Seasonal Kobuci is a great live-music venue, with scores of cool Hungarian bands on stage.

PETER STERLING/GETTY IMAGES ©

Cogwheel Railway

als, which shimmer with ethereal beauty. Hourly 40-minute tours depart between 10am and 4pm daily, except Monday. Paths are easier to walk here, and some sections are accessible by wheelchair. This is a fun destination for families; don't miss the interactive visitor centre. To get here, take bus 29 from Szentlélek tér to the ninth stop.

Hike for Your Heart

CARDIO HIKE IN THE BUDA HILLS

Enjoy hiking around the Buda Hills? Why not test your cardio performance while you're at it? The Szent Ferenc Hospital has created a special **cardio hike** for those with heart disease, high blood pressure and diabetes – though the curious and health-conscious can also give it a go.

To get here, take bus 65 from Kolosy tér to the last station. From here, there are two paths to choose from: follow the blue hearts painted on trees for a shorter 3.5km-long hike, and the red hearts for a longer 5.2km-long trail. You have to measure your pulse at the starting point – as well as every time you see a sign – and record the result in one of the provided leaflets. Both the leaflets and the signs indicate a healthy heart rate for each stop, which you can compare with your results. Need a breather? There are plenty of benches scattered along the trail. At the end of the hike, you can drop off your leaflet in a post box (include your email address) and doctors will notify you in the event you need a medical follow-up.

There are similar cardio hikes throughout Budapest on Hárs Hill, Normafa and in the Farkas Forest in Újpest.

SZIGET FESTIVAL

Budapest's answer to Glastonbury is the Sziget Festival, which takes place on Óbuda Island every August. Concerts and musical performances go from early afternoon, through the witching hour, and continue on until the break of dawn. The five-day festival is also home to countless other attractions, including art performances, film screenings, a beach, travelling funfair, photo booths and bungee jumping. Also known as the 'Island of Freedom', Sziget invites you to leave those grey days behind and party your heart out every summer.

WHERE TO STAY IN ÓBUDA & THE BUDA HILLS

Aquincum Hotel
Complete with thermal pools, saunas, steam rooms and a hot tub, this hotel is big on relaxation. **€€**

M&M Apartman
Two-room apartment comes equipped with a kitchen; it's a five-minute walk to the riverside. **€€**

Vendégház a hegyen
The 'Guest House on the Hill' is a charming wooden house set amid ample greenery; there's a hot tub too. **€€**

BELVÁROS

WELL-HEELED SHOPPING CENTRE

The 'Inner Town' is the centre of Pest's universe, especially when it comes to high-end tourism and shopping. This is where you'll find Váci utca, with its luxury shops, restaurants and bars, and Vörösmarty tér, home to the city's most celebrated *cukrászda* (cake shop). The centre is Deák Ferenc tér, the main square where three of the city's four metro lines converge. Belváros is the most heavily visited part of town, and justifiably so, given the splendid Art Nouveau architecture and dense concentration of dining and drinking venues.

But Belváros has something of a split personality. The area north of busy Ferenciek tere is full of flashy boutiques and well-frequented bars and restaurants. The neighbourhood to the south is more student-driven, quieter and local, with much of it reserved for pedestrians. Still, there's an increasing number of trendy cafes and restaurants here too, along with the usual souvenir shops and boutiques.

TOP TIP

The easiest way to get your bearing is on public transport. Tram 2 (or 2B or 2M) will take you along the western edge by the Danube – though you may be distracted by the impressive views of Castle Hill. Trams 47 and 49 follow the eastern perimeter of the Inner Town.

Street scene, Belváros

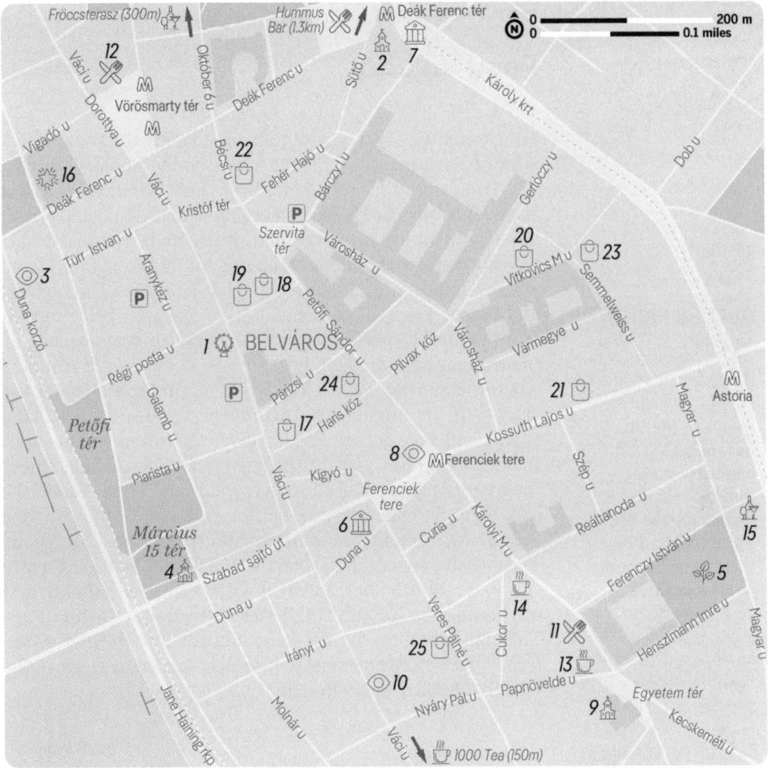

SIGHTS
1 Budapest Eye
2 Deák tér Lutheran Church
3 Duna Korzó
4 Inner Town Parish Church
5 Károlyi kert
6 Matild Palace
7 Millennium Underground Museum
8 Párisi Udvar
9 University Church
10 Váci utca

EATING
11 Belvárosi Disznótoros
12 Gerbeaud

DRINKING & NIGHTLIFE
13 Asterisk
14 Centrál Kávéház
15 Csendes Vintage Bar & Cafe

ENTERTAINMENT
16 Pesti Vigadó

SHOPPING
17 Balogh Kesztyű Üzlet
18 Bomo Art
19 Folkart Kézművésház
20 Holló Műhely
21 Mono
22 Nanushka
23 Rododendron
24 Vass
25 wonderLAB

Millennium Underground Museum

PARADISE FOR TRAINSPOTTERS

V Deák Ferenc tér is where three of Budapest's four metro lines converge. In the pedestrian underpass below the square, this small but fascinating museum traces the development of the capital's underground lines, including the M4 which opened in 2014. Much emphasis is given to the little yellow metro (M1), continental Europe's first underground railway, which opened for the millenary celebrations in 1896. The museum is atmospherically housed in a stretch of disused tunnel with the original station name, 'Gizella tér', spelled out in Zsolnay tiles. It features three wonderfully restored antique carriages used as recently as 1973, an excellent array of historical posters, documents and maps, and a wonderful exhibit of items lost and found. The museum entrance is within the metro's main ticket office.

Pesti Vigadó

WHERE MUSICAL TITANS PERFORMED

This Romantic-style concert hall, built facing the Danube just west of Vörösmarty tér in 1865, was badly damaged during WWII. Restorations took place over three dozen years and it is now fully restored to its former grandeur. The Vigadó boasts quite the historical pedigree; this is where Buda, Pest and Óbuda were forged into the single capital city of Budapest in 1873 and where composers and musicians Johann Strauss, Ferenc Liszt and Ferenc Erkel all performed. It's a fantastic place to visit and to catch a classical concert or a dance performance by the Hungarian State Folk Ensemble in glamorous surrounds.

Before entering, have a look at the main facade facing the river with its huge arched windows, statues representing various musical genres and busts of celebrated Hungarians. Inside, start your visit in the Vigadó Gallery, which traces the history of this 'Place for Merrymaking'. Then ascend the ornamental stone staircase whose walls are festooned with murals by Romanticist painters Mór Thán and Károl Lotz. The massive concert hall is on the 2nd floor. There are theatre spaces on the 4th floor, and a lift will whisk you to the 5th and 6th floors, which contain galleries for temporary exhibitions. The highlight is on the 6th floor; step out onto the *panoráma terasz* (panoramic terrace) to take in spectacular views of the Danube, Buda and Castle Hill.

GETTING HIGH IN THE INNER TOWN

Nowadays, it's quite easy to get high in Belváros. The 6th floor of the Vigadó has its own terrace with both jaw-dropping views and a small cafe, and a short distance south on Március 15 tér, the Inner Town Parish Church (p90) has now opened its South Tower to visitors. Should you prefer a tipple with your views, head for the St Andrea Wine & Skybar in the erstwhile Bank Palace (now Vácil; p95) behind the Vigadó. And then there's the Budapest Eye in Erzsébet tér...

Pesti Vigadó

PETER MOCSONOKY/ALAMY STOCK PHOTO ©

Budapest Eye

SHORT BUT SWEET VIEWS

Dominating V Erzsébet tér, this attraction exaggerates just a titch when it claims, 'The Budapest Eye is to Budapest what the London Eye is to London'. Huh? At just 65m, it's less than half the height of London's wheel, and the ride is over in just three twirls. Still, it does offer stunning panoramic views of Pest and across the Danube to Buda and it's an easy way to get an overview of the capital. Board after dark; the flight is particularly impressive at night.

Budapest Eye

Deák tér Lutheran Church

WHERE THERE'S A WILL

This central church on the south side of V Deák Ferenc tér doesn't sound like a crowd-pleaser, but it was designed by Mihály Pollack in 1799 and is one of the best examples of early neoclassical architecture in Budapest. And frankly, in this overwhelmingly Catholic country (especially the western part), a Protestant church is a rarity. The attached presbytery, which once functioned as a school attended by the poet Sándor Petőfi, contains the National Lutheran Museum, tracing the history of the Reformation and the Hungarian reform movement. Exhibits include church plate and a copy of Martin Luther's will.

Deák tér Lutheran Church

Inner Town Parish Church

CHURCH FOR ALL TIMES

This often overlooked church, sitting uncomfortably close to the Elisabeth Bridge flyover, but there are worthy views from its 55m-high South Tower. It was rebuilt on the site of a 12th-century Romanesque church, itself situated within a Roman fortress. A short distance north of the church entrance you can spot the remains of that **fortress** – called Contra Aquincum and an outpost of the Roman town of Aquincum – which dates back to the 3rd century AD. The present church was reconstructed in the 14th century and again in the 18th century, so you can easily spot Gothic, Renaissance, baroque and even Turkish elements. Indeed, in the ambulatory around the main altar are two dozen sedilia (medieval stone niches), one of which was turned into a mihrab (prayer niche facing Mecca) in the 15th century when the Ottomans converted the church into a mosque. In the sanctuary is a 14th-century fresco of an enthroned Madonna, only uncovered in 2010. The crypt contains an exhibition on the church's history, a treasure of liturgical objects and vestments, and a recently constructed chapel used for chamber music performances. Gain access to the tower at the end of the south aisle to the right of the main entrance; there's a small lift or you can climb the 98 steps. At the top you can cross through a dense network of beams to the North Tower from where the bells ring.

AQUINCUM

The most complete Roman town in Hungary was built around 100 AD. Visitors today can explore the remains of its houses, baths, courtyards and fountains. The on-site Aquincum Museum helps put the ruins in perspective (p78).

WHAT SPANS BELOW

Elisabeth Bridge (p69), dating from 1964, enjoys a special place in the hearts of Budapesters as it was the first newly designed bridge to reopen after WWII, when the retreating Germans destroyed everything that crossed the Danube. With a higher arch than the other bridges spanning the river, it offers dramatic views of both Castle and Gellért Hills, as well as the river itself. Look for the renovated Liberty Bridge (p68) to the south, which originally opened in time for the Millenary Exhibition in 1896.

Inner Town Parish Church

EYE UBIQUITOUS/ALAMY STOCK PHOTO ©

Somlói galuska

DIY FRÖCCS

If you want to make your own *fröccs* then you'll need to master the water-to-wine ratios for the four main styles: *kisfröccs* (small spritzer), *nagyfröccs* (big spritzer), *hosszúlépés* (long step) and *házmester* (janitor). Check out our suggestions on p258.

MORE IN BELVÁROS

Spritzers à la Magyar

SUMMER WINE COOLERS

Hungarians love their wine in more ways than one. In the summertime, spritzers *(fröccs)* of red or white wine mixed with sparkling water are consumed in enormous quantities; knowing the hierarchy and the art of mixing a spritzer to taste – from *kisfröccs* (small spritzer) to *házmester* (janitor) – will definitely win you kudos as an honorary local. The best place to try them is the huge **Fröccsterasz** complex near the Budapest Eye. When you're fully spritzed, follow the crowds next door to Akvárium, a large club with several halls staging a variety of live music.

Sweet-Tooth Paradise

A CAKE SHOP FOR EVERYONE

Every Hungarian has a sweet tooth. Desserts eaten at the end of a meal include *Somlói galuska* (sponge cake with chocolate and whipped cream) and *Gundel palacsinta* (flambéed pancake with chocolate and nuts). More complicated pastries are usually consumed mid-afternoon in a *cukrászda*

WHERE TO DRINK IN BELVÁROS

Good Spirits
A welcoming watering hole fully stocked with more than 300 types of whisky. The signature cocktails here are superb.

Why Not
Perennial favourite gay/mixed hangout celebrated for its parties and fabulous views of Buda Castle and the river.

Három Holló
New-style cafe and boozer for intellectual types, with cultural, literary and musical events almost every night.

Solid
Chichi wine bar on the 7th floor of the Hotel Rum. Come here for views and to chill out.

WHERE TO SEE A SHOW IN BELVÁROS

Puskin Art Mozi
Historic movie hall built as casino in 1926, screens a healthy mix of arthouse and popular releases.

József Katona Theatre
Brave a Hungarian production at the nation's best-known playhouse; shows are infrequently subtitled in English.

Pesti Vigadó
Catch a classical music or dance performance at this opulent mid-19th-century hall.

INNER TOWN TIPS

Judit Marothy, co-founder of the travel agency Budapest Underguide and currently commis chef at Costes Downtown, shares some of her favourite spots in the centre of Budapest.

Károly Garden
This is a cosy little park with a playground, outdoor exhibits and a famous rabbit just off the Inner Ring Roads.

Erzsébet tér
A green space that's easy to find: follow the Budapest Eye to meet Gen Z locals at the skate park.

Gerlóczy Café
Head here for the perfect breakfast or brunch. It has menus for every taste and diet, a lovely terrace and a chic, laid-back atmosphere.

Foton Gallery
This gallery features emerging artists from diverse fields of photography.

(patisserie) of which Belváros counts many, including the traditional **Auguszt Cukrászda** and the more up-to-date **Centrál Kávéház**. But nothing compares with **Gerbeaud**, Budapest's most famous cake shop and a fashionable meeting place at the northern end of the Vörösmarty tér since 1870. Grab a seat on the terrace and don't fail to order the *Dobos torta*, a seven-layer sponge cake layered with chocolate buttercream and topped with caramelised brown sugar, invented by the Hungarian confectioner József C Dobos in 1884.

Show Me the Way

GUIDED TOURS

If you want to make the most of your time, a guided tour can be a great way to glean some local insights. Go on foot, on two wheels (or even three) or by water: Belváros has a number of quality options departing from this central neighbourhood.

Trip to Budapest offers 'free' 2½-hour walking tours of Budapest's top sights in English; guides work for tips only, so dig deep. **Yellow Zebra Bikes** has four-hour guided cycle tours taking in Heroes' Square, City Park, central Pest and Buda via the Margaret Bridge. Less conventional and closer to the ground are the electric-scooter tours from **Urban Tours**, which last 2½ hours and basically follow the Danube on both sides from Margaret to Liberty Bridges.

Tuk Tuk Taxi has popular guided tours that whisk two or three people around in Bangkok-style three-wheelers. From your open-air vantage point, you get to see Castle Hill, Heroes' Square, Gellért Hill, Parliament and other popular sites. Tours last from 1½ to four hours. **Mahart PassNave** has a conventional one-hour cruise with taped commentary along the Danube. More exhilarating is the **River Ride** in a bright yellow amphibious bus that takes you on a 1½-hour heart-stopping tour of the city by road and river.

Sexy Sentries by the Danube

LOVINGLY RESTORED PALACES

Don't miss a closer look at the **Párisi Udvar** and the **Matild**, two palaces conveniently located on opposite sides of the same road. Even though both now contain five-star hotels, you can still enjoy their unbridled opulence for the price of a cup of coffee. The Párisi Udvar (1909) displays Moorish, Gothic and Art Nouveau elements – a classic example of Eclectic architecture. For decades it was a delightful but down-at-heel shopping arcade; now, following a total renovation, its tiles, mosaics and arched glass ceilings once again glisten. At its heart is the Párisi Passage Café; enjoy a drink here or head

WHERE TO STAY IN BELVÁROS

Hotel Rum
A locally designed hotel with four room categories, from Light Rum to Black Rum. €€€

Three Corners Hotel Art
This totally revamped corner hotel has Art Deco touches and well-kept guestrooms and apartments. €€€

Gerlóczy Boutique Hotel
An 1890s building on an attractive square, Gerlóczy offers excellent decor, atmosphere and value. €€

RAKETIR/SHUTTERSTOCK ©

Duna korzó

to the adjoining brasserie for something more substantial. Just across the road is the Matild Palace (1902), which has been restored to its neo-baroque glory. Its eponymous cafe is a sumptuous reimagining of the Belvárosi Kávéház, a popular meeting place during the belle époque.

Stroll Along the River

DANUBE PROMENADE

Enjoy splendid views of Buda while walking along the **Duna korzó**, the 'Danube Promenade', between Elisabeth and Chain Bridges. It sits just above the riverside Belgrád rakpart and is lined with cafes and restaurants; the street performers and handicraft stalls by day turn into strolling lovers by night. The promenade passes two leafy squares: Petőfi tér, named after the poet of the 1848–49 War of Independence, and Március 15 tér, which marks the date of the outbreak of that war.

Everthing's for Sale

SHOPPING IS MORE THAN A PASTIME

It may sound like a cliche, but shopping is a way of life in Belváros. If you're in the neighbourhood, take note: everything from locally produced fashion to high-quality folk art is available. In general, the areas around the northern part of Váci utca (above Ferenciek tere) caters mostly to the well-to-do crowd, with its Fashion Street (Deák Ferenc utca) of recognisable name brands. Lower Váci utca is where you'll find many of the more unusual independent shops.

PEACE & QUIET IN BELVÁROS

Ágnes Fazakas, owner of the Asterisk Antiques Gallery and Café, reveals some of her favourite spots to find peace in the lower Váci utca area.

Bástya Park
This park incorporates parts of Pest's medieval city walls, erected by the legendary king Matthias Corvinus.

Saint George Serbian Orthodox Church
Just a stone's throw away from the park, this churchyard and the cemetery behind its walls offer a tranquil oasis.

The Sliced Palazzo
A grand 19th-century building stands at Szerb utca 15, reminiscent of a Renaissance palazzo with intricate stonework and loggias. A real curiosity, it has essentially been cut in half in order to allow entry to narrow Fejér György utca, flanked by 1930s Bauhaus buildings.

Leo Boutique Rooms
This once simple *panzió* (pension) has metamorphosed into a very cool and quiet oasis. **€€**

Katona Apartments
Simply furnished and cleverly arranged apartments in an old block in the heart of Belváros. **€€**

Loft Hostel
Friendly backpacker magnet with great kitchen, mini-gym and skylit lounge. **€**

For fashion, **Mono** showcases the work of a couple of dozen up-and-coming Hungarian designers, while **Nanushka** sets off Sandra Sandor's cutting-edge women's clothing. Quirkier fare can be found at **wonderLab**, with Hungarian-designed clothing, handbags and jewellery, and at **Rododendron**, with similar offerings as well as toys and prints.

Vass is a traditional shoemaker that stocks high-quality ready-to-wear shoes and also cobbles to order. Nearby **Balogh Kesztyű Üzlet** can stitch you up a pair of custom-made leather gloves complete with cashmere lining.

Our favourite place for Hungarian folk art is **Holló Műhely**, though the painted eggs and boxes are heavily influenced by Saxon folk art in Romania. A wider and more conventional selection (but still first-rate and Hungarian-made) is available at **Folkart Kézművésház**. For the finest locally made paper and paper goods in Budapest, including leather-bound notebooks, photo albums and diaries, visit **Bomo Art**.

BEST PLACES FOR SWEETS IN BELVÁROS

Rózsavölgyi Csokoládé
Tiny boutique sells award-winning bean-to-bar chocolates handmade in nearby Budafok in a wide range of unusual flavours.

Szamos Marcipán
'Many Kinds of Marzipan' sells just that – in every shape, size and flavour imaginable.

Cadeau
The delectable filled bonbons sold here are handmade by a celebrated patisserie in Gyula, in Hungary's southeast.

Chez Dodo
Arguably has the largest (80 at last count) and definitely the most colourful macaron selection in Budapest.

Live Like a Local

POPULAR STUDENT HAUNTS

It's easy to experience local life in Budapest. People are friendly, the food is excellent and the wine is fine. For a true local's day out, try out the neighbourhood around Egyetem tér, where students proliferate.

Start your day at **Asterisk**, a wonderful cafe that serves all-day breakfast, cold plates and mezze. There are galleries here too, which display Art Deco bric-a-brac, antique Japanese silk cushions and artwork.

Egyetem tér (University Sq) takes its name from the prestigious Loránd Eötvös Science University (ELTE). Attached to the main university building is the lovely baroque **University Church**, which was built in 1742 on the site of an Ottoman mosque. Over the altar is a copy of the Black Madonna of Częstochowa, revered in Poland.

At **Belvárosi Disznótoros** chow down on huge portions of sausages and salad while standing up alongside local students. Then head for **Károlyi kert**, a quiet garden with colourful flowerbeds and shady benches.

At teatime, pop over to **1000 Tea** to sip a soothing blend in a Japanese-style tearoom. If coffee is more your thing, another grande dame of traditional cafes, **Centrál Kávéház**, has been serving great pastries since 1887.

And then there are the cocktails: seek out the quirky **Csendes Vintage Bar**, with junkyard chic decorating the walls. Feeling peckish? The evergreen **Hummus Bar** round the corner serves inexpensive veggie dishes.

WHERE TO EAT IN BELVÁROS

Salt
Michelin-starred anchor at the Hotel Rum serving 15-course tasting menus; bring buckets of cash. €€€

Baalbek
Stylish Lebanese on the river, serving favourites like Kibbeh labanieh and lamb kebabs. €€€

Monk's Bistrot
Contemporary reimagining of Hungarian dishes served in hip industrial surrounds. €€

VÁCI UTCA WALKING TOUR

Váci utca is the capital's premier shopping street, a pedestrian strip crammed with chain stores, touristy restaurants and a smattering of shops and notable buildings. A good place to start is at the **1 Párisi Udvar** (p92). Built in 1909, this is a stunning, ornate example of Eclectic architecture, with Moorish, Gothic and Art Nouveau elements; it now houses a cafe, brasserie and hotel. Head up Váci utca to **2 Philanthia**, a shop with a rare Art Nouveau interior from 1906. Next door, **3 Thonet House** is a masterpiece built by Ödön Lechner in 1890; to the west, at Régiposta utca 13, there's a **4 relief** of an old postal coach by the celebrated ceramicist Margit Kovács. Facing Szervita tér is **5 Török Bank House**, built in 1906, with a glass-covered facade. In the upper gable there's a Secessionist mosaic by Miksa Róth of the 'patroness' Hungary surrounded by her celebrated sons. Back on Váci utca is the sumptuous **6 Bank Palace**, built in 1915 and once the home of the Budapest Stock Exchange. It has since been converted into a shopping gallery called Váci1, with the Hard Rock Cafe as anchor tenant. Váci utca disgorges into **7 Vörösmarty tér**, a large square of smart shops, galleries, cafes and artists, who will draw your portrait or caricature. In the centre is a statue of Mihály Vörösmarty, the 19th-century poet after whom the square is named. At the northern end is **8 Gerbeaud** (p92), the city's most famous patisserie. A pleasant way to return to Ferenciek tere is along the **9 Duna korzó** (p93), the riverside 'Danube Promenade' between Chain and Elisabeth Bridges.

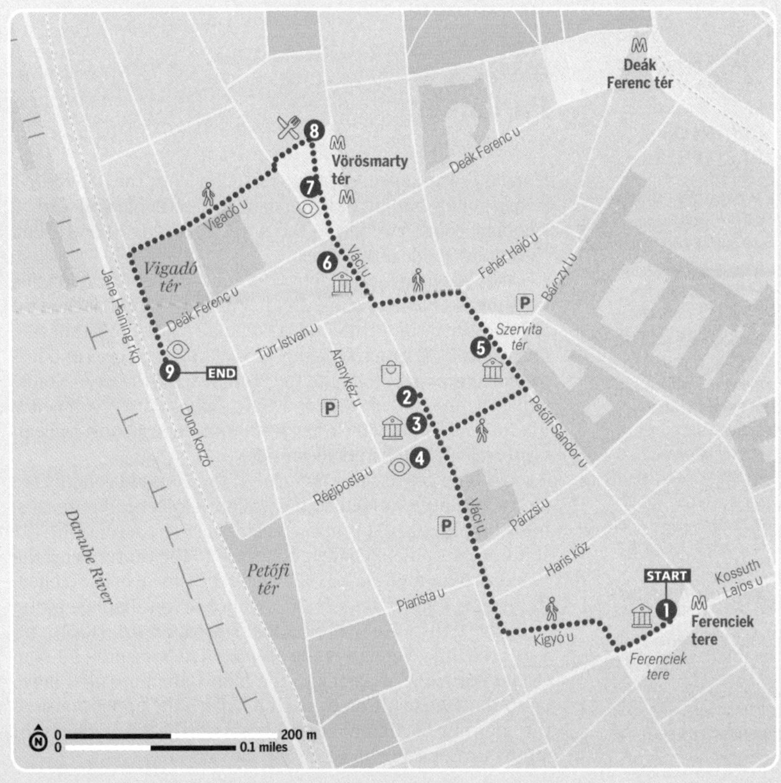

PARLIAMENT & AROUND

SIGNATURE SIGHTS AND SQUARES

North of Belváros is Lipótváros (Leopold Town), with the landmark Parliament facing the Danube to the west and the equally iconic Basilica of St Stephen to the southeast. This is prime sightseeing territory; along with those two icons you'll also discover great galleries and exhibits, some lovely squares and Art Nouveau buildings.

Lipótváros is easy to explore on foot, and its defining squares are V Széchenyi István tér, facing the river; V Szabadság tér, with the only marked Soviet memorial left in the city; and V Kossuth Lajos tér, fronted by Parliament. This neighbourhood has excellent high-end restaurants, welcoming cafes and good bars.

East of Lipótváros lies Terézváros (Theresa Town), named in honour of Empress Maria Theresa. This is a district that gets busy after dark: here you'll also find VI Nagymező utca, lined with theatres and music halls, as well as the city's largest gay club.

TOP TIP

The centre of the neighbourhood is the area around Október 6 utca, due west of the basilica, where you'll find the erstwhile headquarters of the Central European University (now based in Vienna). Come here for the lion's share of the district's restaurants, bars and cafes.

CROWN OF ST STEPHEN

The two-part crown, with its bent cross, pendants and enamelled plaques of the Apostles on the band, dates from the late 12th century and has become the very symbol of the Hungarian nation. The crown has disappeared several times over the centuries, most recently in 1945 when Hungarian fascists fleeing the Soviet army took the crown to Austria; the US army then transferred it to Fort Knox in Kentucky. In 1978 it was returned to Hungary with great ceremony – and relief.

Parliament

HUNGARY'S MOST ICONIC BUILDING

Hungary's Parliament stretches for 268m along the Danube. It's a vast, stately building and repository of national treasures, a symbolic counterweight to the Royal Palace on Buda Hill on the opposite side of the river.

Designed by Imre Steindl in 1885 and completed in 1902, the building is a blend of many architectural styles and is thought to have been inspired by London's rebuilt Palace of Westminster, opened in 1860. Some 90 sculptures of kings, princes and historical figures gaze out onto the Danube from the west facade, while the main door, the Lion Gate, opens onto revamped V Kossuth Lajos tér, which has a state-of-the-art subterranean visitors centre on its northern side.

You'll only get to see a handful of the 700-odd rooms here on a 45-minute guided tour (available in seven languages, including English). From the visitors centre, ascend the 132 steps of the opulent Golden Staircase to the centrepiece: the 16-sided, 66m-high Dome Hall where the Crown of St Stephen, the nation's most important symbol, is on display, along with the 15th-century ceremonial sword, an orb (1301) and a 10th-century Persian-made sceptre. The sweeping 96-step Grand Staircase descends to the Lion Gate, but you'll move on to the 400-seat Congress Hall, where the upper house of the one-time bicameral assembly sat until 1944. Book ahead online through Jegymester (jegymester.hu).

HIGHLIGHTS
1 Basilica of St Stephen
2 Parliament

SIGHTS
3 Budapest Retro Interactive Museum
4 House of Hungarian Photographers
5 In Memoriam: 1956 Revolution Memorial
6 Kossuth Lajos tér
7 Robert Capa Contemporary Photography Center
8 Shoes on the Danube
9 Szabadság tér
10 Széchenyi István tér
11 Urban Betyár Ethnographical Visitors Centre

DRINKING & NIGHTLIFE
12 Bortodoor City
13 DiVino
14 Drop Stop
15 High Note Sky Bar
16 Marlou

ENTERTAINMENT
17 Aranytíz House of Culture
18 Budapest Operetta
19 Hungarian State Opera House

SHOPPING
20 Anna Antikvitás
21 Dárius Antiques
22 Kieselbach Galéria
23 Moró Antik
24 Pintér Galéria

Basilica of St Stephen

HUNGARY'S MOST SACRED CHURCH

Budapest's neoclassical cathedral is the largest and most sacred Catholic church in all of Hungary. It also contains the country's most revered relic: the mummified right hand of the church's patron, King St Stephen. It took over half a century to build, and was finally completed in 1905 (when the dome collapsed in 1868, the structure had to be rebuilt from the ground up).

The basilica's interior glimmers in low-lit splendour, with Károly Lotz's golden mosaics on the inside of the dome seeming to produce a light all of their own. Noteworthy items include Alajos Stróbl's statue of the king-saint on the main altar and Gyula Benczúr's painting of St Stephen dedicating Hungary to the Virgin Mary and Christ Child, to the right in the north aisle. Below the painting in a glass case is the basilica's major drawcard – the Holy Dexter. View it (naturally) from the right-hand side to see the knuckles.

The facade of the basilica is anchored by two hefty towers, one of which contains a bell weighing more than nine tonnes. Behind the towers is the 96m-high dome, which can be reached by a lift and 42 steps (or 302 steps if you walk all the way). The 2nd floor contains a treasury of ecclesiastical objects, including censers, chalices, ciboria and vestments. Don't miss the Art Deco double monstrance (1938). Tickets are valid for the basilica, the dome or treasury or all three.

HOLY DEXTER

King St Stephen's mummified right hand, an object of great devotion, was restored to Hungary by Habsburg empress Maria Theresa in 1771 after it was discovered in a monastery in Bosnia. Like the Crown of St Stephen, it too was snatched by the bad guys after WWII, but was soon, er, handed back. In 1996, to mark the millennium of Stephen's marriage to the Bavarian princess Gizella, the bishop of Passau sent the queen's hand to Hungary, where they finally reunited in marital bliss.

Basilica of St Stephen

DAVE Z/SHUTTERSTOCK ©

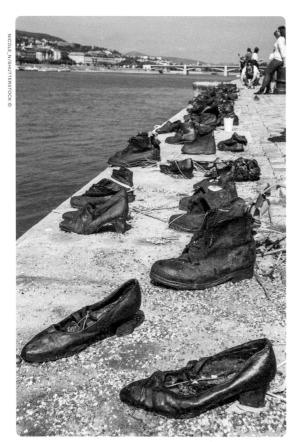

NICOLE_N/SHUTTERSTOCK ©

Shoes on the Danube

Shoes on the Danube

A POIGNANT REMINDER

On the Danube embankment south of the Parliament is a monument to Hungarian Jews shot and thrown into the river by members of the fascist Arrow Cross Party in 1944. Sculptor Gyula Pauer and poet and filmmaker Can Togay named the monument *Shoes on the Danube;* it's a simple but poignant display of 60 pairs of old-style boots and shoes in cast iron, tossed higgledy-piggledy along the riverbank. Ukrainian president Volodymyr Zelensky famously made a reference to the sculpture in 2022, early in the war with Russia, while criticising President Orbán during a teleconference.

Széchenyi István tér

A SQUARE WITH A VIEW

This square, which was called Roosevelt tér for more than a half-century, offers one of the best views of Castle Hill across the Danube. On its northern side is the Hungarian Academy of Sciences and Letters, which was founded in 1825 by Count István Széchenyi, whom fellow reformer Lajos Kossuth dubbed 'the greatest Hungarian'. The sumptuous Art Nouveau building to the east, with its gold tiles, mosaics and celebrated wrought-iron Peacock Gates, was built by an English insurance company in 1907. It underwent a massive renovation in the late 1990s and now houses the luxury Four Seasons hotel. On the southern end is a statue of Ferenc Deák, the Hungarian minister largely responsible for the Compromise of 1867, which brought about the dual monarchy of Austria and Hungary. Below Deák is a likeness of an Austrian and a Hungarian child holding hands in peaceful bliss. The Magyar kid's hair is tousled, and he is naked; the Osztrák is demurely covered by a bit of the patrician's robe, his hair neatly combed.

Szabadság tér

MEMORIES OF PAST AND PRESENT

At the northern end of the large 'Liberty Square' stands a Soviet Army memorial, still sporting its wreathed hammer and sickle and huge gold star.

On the eastern side is the fortress-like US Embassy, now cut off from the square by high steel fencing and concrete blocks. It was here that Cardinal József Mindszenty sought refuge after the 1956 Uprising, staying for 15 years until his departure for Vienna in 1971. The embassy backs onto Hold utca (Moon St), which, until 1990, was named Rosenberg házaspár utca (Rosenberg Couple St) after the American couple Julius and Ethel Rosenberg who were executed as Soviet spies in the US in 1953. Today, statues of the late US presidents Ronald Reagan and George HW Bush grace the northern end of the park.

At the southern end is the Antifascist Monument, which was dedicated to the 'victims of the German occupation' in 2014. It remains extremely controversial as many people believe that Ferenc Szálasi, the leader of the puppet government and the ultranationalist Arrow Cross Party, fully supported the Nazis when he came to power in 1944. Protesters established an alternate memorial of candles, letters and personal memorabilia, which continues to be maintained.

Facing it all from a Presbyterian church across the street is a statue of Hungary's interwar leader Miklós Horthy, called a hero by the right wing but reviled as a fascist dictator by many others. The pedestal he stands on is labelled 'Trianon'.

BANKING ON ART NOUVEAU

Just east of Szabadság tér is one of the most beautiful buildings in Pest. It's the former Royal Postal Savings Bank, a Secessionist extravaganza of colourful tiles and folk motifs, built by Ödön Lechner in 1901. To the southeast is the delightful seat of the National Bank of Hungary. It has terracotta reliefs on all four sides that illustrate trade and commerce through history: Arab camel traders, African rug merchants, Egyptian grain farmers, Chinese tea salesmen and the inevitable solicitor witnessing contracts.

Soviet Army memorial, Szabadság tér

PJRTRAVEL/ALAMY STOCK PHOTO ©

Kossuth Lajos tér

A GRANDIOSE SQUARE

The site of the Parliament, Budapest's most photographed building, this riverside square has been restored to its original pre-war design. The two grand buildings facing Parliament to the east are the Ministry of Agriculture (1887), where you can still see markers showing bullet holes from the 1956 Bloody Thursday massacre, and the Palace Justice (1896), which housed the Museum of Ethnography until it moved to City Park. The ceremonial guards at the flagpole outside Parliament change every hour between 8am and 7pm (earlier in winter).

Changing of the guard, Parliament

Parliament

Lapidary

PARLIAMENT'S NEW LEASE OF LIFE

The Parliament building's architect, Imre Steindl, originally designed a brick cladding for the exterior but later modified it into a stone facing more befitting its Gothic style. Unfortunately, he used a porous type of limestone that rapidly eroded amid the urban pollution and high winds along the Danube. Due to its extensive surface and detailed handiwork, the building remained under scaffolding for decades while it was being repaired. Now that the facing has been replaced, some of the original sculptures and other stonework have been put on display in the lapidary below the northern side of Kossuth Lajos tér. Archival and contemporary photographs displayed side by side present a fascinating contrast of what the square looked like then and now.

1956 Revolution Memorial

IN MEMORIAM

This underground memorial, created in the Parliament's ventilation tunnel on the south side of Kossuth Lajos tér, examines the events of Bloody Thursday – 25 October 1956, the second day of the anti-Soviet Uprising – when soldiers opened fire from the roof of the Agricultural Ministry on a peaceful crowd gathering in the square, killing hundreds of people. Follow the red neon line on the floor, evoking a river of blood, past videos, photos and memorabilia of the period. The hologram of a tank opening fire is especially frightening. Photography is not allowed, and visitors are asked to maintain a respectful silence.

LIPÓTVÁROS SURPRISES

Virág Vántora, owner and manager of Katona Apartments, reveals some of her favourite spots in Lipótváros.

Tiny Sculptures
Mihály Kolodko deposits his tiny bronze sculptures throughout the city. Look for Kermit the Frog on Szabadság tér, a lifeless squirrel next to Peter Falk on Falk Miksa utca, and Franz Joseph on a railing of Liberty Bridge.

Teqball
Want to try out a new sport? Teqball combines football and table tennis. Find the curved tables in the V30 Downtown Sports Center.

Olimpia Park
The district's only Rekortan running track is just north of the Parliament in Olimpia Park, a multifunctional green space. The track is about 435m in length and is equipped with a speed indicator.

Budapest Retro Interactive Museum

MORE IN PARLIAMENT & AROUND

Wine Tasting with the Experts

WHERE TO TASTE THE BEST

Wine is very much part of the social scene in Budapest, and you can't miss the chance of trying a local tipple or two. It's sold by the glass or bottle across the city, and prices are usually quite reasonable. Old-fashioned wine bars ladle it out by the deci (decilitre, or 100 ml), but if you're serious about wine, you should visit one of Budapest's excellent wine bars in the Parliament area, where staff will be able to guide you in the right direction. These newer wine bars use 1.5dl tasting glasses.

Near the basilica and always busy, **DiVino** is where wine first became the all-singin', all-dancin', all embracin' obsession that it is today. Choose from more than 120 wines produced by some three-dozen winemakers. Just off Nagymező, Budapest's 'Broadway', popular **Bortodoor City** is always fun and festive, but the America-British pair who own it take their wine list seriously – there are more than 50 wines that change weekly.

WHERE TO STAY IN PARLIAMENT & AROUND

Four Seasons Gresham Palace Hotel One-of-a-kind luxury hotel created out of the long-derelict Art Nouveau Gresham Palace. €€€

Aria Hotel Budapest
Music-themed luxury digs with Jazz, Opera, Classical and Contemporary wings and a breathtaking rooftop bar. €€€

Cotton Tree
Smallish hotel with a fun speakeasy theme and comfortable rooms with shower, tub or Jacuzzi. €€

Drop Stop is a discreet and independent wine bar and shop near the Margaret bridge; it has a well-conceived selection of wines in the higher categories and knowledgeable staff.

The new kid on the block is **Marlou**. Located behind the Opera House, it specialises in natural wines. It has a well-curated list, although it's a bit on the pricey side.

In Search of Things Ancient

A STROLL DOWN ANTIQUE STREET

While away a Saturday morning along V Falk Miksa utca, which is lined with antique and curio shops and known to some as 'Art and Antique St'. Start at the northern end, where the statue of TV detective Columbo, played by Peter Falk (1927–2011), greets shoppers. **BÁV Art**, a branch of the auction-house chain, is on the corner and features upmarket retro stock. Opposite is the **Kieselbach Galéria**, which auctions established Hungarian painters.

Head south to **Moró Antik**, with its considerable collection of antique swords and pistols, as well as porcelain, paintings and other items from China, Japan and elsewhere in Asia; the owner is exceptionally knowledgeable and helpful. Opposite is **Dárius Antiques**, with furniture, paintings, glass, porcelain, clocks and weapons. **Anna Antikvitás** specialises in folksy embroidered antique tablecloths, bed linen and other textiles; it's piled high throughout the shop and is of top quality. Anna also has pieces of folk costumes.

At the end of the road is **Pintér Galéria**, with an enormous antiques showroom measuring some 2000 sq m, spread across a series of cellars just north of the Parliament building. Pintér has everything – from furniture and chandeliers to oil paintings and china – and is arguably the most interesting place on Falk Miksa utca for browsing. The helpful staff always give a warm welcome.

A Trip Back to the Not-So-Distant past

COMMUNIST BUDAPEST

The **Budapest Retro Interactive Museum** parts the curtains on life in Hungary (with a particular focus on Budapest) between 1960 and 1989, taking visitors along for the ride. Here you can get behind the wheel and drive a Lada, visit typical shops of the day (including a very dated appliance store), sit in on an official news broadcast from a contemporary television studio and enjoy the delights of a typical Budapest home,

BEST HUNGARIAN RESTAURANTS IN THE PARLIAMENT AREA

Borkonyha
Michelin-starred restaurant with a contemporary approach to Hungarian cuisine. €€€

Kispiac
Intimate retro-style restaurant that prepares hearty fare such as wild boar spare ribs. €€

Pick Bistro
Hungarian-style bistro and deli where you can try the most famous salami in the country. €€

Első Pesti Rétesház
Fine for a meal amidst the olde-worlde decor, but come for its signature strudel. €€

Kisharang
This *étkezde* (diner) serves some of the best and most affordable Hungarian dishes in town. €

Hotel Medos
Affordable hotel with upgraded rooms facing the restaurants and bars of Liszt Ferenc tér. €€

Full-Moon Budapest
Hostel-cum-budget hotel with oversized portraits of Joplin and Hendrix in the lobby and an upbeat atmosphere. €€

Pal's Hostel
A cut above the rest, Pal's has accommodation in a string of apartments spread across Lipótváros. €€

BEST ASIAN RESTAURANTS IN THE PARLIAMENT AREA

Jin Galbi
Arguably the best Korean barbecue and the greatest selection of *banchan* (side dishes) are to be found here. €€€

Bombay Budapest
This sleek and authentic new Indian stands out with a wide range of vegetarian offerings. €€

Parázs Thai Étterem
Reliable Thai eatery has all the favourites, from tom yum soup to a full range of curries. €€

Momotaro
A favourite pit stop for Taiwan-style noodles – especially the soup variety – and dumplings. €

S4SVISUALS/SHUTTERSTOCK ©

Hungarian State Opera House

complete with the inevitable orange kitchen furnishings. It might feel a bit hokey at times, but the museum does bring forward a past that was not that long ago. Best of all, everything has been translated, so reading about, phoning or driving into days gone by is accessible to all.

Once Upon a Time on the Farm

A TASTE OF RURAL LIFE IN HUNGARY

Urban Betyár Ethnographical Visitors Centre, a little museum above the Urban Betyár restaurant, does an excellent job portraying Hungarian rural life in the 19th and early 20th centuries with original artefacts and modern interactive displays. Each room captures different aspects, eras and locations in Hungarian peasant culture, from carved and painted furniture, glazed ceramics and paintings. There's also a

WHERE TO SHOP IN PARLIAMENT & AROUND

Bestsellers
Top dog among English-language bookshops with helpful staff, this place stocks heaps of novels and nonfiction.

Cartographia
This outlet of the national mapmaking company stocks a full range of city and provincial maps.

Memories of Hungary
Located in the Parliament visitor centre, this shop has a good selection of mostly genuine handicrafts.

wonderful collection of traditional costumes, as well as lots of weapons, especially pistols. Admittedly, this might just be a marketing tool to get people to eat at the restaurant downstairs, but there's no shame in that: the Urban Betyár merges Hungarian tradition with contemporary flair.

Hungarian Photography in Focus

TOP LOCAL GALLERIES

Hungary has always punched well above its weight in the art of photography. Visit two galleries in the heart of the city's theatre district to help put everything into perspective. The **House of Hungarian Photographers** has top-class exhibitions with everything from the humorous work of Finnish photographer Maija Astikainen, whose portraits give dogs human qualities, to Ata Kandó, who photographed children on the Austrian border fleeing Hungary after the 1956 Uprising. The gallery is located in Mai Manó Ház, a beautiful eight-storey Art Nouveau building that was built in 1894 and was once the home and studio of the eponymous photographer. In his time, Manó Mai (Emánuel May; 1855–1917) was one of the best and most established child portraitists and was named 'imperial and royal court photographer' in 1885. Don't miss his extraordinary Daylight Studio on the top floor, which was used to take studio photographs in natural light.

Just a block south is the **Robert Capa Contemporary Photography Center**, named after Hungarian-born photographer and Magnum Photos cofounder Robert Capa (born Endre Friedmann; 1913–54). Housed in a renovated cultural centre that dates back 100 years, the gallery shows the best in contemporary visual arts, with exhibitions that change quarterly. Take a close look at the magnificent stained-glass window by Miksa Roth in the stairwell.

A Night at the Opera

MUSIC, LAUGHTER AND BEAUTIFUL BUILDINGS

The neo-Renaissance **Hungarian State Opera House** was completed in 1884 and is among the most beautiful buildings in Budapest. It's worth a visit as much to admire the incredibly rich decoration inside as to view a performance and hear the perfect acoustics. The facade is decorated with statues of muses and opera greats such as Puccini, Mozart, Liszt, Verdi and Ferenc Erkel, while its interior dazzles with marble columns, gilded vaulted ceilings, Zsolnay mosaics and chandeliers. Ferenc Erkel (1810–93) is the father of Hungarian opera, and two of his works – the nationalistic *Bánk Bán* and

HUNGARIAN THROUGH AND THROUGH

Hungarians have made impressive contributions across a number of fields – from cinema to fine arts – especially when you consider the nation's relatively small population.

Brassaï (Halász Gyula; 1899–1984) Known for his dramatic photographs of Paris at night

George Cukor (1899–1983) American film producer and director

Tony Curtis (Bernard Schwartz; 1925–2010). Perennial American actor

Joe Eszterhas (1944–) American scriptwriter

Harry Houdini (Weisz Ehrich; 1874–1926) Celebrated escape artist

Bela Lugosi (Blasko Béla; 1884–1956) Cinema's only true Dracula

Ernő Rubik (1944–) Inventor of the iconic cube-shaped puzzle

Billy Wilder (Samuel Wilder; 1906–) American film director and producer

Originart Galéria
Playful Hungarian handicrafts guaranteed to put a smile on your face, and with kiddie appeal too.

Wave
Cubbyhole shop is packed to the rafters with alternative LPs and some rarer Eastern European sounds.

Culinaris Parliament
This gourmet haven has items and ingredients not stocked in most other Budapest food-and-drink shops.

FOODIE'S FAVOURITES IN THE CENTRE

Long-time Budapest resident and unabashed foodie **Brandon Krueger** offers tips on where to find Mediterranean and Middle Eastern fare within the city's central districts.

Leila's
Fans of Lebanese food will enjoy the selection of grilled dishes and mezzes, prepared by a chef who is originally from Beirut.

Garden Studio & Cafe
Offering a Turkish breakfast that's perfect for vegetarians, this cafe is also known for its cocktails – and it has a shop selling local crafts.

Dobrumba
Always packed with locals and foreigners, this was one of the first restaurants in Budapest to popularise the region's cuisine. The chicken tagine is highly recommended. Reserve.

László Hunyadi – are standards here. Tickets range from affordable to astronomical, but standing room only costs next to nothing. If you can't attend a performance, join one of the three 45-minute daily tours in English, which include a 10-minute performance.

Opposite the Opera is **Drechsler Palace**, currently under renovation. Go behind for a look at the **New Theatre**, an Art Deco gem that opened as the Parisiana music hall in 1909 and is embellished with monkey faces, globes and geometric designs.

One block north along Nagymező utca is a theatre-lined street known locally as Budapest's Broadway. The **Budapest Operetta** stages campy shows like *The Gypsy Princess*, *Countess Marica* and *The Merry Widow*, with over-the-top staging and costumes. Think baroque Gilbert and Sullivan – and then some. There's an interesting bronze statue of Kálmán outside the main entrance.

Take a Ride on the Historic Underground

THE CONTINENT'S FIRST METRO

Trainspotters (or 'ferro-fanatics' as they are known in central Europe) will waste no time in riding the M1 line, also known as the **Millennium Underground Railway** or Kisföldalatti ('Little Underground'). One of Budapest's four metro lines, it is by far the oldest. Indeed, it was the first underground railway to open in continental Europe, beating the Paris metro by 14 years.

Today it runs for 4.4km below Andrássy út, making 11 stops; to change direction you must exit and cross the street. The line's original raison d'être was to facilitate public transport to City Park without having to mar the elegant streetscape above. Originally named the Franz Joseph Underground Railway, the ruler himself travelled on it while visiting Budapest for the millenary celebrations that marked 1000 years of Magyar settlement in Hungary. Hop aboard and feel like an emperor or empress.

Going Up...

BEST VANTAGE POINTS AROUND PARLIAMENT

The area around Parliament has plenty of dramatic vantage points. The Chain Bridge is good for views of Buda, Pest and the Danube; the dome of St Stephen's Basilica takes in all three equally well. Should you want your view with music and

WHERE TO EAT IN PARLIAMENT & AROUND

Costes Downtown
This self-described 'fine-dining bistro' with a Michelin star brings a new dimension to Budapest's dining scene. €€€

Mák
'Poppy' offers international dishes that lean in Hungary's direction from several inventive tasting menus. €€€

Bigfish
Super fresh fish and shellfish that you can select yourself right from the ice trays. €€

BRIAN_KINNEY/ALAMY STOCK PHOTO ©

Millennium Underground Railway

a libation, head for what is arguably the most impressive of Pest's rooftop bars: the **High Note Sky Bar** atop the Aria Hotel. From here you can almost reach out and touch the basilica's dome, and virtually every city landmark lies at your feet.

Traditional Music after Dark

LEARN TO DANCE HUNGARIAN STYLE

One of the best places in all of Budapest for catching music and dance performances is the **Aranytíz House of Culture** in Lipótváros. Here, you are likely to catch entertainment as diverse as theatre performances, pop and classical music concerts, exhibitions, film, children's ballet and visual arts. But their forte is traditional music and dance, especially *táncház* (folk music and dance workshops). This is an excellent way both to hear Hungarian folk music and to learn to dance. You might even get lucky and catch a performance by Kalamajka Táncház, who were the major players behind the movement a half-century ago. Look out for the extravagant Rajkó Gypsy Orchestra and Folk Ensemble too.

PARLIAMENT BY THE NUMBERS

Budapest's Parliament is the largest building in Hungary, and can claim all sorts of superlatives: the largest number of rooms (691), the longest riverfront footage, and even the most sacred objects in the land on display. About 100,000 people were involved in the construction of the gargantuan edifice, laying roughly 40 million bricks in the process. The interior is decorated with half a million precious and semiprecious stones, plus 40kg of gold. And that's not all. Here are some other fun Parliament facts to know: there are 27 gates and 10 courtyards; 29 staircases and 13 lifts; 8730 light bulbs and 108 clocks; and three times as many employees (700) as there are statues (242).

Lokum
Bright and airy restaurant that excels with Turkish breakfasts and brunches. **€€**

Iguana
This lively place has decent Mexican options for those who need an enchilada or burrito fix. **€€**

Pizzica
If there is a finer pizza in all of Budapest, we don't know where to find it. **€**

BEST PLACES TO PARTY IN THE PARLIAMENT AREA

Alterego
Budapest's top gay club, this has a chic crowd, great music and inspired drag shows.

Morrison's 2
The biggest party venue in town; six dance floors and just as many bars attract a younger crowd.

Ötkert
This daytime *lángos* joint transmogrifies into a popular dance club from Wednesday into the weekend.

Caledonia
This expat mecca lures in the punters with its 140 types of whisky and big-screen sports coverage.

Choral performance, Basilica of St Stephen

Sacred Music

CATCH A CONCERT IN A CHURCH

Churches are popular venues for classical music concerts in Budapest. The focus is on organ music, but this is often accompanied by violins, trumpets and vocals. Few concert halls – with the possible exception of the Liszt Music Academy – offer such ornate surrounding in addition to providing exceptional acoustics. Concerts generally last just over an hour and tickets are affordable (starting at about €20). The most popular place in Lipótváros is the Basilica of St Stephen, where concerts usually take place on Tuesday and Sunday at 8pm and more frequently in summer. Other popular venues are largely in Belváros and include St Michael's Church on V Váci utca, St Anne's Church on V Szervita tér and University Church on Egyetem tér.

WHERE TO DRINK COFFEE IN PARLIAMENT & AROUND

Espresso Embassy
Some say this upbeat cafe has the best espressos, flat whites, cappuccinos and lattes in town.

Artizán
This wonderful modern cafe serves whole food with no additives, housemade bread and superb coffee.

Ételem Étterem
Effectively a vegetarian and vegan cafe, this place serves some of the best organic coffee in town.

MARGARET ISLAND & NORTHERN PEST

PARKLAND WITH TRAILS AND RUINS

Neither Buda nor Pest, Margaret Island (Margit-sziget) sits in the middle of the Danube. Just 2.5km long, it is not graced with many significant sights, but you can easily spend half a day exploring its swimming complexes, thermal spa, gardens and centuries-old ruins – and on a hot afternoon, it makes for a lovely escape. Cars are allowed on Margaret Island only as far as the hotels at the northern end; the rest is reserved for pedestrians and cyclists.

Szent István körút, the northernmost stretch of the Big Ring Road (Nagykörút) in Pest, runs in an easterly direction from Margaret Bridge to Nyugati tér. The area north of Szent István körút is known as Újlipótváros (New Leopold Town) to distinguish it from Lipótváros (Leopold Town) to the south of the Big Ring Road. It's a wonderful neighbourhood with tree-lined streets, boutiques, cafes and restaurants, and is best seen on foot.

TOP TIP

Margaret Island is bigger than you think, so consider touring on two wheels. Bike-share scheme Bubi Bikes, has a docking station on XIII Jászai Mari tér just before Margaret Bridge. Bringóhintó rents multiseated pedal contraptions and e-scooters from a stand near the Musical Fountain.

Church and Monastery Ruins

REMINDERS OF THE ISLAND'S RELIGIOUS PAST

Margaret Island was always the domain of one religious order or another until the Turks arrived in the mid-16th century. They proceeded to turn what was then called the Island of Rabbits into – appropriately enough – a harem, from which all infidels were barred. A few reminders of those times remain.

On the northeast side, the Romanesque **Premonstratensian Church**, dedicated to St Michael by the order of White Canons, originally dates to the 12th century though it was largely rebuilt in 1931. Its 15th-century bell mysteriously appeared one night in 1914 under the roots of a walnut tree knocked over in a storm. It was probably buried by the canons during the Turkish invasion. Just south are the ruins of the 13th-century **Dominican convent** built by Béla IV, where his daughter St Margaret took the veil. It remained a working convent until the Ottoman occupation. Adjoining are the remains of a medieval palace.

To the southwest, almost in the island's centre, are the ruins – no more than a tower and a wall – of a one-time **Franciscan church and monastery** that dates back to the late 13th century. Still visible in the western wall is a doorway leading to the organ loft as well as a spiral staircase and fine arched window. Habsburg Archduke Joseph built a summer residence here when he inherited the island in 1867. It was later converted into a hotel, which operated until 1949.

ST MARGARET

The island's most famous resident was Margaret (1242–71), daughter of Béla IV. According to legend, the king pledged her to a nunnery in exchange for the expulsion of the Mongols, who had overrun Hungary in 1241. If we're to believe *The Lives of the Saints*, she enjoyed her life of devotion, especially the mortification-of-the-flesh parts. Canonised in 1943, St Margaret commands something of a cult following in Hungary. A red-marble sepulchre cover surrounded by a wrought-iron grille marks her original resting place.

MARGARET ISLAND & NORTHERN PEST

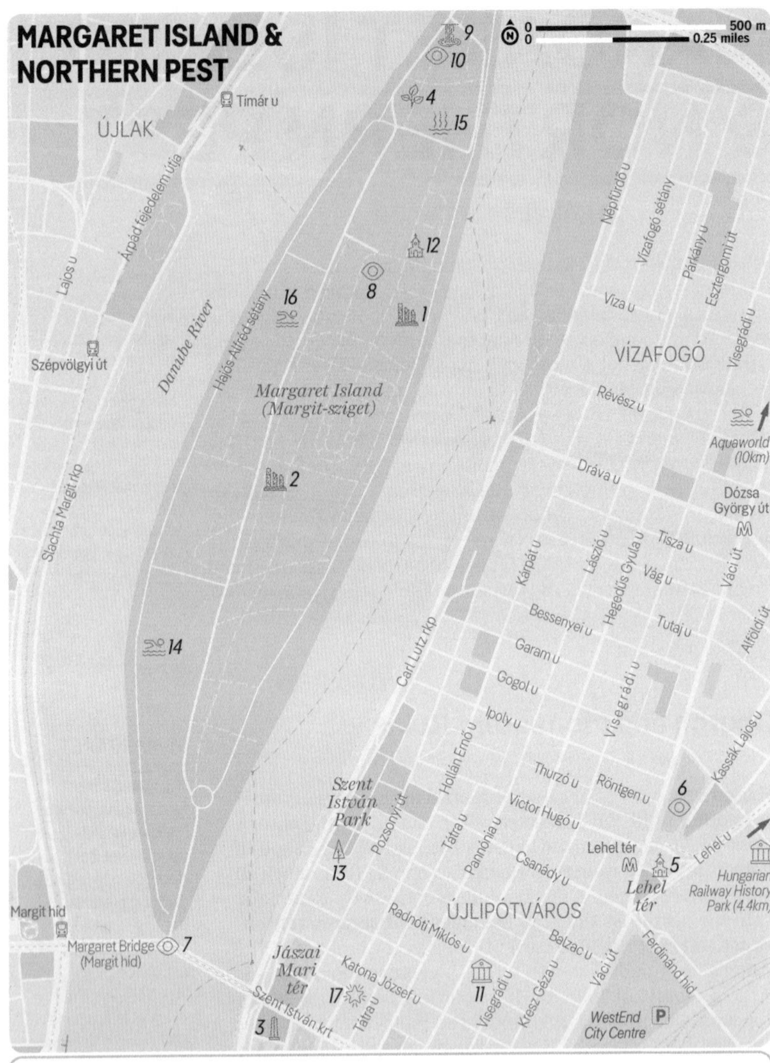

SIGHTS
1 Dominican Convent
2 Franciscan Church and Monastery
3 Statue of Imre Nagy
4 Japanese Garden
5 Lehel Church
6 Lehel Market
7 Margaret Bridge
8 Margaret Island Water Tower & Open-Air Theatre
9 Musical Fountain
10 Musical Well
11 Pinball Museum
12 Premonstratensian Church
13 Szent István Park

ACTIVITIES
13 Alfréd Hajós National Sports Pool
14 Ensana Medical Spa
15 Palatinus Strand

ENTERTAINMENT
16 Budapest Jazz Club

Imre Nagy Statue

NEW HOME FOR AN OLD HERO

At the eastern foot of the bridge in V Jászai Mari tér is an unusual statue of Imre Nagy. He's standing in the centre of a small footbridge, having moved Hungary 'halfway to freedom'. Nagy was a communist prime minister who was executed in 1958 for his role in the uprising two years earlier. The statue was unveiled opposite the Parliament building with great ceremony in the summer of 1996, but moved to its present location in 2019 for what some people say were political motives.

Imre Nagy statue

Margaret Bridge

THE CITY'S SECOND-OLDEST BRIDGE

Margaret Bridge

Margaret Bridge introduces the Big Ring Rd to Buda. It's unique in that it doglegs in the middle in order to stand at right angles to the Danube where it converges at the southern tip of Margaret Island. The bridge was originally built in 1876 as the second permanent bridge over the Danube. The spur leading to the island was added in 1901. Like all of the other spans across the Danube, Margaret Bridge was destroyed during WWII and only rebuilt in the aftermath. During reconstruction, much of the original steel material was lifted from the river and incorporated into the new structure.

Margaret Island Water Tower

A MARRIAGE OF FUNCTION AND STYLE

Erected in 1911 in the north-central part of Margaret Island according to a design by the architect Zielinski Szilárd, this Secessionist-style water tower rises 57m above the open-air theatre to the south, which is used for concerts and plays in summer and can seat 3500 spectators. The octagonal structure is both decorative and functional as a water supply for the island. Climb up 152 steps to reach the tower's Lookout Gallery. While pleasant, the 360-degree view of the island mostly consists of treetops, although you will get some nice views of the Parliament building and the Buda Hills. Make sure to check out the art and photography exhibitions in the galleries on your way out.

Lehel Church

Lehel Church & Market

BEAUTY AND THE BEAST

On Lehel tér you'll see the twin spires of the eponymous church, which is a 1933 copy of a celebrated 13th-century Romanesque structure now in ruins at Zsámbék, 33km west of Budapest. That church was destroyed by the Mongols in 1241, rebuilt but levelled again by an earthquake in 1763. Just north is a large market now housed in a hideous boatlike postmodern structure designed by László Rajk, son of the communist minister of the interior executed for 'Titoism' in 1949. Wags say this building is his revenge.

Hungarian Railway History Park

MECCA FOR TRAINSPOTTERS

Though a bit out of view from Újlipótváros – it's about 4.5km northeast of Lehel tér – the Hungarian Railway History Park will be irresistible to trainspotters and fellow travellers. The largely outdoor museum claims to be Europe's largest open-air railway entertainment park, with 100 examples of locomotives and other rolling stock, plus an exhibition on the history of the railway in Hungary. There's a wonderful array of hands-on activities for kids, mostly involving getting behind the wheel. Riding the miniature locomotive is a real treat. Reach it on tram 14 from Lehel tér 30 or 30A from Keleti train station.

Memorial to Raoul Wallenberg, Szent István Park

Szent István Park

THE SERPENT SLAYER

St Stephen's Park contains a memorial to Raoul Wallenberg, portraying a warrior doing battle with a snake. Erected in 1999 and titled *Kígyóölő* (Serpent Slayer), it's a copy of another sculpture that the communist regime removed in 1949. Of all the 'righteous gentiles' honoured by Jews around the world, Wallenberg – a Swedish diplomat who rescued as many as 60,000 Hungarian Jews during WWII – is the most revered. You can still make out the remnants of a yellow Star of David at the entrance to an apartment block at XIII Katona József utca 2/E, where Jews were forced to identify themselves during the Holocaust. Facing the river south of the entrance is a row of Bauhaus apartments, built in the late 1920s.

Alfréd Hajós National Sports Pool

MORE IN MARGARET ISLAND & NORTHERN PEST

Water, Water Everywhere

DIVE IN

If you fancy taking the plunge, Margaret Island is just the place to do it – whether it be swimming laps in an Olympic-size pool, splashing around in Budapest's largest swimming complex or relaxing in a modern spa.

The **Alfréd Hajós National Sports Pool**, named after Hungary's first Olympic champion, contains some eight indoor and outdoor pools open to the public at various times. Take note: this is where the Olympic swimming and water polo teams train. Further north on the west side is **Palatinus Strand**, the largest swimming complex in the capital, with 11 pools (two with thermal water), wave machines and water slides. This is the best place to bring the kids in summer, and with four of the pools now covered, it stays open year-round. Close to the island's northern end, the **Ensana Medical Spa** is modern and spic-and-span, but a bit soulless. A daily ticket includes entry to the swimming pools, sauna and steam room; the list of available medical treatments is enviable.

BEST SHOPS ON MARGARET ISLAND

Mézes Kuckó
Come here for nut-and-honey cookies and colourful heart-shaped *mézeskalácsok* (honey cakes).

Ligeti Bolt
This package-free shop sells pasta, nuts, jam, dairy products and kitchen accessories.

Sarki Fűszeres
A retro-style cafe that's a delight for brunch; it also doubles as a deli and wine shop.

Fromage
Stacked high with cheeses and other picnic supplies for an afternoon on Margaret Island.

Zsebi
This stylish bakery has a mouthwatering assortment of baked goods and shop-made jams, preserves and honey.

WHERE TO STAY ON MARGARET ISLAND & IN NORTHERN PEST

Grand Margaret Island Hotel
Constructed in the late 19th century, this comfortable, tranquil hotel is connected to the Ensana spa. **€€€**

NH Budapest
Minimalist, welcoming hotel with bright atrium lobby and a flash fitness centre on the 8th floor. **€€**

Hotel City Ring
Renovations have brought this hotel up several notches, and its central location is stellar. **€€**

TOURING ÚJLIPÓTVÁROS' 'STRIP'

Ildikó Moran, retired university external relations vice president, takes us on a mini-tour of her neighbourhood.

If you want to get a real taste of urban community life along the 'strip' Pozsonyi út in Újlipótváros, catch the Pozsonyi Piknik (Cultural Village Day) on a Saturday in late summer, when friends meet with their children for amusement rides and other attractions. Or, while patiently queuing for challah bread at the Sommer Dunapark bakery, you are greeted by an acquaintance from the doggie run. In the morning, the waiter at Sarki Fűszeres silently brings your latte. And as night falls the jovial American who runs Gaby's by the river bank is putting out notices about Drag Nite Bingo.

Still feeling like a fish out of water? Head for **Aquaworld**, one of Europe's largest water parks, in the far north of Pest, with an adventure centre covered by a 72m-high dome, pools with a dozen slides and an array of saunas to keep the whole family at play all year long. Reach it on tram 14 from Lehel tér.

Water, Music & Bright Lights

ISLAND ATTRACTIONS

On Margaret Island, you don't always have to entertain yourself; several attractions will do the work for you.

At the northwestern end of the island, the unexpected **Japanese Garden** has ponds filled with koi fish and lily pads, as well as bamboo groves, miniature maples, dawn redwoods, cypresses, a small wooden bridge and a waterfall. But don't be surprised if you hear some rather incongruous music in the background, and even a few trumpet blasts emanating nearby. It's coming from the **Musical Well**, which sits on a raised gazebo a few steps away. This is a replica of a 1936 fountain in Marosvásárhely (now Târgu Mureș) in Transylvania, and is topped with a statue of Neptune that revolves (in theory) in line with the sun. The structure plays Hungarian melodies every hour on the hour and a four-trombone ditty on the half-hour. At ground level it earns the second part of its name: three taps pump out potable well water.

A much bigger show is waiting to happen at the southern end of the island. Here, the **Musical Fountain** puts on a dramatic display five times a day with jets 'dancing' to music and shooting up to 10m into the air. The soundtrack ranges from Vivaldi to the Rolling Stones. Catch the last show at 9pm, when the fountain is illuminated by hundreds of coloured lights.

Pinball Wizardry

TEST YOUR REFLEXES

Release your inner Elton John – with or without the 1.5m-high boots (see the 1975 film *Tommy*) – for the **Pinball Museum** in Újlipótváros. Though rather specialised and quirky, this basement museum frequently makes it into Budapest's top 10 sights. It's home to 140 vintage pinball machines and you can play all but the oldest wooden models dating back as far as 1947. As the largest collection in Europe that's not only open to the public but also interactive, it has quite a cult following. As they say, there are two kinds of people: those who play pinball and those who play video games. Come here and decide which camp you fall into.

WHERE TO EAT ON MARGARET ISLAND & NORTHERN PEST

Dunapark
A 1938 Art Deco landmark that's good for a light meal or coffee and cake. **€€**

Firkász
An unmissable 'nostalgia' spot thanks to the memorabilia on the walls and great homestyle dishes. **€€**

Babka
Come to this Israeli-style place for excellent food, friendly service and a hip crowd. **€€**

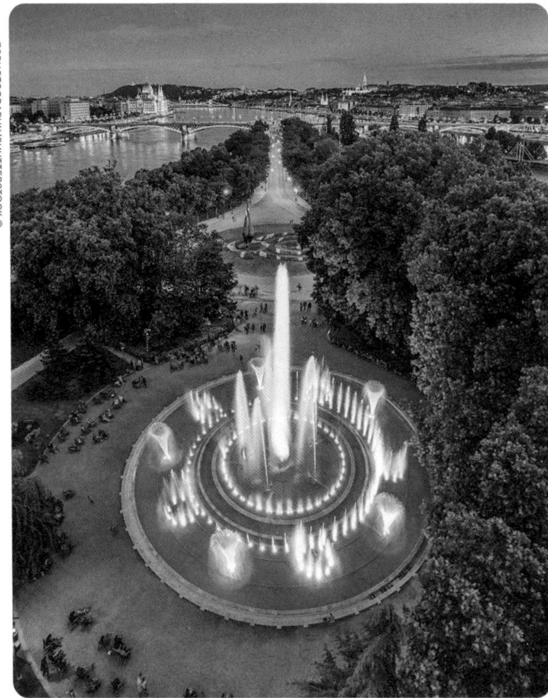

Musical Fountain

BEST PLACES TO DRINK ON MARGARET ISLAND & IN NORTHERN PEST

Gaby's
The American-run, gay-friendly bar and restaurant on the Danube is just the ticket for a cocktail or three.

Blue Tomato
This popular boozer is like something out of the classic American sitcom *Cheers*.

Hippie Island
With peace signs everywhere, this throwback is a comfortable seasonal cafe on Margaret Island.

Mosselen
Wide selection of Belgian beers, including seven on draft and two-dozen fruit-flavoured bottled brews.

Figaró Kert
This seasonal bar and cafe is as an oasis in the Újlipótváros' concrete jungle.

All that Jazz

THE MOST SERIOUS VENUE IN BUDAPEST

The sophisticated **Budapest Jazz Club** – now the most serious game in town – is the place to go if you want to hear jazz, be it traditional, fusion, Latin or vocal. Both international and local performers take to the stage in the modern concert hall, which is equipped with a state-of-the-art sound system. Past international performers have included John Schofield, Emmet Cohen, Terrence Blanchard, the Yellowjackets and Liane Carroll. Concerts take place most nights at 8pm, with jam sessions usually at 10pm; there's a kids' jazz club some Saturday mornings and Sunday afternoons. The in-house BJC Bistro serves full meals. In addition, the **Jazz Café** is open daily from late morning.

Figi & Lipike
A bit far but worth the journey, this breakfast-to-dinner place doubles as a deli. **€€**

Pozsonyi Kisvendéglő
Visit this throwback restaurant for gargantuan portions of Hungarian classics and a cast of local characters. **€**

Oriental Soup House
This Vietnamese soup house (a legacy of communist days) has authentic pho and bun cha. **€**

ERZSÉBETVÁROS & THE JEWISH QUARTER

EPICENTRE OF FUN AND GAMES

You'll probably be spending the bulk of your time in this neighbourhood: it has a broad range of accommodation, restaurants serving everything from Indian to Jewish cuisines, as well as the city's hottest nightspots. This is where the ruin pub (*romkocsma*) phenomenon was born and where it continues to thrive.

Bounded by the Little Ring Rd, the western side of Erzsébetváros is where nocturnal Budapest comes alive. Here you'll find most of its famous ruin pubs and garden clubs, including Szimpla Kert. It heaves most nights after dark with tourists and locals jumping from bar to bar. By day, it's an atmospheric place to wander, with plenty of evidence of the large Jewish community that has always been here, as well as great shops, cafes and restaurants. The eastern side of Erzsébetváros is rundown, with little of interest except for all-important Keleti train station on Baross tér.

TOP TIP

The best way to get the measure of this neighbourhood is to stroll the length of Andrássy út, starting at Deák Ferenc tér and ending at Heroes' Sq (Hősök tere). Along the way you'll pass several museums and notable buildings, including the House of Terror and the Hungarian State Opera House.

Great Synagogue

Great Synagogue

THE LARGEST IN EUROPE

Budapest's Great Synagogue, with its crenellated red-and-yellow glazed-brick facade and two Moorish-style towers, is the largest Jewish temple in the world outside New York. Designed by non-Jewish architect Ludwig Förster and completed in 1859, the copper-domed 3000-seat Neolog house of worship has some distinctive Christian elements, including pulpits, a 5000-pipe organ and a central rose window. For that reason, it is sometimes referred to as the 'Jewish cathedral'. Don't miss the decorative carvings on the Ark of the Covenant by National Romantic architect Frigyes Feszl, who also did the wall and ceiling frescoes of multicoloured and gold geometric shapes. Your ticket includes an informative one-hour tour by a member of the local Jewish community.

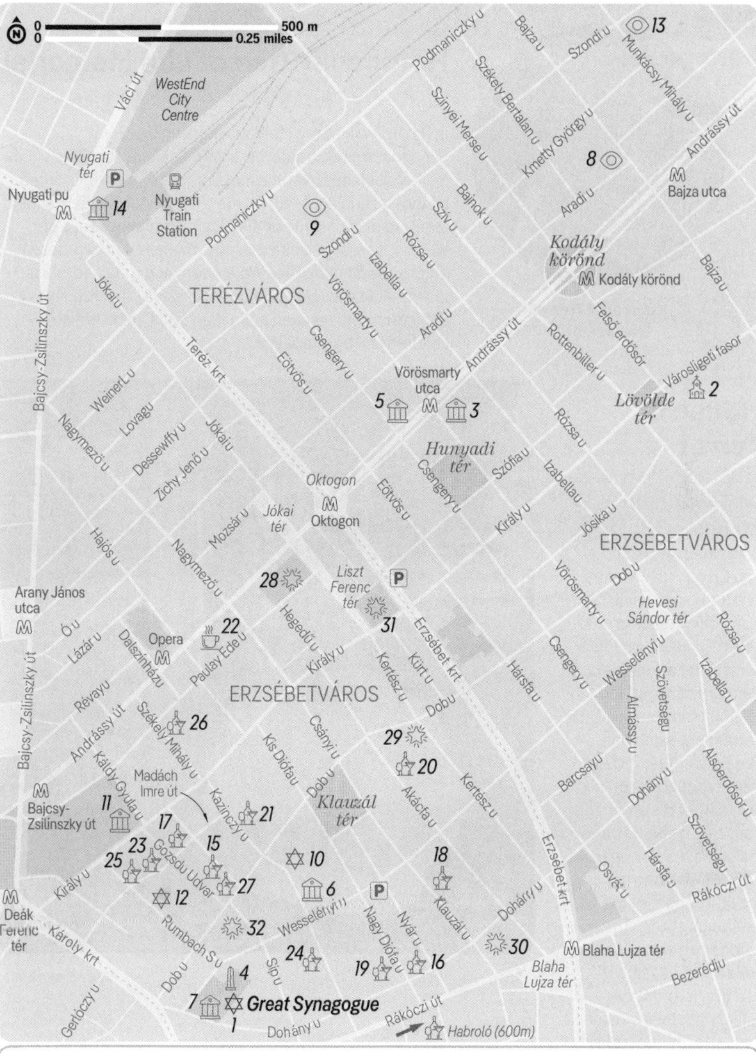

HIGHLIGHTS
1 Great Synagogue

SIGHTS
2 City Park Calvinist Church
3 Ferenc Liszt Memorial Museum
4 Holocaust Tree of Life Memorial
5 House of Terror
6 Hungarian Electrical Engineering Museum
7 Hungarian Jewish Museum & Archives
8 Léderer House
9 Lindenbaum House
10 Orthodox Synagogue
11 Pálinka Museum
12 Rumbach Sebestyén utca Synagogue
13 Sonnenberg House
14 Western Train Station

DRINKING & NIGHTLIFE
15 Blue Bird Karaoke
16 CoXx
17 Feri's Kitchen & Bar
18 Füge Udvar
19 Grandio Jungle Bar
20 Instant-Fogas
21 Kőleves Kert
see 21 Mika Tivadar Kert
22 Művész Kávéház
23 Spíler
24 Szimpla Kert
25 Telep
26 Tuk Tuk Bar
27 Vicky Barcelona

ENTERTAINMENT
see 3 Budapest Puppet Theatre
28 Giero Pub
29 Havana
30 Ladó Café
31 Liszt Music Academy
32 Spinoza Café

Holocaust Tree of Life Memorial

Holocaust Tree of Life Memorial

POIGNANT MONUMENT TO SHOAH VICTIMS

In Raoul Wallenberg Memorial Park on the Great Synagogue's north side, Imre Varga's Holocaust Tree of Life Memorial stands over the mass graves of those murdered by the Nazis in 1944–45. On the tree's metal leaves are the family names of some of the hundreds of thousands of victims. Nearby is a black-marble memorial to two-dozen 'Righteous Gentiles' like Wallenberg and a stained-glass memorial to Nicholas Winton (1909–2015), the 'British Schindler' who rescued more than 600 Czech Jewish children just before WWII.

House of Terror

ATROCITIES ON THE LEFT AND RIGHT

This prison – set up by the Hungarian fascists (the Iron Cross Party) before WWII – now houses the disturbing House of Terror, focusing on the crimes and atrocities of Hungary's fascist and Stalinist regimes in a permanent exhibition. The building served as the headquarters of the dreaded ÁVH secret police after the war, and the years leading up to the 1956 Uprising get the lion's share of the exhibition space. The reconstructed prison cells in the basement and the Perpetrators' Gallery on the staircase, featuring photographs of the turncoats, spies and torturers, are especially chilling. The (communist) star and the (fascist) pointed Greek cross at the entrance and the tank in the central courtyard make for jarring introductions to the museum; the wall outside, displaying metallic plaques and photos of the many victims, speaks volumes.

Művész Kávéház

Művész Kávéház

A PORT IN A STORM

We know of no better place to calm fraught nerves after the House of Terror than the 'Artist's Cafe', a half-kilometre to the southwest. Located diagonally opposite the Hungarian State Opera House, this cafe is an interesting place to people-watch and enjoy a slice of gateau along the Unesco-listed Andrássy út on which it stands. Choose the inner room where the late Biedermeier furnishings earned it the nickname 'the Little Gerbeaud'. The clientele here is generally older and quieter than the tourists who throw themselves into the seats on the pavement terrace – just the ticket after your harrowing visit.

Orthodox Synagogue

ART NOUVEAU EDIFICE

The Orthodox Synagogue – sometimes called the Kazinczy synagogue – is the second of a half-dozen synagogues and prayer houses that once stood in the Jewish Quarter before WWII. It was designed by the brothers Béla and Sándor Löffler and completed in 1913. Along with the house of worship seating 1000 on two levels, the project included a community centre, a school, a kindergarten and a restaurant (which still functions as Hanna Garden). At the time it was considered something of a rarity, as the tendency was to build synagogues for more liberal communities like the Neologs (eg the Great Synagogue). It was also considered a modern design, and there are late Art Nouveau touches and brightly coloured geometrical decorations throughout. The stained-glass windows in the ceiling are especially fine; those you see today are reconstructions, as Miksa Róth's originals were destroyed during WWII.

Stained glass window, Hungarian Jewish Museum

Hungarian Jewish Museum & Archives

PRICELESS TREASURY OF JUDAICA

The Hungarian Jewish Museum & Archives, in an upstairs annexe of the Great Synagogue, contains objects related to both religious and everyday life. Interesting items include a 3rd-century Jewish headstone from Roman Pannonia, discovered in the Danube near Esztergom; a vast array of liturgical items in silver, including Torah finials from 1602; a dozen stained-glass windows of Biblical scenes, salvaged from a local high school; and manuscripts, including a handwritten book of the local Nagykanizsa Burial Society from the late 18th century. Behind the museum is the 250-seat Art Deco Heroes' Temple built in 1931 to honour the fallen in WWI.

Rumbach Sebestyén utca Synagogue

VESTIGE OF THE HUNGARIAN SCHISM

The Moorish-style Rumbach Sebestyén utca Synagogue, named after the small street on which it stands, was designed by the Austrian Secessionist architect Otto Wagner and completed in 1874 to accommodate 1265 worshippers. It was financed by the Status Quo Ante (moderate conservative) community, who had effectively broken away from the Neolog congregation of the Great Synagogue. The building has emerged from a protracted renovation and the interior is awash in red, blue and gold, symbolising the heart, the intellect and wealth. There's a small exhibition on the upper floor.

Hungarian Electrical Engineering Museum

QUIRKY EXHIBITS & COLOURFUL NEON

Housed in what was originally a transformer station, this museum may not sound like much of a crowd-pleaser, but the Bauhaus-style building is full of such unusual and quirky exbibits that it warrants a visit. The staff, retired workers in long white coats, will guide you through the eight permanent exhibitions in four rooms, which focus on the development and history of the Hungarian electrical industry. If you've ever wondered just how the communist-era alarm system functioned on the barbed wire fence that separated Hungary and Austria, this is your spot. Staff will also point out and explain the stork-friendly nesting platforms that the electricity company builds, in order to keep the long-legged birds from interfering with the wires and electrocuting themselves.

There are also tons of old household appliances (many still work), but the highlight is the collection of colourful communist neon shop signs that adorn the outside courtyard in a unique exhibition entitled Neonparade. Wait till it gets dark and don't miss the iconic white swan of the Patyolat laundry, the shopping basket of the Csemege grocery store and the winking owl of the Antikvárium second-hand bookshop. The weirdest display of all is the assortment of electricity-consumption meters, one of the largest in the world, which includes one installed in the apartment of 'Rákosi Mátyás elvtárs' (Comrade Mátyás Rákosi), the Communist Party secretary, on his 60th birthday in 1952, and another recalling Stalin's 70th birthday in 1948.

A SNIP IN TIME

Hungary's role in the dissolution of communism was far greater than many people remember. It began in June 1989 when the Hungarian and Austrian foreign ministers symbolically cut through a section of the barbed wire that had divided their countries for decades. Three months later, a festive picnic was held to finish the job. On 11 September, Hungary opened its borders with Austria altogether and more than 70,000 people fled to the West. The East German government collapsed weeks later, followed by the fall of the Berlin Wall.

Hungarian Electrical Engineering Museum

PE FORSBERG/ALAMY STOCK PHOTO ©

Ferenc Liszt Memorial Museum

WHERE LISZT LAY HIS HEAD

This wonderful little museum is housed in the Old Music Academy, where the great composer lived in a 1st-floor apartment for five years until his death in 1886. As the founding president and a professor of the academy, Liszt did not accept any money for his teaching. Instead, he was offered this furnished three-room flat. The rooms are filled with his instruments, furniture, books, portraits and personal effects – all original. Central to the collection are the pianos he donated to the academy, including two American Chickerings and a tiny glass one, as well as a lovely walnut composing desk that he cherished. Concerts are usually held in the adjoining Chamber Hall at 11am on Saturdays, except in summer.

Ferenc Liszt Memorial Museum

Liszt Music Academy

Liszt Music Academy

BUDAPEST'S FOREMOST CONCERT HALL

The Art Nouveau Liszt Music Academy, built in 1907, attracts students from around the world and is Budapest's top classical-music venue. The renovated interior, which has two concert halls and is richly embellished with Zsolnay porcelain and frescoes, is worth visiting on a guided tour if you're not attending a performance. Tours last just under an hour, and will take you into the wings and treat you to a 20-minute mini-concert performed by students of the academy. Full-on performances are usually booked up at least a week in advance, but more expensive (though still affordable) last-minute tickets are usually available.

Giero Pub

THE REAL DEAL

Composer Ferenc Liszt liked to describe himself as 'part Gypsy' and some of his works, notably his 20 Hungarian Rhapsodies, do echo the traditional music of the Roma people. But if you'd like to hear something authentic, head south on Andrássy út to this basement bar presided over by Gizi néni (Aunt Gizi) for live Roma music. Local musicians congregate here to jam from 10pm onward, after they've finished up providing a more saccharine soundtrack for top-end hotels. Expect a warm welcome but no frills.

ERZSÉBETVÁROS & THE JEWISH QUARTER WALKING TOUR

Begin your walk in restaurant- and cafe-packed VI Liszt Ferenc tér and poke your head into the sumptuous 1 **Liszt Music Academy** (p121). Walking southwest along Király utca you'll pass the 2 **Church of St Teresa**, built in 1811, with a tower by Miklós Ybl and a massive neoclassical altar designed by Mihály Pollack in 1824. At Király utca 47 (and directly opposite the church) is 3 **Pekáry House**, an interesting neo-Gothic house built in 1847, with a stepped gable and charming double balcony. Turning into Csányi utca, head south over Dob utca to the heart of the old Jewish Quarter, 4 **Klauzál tér**. The square still has a feeling of pre-war Budapest. A continued Jewish presence is evident in the surrounding streets, with kosher 5 **Hanna Deli** next to the 6 **Orthodox Synagogue** (p119) and a convenient pit stop. Turn right into Holló utca. If the gate at Király utca 15 is open, walk to the courtyard's rear to see a 30m-long piece of the original 7 **ghetto wall**, rebuilt in 2010. Otherwise, you can peer through the hole cut into the gate. The next turn on the left is the passageway called 8 **Gozsdu udvar** (p127), now the district's number-one nightlife destination. At Dob utca 12 is an unusual antifascist 9 **monument to Carl Lutz**, a Swiss consul who, like Raoul Wallenberg, provided Jews with false papers in 1944. Just around the corner, bordering a car park, are 10 **two murals**. The one on the left commemorates the football victory of Hungary's 'Golden Team' against England at Wembley (6–3) in 1953. The one on the right is an oversized Rubik's cube, the 3D puzzle invented in 1974 by Hungarian sculptor and architecture professor Ernő Rubik.

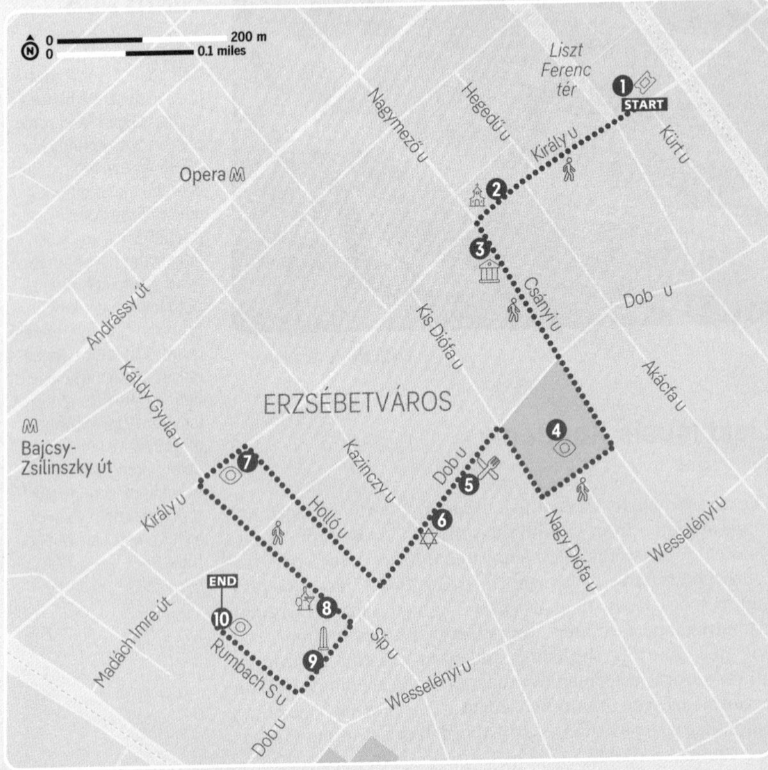

Mafia Mission escape room, Gozsdu Mission

MORE IN ERZSÉBETVÁROS & THE JEWISH QUARTER

Budapest's Challenging Escape Rooms

GET ME OUTTA HERE

Budapest is the undisputed European capital of live escape games, in which teams of two to six people willingly lock themselves in a room, and then proceed to spend the next 60 to 90 minutes trying to solve numerous riddles that will help unlock the door that leads to freedom. History's most famous escape artist, Harry Houdini, was a born and bred Hungarian. Could there be a connection?

Like the city's ruin pubs, these games are often set in empty, disused apartment blocks; their atmospheric basements are a favorite locale. Each game has a distinct theme and story – ancient Egypt, the medieval era, the Cold War, a sci-fi future – and involves not only solving puzzles but, crucially, the ability to identify the puzzles in the first place.

Inspired by escape-the-room video games, the idea was first developed in Japan in 2007; five years later Europe's first escape room opened in Budapest. Mentally challenging (teams frequently get 'locked in'), the games are incredibly addictive and popular with tourists and locals alike. Some of the first venues to open their doors are still going strong, like

BEST ESCAPE ROOMS IN ERZSÉBETVÁROS & THE JEWISH QUARTER

Gozsdu Mission
Four sophisticated rooms, including an ultra-secure prison and an empty white space.

Locked Room Budapest
Six very different games, from Zodiac Killer (beginner) to Bunker Heist (expert).

A Room Budapest
Pirate Ship and Ghostland are for the kids; Deadland's zombie hordes for a serious fright.

Time Trap
Seven terrifying rooms containing a psychopathic killer, a butcher and the Chernobyl trap.

e-exit
Four rooms in two locations, featuring Mexico's Day of the Dead and Orwell's Big Brother.

WHERE TO BUY VINTAGE CLOTHING IN ERZSÉBETVÁROS

Retrock
Hip store with a vast collection of vintage clothing, bags, jewellery, shoes and Hungarian streetwear.

Szputnyik Shop D-20
Bright, open space, stuffed with retro fashion like US college jackets and Converse sneakers.

Ludovika
Small clothes shop that stocks select pieces for women from a range of eras; great handbags.

WHY I LOVE BUDAPEST

Steve Fallon, writer

I love Budapest for all the right reasons: architecture (especially Art Nouveau), romance (particularly the views from the bridges) and sticky apricot jam. I love Budapest for some of the wrong reasons, too: killer *pálinka* (fruit brandy), reminders of the socialist era and spending way too much time in the Turkish baths. When I first came to Budapest, I was bowled over by an often sad but confident city whose history seemed too complex to comprehend, by a beautiful but impenetrable language, and by a people I thought I'd never know. I stayed on to learn more about all three.

Gozsdu Mission, while newcomers like **Time Trap** have added lots of new features.

You don't need to be able to speak Hungarian in order to play. However, you should book your session in advance.

Ruin Pubs & Gardens

POP-UPS ARE WHERE IT'S AT IN ERZSÉBETVÁROS

A visit to Budapest during the hot summer months is not complete without an evening in one of the Erzsébetváros' *kertek,* gardens that have been converted into entertainment zones. Not sure where to head first? Here are a few of our favourites.

Szimpla Kert was Budapest's first ruin pub, and some say it's still the best and the quirkiest. **Instant-Fogas** is where two ruin bars merged to form the biggest in town, with dozens of rooms to get lost in. Another enormous venue is **Füge Udvar**, which has a large covered courtyard and lots of side rooms with music and games. Among the most sophisticated garden clubs is **Mika Tivadar Kert**, with DJs and live music most nights. **Grandio Jungle Bar** is set below a hostel in a large courtyard overtaken by urban weeds, making it more of a jungle rather than a garden club. The chilled, brightly decorated garden club of **Kőleves Kert** features hammocks, and is popular with diners from parent restaurant Kőleves next door.

Toe-Tapping Concerts

KLEZMER, SWING AND SALSA

Tired of the same old, same old? Seek out Erzsébetváros' lesser-known music venues. **Spinoza Café** stages *klezmer* (Jewish folk music) concerts on Friday nights. **Ladó Café**, unassuming by day, comes into its own most evenings when it hosts live jazz and swing. Meanwhile, **Havana**, a Cuban restaurant located in the city's most beautiful leafy courtyard, welcomes bona fide salsa musicians nightly.

The Gay Side of Budapest

SMALL BUT PERFECTLY FORMED SELECTION

In a city with such a bustling night life, Budapest's gay bar scene is not as big as you might expect. But as we all know, size isn't everything and the half-dozen or so LGBTIQ+ bars, cafes and clubs here cater to most needs. In Erzsébetváros, **Habroló** is a small and welcoming cafe and bar on two levels that takes its name from a flaky rolled pastry filled with sweet

WHERE TO STAY IN ERZSÉBETVÁROS

Mamaison Residence Izabella
Fabulous conversion of a 19th-century building hosts 38 apartments off swanky Andrássy út. €€€

Continental Hotel Budapest
A sympathetic renovation of the glorious Hungaria Bath, the Continental has atmosphere in spades. €€€

Soho Hotel
This stylish boutique hotel feels very much like its Big Apple namesake. €€€

Szimpla Kert

cream. It's a good option for meeting people at the start of a night out. Literally around the corner and beckoning to the daring and/or desperate is **CoXx**, the city's only gay cruise club, with a mammoth bar, 400 sq m of hunting ground and some significant play areas in back. Much more subdued and a 10-minute walk north is the **Tuk Tuk Bar**, with ever-so-Asian-inspired design. Set in the Casati Budapest Hotel, it's great for both the art on the walls and the cocktails.

Gay venues in other neighbourhoods include **Alter Ego**, still the city's premier gay club – and don't you forget it. It's in Nagymező utca, near the Parliament. And a couple of cafe-bars worth a look include the LGBTIQ+-friendly **Why Not** in Belváros and new-kid-on-the-block **Gaby's** in the Újlipótváros area of north Pest. It's a gay-owned American-style bar and restaurant with lots of parties and themed events. Drag-night bingo, anyone?

BEST HOSTELS IN ERZSÉBETVÁROS & THE JEWISH QUARTER

Netizen Budapest Centre
Super modern budget accommodation in primary colours over six floors. €€

Hive Party Hostel
Enormous, central place with a rooftop bar – the name says it all. €€

Wombat's
This slick and well-equipped hostel has multibed dorms and doubles, all en suite. €€

A&O Hostel
New generation hostel-hotel hybrid spread over four floors in a former playing-card factory. €

Maverick Urban Lodge
Three floors of dorms and private rooms in bold colours, decorated in a modern warehouse style. €

Hotel Mika Downtown
Intimate and understated boutique hotel close – but not too close – to bustling Gozsdu udvar. €€

Casati Budapest Hotel
Classy art-adorned hotel in an 18th-century building retains a number of original features. €€

Connection Guest House
A central guesthouse above a leafy courtyard attracts guests of all ages; delightful owners. €

STREET ART

Art curator and private chef **Noémi Nádudvar** walks us past some of her favourite street art in Budapest's district VII.

Angel of Budapest (Walls for Freedom)
Near the Great Synagogue, this vibrating, almost cubist mural by Okuda San Miguel on a Dob utca gable portrays the Spanish diplomat Ángel Sanz Briz (1910-1980), the 'Spanish Schindler' credited with having saved more than 5000 Hungarian Jews from the Holocaust in 1944.

Motivation is a Wonderland
A masterpiece by Spanish artist Dan Ferrer, this mural in a carpark on Kertész utca of a child in a cramped room looks at how both motivation and demotivation affect growth and development.

AkaCorleone mural
This stunning painting by the Portuguese artist welcomes visitors at the Kőleves garden ruin bar.

On the Prowl for Art Nouveau

HIDDEN ARCHITECTURAL GEMS

Budapest's architectural waltz through history begins with Roman Aquincum and carries on to modern times. But taking centre stage is the Art Nouveau found in abundance here.

Erszebetváros can't claim any great Art Nouveau palaces like the Museum of Applied Arts in Southern Pest or the National Institute for the Blind near City Park. But it counts a number of schools, churches and private homes that are exceptional examples of the style and worth an admiring glance. All are east of the Big Ring Road in districts VI and VII.

Lindenbaum House (VI Izabella utca 94) was designed by Frigyes Spiegel in 1896 as the city's first Art Nouveau block. Its entire front elevation is covered with suns, stars, peacocks, flowers, snakes, foxes and long-tressed nudes. Albert Kálmán Kőrössy designed **Sonnenberg House** (VI Munkácsy Mihály utca 23) in 1903; the two women sculptures framing the main door are rare.

Zoltán Bálint and Lajos Jámbor built the **Léderer House** (VI Bajza utca 42) in 1902, with lovely mosaics under the main ledge. Aladár Arkay designed the **City Park Calvinist Church** (VII Városligeti fasor 7); it's a stunning example of late Art Nouveau (1913), with carved wooden gates, stained glass and ceramic tiles.

Finally, don't miss the **Erzsébetváros Bilingual Elementary School** (VII Dob utca 85), designed by Ármin Hegedűs in 1906 with front-elevation mosaics on its facade.

More than a Train Station

DIRECTIONALLY CHALLENGED RAILWAY STATION

The large iron-and-glass structure on Nyugati tér is Nyugati train station (**Western Train Station**), built in 1877 by the Paris-based Eiffel Company and seriously misnamed – it serves trains bound for the east and the north. In 1962, a train crashed through the enormous glass screen on the main facade when its brakes failed; it came to rest on the tram line where the Nos 6 and 4 now pass by. The old dining hall on the south side of the station has housed one of the world's most elegant McDonald's since the 1980s. To the north is Westend, a 400-store shopping centre and once the largest in central Europe.

WHERE TO EAT IN ERZSÉBETVÁROS

Twentysix Budapest
Gets a Wow! both for its location in a plant-filled atrium and the Mediterranean menu. €€€

Fleischer Resto
This 'piece of New York' garners rave reviews for its inspired shared plates. €€€

Kőleves
Always buzzy, the 'Stone Soup' attracts a young crowd with its Jewish-inspired menu. €€

In Hand, on Strings

PUPPETS FOR ALL AGES

The **Budapest Puppet Theatre** might be just the ticket if you've got kids in tow. They stage shows for children of all ages, using everything from rod-and-glove puppets to marionettes and bunraku. And there's usually no need to understand Hungarian. Who doesn't know the story of Nyúl Péter (Peter Rabbit) back to front?

Sipping the Strong Stuff

MUSEUM OF GOOD TASTE

The **Pálinka Museum**, just opposite the northern entrance to buzzing Gozsdu udvar, will teach you all about the production and consumption of *pálinka* and its special place in in Hungarian culture – you can even try your hand at making some yourself (digitally). But most people are here for the shots – one, two, three – of the potent fruit brandy that are included in the entrance fee.

Let the Party Begin

ONE LONG COURTYARD, LOTS OF FUN

Erzsébetváros has Budapest's most exciting nightlife, and **Gozsdu udvar** is its heart. It's a continuous 'courtyard' running a few hundred metres between Király utca 13 and Dob utca 16, with a third access point at Madách Imre út. A residential complex of seven blocks and six interconnecting courtyards when it was built in 1901, and part of the Jewish Ghetto during WWII, it's now lined with bars, clubs, cafes and restaurants, and pulses with music and merrymakers from dusk to dawn.

The choice of venues is enormous, but you might start at **Telep**, a hipster haunt with a small art gallery upstairs that also holds gigs and hosts DJs. If you want something just a titch more sophisticated (read: older), move next door to **Spíler**, a big, bold and bustling bistro bar catering to an up-for-it crowd, with DJs at weekends and a street-food menu too. More decent blotter is available at **Feri's Kitchen & Bar** a few steps south (try their Brooklyn Burger).

If making your own music is your thing, head to **Blue Bird Karaoke**, where you'll be belting out your favourite tunes with the best (and worst) of them. Practically next door is **Vicky Barcelona**, a tapas bar until 11pm, after which it turns into one big salsa party till the wee hours. And then it's time for breakfast...

BEST PLACES FOR BREAKFAST IN ERZSÉBETVÁROS

London Coffee Society
Little place on two levels (look for the sign 'I was born in Hackney') with day-long breakfast menu. €

Blue Bird Café
This cozy cafe serves all-day breakfast and some of the best coffee in town. €

Cirkusz
Colourful breakfast venue near the Gozsdu udvar; open till late afternoon. €€

Anyam Szerint
Mama's homemade breakfast dishes and a darling little garden out back. €€

New York Café
For breakfast in style, head for what's been called the most beautiful cafe in the world. €€€

Halkakas Halbistró
Charming seafood bistro in the heart of the Jewish Quarter, this place serves great-value fish dishes. €€€

Macesz Bistro
The chefs at this handsome dining room marry modern and traditional Hungarian Jewish dishes. €€

Ghettó Gulyás
The best place to try *pörkölt* – what everyone else calls goulash – and *gulyás*, a thick beef soup. €€

SOUTHERN PEST

TWO DISTRICTS ON THE UP AND UP

The colourful districts of Józsefváros (Joseph Town) and Ferencváros (Francis, or Franz, Town) bearing the names of two Habsburg emperors, are traditionally working class and full of students. It's a lot of fun wandering the backstreets and peeping into courtyards and the small, often traditional, shops. Both are evolving areas, with new venues popping up constantly around hubs like Mikszáth Kálmán tér and Ráday utca.

From Blaha Lujza tér, the Big Ring Rd runs through Józsefváros. The western side of the district transforms from a neighbourhood of lovely 19th-century townhouses and villas around the Little Ring Rd to a large student quarter; east of the boulevard is a once rough-and-tumble district that is now being developed at breakneck speed. The neighbourhood south of Üllői út is Ferencváros, home to the city's most popular football team, Ferencvárosi Torna Club (FTC), and many of its tough, green-and-white-clad supporters.

TOP TIP

Pick a major sight and then spend some time wandering the nearby streets. Start with the Hungarian National Museum and mosey round Gutenberg tér, Rákóczi tér and Mikszáth Kálmán tér, or head to the Museum of Applied Arts and then take in the streets that stretch to the Danube.

Hungarian National Museum

HUNGARY'S EPIC SAGA

If you visit just one museum in Budapest, make it this treasure trove of the nation's most important historical relics. The museum was founded in 1802, when Count Ferenc Széchényi donated his personal collection of more than 20,000 prints, maps, manuscripts, coins and archaeological finds to the state.

On the 1st floor, exhibits in eight rooms look at the development of the Carpathian Basin from prehistory to the 9th-century arrival of the Magyars. On the floor above, the history lesson continues through a dozen rooms from the Árpád dynasty to the fall of communism. In the basement is a Roman lapidary, which includes a stunning 2nd-century mosaic.

In its own room to the left on the 1st floor, you'll find King Stephen's beautiful crimson silk coronation mantle, stitched by nuns in 1031. It was refashioned in the 13th century and the much-faded cloth features an intricate embroidery of fine gold thread and pearls. But the highlight for many will be the rooms that examine Hungary's role in WWII, the 1956 Uprising and the decades of communist rule that followed. There's the hand of the monster-sized Stalin statue that once graced the city, footage from 1956, a mock-up of a secret police office, samizdat publications and the town sign from Leninváros (Lenin Town) which reverted back to its original name Tiszaújváros in 1991.

The museum gardens, laid out in 1856, are also worth a stroll.

STEPS TO INDEPENDENCE

Less than a year after the national museum moved into its new purpose-built premises, an impressive neoclassical building designed by Mihály Pollack in 1847, it was the scene of a momentous event. On 15 March, a crowd gathered to hear the poet Sándor Petőfi recite his 'Nemzeti Dal' (National Song) from the front steps, sparking the 1848–49 revolution. Should you be in the area on National Day, expect a lot of pomp and circumstance as the reading of Petőfi's poem is re-enacted.

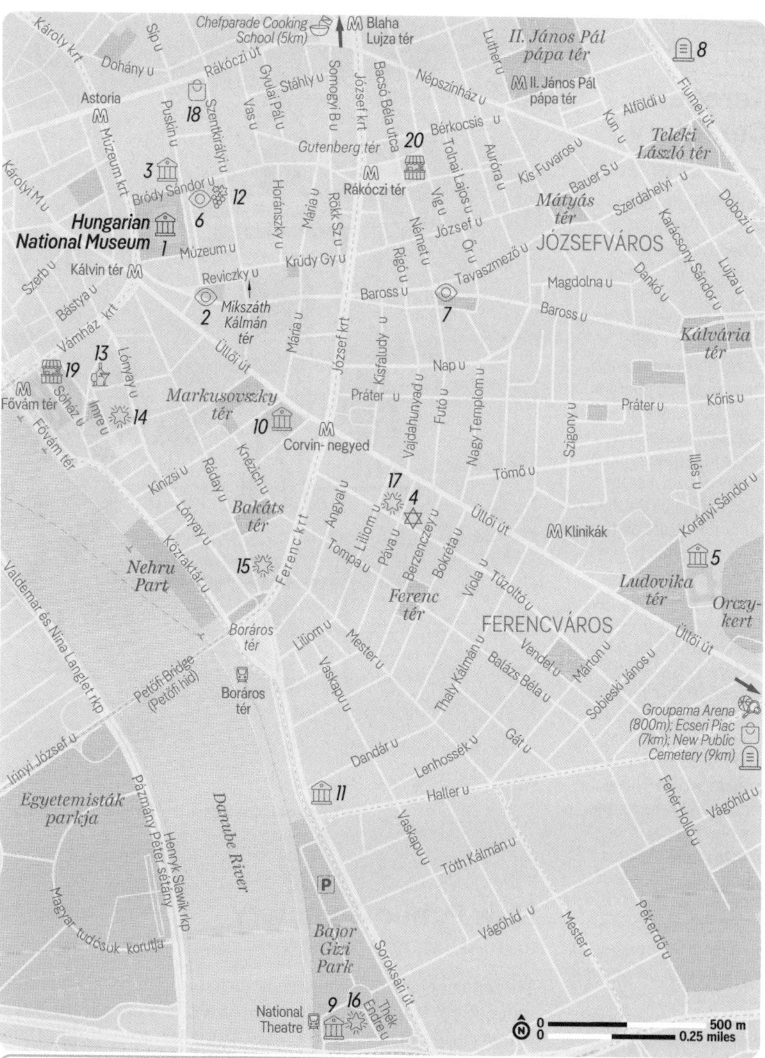

HIGHLIGHTS
1 Hungarian National Museum

SIGHTS
2 Ervin Szabó Central Library
3 Gschwindt Mansion
4 Holocaust Memorial Center
5 Hungarian Natural History Museum
6 Hungarian Radio Headquarters
7 Józsefváros Telephone Exchange Building
8 Kerepesi Cemetery
9 Ludwig Museum of Contemporary Art
10 Museum of Applied Arts
11 Zwack Museum & Visitors Centre

ACTIVITIES
12 Tasting Table

DRINKING & NIGHTLIFE
13 Borbíróság

ENTERTAINMENT
14 Budapest Music Center
15 Jedermann Café
16 Palace of the Arts
17 Trafó House of Contemporary Arts

SHOPPING
18 Magyar Pálinka Háza
19 Nagycsarnok
20 Rákóczi tér Market

Kerepesi Cemetery

FINAL RESTING PLACE

Established in 1847, Kerepesi Cemetery is Budapest's answer to London's Highgate or Paris' Père Lachaise. Some of the 3000 mausoleums in this 56-hectare necropolis are worthy of a pharaoh, especially those of political leaders and national heroes such as Lajos Kossuth, Ferenc Deák and Lajos Batthyány. Other tombs are quite moving, like those of the actor Lujza Blaha and the poet Endre Ady. Plot 21 contains the graves of many who died in the 1956 Uprising. Sitting uncomfortably close by is the huge Workers' Movement Pantheon for party honchos, topped with the words 'I lived for Communism, for the people'. Nearby is the simple grave of János Kádár (1912–89), whose tomb was desecrated in 2007, his skull and a number of bones carted away. Also on the grounds is the Piety Museum, which offers insights into the Hungarian approach to death and mourning. Near the main entrance is the sublime horse-drawn Aponyi Hearse, built in 1932 for state funerals. Pick up a free map of noteworthy graves at the entrance.

Tomb of Lajos Kossuth, Kerepesi Cemetery

New Public Cemetery

HALLOWED GROUND FOR FALLEN HEROES

This enormous 207-hectare cemetery, dating to 1886 and easily reached by tram from Blaha Lujza tér, is where Imre Nagy, prime minister during the 1956 Uprising, and 2000 others were buried in unmarked graves (plots 298–301) after executions in the late 1940s and 1950s. The area has been turned into a moving National Pantheon and is a 30-minute walk from the entrance; follow the signs pointing the way to '298, 300, 301 parcela'. A large monument marks their graves. At peak periods you can take a minibus around the cemetery or hire a taxi at the gate.

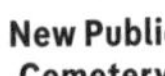

New Public Cemetery

Holocaust Memorial Center

UNRIVALLED DOCUMENTING OF THE SHOAH

The memorial center is the only public collection in the country that deals exclusively with the history of the Holocaust, both here and elsewhere in Europe. Housed in a striking modern building, it opened in 2004 on the 60th anniversary of the start of the Holocaust in Hungary. The thematic permanent exhibition traces the rise of anti-Semitism in Hungary and follows the path to the genocide of the country's Jewish and Roma communities. A sublimely restored synagogue in the central courtyard, designed by Leopold Baumhorn and completed in 1924, hosts temporary exhibitions. An 8m-high wall bears the names of Hungarian victims of the Holocaust.

The exhibits consist of a series of maps, photographs, diaries, personal effects and graphic videos. The music starts off rather festive, but the exhibits are accompanied by the sounds of a pounding heartbeat and marching as the doomed are deprived of their freedom and dignity and deported to death camps in Germany and Poland. The films of the camps, taken by the liberators, are particularly harrowing, featuring piles of corpses and emaciated survivors. The personal effects contained in glass columns in the synagogue are especially poignant. Outside in the small garden, a number of plaques and memorials honour 'righteous gentiles', including Jan Karski, who acted as a courier during WWII, reporting on the Warsaw Ghetto and extermination camps.

Holocaust Memorial Center

HERCULES MILAS/ALAMY STOCK PHOTO ©

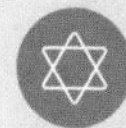

WALL OF MEMORY & LOSS

The names that appear in the memorial wall in the inner courtyard are carved into the glass using a special laser technique. Some 60,00 names were engraved there at the opening of the of the center and since that time the number has more than trebled. Symbolic nametags simply reading 'anonymous' remind visitors of the many victims whose identities are not and probably never will be known. At the bottom of the wall, visitors have laid small pebbles as a sign of respect and loss.

Rákóczi tér Market

Borbíróság

A HUNGARIAN WINE PRIMER

At the simple yet classy 'Wine Court', almost five dozen Hungarian wines are available by the glass and the food – especially the duck and goose – is taken pretty seriously. It's an excellent introduction to well-prepared Hungarian cuisine and is just next to the Nagycsarnok (Great Market Hall). Dining is on two levels, but the terrace on a quiet square is a delight in the warmer months. You might even just pop by for a glass of Etyek Sauvignon Blanc or a Tokaj Furmint.

Rákóczi tér Market

WHERE THE LOCALS SHOP

To get a feel for how local people in Budapest shop and what they shop for, head for this market on Rákóczi tér, which has occupied a handsome blond-brick market hall since 1897. It was renovated in the early 1990s following a fire and contains all the usual staples: fruit, veg, cured meats, pasta, cheese and baked goods, as well as a Spar (supermarket). But best of all, it's one of the few markets where growers still come in from the countryside with produce and foodstuffs like honey, smoked paprika and homemade jams.

Nagycsarnok

Nagycsarnok

THE BIGGEST DEAL IN TOWN

The **'Great Market Hall'** opened in 1897 and is the city's biggest market. It became something of a tourist magnet after massive renovations a century later and still attracts a disproportionate amount of foreign customers alongside the regular shoppers. Gourmets will appreciate the variety of treats available here for less than you'd pay in the shops on nearby Váci utca: potted foie gras, garlands of dried paprika, souvenir sacks and tins of paprika powder, and as many kinds of honey as you'd care to name. Head up to the 1st floor for Hungarian folk costumes, dolls, painted eggs, embroidered tablecloths, carved hunting knives and other souvenirs, as well as prepared foods like *kolbász*, *pörkölt* and *lángos*.

Art Nouveau Peeping

MUSEUM OF APPLIED ARTS

Housed in a gorgeous Ödön Lechner-designed Art Nouveau building (1896) decorated with Zsolnay ceramic tiles, the **Museum of Applied Arts** houses two permanent collections. One contains Hungarian and European furniture from the 18th and 19th centuries, Art Nouveau and Secessionist artefacts, and objects relating to trades and crafts (glassmaking, bookbinding, goldsmithing). The other consists of Islamic art and artefacts from the 9th to the 19th centuries. Unfortunately, the museum is currently undergoing protracted renovations and much of it is closed. You might get lucky and chance upon one of the special exhibits occasionally held in the completed Central Hall, a blindingly white extravaganza supposedly modelled on the Alhambra in Spain.

Otherwise, content yourself with some exterior tile-watching or visit the **György Ráth Museum** and its fine collection of Art Nouveau objects near the City Park.

Wine Tasting with the Experts

HUNGARIAN WINE FROM A TO Z

Looking for a crash course in Hungarian wine? Head for the attractive cellars of **Tasting Table**. Tastings of between five and eight wines, accompanied by a sumptuous cheese and charcuterie board, are held twice a day, and the knowledgeable staff will walk you through each selection. Their shop across the road has a huge selection of local wines, especially from smaller producers, and the largest selection of Tokaj wines available in Budapest. Here, you can taste and order flights without pre-booking. They also host weekly three-course dinners, paired with six wines.

Playing with the Fradi Boys

AT HOME WITH FERENCVÁROSI TC

Hungary's descent from being at the top of European football to *béka segge alatt* ('under the arse of the frog') remains one of sport's great mysteries. Hungary's antediluvian victories over England, both at Wembley (6–3) in 1953 and at home (7–1) the following year, are still talked about as if the winning goals were scored yesterday. If you want to watch Ferencvárosi Torna Club, the country's loudest, brashest and

BEST CAFES IN SOUTHERN PEST

Hauer Cukrászda és Kávéház
This fin-de-siècle confectionery is the Central European coffeehouse you came to Budapest to experience.

Rengeteg RomKafe
A rabbit-warren cafe for kids and adults, cluttered with teddy bears, old sewing machines, books and games.

Nem Adom Fel Kávézó
'I Won't Give Up' is Hungary's first cafe operated by people with special needs and disabilities.

Nándor Cukrászda
This tiny patisserie with excellent biscuits and cakes has been here since 1957. Take a number and join the queue.

WHERE TO DRINK IN SOUTHERN PEST

Café Csiga
The popular 'Snail Cafe' has an agreeable location alongside the Rákóczi tér market.

Lumen Café
This enormous venue with multiple rooms, and covered and open courtyards, has music most nights.

Tilos a Tilos
The anchor tenant in a car-free square. The huge terrace here is often overflowing with students.

most popular football team, head for their home stadium, **Groupama Arena**. Like everyone else, you'll either love the Fradi boys or hate 'em.

LOCAL PICKS IN SOUTHERN PEST

Tony Dabbous Láng is the founder of independent bookshop Bestsellers.

Nagycsarnok
I live right next door to the Great Market Hall; in fact, I can look into it from my windows. I come here almost daily for fresh produce and the excellent butcher's shop in the basement.

Ázsia
I buy all my spices, fresh herbs, sauces and condiments from the Asia shop right behind the Great Market Hall.

Trattoria La Coppola
My favourite restaurant, an authentic Sicilian trattoria, is walking distance from my home.

Danube Promenade
For exercise and relaxation, I walk south along the Danube past the distinctive Bálna shopping centre, enjoying views of the river, cruise ships, barges and Gellért Hill.

A Walk Among the Palaces

ELEGANT ARCHITECTURE

The area around the Hungarian National Museum is sometimes referred to as the Palotanegyed – the Palace Quarter – because of its impressive 19th-century palaces and leafy squares. Today, it's an up-and-coming district, full of restaurants, artsy boutique hotels and independent galleries. At one time the buildings here were owned by individual families, and many still bear the names of their original residents. A favourite is the **Gschwindt mansion** on the corner of VIII Bródy Sándor 12 and Puskin utca. It was built at the turn of the century by a successful wine producer and merchant, whose bust you can see above the entrance. A short distance to the east at VIII Bródy Sándor utca 5-7 is the former **headquarters of Hungarian Radio**, where shots were fired on 23 October 1956, sparking the anti-Soviet Uprising.

Down the Hatch

TWO ICONIC SPIRITS

Unicum, the thick, almost medicinal-tasting aperitif made from 40 herbs and spices, is as bitter as a loser's tears and a favourite drink in Hungary. To delve into its history, head for the **Zwack Museum & Visitors Centre**, which starts with a rather schmaltzy video, has an enormous collection of 17,000 miniature bottles from across the globe and concludes with an educated tasting session. You can buy more – in quantities both small and large – from the adjacent shop.

The fruit-based brandy *pálinka* is available in bars across town, but should you want a souvenir bottle, the largest and best selection is available at **Magyar Pálinka Háza**. This large shop stocks hundreds of varieties – from the traditional plum to more exotic flavours like apricot, pear and raspberry. Looking for something a bit smaller? *Pálinka*-filled chocolates make for a great gift.

Cooking Up a Storm

HUNGARIAN CULINARY CLASSES

Want to learn the difference between *gulyás* (a beef-based soup) and *pörkölt* (more akin to what we call goulash, most commonly made with veal or pork)? Even better, want to don

WHERE TO EAT IN SOUTHERN PEST

Costes
The first restaurant in Hungary to gain a Michelin star, Costes offers exceptional tasting menus. **€€€**

Padrón
An authentic slice of Spain in the backstreets of Pest, with a great range of tapas. **€€**

Paletta Bistró
International bistro serving every Hungarian kid's favourite: *rántott sajt* (breaded deep-fried cheese). **€€**

Zwack Museum

an apron and give it a stir? The **Chefparade Cooking School** is a contemporary, cosmopolitan kitchen for those who'd like to learn to cook Hungarian cuisine. A popular course is the four-hour morning class, which includes a market visit and the preparation of three dishes. Finish up with your very own gourmet meal.

Mother Nature Square in the Face

NATURAL HISTORY FOR YOUNG AND OLD

If you've got kids in tow, don't miss the **Hungarian Natural History Museum**. The impressive skeleton of a two-tonne finback whale greets visitors just inside the entrance, hinting at the treasures that await e over four floors of interactive exhibits. Interesting displays focus on topics as varied as the biodiversity of coral reefs, the natural resources of the Carpathian Basin, and the secret world of gems, meteorites and minerals. The Ark of Biodiversity explores Hungary's natural world, while the excellent Age of Dinosaurs will keep many a preteen entertained. Temporary exhibitions are generally excellent, with a particular focus on wildlife photography.

THE SPIRITS OF HUNGARY

Budapest's two most famous spirits are *pálinka* and Unicum. *Pálinka* is distilled from a variety of fruits and is akin to a strong brandy or eau de vie. It kicks like a mule and is served in most bars, some of which carry an enormous range. Unicum's medicinal-looking bottle is instantly recognisable. The bitter aperitif has been around since 1790 – it's prepared according to a secret formula and is aged in oak casks; it's now available in four different tastes. The liqueur was apparently baptised by Austro-Hungarian Emperor Joseph II; when tasting it for the first time, he exclaimed, 'Das ist ein Unikum!' (This is unique!). We still wonder what it was called before his outburst...

Petrus
This French-style bistro has all the classics: boeuf bourguignon, duck confit and escargots. **€€**

Öcsi
For the closest thing to homemade Hungarian food, head for this very authentic *étkezde* (diner). **€**

African Buffet
Colourful ultra-budget oasis: order spicy goat soup and the Zanzibar fried rice studded with goodies. **€**

All-Night Entertainment

A TRIO OF JAZZ AND DANCE VENUES

Three hip venues within 15 minutes' walk of one another offer a nightly array of music and dance performances. The **Budapest Music Center** hosts a fantastic lineup of classical performances in its classy 350-seat concert hall, while Hungarian and international jazz groups take to the stage at the in-house **Opus Jazz Club**, with concerts five nights a week. If that's not to your taste, head for the lovely, old-style **Jedermann Café**, which turns into a great music venue at night, focusing primarily on jazz. If you're in a more eclectic mood, up for a mixture of music, theatre and dance, the **Trafó House of Contemporary Arts** presents a great selection of local and international acts – Patti Smith recently played here – with a gallery and club in the basement.

BEST ASIAN RESTAURANTS IN SOUTHERN PEST

Enso
Contemporary izakaya and ramen bar, hidden like a speakeasy inside a disused building. Reserve. €€

Hanoi Xua
This spacious, functional-looking restaurant has an authentic menu of pho (noodle soup), *bún* (rice noodles) and other Vietnamese favourites. €

Barako Kávéház
Barako Kávéház specialises in 'boodle fights', trays lined with banana leaves and overflowing with Filipino specialities. €

Pesti Chutney
Good selection of vegan and veggie dishes, even if the curries are somewhat tailored for Central European tastes. €

Discovering Architecture in the 'Hood

HIDDEN TREASURES IN THE LIBRARY

Southeast of the Hungarian National Museum is the **Ervin Szabó Central Library**, which holds some 2.4 million books and periodicals. Completed in 1889 and exquisitely renovated, the public reading room has gypsum ornamentation, gold tracery and enormous chandeliers. Do yourself a favour and buy the cheap one-day visitor's pass to have a close look at this gem. Alternatively, visit the ground-floor cafe to get a sense of the building. A short walk to the east is the **Józsefváros Telephone Exchange Building**, built in 1910. It's an impressive structure adorned with reliefs of classical figures tracing communications through the ages: Mercury, homing pigeons and that newfangled invention, the telephone.

Flea-Market Finds

DIAMONDS (AND RUST) FOR SALE

Some people consider a visit to the celebrated **Ecseri Piac** a highlight, not just as a place to indulge their consumer vices, but also as the consummate Budapest experience. One of the biggest flea markets in Central Europe, Ecseri sells everything from antique jewellery and Soviet army watches to Fred Astaire–style top hats (and a fair amount of stolen antique goods too, it's said). Early Saturday is the best time to go for the diamonds in the rough. Ecseri is about 10km southeast of the Great Market Hall. To get there, take bus 54 from Pest's Boráros tér, or for a quicker journey, express bus 84E, 89E or 94E from the Határ út stop on the M3 metro line.

WHERE TO STAY IN SOUTHERN PEST

Hotel Palazzo Zichy
Sumptuous 19th-century aristocrat's residence, now a lovely hotel with many original features intact. €€€

Escala Hotel & Suites
These spacious serviced apartments come equipped with living and dining areas, plus full kitchens. €€€

Brody House
One-time residence of the prime minister, offering retro chic at its hippest. No lift. €€

National Theatre

An Evening of Culture

CLASSICAL MUSIC AND DRAMA

They may not have the romantic surrounds of the Hungarian State Opera House or the Liszt Academy of Music, but the two concert venues in the **Palace of the Arts** (Művészetek Palotája or Müpa for short) on the Danube embankment make up for that with near-perfect acoustics. Catch a full orchestral performance at the 1700-seat **Béla Bartók National Concert Hall** or a string quartet at the more intimate Festival Theatre, which seats 450 people. Should you want to brave a play in Hungarian (or just check out the theatre's bizarre architecture) head for the **National Theatre** next door. Designed by Mária Siklós, it is supposedly 'Modern Eclectic' style, mirroring other great Budapest buildings like the Parliament. The overall effect, however, is a postmodern pick-and-mix of classical and folk motifs, porticoes, balconies and columns.

Seeking Modern Art

CONTEMPORARY ART STOP

While visiting the **Millenniumi negyed** (the 'Millennium Quarter'), originally intended to be the site of a joint World Expo with Vienna in 1996, have a look at the **Ludwig Museum of Contemporary Art**, which is on the side of the building overlooking the Danube. The Ludwig Museum holds Hungary's most important collection of international contemporary art; works by Hungarian, American, Russian, German and French artists span the past half-century, while works by Central and Eastern European artists date mostly from the 1990s. The museum's temporary exhibitions are invariably well received.

UNKNOWN SOUTHERN PEST

Gábor Bánfalvi, oenophile and owner of Tasting Table, introduces his favourite spots in Distict VIII.

Garden with Cake
The garden at the Hungarian National Museum is a great place to lay on the grass and admire the surrounding architecture. Bonus: behind the museum, the celebrated Auguszt pastry chain has opened a branch called Geraldine.

Art Galleries, Cafes & Strudel
Stroll along Bródy Sándor utca, which is bursting with cafes and art galleries. At the start of nearby Vas utca you'll find Rétesbolt Anno 1926, with excellent poppy-seed and *túró* (farmer's cheese) strudel.

Stress-Free Square
The restaurants and bars on Mikszáth tér are the preferred haunts of the district's many students, who come here to unwind.

BO18 Hotel Superior
Stylish independent hotel on a quiet street, with small sauna, gym and garden. **€€**

Corvin Hotel Budapest
Sleek, minimalist and comfortable rooms at this fusion of two separate hotels. **€€**

Thomas Hotel
Three dozen bargain rooms – some with balconies over an inner courtyard – in a very central location. **€**

CITY PARK & BEYOND

GREEN LUNG WITH MONUMENTS & MUSEUMS

Sserene City Park (Városliget) is Pest's favourite recreational space. It has a little bit of everything: it's home to the city's most famous plaza, Heroes' Square, the world-renowned Széchenyi Baths, the faux-historic but fairy-tale Vajdahunyad Castle, the enormous Budapest Zoo and Botanical Garden, a handful of outstanding museums and a lovely lake. And all this is within just 15 minutes of downtown. This is where local families flock for cool playgrounds and amateur athletes gather for street workout facilities, table tennis, football, volleyball, teqball and basketball courts. And let's not forget the dog walkers.

During Hungary's millenary celebrations in 1896, City Park hosted most of the events. In recent years, the controversial Liget Budapest project has been undertaking renovations here, opening the House of Music and the Museum of Ethnography, with a new building for the National Gallery to follow.

TOP TIP

To reach City Park, you can either stroll along Andrássy út, a street lined with towering trees and century-old villas, or, if you prefer a speedier journey, take the charmingly retro Millennium Underground (M1; p106), which is the oldest metro line in Europe.

HISTORIC HORSE RACE

Heroes' Square often plays host to the city's major events and celebrations. Every autumn, this monumental landmark is filled with sand when it turns into a rowdy racecourse for the **Nemzeti Vágta** (National Gallop), a crowd-pleasing showcase of Hungarian horsemanship. Young racers dressed as Hungarian hussars race around the square competing for the grand prize, while crowds cheer from the grandstands set up in front of the Museum of Fine Arts and Kunsthalle.

Heroes' Square

Heroes' Square

THE CITY'S MOST EMBLEMATIC SQUARE

The city's largest and most emblematic square lies at the end of tree-lined Andrássy út, forming an elegant gateway to City Park. A World Heritage site, it showcases all of Hungary's history in one place. Its centrepiece is the semi-pherical Millennium Monument (Ezeréves Emlékmű), erected in 1896 for the country's millenary celebrations. Two colonnades display 14 key leaders, from King Stephen (far left), the country's first king, to Lajos Kossuth (far right), an emblematic figure of the

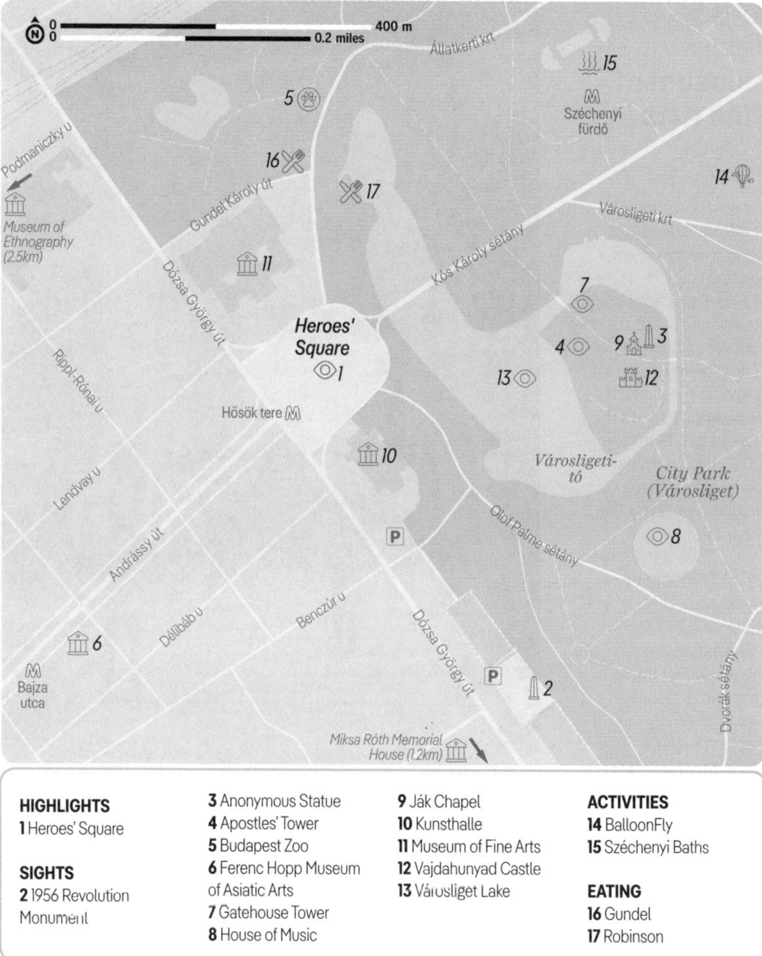

HIGHLIGHTS
1 Heroes' Square

SIGHTS
2 1956 Revolution Monument
3 Anonymous Statue
4 Apostles' Tower
5 Budapest Zoo
6 Ferenc Hopp Museum of Asiatic Arts
7 Gatehouse Tower
8 House of Music
9 Ják Chapel
10 Kunsthalle
11 Museum of Fine Arts
12 Vajdahunyad Castle
13 Városliget Lake

ACTIVITIES
14 BalloonFly
15 Széchenyi Baths

EATING
16 Gundel
17 Robinson

1848–49 Revolution. The colonnades are topped by the chariots of War and Peace, as well as the allegorical bronze figures of Labour and Wealth, and Knowledge and Glory.

In the middle, an obelisk towers above the square, topped by the statue of Archangel Gabriel, holding the Hungarian crown and a patriarchal (two-barred) cross. Legend has it that Pope Sylvester II saw Gabriel offer Stephen the crown of Hungary in a dream. The pope then sent a crown to Stephen, granting him the title 'Apostolic Majesty' – hence the patriarchal cross. At the column's base are the seven chieftains who led the Magyars into the Carpathian Basin in the late 9th century. In front of the obelisk lies the Tomb of the Unknown Soldier, commemorating those who died defending the country throughout history. Visit at night for a particularly majestic experience.

Museum of Fine Arts

HISTORY'S MASTERPIECES

Set on the northern side of Heroes's Square in a grand neoclassical building is the Museum of Fine Arts. Completely renovated in 2018, it's now home to an outstanding collection of foreign art, spanning the centuries from antiquity up to the present day. More than 100,000 masterpieces are on display here, including works by the likes of Raphael, El Greco, Toulouse-Lautrec, Chagall, Velázquez, Rembrandt, Goya, Manet, Monet and Cézanne.

The museum comprises six main collections: Egyptian Antiques, Classical Antiques, Old Masters, Sculptures, Prints and Drawings, and Old Hungarian. Don't miss one of the most famous pieces of all, Raphael's *Esterházy Madonna* (c. 1508). Although unfinished, it still manages to achieve the beauty and harmony for which the paragon of classicism is acclaimed. However, its real claim to fame is that it was among the seven artworks stolen in 1983, the greatest art theft in Hungary's history. With Interpol's help, the paintings were found and returned to the museum, but not without damage – the *Esterházy Madonna* was broken in half.

Museum of Fine Arts

Kunsthalle

CONTEMPORARY ART MUSEUM

Facing the Museum of Fine Arts on the opposite side of Heroes' Square is a beautiful neo-Renaissance building, reminiscent of a Greek temple: the Kunsthalle or Palace of Arts (Műcsarnok). This is the best place to see contemporary art in the city. Following the German Kunsthalle model, the Palace of Arts does not have a permanent collection but instead stages five to six major temporary exhibitions throughout the year, promoting Hungarian and international visual arts like photography, sculpture and various installations. The museum is home to a lovely cafe and gift shop. Concerts are sometimes staged here as well.

Kunsthalle

Széchenyi Baths

SPA SESSIONS IN A WEDDING-CAKE BUILDING

One of the largest spa complexes in Europe, splendid Széchenyi Baths is Budapest's most popular bath alongside Gellért. Even though it's packed with tourists in the high season and during the holidays, locals love it too. Want proof? Look no further than all those old chaps playing chess in the outdoor pool on floating boards.

While the indoor section feels like a labyrinth, where getting lost is part of the fun, the exterior is simply stunning: the bright sunflower-yellow neoclassical architecture contrasts vividly with the blue waters. There are three outdoor pools: the coldest is for swimming (caps required), the warm one is for fun, with a whirlpool in the middle, and the hot one is for relaxing. There are also a variety of indoor thermal pools, as well as saunas, steam cabins and therapeutic services, including massages. A cafeteria serves both cold and warm dishes should you plan to stay for the day.

Like at other thermal baths throughout the city, the water is curative and pleasantly hot. In winter, nothing beats soaking in the outdoor pools of Széchenyi, steam rising into the frigid air while snowflakes fall from the sky.

THERMAL SPAS

Budapest's most popular baths, Széchenyi's palatial complex was constructed in 1913. But Budapest's hot springs history dates back much further – the ancient Romans were the first to harness Hungary's abundant healing waters (p36).

Széchenyi Baths

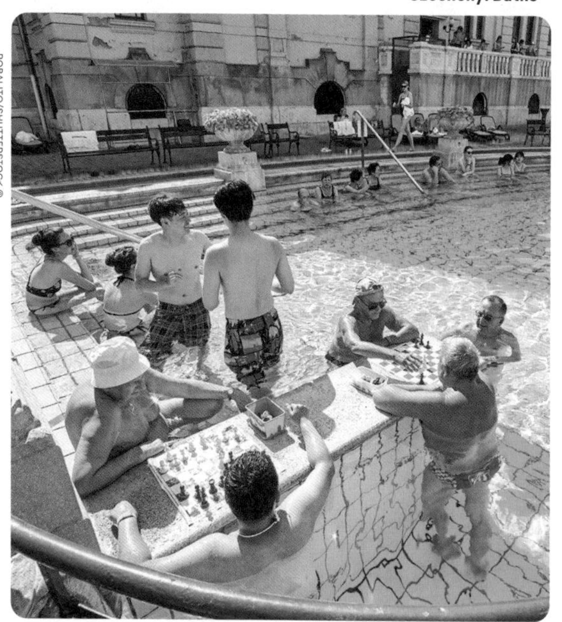

ROBALITO/SHUTTERSTOCK ©

TO CABIN OR NOT TO CABIN

Visitors to Széchenyi often have a hard time deciding whether to choose a ticket with a locker or a cabin. Although cabins are more expensive, you'll have the luxury of a private changing booth where you and a friend can store all your belongings. If you choose the cheaper ticket, your electronic wristband will only open one locker, and you'll have to get changed in one of the common rooms, which are often quite crowded. Locker numbers are not assigned.

Vajdahunyad Castle

A FAUX FAIRY-TALE CASTLE

Majestic Vajdahunyad Castle in the heart of City Park was never inhabited by kings and queens. Modelled after the eponymous castle of the Hunyadis in Transylvania, it was built in 1896 for the millenary celebrations and was only intended to be a temporary structure made of wood. The crowds loved it so much, however, that a permanent structure was later erected from stone. At the time, the castle aimed to showcase Hungary's different architectural styles over the previous 1000 years, hence the intermingling of Roman, Gothic, Renaissance and baroque elements.

Currently, only the Renaissance-baroque wing is open to visitors. Here you'll find the Hungarian Agricultural Museum, which showcases Europe's largest collection of all things agricultural. Farming, hunting, fishing and viticultural equipment abound, as do...antlers. As you walk around the 12 palatial halls, be sure to check out the 18th-century canoe carved from a single tree trunk and the section showcasing the history of Hungarian grape and wine culture. Vajdahunyad Castle is particularly breathtaking when illuminated at night.

Vajdahunyad Castle

Apostles' & Gatehouse Towers

TURRETS TO CLIMB

If you take the 150 steps up the 30m-tall Apostles' Tower at Vajdahunyad Castle, you'll be rewarded with a sweeping panorama of Budapest (guided tours only). Test your knowledge of the city and try to pick out landmarks like the basilica and Gellért Hill, or take the opportunity to peer down on otherwise hidden parts of the castle. If you'd rather explore on your own, head to the Gatehouse Tower, where the footbridge leads into the castle. The view from here is a little less impressive, but an exhibition of old photos showcases the castle's history on two floors.

Gatehouse Tower

Ják Chapel

Ják Chapel

SNAP A SELFIE

This tiny little church is hidden in the courtyard of Vajdahunyad Castle. The intricately carved stonework of the multi-layered portal, with small statues above depicting Christ and 10 apostles (the two others are off to the sides), makes this a fabulous photo-op. A copy of the 13th-century Abbey Church in Ják in western Hungary, it was originally built as the castle library. The church was eventually consecrated in 1915, though today it is only occasionally used for religious purposes. Visitors are welcome to enter on Wednesday and Friday, however the interior is far less impressive. This is a popular wedding venue.

Anonymous Statue

A TOUCH OF LUCK

Walking through the Vajdahunyad Castle courtyard, you may spot a line of people queuing up to take photos with a mysterious statue of a hooded figure, seated on a bench with an open book to one side. No, it's not a pensive death eater from the Harry Potter series but Anonymous, an unknown chronicler at the court of an early king, famous for writing the earliest book on Hungarian history. Gesta Hungarorum (The Deeds of the Hungarians), provides a detailed history of the arrival of the Magyars in the Carpathian Basin in the 9th century. Written around 1200, it exists as a single manuscript, written in medieval Latin. Held in Vienna for centuries, it is now part of the Széchényi National Library's collection in the Royal Palace. So why is everyone lined up in front of the statue? According to local lore, Anonymous bestows inspiration and good fortune to all writers who touch the quill in his right hand.

Anonymous

Gundel Restaurant

THE EMBLEM OF HUNGARIAN GASTRONOMY

This timeless City Park landmark is one of the most famous restaurants in all of Hungary. While an establishment has been operating here since 1860, Gundel's story really started in 1910, when Bavarian-born restauranteur Károly Gundel took over and made history. Gundel was a legend, with an unmatched aptitude for hospitality, treating every guest like an old friend. His name gradually became synonymous with Hungarian gastronomy, and at the 1939 World's Fair in New York, he was responsible for running the Hungarian pavilion's restaurant and was the man to meet – people lined up outside just to talk to him. And with that, he put Hungary on the world culinary map.

Gundel created dishes that would form the foundations of Hungarian cuisine, such as the Gundel crêpes, which are filled with walnut cream and enlivened with rum, soaked with rich chocolate sauce, and served flambéed at the table. Order the menu's National 11, and you'll get to sample eleven iconic Hungarian dishes that are considered to be the restaurant's most important contributions to the local cuisine.

Gundel

Robinson Restaurant

DATE NIGHT

Robinson is the perfect place for a romantic rendezvous: it's located on a small island on the lake at City Park, so you can wine and dine under the open sky while ducks waddle around and live music plays. Downstairs, a seasonally changing menu offers traditional Hungarian, French or Italian dishes; upstairs, a steakhouse is a draw for meat lovers. The Florentine T-bone steaks, shipped in straight from world-renowned Tuscan butcher Dario Cecchini, are unmissable. Pair your dishes with fine Hungarian wines and be sure to make a reservation in high season.

Robinson

TOP: MILENA BOEVA/ALAMY STOCK PHOTO ©, BOTTOM: PHILIPP ZECHNER/ALAMY STOCK PHOTO ©

Miksa Róth Memorial House

Miksa Róth Memorial House

ART NOUVEAU MASTERPIECES

There's hardly a single Budapest building from the belle époque that doesn't contain Miksa Róth's distinctive artistic touch in its interior, from intricate stained-glass windows to colourful mosaics. Without this man, many buildings would look entirely different, including Parliament, Széchenyi Baths and Gresham Palace, in addition to scores of private mansions. He even added his signature design to the cupola of Mexico City's Palace of Fine Arts.

A great museum on Nefelejcs utca, not too far from City Park, exhibits the works of the artist over two floors, in the apartment and studio where he lived and worked from 1911 until his death. The first floor still looks the same as the Róth family once left it, and will give visitors an idea of what the living quarters of a middle-class Hungarian family looked like in the 20th century – though, of course, it was enhanced with masterpieces of Art Nouveau design. Downstairs, an array of Róth's outstanding glass art is on display. It's closed on Monday.

Ferenc Hopp Museum of Asiatic Arts

TRAVEL THE WORLD

The Ferenc Hopp Museum of Asiatic Arts is the only museum in Hungary with a focus on Asian cultures and arts. The collection was founded in 1919 by world traveller and art collector Ferenc Hopp and is displayed in his own lavish mansion. Temporary exhibitions take place throughout the year, showcasing Chinese and Japanese ceramics, porcelain, textiles and sculptures, among other artefacts from Indonesia, India and Tibet. The museum also houses Hungary's only Asian arts library and a peaceful garden. It's located close to City Park on Andrássy út; the pagoda in front gives the game away.

Ferenc Hopp Museum of Asiatic Arts

House of Music

A CONCERT VENUE AND EXHIBITION SPACE

The celebrated Japanese architect Sou Fujimoto designed Budapest's House of Music – an astonishing building that seems to have sprung up organically amid the park's trees. Humongous floor-to-ceiling glass panels form a completely translucent facade, merging interior and exterior, while the perforated roof merges into the surrounding canopy. Inside, you'll find a concert venue, museum and education centre; the main exhibit is the intriguing interactive gallery, 'Sound Dimensions - Musical Journeys in Space and Time'. This showcase allows you to walk (literally) through centuries of European and Hungarian music, from the mysticism of shamanic drumming to modern movie soundtracks. The best part is the special audio headset that follows your every move - whenever you pass by or stop in front of an exhibit, the content changes. Interactive displays allow you to try out drumming, playing in a string quartet or making music on a chessboard. Attending a concert here, with the illuminated Vajdahunyad Castle in the background, is not to be missed.

BODY RHYTHMS

A constant stream of cacophony fills the air outside the House of Music. A unique playground is set in the music centre and museum's garden, where an unusual collection of instruments invites visitors to explore a variety of sounds and rhythms. Kids and adults alike can play congas, windpipes and cajón drums; jump up and down on musical cushions and step on tiles that imitate the sounds of pianos, guitars and harps; and have heaps of fun making music with their every move.

House of Music

KRISZTIAN TEFNER/SHUTTERSTOCK ©

Rooftop garden, Museum of Ethnography

Museum of Ethnography

SUBTERRANEAN CULTURE TRIP

Presenting Hungarian culture and way of life, the Museum of Ethnography's collection comprises some 250,000 ethnographic objects, as well as exceptional photographic and film materials, manuscripts and music recordings. Alongside priceless relics of Hungarian folk culture, the museum also holds a vast collection of ethnographic objects representing cultures from the far-flung corners of the world.

Opened in 2022, the immense building – defined by its signature parabolic rooftop garden – is a new addition to City Park. While most of the museum is actually located underground, the above-ground portions are hugged by a glass curtain wall that's covered with an aluminium mesh, decorated with half-a-million pixels depicting 20 Hungarian and 20 international contemporary ethnographic motifs from the museum's collection (Venezuelan, Congolese, Cameroonian, Mongolian, Chinese, Melanesian and more). A special attraction is the rooftop garden that's planted with shrubs and trees, which is meant to be a communal space for visitors to climb and picnic upon, and which provides great views of the city from its highest point.

1956 Revolution Monument

A MEMORIAL MARKS THE SPOT

Located in between the two wings of the Museum of Ethnography, this triangular monument made of gleaming metal and rusting steel was erected in 2006 to mark the 50th anniversary of the 1956 Uprising. On the first night, a giant statue of Stalin was pulled down by demonstrators here. The statue's plinth was the terrace from where communist leaders used to watch May Day processions, waving to the crowds below. The monument is shaped like a wedge that forms a 56-degree angle with Dózsa Görgy út, symbolising Hungarians who joined forces to break through communist rule.

1956 Memorial Monument

SPARTY UP!

Every Saturday night, Széchenyi Baths goes wild when a DJ starts spinning disks – mostly blasting electronic music – and a laser show lights up the historic walls outside. This is the so-called Szecska sparty (pun intended) that starts after the official closing hours at 9.30pm and lasts until 2am. Regular entry tickets include a standard locker. More expensive tickets include a cabin and a drink coupon, while a VIP room is also available. You can book ahead online or pay by cash at the door if there's still space inside. Note that daytime services like saunas and massages are not available during the sparties, and there are generally more guys than girls.

Széchenyi Baths

MORE IN CITY PARK & BEYOND

Sudsy Soak

BUDAPEST'S BEER BATH

While visiting Budapest's **Széchenyi Baths** (p141) is a special experience in itself, those after something even more unique should consider the spa's beer bath: an acacia tub for two, filled with hot mineral water (36°C), plus malts, hops, barley, brewer's yeast, and beer bath salts from the Czech Republic. If this sounds like some sort of hokey gimmick, think again. Brewer's yeast is one of those time-honoured grandmotherly cure-alls (it improves digestion and boosts the body's immune system, in addition to being rich in B vitamins that restore hair and skin), while hops are a natural sedative. Thus, no surprise that the practice has been around since the 16th century – at least in Prague.

WHERE TO GRAB A QUICK BITE IN CITY PARK

Léghajó Kert
Coffee, hot dogs and pastries feature at this cafe next to the park's main playground. €

Nyereg Bar & Grill
Sporting a spacious terrace by the lake, Nyereg is perfect for a quick drink and a bite. €€

Pavilon Kert
Near Széchenyi Baths, a series of stalls offer Hungarian favourites like *lángos* and deep-fried meats. €

There are two beer spa halls at Széchenyi, both equipped with six tubs – one for those who want to try the beer spa only and one for those who plan on entering the main baths afterwards. Emerald-coloured Zsolnay tiles and hops motifs adorn the walls.

And if soaking in hops and barley isn't enough, there's a tap right next to each tub, so you can pull unlimited amounts of Czech beer to sip while soaking. Sessions are 45 minutes long and are said to stimulate the metabolism, remove toxins from the body and ease fatigue, stress and hangovers. A beer spa is also available at Lukács Baths (p83). Cheers!

Budapest's Favourite Lake

YEAR-ROUND FUN

If you ask locals, **Városliget Lake**, found just behind Heroes' Square, is one of City Park's best features. It was created at the turn of the 19th century when the development of the park began. The lake is only about 60cm deep and is fed by used water from Széchenyi Baths, thus no swimming is allowed. That doesn't stop the neighbourhood pups from plunging in, though.

From spring to autumn, you can rent colourful rowboats and pedalos (paddleboats) to float around and enjoy the views to Vajdahunyad Castle. When winter comes, it's time to lace up your skates as the lake turns into Europe's largest outdoor **ice-skating rink**. This winter wonderland is especially charming when darkness descends and ethereal lights illuminate the massive space while music plays in the background. There's a dedicated area for beginners, where staff can help you learn to skate, while the side close to the bridge is where the pros generally gather, gliding gracefully across the ice. Between laps, you can refuel with warm mulled wine or tea. Skates are available to rent.

Fly High in a Hot-Air Balloon

LEAVE GRAVITY BEHIND

No matter where you are in Budapest, you'll likely spot a hot-air balloon floating high above the city, adding a dash of red-and-white stripes to the Pest skyline. This is **BalloonFly** in City Park, whose 15-minute flights offer a perspective like no other. BalloonFly is located on Mimóza Hill, the very spot from where another hot-air balloon, the Balloon Captif, piloted by French captain Louis Godard, took people up above City Park in 1896 during the millenary celebrations.

BEST ART NOUVEAU BUILDINGS NEAR CITY PARK

Hungarian Institute of Geology and Geophysics (14 Stefánia út)
This institute, originally built in 1869, sports a stunning sky-blue roof covered in Zsolnay tiles.

Institute for the Blind (39 Ajtósi Dűrer sor)
Breathtaking inside and out, this 1898 edifice hides the country's biggest stained-glass composition in its Nádor Hall.

Kőrössy Villa (47-49 Városligeti fasor)
Looking like a creamy wedding cake, the Kőrössy Villa is the oldest home on the street, erected in 1899.

Pántlika
Communist-era kiosk with a cool wavy roof and a great terrace shaded by tall trees. €

Piknik
Prepared picnic baskets for those who'd like to sit on the grass; tables are also available. €€

Zöld Küllő
Steps from Vajdahunyad Castle, with fairy lights in summer and transparent igloos in winter. €

CITY PARK'S OLDEST BUILDING

The former Olof Palme House – built for the 1896 millenary celebrations that marked the 1000-year anniversary of the Hungarian conquest of the Carpathian Basin – was fully renovated in 2019 with 21st-century touches and reopened as **Millennium House**. With intricate decorations and Zsolnay tiles adorning the facade, the building is absolutely breathtaking. Inside, visitors will find a cultural space that displays temporary exhibitions and events, and an elegant restaurant and cafe that occupies the building's terrace during the warmer months. Outside, a splendid rose garden provides ample space for relaxation, with a colourfully tiled fountain at its centre. Be sure to walk around the building, as both sides look splendid.

Budapest Zoo

The present-day attraction flies on a set schedule and never leaves Mimóza Hill, so it essentially operates like a 150m-high open-air lift – it's just a lot prettier and heaps more fun. A maximum of 30 people fit into the basket at a time, and you'll likely be asked to pay attention to weight distribution to avoid an off-kilter journey, so this flight is not recommended for those afraid of heights. The shape and colours of the balloon – which you will spot elsewhere in City Park – are a nod to Pál Szinyei Merse's famous 19th-century painting, *Balloon*, which is on display at the National Gallery within the Royal Palace.

WHERE TO STAY IN CITY PARK

Baroque Hostel & Coworking
Clean rooms, 24-hour reception, shared bathrooms and cool common spaces suitable for coworking. **€€**

D50
This fuss-free 4-star hotel has inviting rooms and a great breakfast within walking distance from City Park. **€€**

Ibis Budapest Heroes' Square
Nice rooms, good breakfast and great views to the Budapest Zoo and Botanical Gardens. **€€**

All you need to do is buy your ticket and wait for your number to be called – there's a digital board that shows you when you're next and an on-site cafe to ease the wait. Get a nighttime ticket for a view of the illuminated cityscape, spread out below. Note that BalloonFly doesn't operate in January or in bad weather. Even if the weather seems pleasant on the ground, it may be windy up above, so always check the website for the daily schedule first (balloonfly.hu).

Family Fun in the Park

FROM ELEPHANTS TO ACROBATS

Lions, tigers and bears...nearly 1000 different species of animals live at the **Budapest Zoo and Botanical Garden** on the fringes of City Park. You can easily spend two to three hours – or even a whole afternoon – wandering around a charming lake that's home to colourful birds, daring to step closer to the big cats or visiting the Australia Zone. Time your visit around the many feeding sessions to see giraffes, penguins or sharks in action. While animals are the main attraction, the zoo also has some architectural points of interest. Admire the Art Nouveau entrance with animals flanking the gate, the Secessionist-style Elephant House adorned with Zsolnay tiles, and the intriguing design of the Palm House, by Gustav Eiffel of Eiffel Tower fame. Adjacent is a children's entertainment centre (Holnemvolt Vár or Once Upon a Time Castle) built on the site of a former amusement park, with a petting zoo, riding stables, a shark school and a hedgehog hospital.

Next door, the year-round **Capital Circus** has everything you'd expect from such a place: acrobatics, aerial acts, mind-boggling juggling and many other daredevil extravaganzas. The circus has a capacity of 1850 seats and can be visited rain or shine. While the shows are mostly in Hungarian, the stories are highly visual and easy to follow.

CITY PARK PLAYGROUNDS

On the southeastern side of City Park, one of the largest playgrounds in the country awaits bigger kids with cool slides, a three-storey jungle gym and swings. Steps away, the playground's little brother has more swings, a zip ride and trampolines built into the ground.

In the heart of the park, by King's Hill, a small playground suited for toddlers has a sand pit and swings. Close to the eastern tip of the park, a miniature city awaits little ones, designed to help them learn the rules of the road. It's got everything from roundabouts and bike lanes to speed bumps, crosswalks and traffic lights.

Mamaison Hotel Andrássy Budapest Sleek boutique hotel on central Andrássy út offering well-appointed rooms and suites; whirlpools too. **€€€**

Mirage Medic Hotel Housed in a classic 19th-century building, book a room here for the holistic healing programmes. **€€€**

Star City Hotel This midrange hotel is a few minutes' walk from Keleti Railway Station and offers special deals for families. **€€**

AROUND BUDAPEST: GÖDÖLLŐ

HUNGARY'S LARGEST BAROQUE MANOR

The town of Gödöllő, 30km northeast of Budapest, is full of lovely baroque buildings and monuments, but the real reason everyone's here is the Gödöllő Royal Palace. Hungary's largest baroque manor house, Antal Mayerhoffer designed the residence in the 1760s for Count Antal Grassalkovich, the confidante of Empress Maria Theresa. It was enlarged as a summer retreat and gifted to Emperor Franz Joseph in the 1870s; soon after it became the favoured residence of his consort, the much-loved Habsburg empress and Hungarian queen, Elisabeth (1837–98), who was affectionately known as Sissi.

Between the two world wars the regent, Admiral Miklós Horthy, also used it as a summer residence, but after the communists came to power part of the mansion was turned into a barracks and then converted into an old people's home. The rest was left to decay. Partial renovation began in the mid-1980s, and it finally reopened in 1996.

TOP TIP

The easiest way to get here is by HÉV train (H8). From Örs vezér tere, which is on M2 metro line, go to Gödöllő's Szabadság tér station, the second of the town's four stops. Those with a travel pass will need to buy a supplement, as Gödöllő is outside the BKK travel zone.

Gödöllő Royal Palace

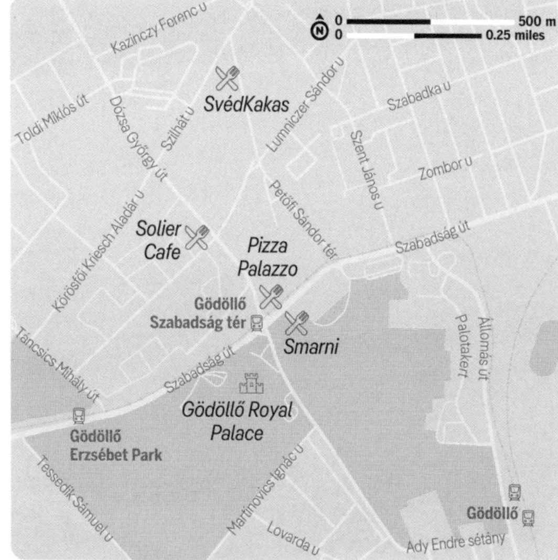

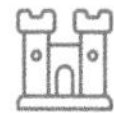

Gödöllő Royal Palace

WHERE KINGS AND DESPOTS SLEPT

Visitors to Gödöllő can tour 34 of the palace's rooms, which have been restored to the period when the imperial couple was in residence. Franz Joseph's suites (largely in burgundy) and Sissi's private apartments (lavender) on the 1st floor are particularly impressive. Check out the Ornamental Hall (room 17) – all gold tracery, stucco and chandeliers – where chamber-music concerts are held throughout the year, and the Queen's Reception Room (room 18), with a Secessionist-style oil painting of Sissi patriotically repairing the coronation robe of King Stephen with needle and thread.

Other parts of the permanent collection before and after the private suites include the Grassalkovich Era Exhibition (rooms 5 to 12), which offers a glance at the palace during its first century (don't miss the impressive Chapel and Oratory overlooking it), and the Queen Elisabeth Memorial Exhibit (rooms 24 to 26), which looks at the queen's early life, marriage to Franz Joseph and her assassination by Italian anarchist Luigi Lucheni, who stabbed her to death with a needle file in Geneva in 1898. It also examines her legacy, which continued to grow in the century that followed her death. Four rooms at the end trace the history of the palace from the interwar years up through the communist era.

Guided tours are available for the splendid Baroque Theatre, the two stable buildings and Horthy's Bunker, a two-room, 55-sq-metre underground shelter built in 1944 for the then-regent and his family.

BEST PLACES TO EAT IN GÖDÖLLŐ

Smarni
Housed in an outbuilding of the royal palace opposite the main HÉV train station, Smarni serves enlightened Hungarian favourites. **€€**

SvédKakas
Charming restaurant with a covered garden is great for à la carte lunch midweek and an all-you-can-eat buffet at weekends. **€€**

Pizza Palazzo
This popular Italian eatery serves pizzas and pastas and is attached to the Szabadság tér HÉV station. **€**

Solier Cafe
In the centre of Gödöllő, this is a wonderful *cukrászda* (cake shop) with a daily lunch menu. **€**

Above: Citadel (p164), Visegrád. Right: Esztergom Basilica (p168)

THE DANUBE BEND & WESTERN TRANSDANUBIA

PICTURESQUE TOWNS AND REMOTE FOREST

North and west of Budapest, historic towns nestle among hills on Europe's second-longest river, giving way to plains, lush forest and sweeping countryside.

Snaking, gushing and bursting unexpectedly with sidearms and wetlands at its flanks, the Danube is etched deeply into the cultural psyche of Hungary. Over the millennia, this river has united, divided and provided a highway for trade, and its banks have offered residence for rulers and invaders. North of Budapest, the Danube Bend is a region of low peaks and attractive river towns steeped in history and the cultures of those who have settled here, including Romans, Magyar tribes, Orthodox Serbs, Jews, and the Ottoman Turks, who conquered the region and held it for a century and a half. Hilltop fortresses are spectacular reminders of power, turbulence and moments of relative tranquility, much like the qualities of the Danube River itself.

Travelling upriver from Budapest, the Danube draws you deeper into its spell as you leave the day-trippers behind in the arts-focused town of Szentendre, round the eponymous bend and pass the impressive Citadel of Visegrád. Beyond that, the Danube swirls past Esztergom, which, like Visegrád, was once a royal seat of sorts, but in contrast, Esztergom is a religious centre dominated by a vast hilltop basilica.

Western Transdanubia reveals its secrets gradually rather than in dramatic landscapes, making it best suited to slow travel, especially once you move south of Sopron into beautiful forests, meadows, and small towns and villages.

THE MAIN AREAS

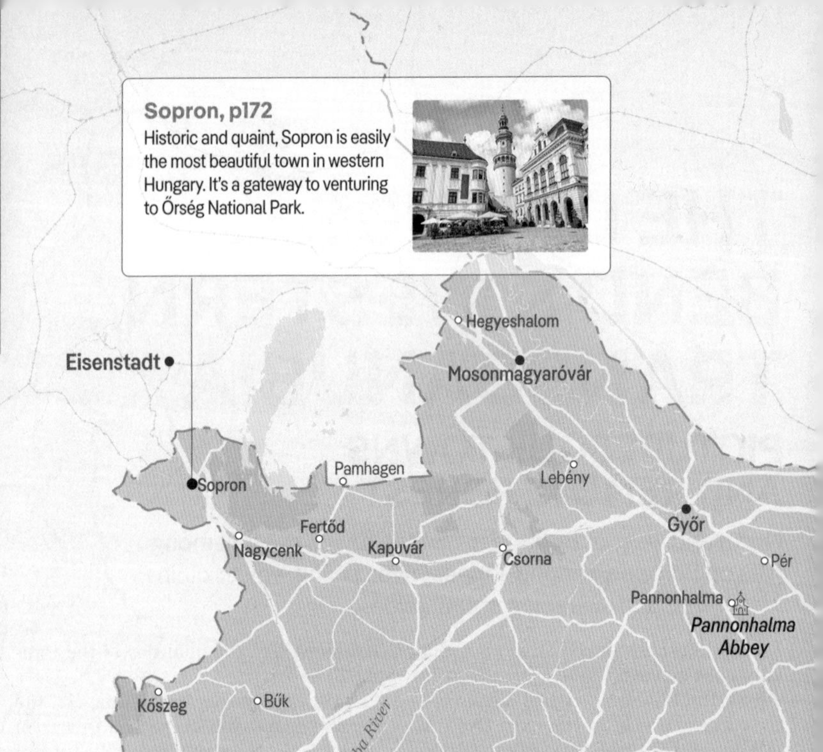

Sopron, p172

Historic and quaint, Sopron is easily the most beautiful town in western Hungary. It's a gateway to venturing to Őrség National Park.

Hegyeshalom
Eisenstadt
Mosonmagyaróvár
Pamhagen
Lebény
Sopron
Győr
Fertőd
Nagycenk
Kapuvár
Csorna
Pér
Pannonhalma
Pannonhalma Abbey
Kőszeg
Bük
Rába River
Pápa
Szombathely
Sárvár
Celldömölk
Zirc
Ják
Jánoshaza
Herend
Devecser
Ajka
Veszprém
Vasvár
Körmend
Nyirád
Szentgotthárd
Sümeg
Kondorfa
Őrség National Park
Szalafő
Zalalövő
Zalaegerszeg
Hodoš
Balaton Uplands National Park
Lake Balaton

Find Your Way

The Danube makes its namesake bend some 50km north of Budapest, flanked by attractive towns. From there, the journey along the river heads to Sopron, and to villages in Őrség National Park some 150km south.

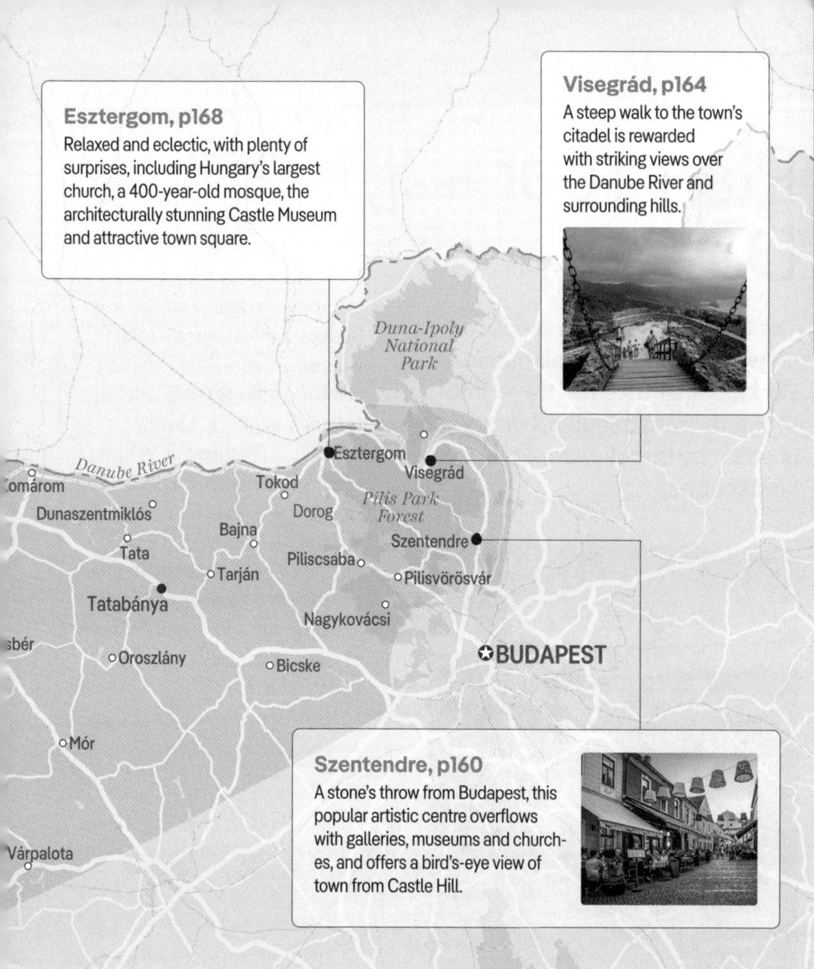

Esztergom, p168

Relaxed and eclectic, with plenty of surprises, including Hungary's largest church, a 400-year-old mosque, the architecturally stunning Castle Museum and attractive town square.

Visegrád, p164

A steep walk to the town's citadel is rewarded with striking views over the Danube River and surrounding hills.

Duna-Ipoly National Park
Danube River
Komárom
Esztergom
Visegrád
Tokod
Dorog
Pilis Park Forest
Dunaszentmiklós
Bajna
Tata
Szentendre
Piliscsaba
Tarján
Pilisvörösvár
Tatabánya
Nagykovácsi
Kisbér
BUDAPEST
Oroszlány
Bicske
Mór
Várpalota

Szentendre, p160

A stone's throw from Budapest, this popular artistic centre overflows with galleries, museums and churches, and offers a bird's-eye view of town from Castle Hill.

BOAT

Excursion boats and faster hydrofoils take you to the Danube towns from Budapest in season, generally May to September. Going by boat is by far the most relaxing and beautiful way to experience the Danube Bend region.

CAR

Travel by bus and train are possible if you plan well, but it can be useful to have a car to explore Western Transdanubia. It's also an alternative mode of transport if you're visiting when boat services aren't running. Hire a car in Budapest or Győr.

TRAIN & BUS

Trains connect Budapest with Szentendre, and a separate line runs to Esztergom. Another route from Budapest stops across the river from Visegrád (with an hourly ferry). Trains also run to Csákánydoroszló, the entrance to Őrség National Park. Regular buses serve towns on the Danube's west bank.

0 50 km
0 25 mile

Plan Your Days

The Danube Bend is a place for slow travel and fresh air outside Budapest, and as you travel into Western Transdanubia, history is offset by bucolic, low-key landscapes.

FEELTHEDRONE/SHUTTERSTOCK ©

Esztergom Basilica (p168)

Day trip from Budapest

- In the river transport season, there's no better way to enjoy the Danube and its towns than by taking a hydrofoil or train from Budapest to **Visegrád** (p164), where in warm weather you can climb the trails to the Citadel and towers. Visegrád is a lovely place to picnic in the forest or by the river, or grab lunch in a restaurant.

- After that, squeeze in a visit to the basilica in **Esztergom** (p168) or return to **Szentendre** (p160) and drop into a museum. From any of these towns, you can return to Budapest by train.

SEASONAL HIGHLIGHTS

Summer is the time to enjoy Danube boat trips, picnics, hiking and cycling. In winter, cosy up in restaurants and bars, and immerse yourself in local culture.

JANUARY

Bundle up and dip into museums and galleries, sip mulled wine (***forralt bor***) and plunge into hot goulash soup (***gulyásleves***).

APRIL

Easter and Szentendre's open-air ethnographic museum celebrate all manner of folk traditions with performances from different regions.

MAY

Perfect month for **boat trips** into the Danube Bend and hopping between towns with a picnic lunch in your daypack.

KARL ALLGAEUER/SHUTTERSTOCK ©, IHSANUNUVAR/SHUTTERSTOCK ©, GTS PRODUCTIONS/SHUTTERSTOCK ©

Three days to travel the region

- Stroll and climb through fortress towns along the magnificent Danube before travelling to Western Transdanubia. Take the train or boat to **Szentendre** (p160) to visit a gallery or museum in this artsy town before hopping on a bus or boat to **Visegrád** (p164) to experience the spectacular Citadel.

- Stay overnight in Visegrád before travelling by bus or boat to **Esztergom** (p168). Spend a day visiting the basilica, Castle Museum and Danube Museum. Journey on to historically charming **Sopron** (p172).

Slow travel

- If you have a week or more, travel by boat (by train out of season) to **Szentendre** (p160) and linger over impressionist works at the Czóbel Museum and changing exhibitions at Art Mill.

- Take the boat or bus to **Visegrád** (p164) and hike the trails to the towers and Citadel. Continue on by boat or bus to **Esztergom** (p168) to explore the basilica and museums, and picnic on the Danube in summer.

- Catch the train to beautiful **Sopron** (p172), stopping over at **Pannonhalma Abbey** (p176), and afterwards cycle through **Őrség National Park** (p178) and villages at your chosen speed.

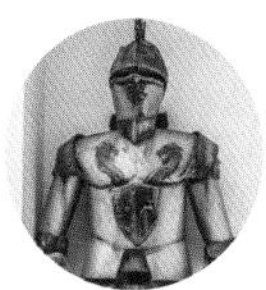

JULY

Don't miss Visegrád's three-day **Palace Festival** of medieval military games, music and more during the second weekend of July.

AUGUST

Hike the hills above the Danube, **cycle** through Őrség National Park or **paddle** a kayak in nice weather.

SEPTEMBER

Enjoy fine wines as Sopron brings in the **grape harvest** and celebrates with drink, folk music and dancing.

NOVEMBER

Celebrate **St Martin's Day** with a meal of goose on 11 November in the saint's region of birth, Western Transdanubia.

Szentendre
Budapest

SZENTENDRE

Szentendre (St Andrew) is the southern gateway to the Danube Bend and an easy day trip from Budapest, just 19km away. The city has a pleasant historic centre, but that's just one reason for its immense popularity. Szentendre became an artists' colony in the 1920s, and late in the week and on weekends, its galleries and museums spring to life. Delving into exhibitions at the superb museums and art galleries is what brings most people to town, but you can enjoy Szentendre in many different ways. One is by simply walking its streets and soaking up its 'Mediterranean' feel. The city also has numerous Serbian Orthodox churches with excellent collections of religious art and liturgical objects, the legacy of Serbs who fled in waves from the Ottomans. Outside Szentendre, the open-air ethnographic village is impressive, making for a pleasant stroll through a cross-section of regional Hungarian villages.

TOP TIP

By far the best days of the week to visit Szentendre are Thursday and Friday, as weekends are crowded and most of the museums are closed from Monday to Wednesday. The open-air ethnographic village museum is shut in winter. If you're day-tripping from Budapest, the last train back is around 11.30pm.

SZENTENDRE'S MUSEUMS

Ferenczy Múzeumi Centrum *(femuz.hu)* administers Szentendre's 10 major museums. All of them except the Margit Kovács Ceramic Collection are closed from Monday to Wednesday. A ticket to one includes all museums. On the website you'll find a great map of all museum locations, as well as information in English and Hungarian to help you plan your visit. It's especially useful for working out opening times and seasonal closures.

Hungarian Ethnographic Explorations

STROLL THROUGH TRADITIONAL VILLAGES

The **Hungarian Open-Air Ethnographical Museum** (Szabadtéri Néprajzi Múzeum) is the country's most ambitious *skanzen* (folk museum displaying village architecture). It's cleverly arranged into 11 sections covering the regions of Hungary, as well as one on Transylvania in Romania. As you walk or ride a bike (hire available on-site) past the different buildings and even whole villages that have been reconstructed, you're lured into a feeling of actually being in these places. A sense of having been suddenly transported out of Szentendre and into, say, the Balaton Uplands, becomes even stronger and stranger once you encounter village extras – artisans, craftspeople and peasants in costume sitting on church steps, picking flowers or simply acting in character. Churches rise up from hillsides and plains, and houses of various social classes are filled with furnishings. The sheer number of different buildings makes the museum truly remarkable.

When a Romanian–Hungarian border post suddenly appears, you cross and eventually arrive at a stunningly reconstructed town square in Transylvania. The coffeehouse is beautiful, and you can even enjoy a real brew. By this time, you may well have completely relinquished yourself to the reconstructed fiction and believe all this is real – and in a sense, it is, because it's so closely modelled on actual places.

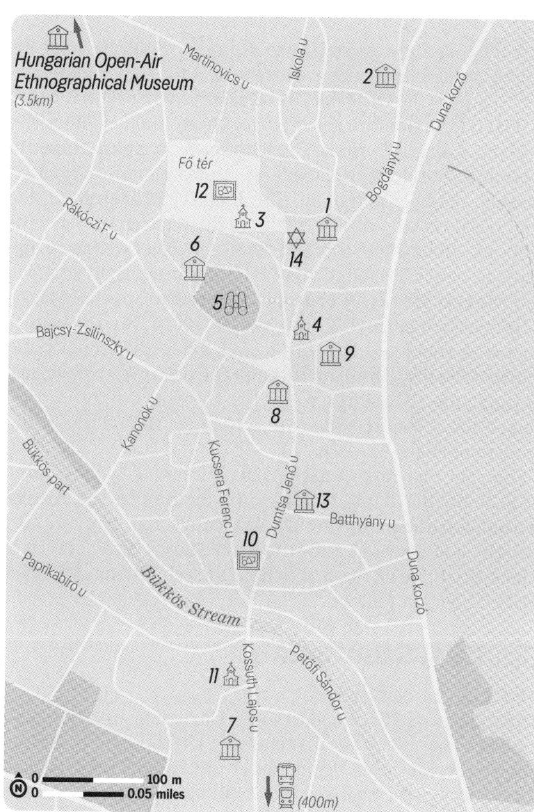

SIGHTS
1 Ámos-Anna Museum
2 Art Mill
3 Belgrade Cathedral
4 Blagoveštenska Church
5 Castle Hill
6 Czóbel Museum
7 Ferenczy Károly Museum
8 Kmetty Museum
9 Margit Kovács Ceramic Collection
10 Old Goat Art Gallery
11 Požarevačka Church
12 Serbian Ecclesiastical Art Collection
13 Szamos Marzipan Museum
14 Szanto Memorial Home & Synagogue

Plan on spending at least two to three hours. It's best enjoyed on weekdays (closed Monday and in winter) when the grounds are more likely to be quiet. It's located around 5km northwest of the centre and is reached by bus 230 from bay 7 of Szentendre's bus station.

Artistic Pursuits

GALLERIES, MUSEUMS AND SPECTACULAR VIEWS

Szentendre has tons of top-notch art museums and galleries. Closest to the train and bus station is the **Ferenczy Museum**. Károly Ferenczy (1862–1917) is attributed with

WHERE TO EAT IN SZENTENDRE

From Sea
Enjoy seafood with an inland twist, like a salmon burger, outside in summer and upstairs in winter. **€€**

Himalaya
Indian dishes, including lots of vegetarian options, with outdoor summer seating. **€€**

Passata
Tasty pizza and with a few summer tables outside in the historic centre. **€**

introducing Impressionism to Hungary, and many of his works are displayed along with those of his sons and daughter. Nearby is the **Old Goat Art Gallery**, with original works by leading Szentendre artist Eszter Győry and her American husband Osiris O'Connor. The **Szamos Marzipan Museum** has namesake creations including a life-size figure of Michael Jackson made of marzipan. The **Kmetty Museum**, on the southwestern side of Fő tér (the main square), displays the work of Cubist János Kmetty (1889–1975), as well as sculptures by Jenő Kerényi. Cross Fő tér and turn right to reach the **Margit Kovács Ceramic Collection** (Kovács Margit Kerámia Gyűjtemény). Margit Kovács (1902–77) was a ceramicist who combined Hungarian folk art with religious and modern themes. Climb up through the pretty narrow streets to the **Czóbel Museum**, which has the works of the impressionist Béla Czóbel (1883–1976), a friend of Pablo Picasso and student of Henri Matisse.

Enjoy the view from **Castle Hill** (dominated by the Church of St John the Baptist) before descending to the **Ámos-Anna Museum**, housing the surrealist and expressionist paintings of husband-and-wife team Margit Anna and Imre Ámos. Continue on to see the changing exhibitions at the **Art Mill** (Művészet Malom).

WHY I LOVE SZENTENDRE

Anthony Haywood, writer

Sure, it's so close to Budapest that these 'Mediterranean' streets can overfill on warm summer weekends, but Szentendre has a lively cultural scene and a unique flavour of its own. I don't mean its sweet Marzipan Museum (although that literally has its own flavour). Szentendre has lots of quirky galleries, ranging from miniature art to textiles and the Retro Design Center, with its Eastern European cars and appliances from the 1960s and 1970s. There's always something new to find in town on a stroll. I love rivers and landscapes, so taking the stairs up to Castle Hill and looking over the Danube is a real favourite of mine.

Spiritual Szentendre

SACRED PLACES AND OBJECTS

The influence of Serbian Orthodox Christians in Szentendre has been enormous over the centuries. Orthodox Serbs arrived here in several waves, fleeing the Ottomans and regional conflicts between the 14th and 19th centuries. The result is a rich legacy of Serbian Orthodox churches, most dating from the 18th century. **Blagoveštenska Church** (Blagoveštenska templom; 1752) on Fő tér has fine baroque and rococo elements. The **Belgrade Cathedral** (Belgrád Székesegyház; 1764) rises up impressively near Castle Hill, and **Požarevačka Church**, between the train and bus stations and the main square, has a lovely iconostasis from 1742.

Just off Fő tér, the **Serbian Ecclesiastical Art Collection** has a dazzling array of icons and other religious objects from Serbian Orthodox churches around Hungary brought together into one museum. The highlight is the Lőrév Codex, a manuscript dating from the 13th or 14th century, but the works in gold are also plentiful and beautiful. Szentendre's 250-strong

WHERE TO DRINK IN SZENTENDRE

Teddy Beer
Some 150 different beers, lots of whisky and rum, and good grilled chow to top it off.

Művész
Drink while listening to live jazz, Latin, rock and more on Fridays and Saturdays from May to October.

National Wine Museum (Nemzeti Bormúzeum)
Taste wines in a labyrinthian cellar where the sommelier gives their background.

Belgrade Cathedral

Jewish community was devastated by the Holocaust. A reminder is the **Szanto Memorial Home and Synagogue** (Szántó Emlékház és Imaház), which has a small collection of relics and is Europe's tiniest synagogue.

SZENTENDRE'S ARTISTS' COLONY

Szentendre became a vibrant artists' colony in 1929, and its artists greatly shaped 20th-century Hungarian painting. Some of the work by Lajos Vajda, who lived here from the early 1920s, showed influences of Serbian religious art, reflecting the multiethnic and multicultural character of Szentendre. Another important figure in the colony was Dezső Korniss, who sometimes used folk motifs in his avant-garde paintings. The works of both artists provided strong inspiration for the European School of Hungarian modernism that took shape after 1945. Later, Béla Czóbel, whose paintings can be seen in the city's museum dedicated to him, was also a major influence.

GETTING AROUND

Szentendre is easy to get around by foot. The only exception is reaching the Hungarian Ethnographical Museum, which is out of town and reached by bus. The easiest way to get to Szentendre from Budapest is on the HEV suburban train (H5) from Batthyány tér in Buda, which takes 40 minutes and leaves every half hour. In addition to your city ticket for Budapest (don't forget to punch it), buy a supplement. The last train back is around 11.30pm. Buses run at least hourly from Újpest-Városkapu train station and on to Visegrád and Esztergom, but it's a dull 30-minute ride. The section of the Danube between Budapest and Szentendre is not particularly interesting by boat, so you won't miss much by taking the train. Low water levels and the COVID-19 pandemic have taken their toll on boat services, but Mahart PassNave runs slow boats and hydrofoils to Szentendre once daily Friday to Sunday from May to September from Vigadó tér in Budapest. Book well ahead for the hydrofoil.

Visegrád

Budapest

VISEGRÁD

Visegrád wears its long history on its sleeve, with the Royal Palace and the Citadel ruin rising out of bucolic forest. Romans and later Slovaks settled here. Mongols rode through in 1241–42, prompting a jittery King Béla IV to begin work on a lower castle by the river and then on the hilltop Citadel. Less than a century later, an embattled King Charles Robert of Anjou moved the royal household to Visegrád. For almost 200 years, Visegrád was Hungary's 'other' (often summer) capital. Visegrád's real golden age came during the reign of King Matthias Corvinus (r 1458–90) and Queen Beatrix, who had Italian Renaissance craftsmen rebuild the Gothic palace. In the 16th century, Ottomans invaded and settled. History aside, the walk up to the Citadel and the view from the top are what make Visegrád such a special place to visit, and you can begin forest hikes here.

TOP TIP

Visegrád's Citadel is open every day for most of the year (limited hours December and January), making it ideal for a visit early in the week when museums in other towns are closed. The hike up and the views are what make it particularly magical, so it's best enjoyed on warmer days.

BLUE TRAIL

The Visegrád INFO office, near the ferry crossing to Nagymaros, has excellent hiking maps of the region. If the walk to the Citadel whets your appetite for more, follow the **National Blue Trail** (Országos Kéktúra) to Pilisszentlászló, an 11km hike with views of the Danube and hills from lookouts. There are places to rest and picnic along the way. To travel back to Budapest or Visegrád, leave the trail at Pilisszentlászló and catch bus 870 to Szentendre. Wear suitable hiking gear and check the weather before setting off.

To the Citadel & Solomon's Tower

STEEP WALK TO STUNNING VIEWS

The climb past **Solomon's Tower** (Salamon-torony) to the **Citadel** (Fellegvár) is easily the highlight of Visegrád, but you need to be fit for the steep Fellegvár trail (40 minutes from the tower). You can also take the easy but less spectacular Calvary Promenade (Kálvária sétány) near the church or a whole circuit with both. The quiet, paved Salamontorony utca leads to the 13th-century tower. This tower was once part of a lower castle, built during the reign of Béla IV and used to control river traffic. If you visit from May to October (closed Monday and Tuesday), you can check out the exhibits on town history.

Above the tower, a hiking track leads off to the right, and you begin a sweaty climb to the Citadel. It's an invigorating hike (wear decent shoes), and once you reach the top, you have some of the region's best views over the Danube. Exhibits inside the Citadel are unlikely to knock your sweaty socks off, but they include a bit of armoury and a large waxwork of the Congress of Visegrád in 1335. Enjoy the view and the walk around the walls, and feel the wind whistling around you from the crown of this 330m hilltop. A spectacular 180-degree panorama opens up over the Danube and the hills beyond. The scene becomes a 360-degree view when you walk along the walls. Completed in 1259, the Citadel was the repository for the Hungarian crown jewels until 1440, when Elizabeth of Luxembourg, the daughter of King Sigismund,

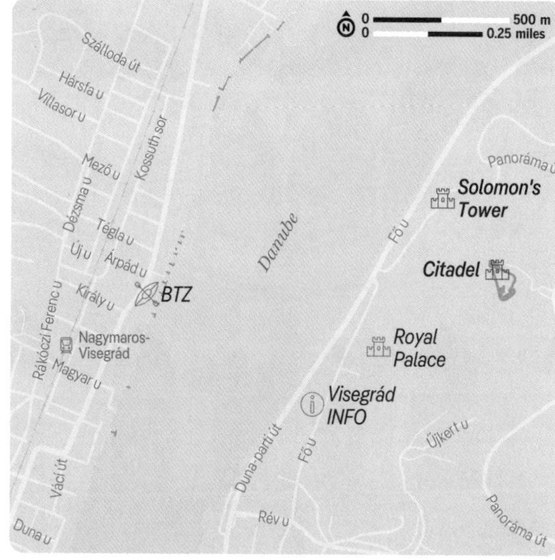

stole them with the help of her lady-in-waiting and hurried off to Székesfehérvár to have her infant son László crowned king in a palace intrigue worthy of a Shakespearean drama. The crown was returned to the Citadel in 1464 and held here – under a stronger lock, no doubt – until the Ottoman invasion in the 16th century.

Renaissance & Late Gothic Visegrád

WANDER THROUGH PALACE ROOMS

The best place to begin exploring the town is from the **Visegrád INFO office** (closed Monday), where you can pick up information, a city map and hiking maps if you're heading into the Pilis Mountains. Follow the road to the late-Gothic and Renaissance **Royal Palace**, set in attractive grounds. Unless it's a Monday, you can enter and stroll through rooms and temporary exhibitions. Visegrád was a royal residence from the 14th century, but the palace blossomed in the late 15th century during the reign of King Matthias, who was the first to introduce Italian Renaissance architecture north of the Alps. The

WHERE TO STAY IN VISEGRÁD

Hotel Silvanus
On a forested hillside near the Citadel. Great views, outdoor pool and delightful spa. **€€€**

Hotel Honti
Homely chalet-style hotel and B&B in the centre with bike hire and a pool. **€€**

Kék Duna
The only campground in the immediate environs, making it convenient for cyclists with tents. **€**

VISEGRÁD GROUP

A **waxwork** inside the Citadel shows how the Visegrád Group began, and the name still lives on today. The year was 1335. The three kings of Bohemia, Hungary and Poland came together in Visegrád to do deals, form an anti-Habsburg alliance, resolve disputes and eat well, judging by this waxy portrayal. This meeting was the first diplomatic cooperation between the so-called 'Visegrád countries', and in 1991, a Visegrád Group was formed between Hungary, Czechoslovakia and Poland to promote cooperation and mutual interests, which later became the Visegrád 4 when Slovakia became an independent country. Differing responses to the 2022 Russian invasion of Ukraine have brought some friction to the group.

Courtyard, Royal Palace

building fell into ruin from the mid-16th century following the arrival of the Ottomans and was buried until archaeologists dug it up in the 1930s. Reconstructions and replicas fill the rooms today: a cold and clammy royal bedchamber from the 1400s, a warmer kitchen, beautiful tile stoves and the red marble Lion Fountain in the courtyard to the east. Look out for a replica of the petite St George's Chapel, originally built in 1366. The most beautiful aspect of the palace is the atmosphere created by the centrepiece Hercules Fountain in the courtyard and Renaissance loggia. If you don't have time to visit the palace, it graces the back of the 1000Ft banknote.

WHERE TO ET IN VISEGRÁD

Don Vito Pizzeria
Delicious stone-baked pizza and a backdrop of gangster pictures. Vegetarians can opt for margherita and add extras. **€**

Sirály
Hungarian and international dishes, with enough to keep vegetarians well fed. **€€**

Kovács-Kert
Hungarian classics from a large menu served on a leafy terrace in summer by efficient staff. **€€**

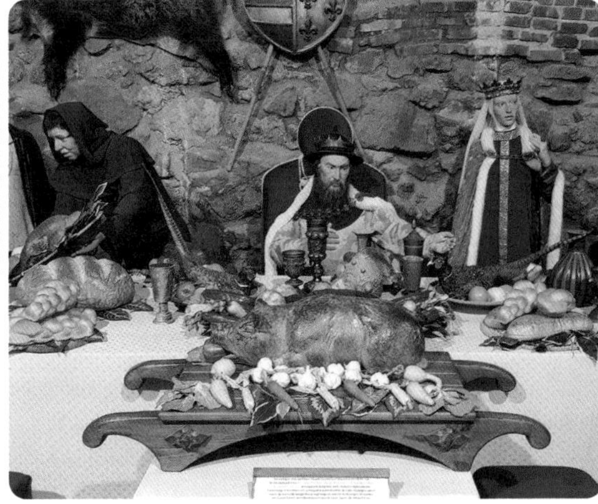

Waxwork of three kings, Citadel

Boat Trips & Kayaking

WETLANDS AND WILLOWED RIVERBANKS

Landlocked Hungarians love to take to the water, whether it's a boat cruise or a long paddle. Travelling upstream by boat from Budapest, the scenery is only moderately interesting until you approach Visegrád, where views open up to the Citadel and vegetation on the riverbanks is more natural. The attractive sections to see by boat are from Visegrád to Esztergom, with interesting inlets, wetlands and shores lined with dense vegetation. If you kayak north of Visegrád, you can see these same verdant banks up close. Edging closer to Esztergom, the basilica rises up in one of the Danube's most spectacular vistas. Drop by **BTZ** in the town of Nagymaros to hire single or double touring kayaks between May and October. The company can also organise kayaks in Esztergom so that you can make a downstream journey of about six hours back to its base.

BEST PLACES FOR A DRINK IN VISEGRÁD

Zugfőzde Pálinkamúzeum
Enjoy *pálinka*, a traditional fruit brandy, in the comfortable tasting section among the distillery's knick-knacks. It's best savoured in winter, and you can buy a bottle to take home.

Rigoletto Cukrászda
Patisserie and cafe with coffee and delicious cakes (some gluten- and lactose-free) to sample in the quiet paved outdoor area.

Schachtel Étterem
Sip a drink with a river view while you wait to take the ferry to the train station in Nagymaros.

GETTING AROUND

If you're visiting between Monday and Thursday, getting around Visegrád can involve a lot of walking, some of it on steep trails. A hop-on hop-off bus runs Friday to Sunday to the Citadel and towers from the information centre. Otherwise, City-Bus runs shuttles for small groups from March to October. Hiring an e-bike from Tekerentyű is also an option. Arriving by boat, walk south from the dock for about 300m and follow the signs to reach the Citadel. Mahart PassNave runs excursion boats from Budapest, as well as a circle line from Visegrád that allows you to change at Zebegény and continue to Esztergom. The hydrofoil from Budapest each morning from Friday to Sunday is the fastest option. Trains run at least hourly from Budapest-Nyugati to Nagymaros, across the river from Visegrád proper. The hourly car ferry schedule is linked to train arrivals, and the river crossing takes 10 minutes.

Esztergom
Budapest

ESZTERGOM

If Szentendre is art and Visegrád is regal history, Esztergom is about its massive basilica, which towers impressively from a hill above the Danube River. It is no coincidence that the city also has a Christian Museum with a breathtaking collection of medieval religious art. The country's first king, St Stephen, was born in Esztergom in 975 and crowned here in 1000. Esztergom was a royal seat from the late 10th to the mid-13th century, as well as the seat of Roman Catholicism in Hungary for more than 1000 years. But Esztergom is much more than royalty and the basilica. It also has a historic mosque, excellent restaurants and places to enjoy fine wine or a beer. Though not as compact as Szentendre or Visegrád, Esztergom has an attractive main square, and the views from the basilica are sensational.

TOP TIP

Esztergom is famous for its basilica, Christian Museum and historic sights, but it is also the most relaxed city in the region. It's generally less crowded than Szentendre (which gets packed with day-trippers from Budapest) and is livelier than Visegrád, with much more of a city flavour.

BEST PLACES TO DRINK IN ESZTERGOM

Café Trafo
Lovely cafe in a glasshouse opposite the Danube Museum.

BorYou Bistro
Wine and good food served by friendly staff at outdoor seating on the main square.

Kaleidoszkóp Ház
Alternative cafe, cultural centre and hostel with occasional live music and open mic sessions.

42 Restaurant
Stylish place to relax and sip a glass of wine. Also has accommodation and a fine restaurant.

Climbing to the Basilica

HUNGARY'S LARGEST CHURCH

If you arrive by boat, the **Esztergom Basilica** can hardly be missed. Perched on top of Castle Hill, it's the country's biggest church, measuring 114m by 47m, and its 72m-high central dome can be seen for many kilometres around. The best approach is through the gate of the Cat's Stairs, a well-hidden set of steps off Berényi Zsigmond utca. It's a brisk climb, with places to rest along the way and views over the Danube River that become even grander as you gradually reach the top.

Building of the basilica began in 1822 on the site of a 12th-century predecessor destroyed by the Ottomans. József Hild, who designed the cathedral at Eger, crowned the basilica with its vast dome. The basilica was consecrated in 1856 with a sung Mass composed by Franz Liszt. Stepping inside, you're greeted with an explosion of frescoes brightly lit by windows around the dome and high on the walls. The red-and-white marble Bakócz Chapel on the southwest side is a splendid example of Italian Renaissance stone carving and sculpture that escaped the worst part of the vandalism by the Ottomans. Gabriel's face has been partially smashed in, and other angels above the altar have lost their heads. The altar painting by Michelangelo Grigoletti (1854) is said to be the world's largest painting on a single canvas.

On the northwest side of the church is the entrance to the treasury, an Aladdin's cave of vestments and church plates in gold and silver, studded with jewels, the richest ecclesiastical collection in Hungary. The door to the right as you enter the basilica leads to the crypt, a series of eerie vaults

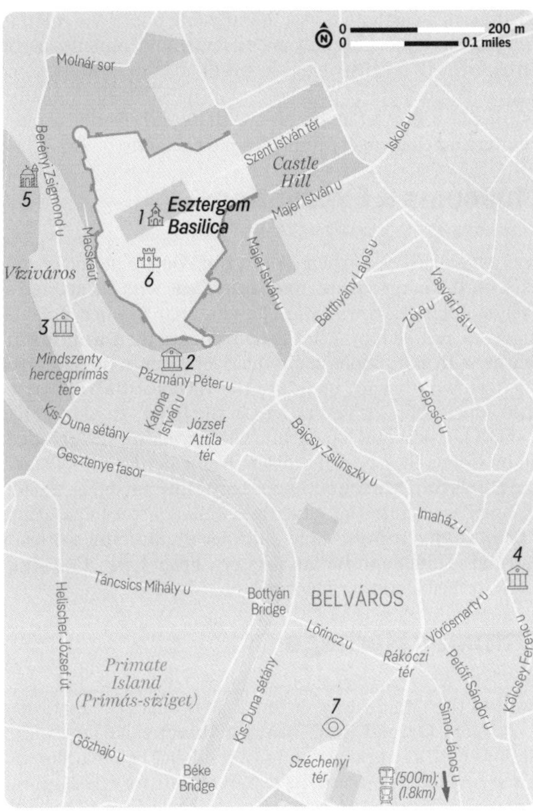

HIGHLIGHTS
1 Esztergom Basilica

SIGHTS
2 Balassa Bálint Museum
3 Christian Museum
4 Danube Museum
5 Öziçeli Hacci Ibrahim Mosque
6 Royal Castle
7 Széchenyi tér

DRINKING & NIGHTLIFE
see 7 BorYou

down 50 steps with tombs guarded by monoliths representing Mourning and Eternity. Once renovations are complete, you will also be able to make the tortuous climb up to the dome for the outstanding views over the city. In the meantime, enjoy the scene over the Danube from outside the basilica or at a panorama cafe.

Alongside the basilica, the **Royal Castle** has a chequered history and saw its first incarnation in the 11th century. Subsequent destruction and rebuilding took place over the years, with the Ottomans taking the castle in 1543 during a two-week siege of the city. It took some 150 years to recapture it.

WHERE TO STAY IN ESZTERGOM

Room42
Stylish suites as well as three large apartments in a prime location in the pedestrian zone. **€€€**

Szent Kristóf Panzió
Close to the basilica and popular with cyclists. Friendly owner offers comfortable rooms with hardwood floors. **€€**

Kaleidoszkóp Ház
Hostel with an indie feel that's part of a cultural centre and alternative bar. **€**

Visiting this castle that was literally dug out of the earth in the 1930s is almost literally an 'underground' pursuit, as you stroll through reconstructed rooms filled with exhibits, some archaeological, others on medieval themes. The Royal Chapel is arguably the most impressive, with its early Gothic vaulted ceiling and elements of Romanesque harmony.

BÁLINT BALASSI: EROTIC POEMS & CANNONBALLS

Although Esztergom was not the birthplace of Bálint Balassi, Hungary's famous 16th-century Renaissance lyrical poet, he did die here, and a museum is named after him. Fluent in eight languages (he wrote some of his poetry in Slovakian), Balassi is considered Hungary's first poet of note and its foremost until the Enlightenment in the 18th century. He converted to Catholicism, and as well as lyrical and sometimes erotic love poems, he turned his hand to religious and military poetry. However, it was the military that would be his downfall. As well as wriggling a good quill, he was a trained soldier, and while fighting Ottomans, he was wounded by a cannonball and died in 1594.

Museums & Excavations

DIGGING THE PAST IN THE PRESENT

Kick off half a day of exploration at **BorYou**, a cafe and restaurant on the main square, **Széchenyi tér**, with its attractive Plague Pillar, the town's way of giving thanks when a plague epidemic passed it by. After that, drop into the **Danube Museum**, with exhibitions about the river. Over in the Víziváros (Watertown) district, step into the **Balassa Bálint Museum**, which contains excavations of the town's castle and has a small but peaceful lapidarium where you can sit surrounded by stone relics. Nearby, inside the former Bishop's Palace, the **Christian Museum** (Keresztény Múzeum) houses a not-to-be-missed collection of early religious art, such as Hungarian Gothic triptychs and altarpieces, plus later works by German, Dutch and Italian masters. From here, it's a short walk to the basilica or mosque.

Ottoman Heritage

400-YEAR-OLD MOSQUE

Built in the 17th century during the Ottoman occupation of Esztergom, **Öziçeli Haci Ibrahim Mosque** had later incarnations both as a granary and as a residence before becoming a museum that showcases its remarkable history. The mihrab (prayer niche facing Mecca) is largely intact, and it's the only two-storey mosque in Hungary. In the back is a waterwheel; a well was here during the Ottoman siege. Having run out of food and water in the castle, the Hungarians surrendered. Cap off your visit in the pleasant cafe downstairs or in the nearby Rózsakert restaurant with great views over the Danube.

WHERE TO EAT IN ESZTERGOM

Rózsakert Étterem
Hungarian and international food next to the mosque. Large windows and a terrace offer dramatic Danube views. **€€**

Prímás Pince
Creative takes on Hungarian cuisine and a good wine list in the cellars beneath the basilica. **€€**

42 Restaurant
Quality Hungarian and pan-European cuisine, with five- and seven-course menus and excellent wine pairings. **€€€**

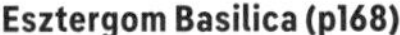

Esztergom Basilica (p168)

WHERE TO CATCH YOUR BREATH IN ESZTERGOM

Balassa Bálint Museum Lapidarium
Sit in the lapidarium surrounded by excavations, gargoyles and other fragments of Esztergom's history.

Cat's Stairs
As you approach the basilica, a strategically placed bench makes a perfect spot to rest and enjoy the spectacular view over the Danube.

Little Danube
Stroll along Kis Duna sétány beneath the large plane trees from the Királyi neighbourhood to the Watertown district to find local life away from big attractions, with a small cafe and outdoor seating along the way.

GETTING AROUND

Getting to the centre from the train and bus station involves a 2km walk, but bus 1 takes you to the pedestrian area. On foot, the nicest route into town is to turn left at Árok utca and then walk along the Little Danube. Frequent buses and trains run to Budapest, and Mahart PassNave operates fast hydrofoils from Friday to Sunday in the morning from Vigadó tér in Budapest. It's best to book ahead. You can also reach Esztergom on the Mahart PassNave circle line from Visegrád by changing at Zebegény. If you're travelling into Western Transdanubia without returning to Budapest, you need to change trains at Komárom.

SOPRON

On Hungary's western edge and just a stone's throw from Vienna in Austria and Bratislava in Slovakia, Sopron is Hungarian (and not Austrian) because it opted to stay that way in a referendum in 1921. Its Jewish citizens played an important role in the 'remain' vote, but their long connection with the city was turbulent and ultimately, during WWII, tragic. Sopron is the most beautiful city in western Hungary, with an attractive medieval Inner Town (Belváros) and cobbled streets that make it a pleasure to wander through while soaking up the city's atmosphere. All of the city's attractions are within walking distance, the most strenuous of which is the climb up its iconic Firewatch Tower, which affords sensational (and blustery on a windy day) views over the surrounding landscape. It is a pleasant and provincial town, modest in terms of restaurants and cafes, but with lots of culture.

TOP TIP

Walk around the historic heart of medieval Sopron on a quiet, warm night to enjoy the peacefulness and shades of light. The Firewatch Tower is lit up in attractive crimson, but don't miss the floodlit fountain at Petőfi téri and minuscule Orsolya tér while exploring the cobblestone streets winding through town.

BEST PLACES TO DRINK IN SOPRON

Kultúrpresszó
Fantastic cultural cafe that serves bagels, sandwiches and drinks for a morning coffee among books.

Cezár Pince
Buried in a 17th-century cellar with a convivial atmosphere, this bar pours good wine to accompany cold platters.

TasteVino Borbár & Vinotéka
A vaulted bar and wine shop to sample the best of Sopron's wineries and purchase tipples of choice.

Exploring Fő tér

HISTORY ON AN ATTRACTIVE SQUARE

Fő tér, Sopron's oddly shaped square, offers lots of surprises. Climb the massive 60m-high **Fire Tower** (Tűztorony) for a great panorama of town. From here, trumpeters warned of fire, marked the hour and watched for merchants trying to smuggle in non-Sopron wine. View the **Lapidary** inside, with its fragments of carved cornices, statues and excavated 13th-century foundations (the entrance to the tower goes through the Lapidary). There are stunning views through oversized windows in the cafe on the 1st floor (where you can drink *pálinka* while surrounded by antiquities).

Fidelity Gate, at the bottom of the tower, depicts 'Hungaria' receiving the kneeling *civitas fidelissima* (Latin for 'the most loyal citizenry') of Sopron, together with the city's coat of arms. It was erected in 1922 after Sopron's citizens rejected the offer of Austrian citizenship in a referendum. Stroll to **Storno House** (Storno Ház) at No. 8, which dates from 1417 and was taken over by the Swiss–Italian family of Ferenc Storno, chimney sweep turned art restorer, whose recarving of Romanesque and Gothic monuments throughout Transdanubia divides opinions to this day. If it's not a Monday, enter and view the interior of lead-light windows, frescoes and the collection of family treasures.

The baroque **Fabricius House** at No. 6 is a place to delve into archaeology, the Roman period and interior furnishings.

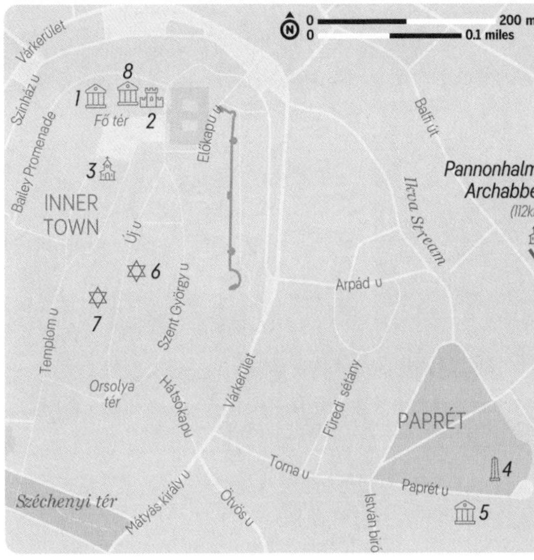

SIGHTS
1 Fabricius House
2 Fire Tower
3 Goat Church
4 Monument
5 Neológ Synagogue
6 New Synagogue
7 Old Synagogue
8 Storno House

Just off the square, duck into the **Goat Church** (Kecsketemplom) for a dose of 13th-century Gothic.

Jewish Sopron

SYNAGOGUES AND MEMORIAL

Jewish settlement in Hungary goes back to Roman times, predating the arrival of Magyar tribes in the 9th century. Many Jews arriving in the 11th century from German principalities and the present-day Czech Republic settled in Danube and Western Transdanubian cities. In Sopron, they were restricted to living in Új utca, where today the **Old Synagogue** stands, built in the 14th century in Gothic style (said to be unique in Eastern Europe). Many of Sopron's Jews left for Austria during an expulsion in 1360, returning five years later, only to be expelled again by the Ottomans in 1526. Some gradually returned, but it was only in the mid-19th century that Jews could legally live here again. When Nazi Germany occupied Sopron in 1944, Jews were confined to a ghetto and shortly afterwards deported to Auschwitz

WHERE TO EAT IN SOPRON

Erhardt
Delicious seasonal dishes in a town with few good options; cherry-pick from the set menus. **€€**

Sopronbánfalvi Pálos-Karmelita Kolostor
Quality dining in the vaulted dining room of a monastery that also offers rooms. **€€€**

Bacha Sushi Shop
Fresh sushi, though generally with mayonnaise in the rolls. Convenient hours and an alternative to Hungarian staples. **€**

HOW HUNGARY SNIPPED THE IRON CURTAIN

The Iron Curtain was a metaphor for the political divide between the Eastern Bloc countries and the West, but it was also an actual barbed wire fence that once separated Europe. The first holes in the Iron Curtain appeared in Western Transdanubia in 1989, when Hungary allowed travel to Austria. East Germans seized the opportunity to flee to West Germany via Hungary, and the sheer number of East Germans leaving was the beginning of the end of the Soviet Union's dominance in Eastern Europe, culminating ultimately in the demise of the Soviet Union itself.

Holocaust memorial

concentration camp. Their history in Sopron is fraught with tragedy and bizarre accusations, such as the 'host desecration libel' that alleges that Jews stole communion wafers and tortured Christ by sticking pins into them. This history becomes tangible through architecture and exhibits such as those in the 14th-century **New Synagogue** on the 'forgotten Sopronians' (the 40 Jewish families deported to Auschwitz), a plaque at the **Neológ Synagogue** in disrepair at Paprét 14 to the '1640 martyrs' from these families, and through the **monument** in the car park across the road.

GETTING AROUND

Sopron is easy to see on foot. Your longest (and least inspiring) walk is from the bus station (1km northwest of the centre) or the train station (1km south). Jump on bus 1, 2, 10 or 20 from the train station going along Várkerület and disembark near the tower. Otherwise, walk 10 minutes from the train station along Mátyás király utca.

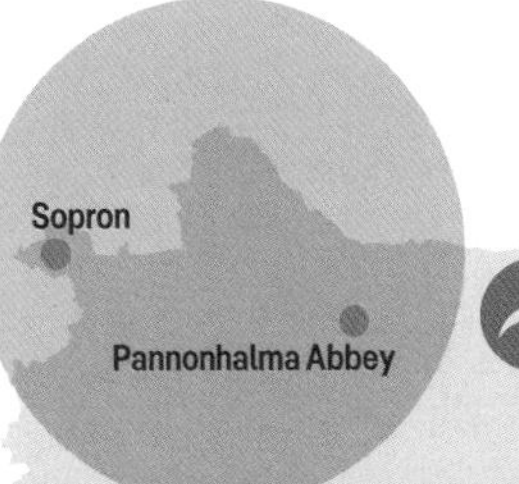

Beyond Sopron

East of Sopron is the remarkable Pannonhalma Abbey, and to the south, you venture into meadows and forests.

Nestled along the borders with Austria, Slovakia and Slovenia, this region is one of green plains, low hills, historic landmarks and cycle routes that make it perfect for slow travel. If coming from Budapest or the Danube Bend, the train takes you via Győr, a town of only moderate interest in itself but the starting point for a trip to the hilltop Pannonhalma Abbey, some 100km east of Sopron. Travelling south of Sopron takes you into Őrség National Park, with lush forests, meadows and farmland sprinkled with villages and small towns such as Őriszentpéter. Explore it by bike – along cycle routes and a few steep hills – or on a drive if you have less time.

TOP TIP

Travelling around Western Transdanubia is best by car, but it's possible with patience, bus connections and the useful transport website menetrendek.hu.

Pannonhalma Abbey (p176)

OUTINGS NEAR SOPRON

Judit Käesz (facebook.com/kulturpresszosopron) is the owner of Kultúrpresszó, a specialty coffee shop in Sopron. She shares her favourite cultural experiences just outside town.

Cave Theatre, Fertőrákos
It's originally a quarry, and the stone blocks were towed to Vienna to decorate the facades of churches, museums and the university. It provides a unique concert venue with a special atmosphere, a natural backdrop for events.

Esterházy Palace, Fertőd
This palace is called the Hungarian Versailles and is the most beautiful baroque palace in Hungary. The great composer Joseph Haydn lived and worked here, and during summer months, concerts are held here, as in Haydn's time.

TAINAR/SHUTTERSTOCK ©

Library, Pannonhalma Abbey

Monastery with a View

STUNNING HILLTOP ABBEY

Founded in 996, hilltop **Pannonhalma Abbey** (Pannonhalmi Főapátság) was the starting point for the conversion of pagan Hungarians to Christianity. It also served as a mosque during the Ottoman occupation and as a refuge for Jews in 1944 under International Red Cross protection. Spend an entire day walking through the abbey complex and discover an eclectic mix of styles cobbled together over the centuries. In the early 1990s, the brethren of Pannonhalma Abbey resurrected the monastery's age-old tradition of winemaking, and you can taste their outstanding vinicultural dedication on a terrace with views. Book tours of the cellars in advance.

WHERE TO EAT BEYOND SOPRON

Bognar Etterem (Őriszentpéter)
Hungarian classics, venison and seasonal specialities like Őrség mushroom soup. €€

Pajta (Őriszentpéter)
Reserve ahead for lunch or the 12-course dinner at one of the best restaurants in the region. €€€

Viator (Pannonhalma)
Excellent views, barbecue Mangalica pork, duck, and other meat and fish dishes near Pannonhalma Abbey. €€€

Strolling through the ensemble, you encounter in the courtyard the first abbot, Asztrik, who brought the all-important Hungarian crown worn by King Stephen to Hungary from Rome. At the entrance to the 12th-century St Martin's Basilica (Szent Márton-bazilika), you pass through the red-limestone Porta Speciosa. On the right, you can see what is probably the oldest graffiti in Hungary: 'Benedict Padary was here in 1578', it reads in Latin. Inside is the austerity of the 13th-century early Gothic period. The red marble niche in the crypt is believed to cover the wooden throne of St Stephen and a marble slab inscribed with 'Ottó 1912–2011' marks the burial spot of the heart of Otto von Habsburg, the last crown prince of Austria-Hungary (the rest of him is buried in Vienna). In the cloister arcade, faces on the wall represent human emotions and vices. Stroll into the sensational neoclassical library, built in 1836 by János Packh, who helped design Esztergom Basilica. The abbey is closed to visitors on Monday, and from around November to March, it's only open Friday to Sunday (you can attend the service on Sunday).

Trails around Pannonhalma Abbey

PATHWAYS IN ATTRACTIVE FOREST

Although Pannonhalma Abbey, some 20km from Győr and 106km from Sopron, is the main drawcard, its grounds and immediate environs are just as enjoyable on a warm day. A Tourinform office at the entrance to the grounds has useful sketch maps to help you find your way. From the info office, a path alongside the road leads towards the abbey, with the lush 10th-century **arboretum** on the left, filled with chirping birdlife and some 1300 different plant species across its 4 hectares. Continuing along the path, you reach the abbey itself, but beyond this is the **Abbey Winery**, which offers tours by appointment. In summer months, it's just as nice to sit in the yard and try some of the wines. Paths continue into the forest, taking you past **Our Lady Chapel** and deeper among the trees to a wooden viewing tower and the nearby **'treetop' curved walkway**, from where you have fantastic views across low, sweeping hills.

CYCLING WESTERN TRANSDANUBIA

Western Transdanubia has lots of great cycling routes. Pick up some wheels from **Bike Like** in the town of Győr and cycle or e-bike on a day trip to Pannonhalma Abbey or along EuroVelo 6 route to the Mosoni-Duna region, where an arm of the Danube disperses into sidearms and wetland near the Slovakian border. Campgrounds abound, and the villages of **Kisbodak** (33km from Győr) and **Dunasziget** (42km) have places where you can hire kayaks and take to the water. To hire a bike for Őrség National Park (which requires at least two days), **Vaskarika Kerékpár Kölcsönző** at Városszer 116 in Őriszentpéter has a good range.

GETTING AROUND

Travelling west from Budapest, trains stop at Győr, where you can change trains or take a bus for Pannonhalma. The bus drops you directly at the abbey, but the train is best if you have a bike. Pannonhalma doesn't have left luggage facilities, but the attendant might store it in the office. The easiest way to reach Őrség National Park by public transport is the train to Csákánydoroszló and connecting bus to Őriszentpéter via Őrségi Patakparti Alpaka Farm and Guesthouse. You can take your bike on most trains (check mavcsoport.hu), and from Csákánydoroszló, it's an easy one-hour cycle to Őriszentpéter. You can stop off at the national park office in Csákánydoroszló on the way.

ROAD TRIP

Cycling or Driving Őrség National Park

Őrség is dotted with sleepy towns in a landscape of lush meadows, farmland, forest, hills and marshland. Numbered bike routes, helpfully marked on maps at the information offices, wind through the national park. You'll find plenty of guesthouses, and the same 75km (two- to three-day) cycle route can also be done by car in one day.

1 Őriszentpéter

Begin in Őriszentpéter, some 17km south of Csákánydoroszló, which is about an hour by bike if you've taken the train. Őriszentpéter has a national park office for maps and information, bike hire, and the best restaurants in this area.

The Ride: Follow the road northwest and turn towards Szalafő, cycling out just beyond the town limits.

2 Outside Szalafő

Flanked by a graveyard and picturesque fields behind, a remarkably well-preserved Romanesque church features a wonderful carved portal and an 18th-century altarpiece painted by a student of Franz Anton Maulbertsch.

The Ride: Continue 5km west to Szalafő-Pityerszer, dog-legging left after Szalafő and following the narrow road between fields and past forest.

3 Szalafő-Pityerszer

The Open-Air Ethnographic Museum has three traditional thatched-roof cottages in grounds that invite a rest.

The Ride: Backtrack to Őriszentpéter and then south for 8km on cycle path 2 to Bajánsenye and

Reform church, Szentgyörgyvölgy

BOTOND HORVATH/SHUTTERSTOCK ©

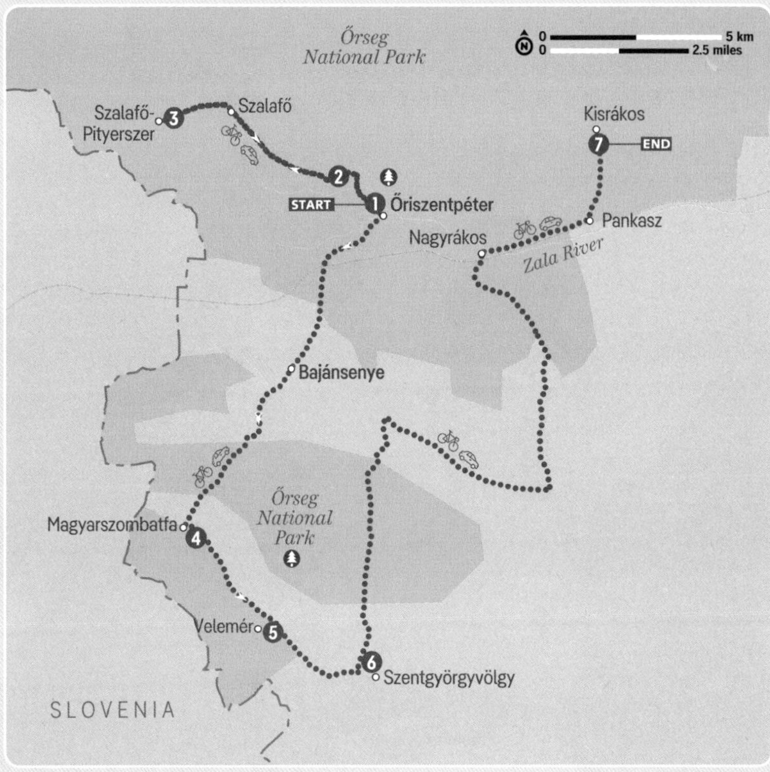

beyond that for another 10km, climbing into forest and descending to fields and your next stop.

4 Magyarszombatfa

For centuries, this area has been known for its pottery, and the craft is still very much alive today. If you don't catch the local potters in action, drop into the thatch-roofed **Fazekasház** (potter's house), dating from 1760, which features splendid unglazed containers and cooking vessels.

The Ride: Head 7km southeast to Velemér and turn right, cycling along the narrow paved road for about 750m up to the architectural and spiritual highlight of the trip.

5 Velemér

Nestled among trees, Velemér's magnificent 13th-century church has frescoes by Austrian painter Johannes Aquila that are designed to be illuminated by the sun at certain times of year. Rest up or take a walk in the delightful mixed-species forest.

The Ride: Return to the road and continue along cycle path 2 for 4km to the small town of Szentgyörgyvölgy, turning left at Kossuth Lajos utca to reach the church.

6 Szentgyörgyvölgy

Look for the splendid Reform church from 1517, with its stupendous wooden interior and panelled ceiling.

The Ride: Backtrack and follow cycle path 2 across fields and through forest, zig-zagging via Kerkáskápolna, Kerkafalva, Nagyrákos and Pankasz to Kisrákos (30km).

7 Őrségi Patakparti Alpaka Farm & Guesthouse

Friendly owner Katalin Könye serves refreshments and cake, and offers rooms upstairs and in three wooden treehouses in a fantastic forest setting. From here, either return to Csákánydoroszló (15km; buses pass here too) or Őriszentpéter (9km).

Above: Benedictine Abbey Church (p190), Tihany. Right: Festetics Palace (p195), Keszthely

LAKE BALATON & SOUTHERN TRANSDANUBIA

THE HAMPTONS OF HUNGARY

Historical wonders, impressive food and wine, and an unparalleled spa scene: Lake Balaton and Southern Transdanubia are where Hungarians relish the good life.

Lake Balaton is where the Magyars (Hungarians) flock to spend their summer holidays. During the dog days, resorts and guesthouses get packed with holidaymakers beaching and boating in opaque, turquoise-hued waters. Beyond the postcard-perfect marinas, Central Europe's biggest (and shallowest!) lake has a depth that may be surprising – Balaton is equal parts quaint and cool. Thermal spas, wellness centres and well-appointed campsites reel visitors in, but it's Balaton's hearty 'everything stew' of varied experiences that proves most memorable, from sipping whites at handsome wineries to exploring hiking trails and historical treasures.

In Southern Transdanubia, whitewashed farmhouses with thatched roofs dominate a countryside that hasn't changed in centuries. Anchoring its centre is Budapest's rival, Pécs, which offers culture and history without the crowds. Its Mediterranean feel permeates streets filled with relics of Hungary's Ottoman and Roman pasts, plus exceptional museums. Pécs is a university city, and students congregate around squares and monuments. But its lively downtown pub and gastronomy scene – with upscale, forward-thinking restaurants and wine bars – caters to hip young professionals. Beyond the city, a clutch of medieval castles and vineyard cellars beckons you to wine-taste your heart out.

THE MAIN AREAS

Find Your Way

Lake Balaton is Hungary's largest body of water. The 235km shoreline is dotted with tiny villages a few minutes' drive from one another. Southern Transdanubia is Hungary's least population-dense area, and the villages are spread out.

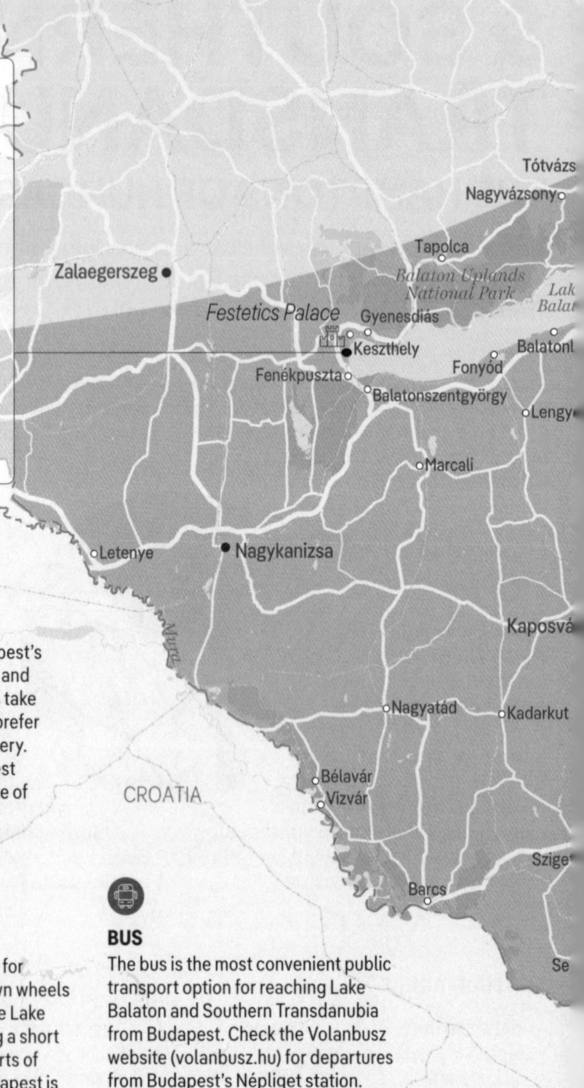

Keszthely, p194

Watch your worries float away against gorgeous sands and grassy knolls. The lavish baroque Festetics Palace is a must-see, and lovely small museums abound.

Tótvázs
Nagyvázsony
Tapolca
Zalaegerszeg
Balaton Uplands National Park
Lak Bala
Festetics Palace
Gyenesdiás
Keszthely
Balatonl
Fonyód
Fenékpuszta
Balatonszentgyörgy
Lengy
Marcali
Letenye
Nagykanizsa
Kaposvá
Mura
Nagyatád
Kadarkut
Bélavár
Vízvár
CROATIA
Szige
Barcs
Se

TRAIN

Frequent trains connect Budapest's Keleti station to Balaton, Pécs and their surrounding areas. Trains take longer than buses, but locals prefer them for extra space and scenery. Express services from Budapest shorten the journey by a couple of hours.

CAR

Hiring a car is the best option for exploring this region. Your own wheels allow you to easily experience Lake Balaton's shoreline (including a short ferry ride) and the hilly outskirts of Pécs. Road tripping from Budapest is straightforward.

BUS

The bus is the most convenient public transport option for reaching Lake Balaton and Southern Transdanubia from Budapest. Check the Volanbusz website (volanbusz.hu) for departures from Budapest's Népliget station. Frequent local bus routes in Pécs and along Lake Balaton's northern and southern shores are handy.

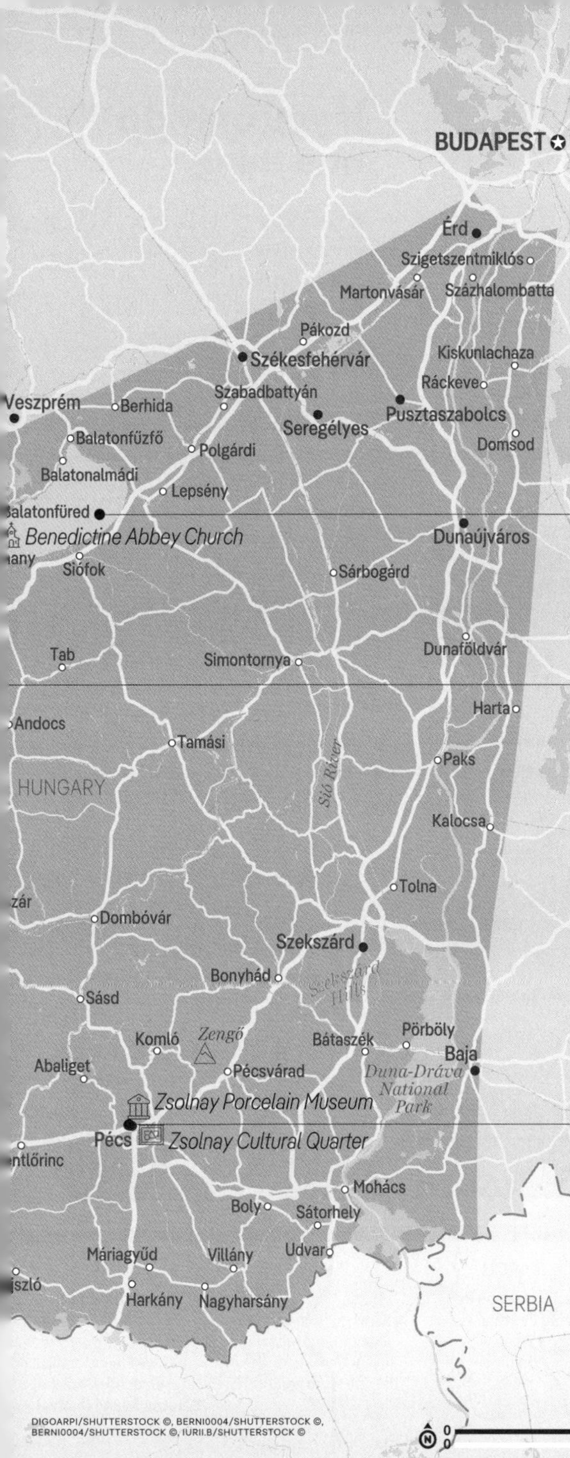

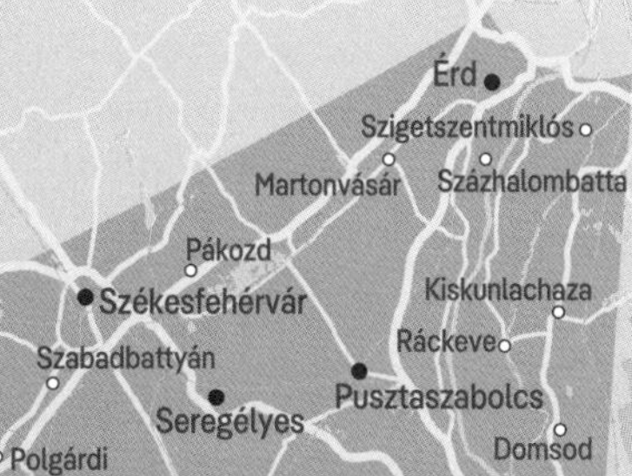

Balatonfüred, p186

Lake Balaton's central hub with posh spa hotels and gourmet dining. On its pretty promenade, happy locals hang out with shoreside wildlife and historic statues.

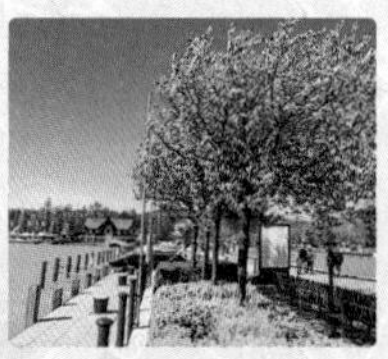

Tihany, p190

Balaton's historical hot spot. Don't miss this picture-perfect Hungarian village with its stunning 18th-century abbey, thatched-roof buildings, beaches and famous lavender fields.

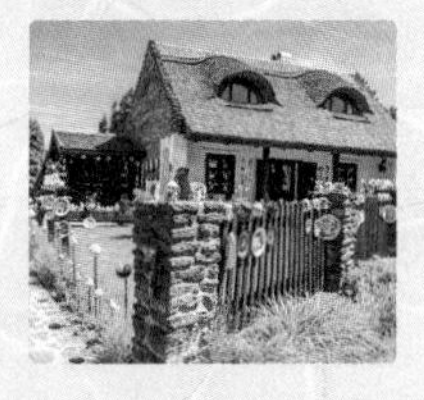

Pécs, p198

Discover a perfect medley of shops, restaurants and excellent museums in this charismatic medieval city defined by an industry of trade and artisanship.

DIGOARPI/SHUTTERSTOCK ©, BERNI0004/SHUTTERSTOCK ©, BERNI0004/SHUTTERSTOCK ©, IURII.B/SHUTTERSTOCK ©

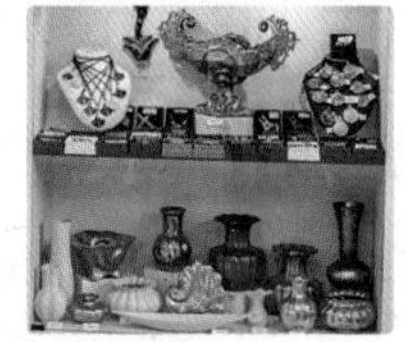

Plan Your Days

Posting up at a wellness centre is mighty tempting, but Balaton's shores have much to explore. Meanwhile, Pécs' compact downtown leaves you eager to venture into the countryside.

UNGVARI ATTILA/SHUTTERSTOCK ©

Zsolnay Cultural Quarter (p198), Pécs

If you only do one thing

● Fed by 80 million litres of thermal water daily, the hot springs in **Hévíz** (p197) are an astonishing sight. Float or indulge in a spa remedy at Europe's largest thermal lake. Swim in protected waters or out into the lake, with some shoreside piers for sunbathing. Afterwards, stroll around the **Zsolnay Cultural Quarter** (p198) in **Pécs** (p198), which has a smorgasbord of beautiful buildings, porcelain exhibitions and a couple of good restaurants. Highlights include the street of artisans' shops, watching porcelain being made by hand at the Zsolnay Factory and the on-site porcelain museum.

SEASONAL HIGHLIGHTS

This region is at its buzziest in summer. Lake Balaton has an expansive programme of concerts and events, and parks and public areas in Pécs come alive.

MARCH

The month-long **Pécs Spring Festival** kicks off the season with live music, exhibitions and more.

MAY

At Pécs' universities, exams go from mid-May to mid-June, followed by students taking to the streets to celebrate.

JUNE

Tihany's **lavender season** peaks in mid-June to early July, overlapping with star-studded DJs at the **Balaton Sound festival.**

ZORAN MILOSAVLJEVIC/SHUTTERSTOCK ©, POSZTOS/SHUTTERSTOCK ©, FESUS ROBERT/SHUTTERSTOCK ©

Three days to travel around

- Treat yourself to a spa day in **Balatonfüred** (p186) or **Hévíz** (p197) and spend another day sightseeing in **Tihany** (p190). Take in Balaton's most important historical attraction, the **Benedictine Abbey Church** (p190), and the quaint shops and cafes along the medieval cobblestone Batthyány utca. On the way out, get a fragrant whiff of lavender fields.

- Pack in a full cultural day in **Pécs** (p198) at the **Zsolnay Cultural Quarter** (p198) and the **Victor Vasarely Museum** (p199). Head downtown for a meal and a stroll on the cobblestone streets around **Széchenyi tér** (p201) before catching a sublime sunset from the **TV Tower** (p200).

If you have more time

- The 200km **Balaton Cycling Route** (p188) runs through Balatonfüred, and riding a bike along the water is a fine way to spend time (but note that heading away from the lake, it's all uphill). The path passes through key destinations such as **Balatonfüred** (p186), **Keszthely** (p194) and **Hévíz** (p197).

- After exploring **Pécs** (p198), venture out to **Mohács** (p203). This sleepy little Danube port wakes up in late February or March for the frenzied annual **Busójárás festival** (p202), a South Slavic tradition where scary masks send off the winter. After that, take your time exploring Mohács' historical battle sights and taking tasting notes at wineries.

JULY

Balatonfüred's **Anna Ball** has been held since 1825. Beyond the outdated beauty pageant, there are violin concerts and opera.

AUGUST

Catch Keszthely's two-day **Wine Festival** and thousands jumping in Lake Balaton for the annual cross-swimming race.

SEPTEMBER

Lake Balaton's high season goes out with a bang with concerts and events focused on yachting and wine.

OCTOBER

Many wineries and restaurants in Balaton are closed for the season, but resorts offer reduced autumn rates.

Budapest
Balatonfüred

BALATONFÜRED

Balatonfüred is not only the oldest resort on Lake Balaton's northern shore, but it's also the most fashionable. In former days, the wealthy and famous built large villas on its streets, and that architectural legacy can still be seen today. Yes, it's touristy, but the predominantly Hungarian tourists (and little to no signage in English) give it an insider feel. Balatonfüred is a fine, central place to base yourself on the lake, with beautiful marinas and some of the region's best lodging options.

Balatonfüred is famed for the thermal waters of its world-famous heart hospital. In the late 18th century, the town was declared a spa with its own chief physician in residence. The 19th century was its golden age, especially the first half when political and cultural leaders of the Reform Era (roughly 1825–48) holidayed here. Today, it's a popular weekend destination for middle-class Hungarians seeking family time and romantic escapes.

TOP TIP

At the centre of Gyógy tér next to the State Hospital of Cardiology, the Kossuth Pump House is a natural spring dispensing sulphuric (but drinkable) thermal water. It tastes bad and is slightly yellow but rich in carbonic acid. The water has allegedly cured stomach ailments over centuries. Bring your own bottle!

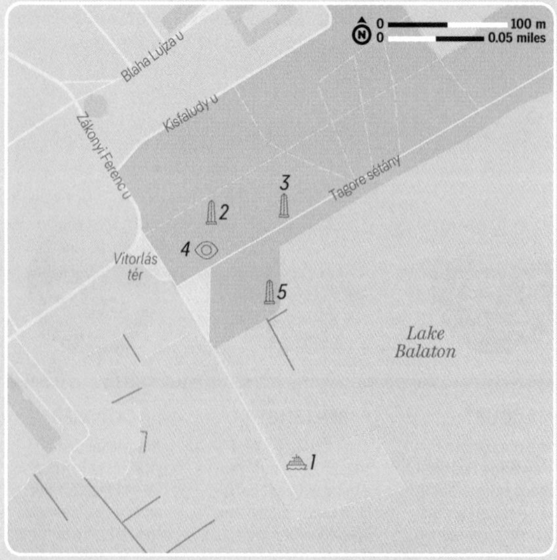

SIGHTS

1 Balaton Shipping Company
2 Bust of Rabindranath Tagore
3 Memorial to the victims of the 1954 Pajtás shipwreck
4 Tagore Sétány
5 The Fisherman and The Ferryman

Tagore Sétány

On the Boardwalk

BALATONFÜRED'S BEATING HEART

Balatonfüred is home to one of Balaton's most stylish marinas. Stroll along **Tagore Sétány**, its lake-hugging promenade, and breathe in the fresh lake air. The promenade, surrounded by restaurants and souvenir shops, is buzzing in summer – a little too much so, some say. In contrast, during off season, it's a laid-back haven where (mostly elderly) locals play cards in the rose garden, yacht spot and feed the ducks. Grab a coffee from one of the cafes near the car park and promenade entrance and ramble around to get acquainted with a range of statues depicting lake history. Start with the **bust of Rabindranath Tagore**, a Bengali poet who was the first non-European to win a Nobel Prize in Literature, near the rose garden. He planted the lime tree beside the statue in 1926 to mark being cured here. Diagonally opposite is a disturbing **memorial to the victims of the 1954 Pajtás shipwreck**: a hand outstretched from the water. **The Fisherman** and **The Ferryman** statues oversee the harbour entrance. It's said that if you rub their boots, you'll return to Balaton. Opposite, Hungarian filmmaker and strongman István Bujtor is immortalised indulging in his favourite pastime, yachting. Further down the promenade, the **Balaton Shipping Company** has been setting sail from Balatonfüred's pier since the 1840s. Take in pink skies during a romantic sunset cruise on a vintage boat from late April to early October.

BEST STAYS WITH SPAS

Lua
Balaton's newest adults-only resort offers over-the-top gourmet breakfasts and free yoga classes. €€€

Aura
Adults-only resort with a boutique feel. Unwind in cosy beds and plush whirlpools. €€€

Club Hotel Füred
Balatonfüred's most expansive resort with 2.5 hectares of parkland, gardens and a private beach. €€€

Hotel Golden Lake Resort
Family-friendly suites with lake views and balconies. Wellness centre includes sauna and gym. €€€

Füred Camping
Bungalows and caravans, plus a pool and direct lake access, offer relaxation on a budget. €

GETTING AROUND

Balatonfüred is small enough to get around on foot, and local buses ensure it's well connected. A car gives the most flexibility, though.

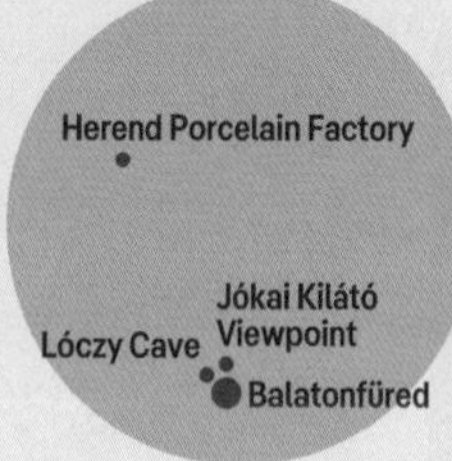

Beyond Balatonfüred

Balatonfüred's countryside is perfect for getting away from the touristy areas and discovering natural wonders.

Balatonfüred's cushy spa hotels make it easy to lose track of time in a bathrobe, but exploring outside the town is a fun and gratifying experience. Balatonfüred is an excellent base for exploring northern shore lake villages, winelands, verdant hiking trails, surprisingly good roadside restaurants and beaches galore. The 200km **Balaton Cycling Route**, running through Balatonfüred, is an unforgettable way to see the region's scenic spoils. Some hotels hire bicycles, and trekking and electric rentals are available at local bike shops. Popular cruises by the Balaton Shipping Company connect Balatonfüred to other port villages several times daily between late May and mid-September.

TOP TIP

The lush, hilly Badacsony wine region has been described as Hungary's most beautiful place, inspiring many Hungarian authors and artists.

Balaton Cycling Route

SHAUN BUSUTTIL/LONELY PLANET ©

Herend Porcelain Factory

Porcelain Dreams

PRIZED POSSESSIONS

In Herend, 33km north of Balatonfüred, the **Herend Porcelain Factory** has been producing Hungary's finest hand-painted china for more than 180 years. Discover how clay becomes delicate porcelain on a guided tour and through museum displays of prized Herend pieces, including kooky 19th-century interpretations of Japanese art, as well as the company's own patterns. Initially, the factory specialised in copying and replacing broken china imported from Asia for the nobility. To avoid bankruptcy in the 1870s, the factory began mass production. Tastes ran from kitschy pastoral scenes to the ever-popular animal sculptures with distinctive scale-like triangle patterns. In 1992, 75% of the factory was purchased by its 1500 workers, and it became one of the first companies in Hungary privatised through an employee stock-ownership plan. The state owns the other quarter.

Subterranean Look-See

EXPLORE A COMPACT CAVE

In the Balaton Uplands, enjoy a quick and easy spelunking experience at **Lóczy Cave**. Around 40m is accessible to the public, lit up with electric lamps to reveal mesmerisingly swirled layers of limestone. It's a cool 12°C all year, so bring a warm top. Combine your underground explorations with a hike up to the **Jókai kilátó viewpoint** and take in Balatonfüred on a clear day.

WINE TIME

Vines have been growing on the lake's hilltops since the 1st century BCE, cultivated by the ancient Romans and medieval monastic orders. Balaton's 100 sq km vineyard region spans six diverse wine areas, including volcanic stone and limestone. The main grape variety is Olaszrizling (which translates as 'Italian Riesling' but has nothing to do with German Riesling). Many of Balaton's wineries are small and family-run. If you want to visit a winery, especially during the off season (April to October), call or email ahead. On the outskirts of Balatonfüred, you can visit family-run winery restaurants for tastings or a meal. **Szent Donát Borküria**, **Figula Pincészet** and **Söptei Winery** all offer great food and sprawling vineyard views.

GETTING AROUND

Buses and ferries leaving from Balatonfüred are the most convenient modes of public transport for visiting other villages around the lake. Most smaller Balaton villages are not served by train.

TIHANY

The place with the greatest historical significance on Lake Balaton is the Tihany Peninsula, which juts 5km into the lake. Tihany village, perched on an 80m-high plateau along the peninsula's eastern coast, is home to Balaton's famous Benedictine Abbey Church. The church is worth visiting, but you can escape high-season crowds by wandering around the lovely thatched-roof houses in the village or board the mini-train chugging its way around town. The hilly peninsula is a nature reserve of marshy meadows with an isolated, almost wild feel. It's a popular recreational area with beaches on its eastern and western coasts and a big resort complex at its southern tip. Two inland basins are fed by rain and groundwater: the Inner Lake (Belső-tó), the crater of an ancient volcano, is visible from the village and the mostly dried-up Outer Lake (Külső-tó) to the northwest. Both attract considerable birdlife, including purple herons and ferruginous ducks.

TOP TIP

The Tihany Lavender Festival coincides with the blossom season from mid-June to early July. Wander the aromatic purple fields and indulge in lavender picking. At Lavender House, learn about local lavender production with activities that include a maze. The fabulous-smelling Lavender Shop on Batthyány utca sells flower-spiked foods and cosmetics.

Sacred Architecture

BALATON'S MOST BEAUTIFUL CHURCH

Built in 1754 on the site of King Andrew I's church, the twin-spired, ochre-coloured **Benedictine Abbey Church** is Tihany's dominant feature. Don't miss the fantastic 18th-century carved altars, pulpits and screens, true baroque-rococo masterpieces. Andrew I's remains lie in a limestone sarcophagus in the Romanesque crypt. Upon entering the central nave, turn your back to the sumptuous main altar and abbot's throne and look right to the side altar dedicated to Mary. The large angel kneeling on the right is said to represent a fisher's daughter who died young. On the Altar of the Sacred Heart across the aisle, a pelican symbolising Christ nurtures the faithful with its blood. Enter the church crypt to the **Benedictine Abbey Museum** (included in admission), with exhibits on Lake Balaton, contemporary art and religious artefacts.

SEE THE ARTEFACT

The priceless Deed of Foundation of Tihany Abbey is on display at **Pannonhalma Abbey** (p176) in western Hungary. The abbey contains the country's largest private library with some 400,000 volumes.

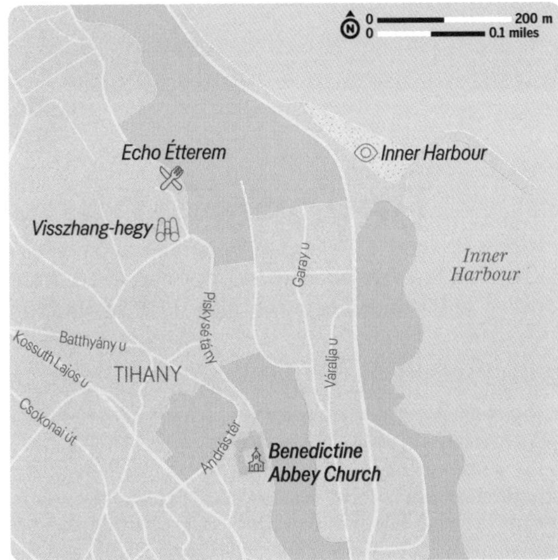

The Tihany Echo

HOWLING AT THE ABBEY

Can you Hungarian yodel? Head up **Visszhang-hegy** (Echo Hill) and try. On a clear, uncrowded day, shout from the **Echo Stone** and hear the echo bounce back from the northern abbey wall 300m away. Years ago, up to 15 syllables would bounce back, but because of new construction (and perhaps climate change), you'll be lucky to get three nowadays. At the top, enjoy the magnificent views at the **Echo Étterem** restaurant and a cold platter of meats, cheeses, pickles and homemade bread inspired by traditional monastery fare. Descend to the **Inner Harbour** and a small beach, or go for a hike on nearby trails.

NATIONAL TREASURE

This area had a Roman settlement, but Tihany first appeared on the map in 1055, when King Andrew I (r 1046–60), a son of King Stephen's great nemesis, Vászoly, founded a Benedictine monastery here. The **Deed of Foundation of Tihany Abbey** is one of the earliest known documents bearing any Hungarian words – some 50 place names within a mostly Latin text. It's a linguistic treasure in a country where, until the 19th century, the vernacular in its written form was spurned – particularly in schools – favouring the more 'cultured' Latin and German. The text has fortuitously survived tumult – for example, a fortress built in 1267 around the church kept Ottoman intruders at bay 300 years later. It is now in the archives of Pannonhalma Abbey.

GETTING AROUND

Buses cover the 14km between Balatonfüred's bus and train stations and Tihany throughout the day. They stop at both ferry landings before climbing to Tihany village.

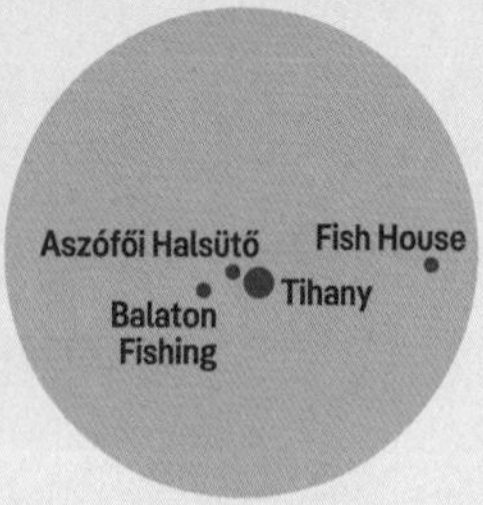

Beyond Tihany

Catch a ferry or boat from Tihany to get a taste of Balaton's busy southern shores and its communist history.

Tihany's port is the gateway between Balaton's northern and southern shores. The ferry from Tihany to Szántód, leaving almost hourly year-round, connects the hilly wine country to the southern piers. Siófok, 13km from Szántód, rivals Balatonfüred as the lake's busiest town, though Siófok tends to lose out because Balatonfüred delivers more culture and history. Siófok has nightlife (although it's quite cheesy) and spa hotels, too. The Blue Ribbon Regatta, Europe's oldest sailing competition, connects Balatonfüred and Siófok across the lake, doubling the population of both towns every summer. Balaton Sound, Europe's largest lakeside electronic-music festival, also takes place near Siófok. Gigantic stages host big-name DJs, and Balaton's waters become packed with floaties and bikini-ravers.

TOP TIP

Club Aliga, 17km from Siófok, was once a Socialist Party resort visited by communist world leaders – it's now a beach club.

Szántód ferry dock

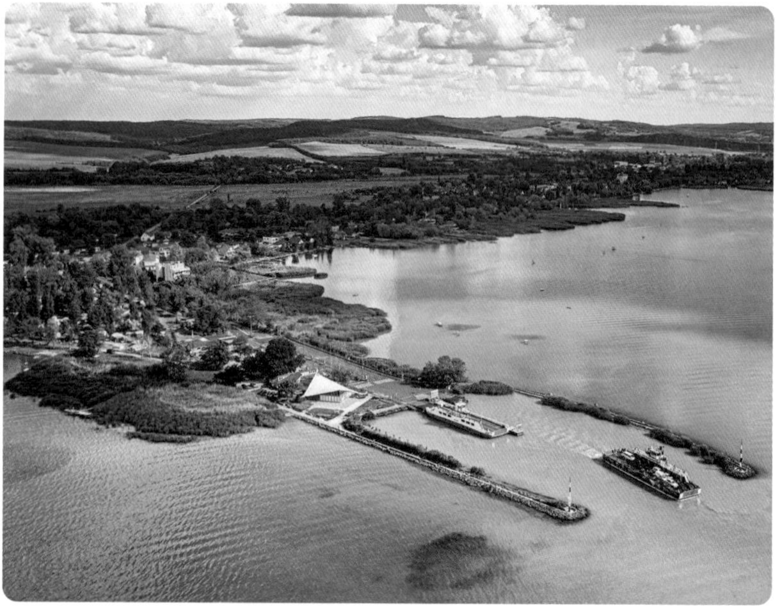

Fried hake

Go Fish!

HOOK YOUR SUPPER

Fishers are often successful on Lake Balaton, which has diverse species including bass, bream, catfish and perch. However, certain lakeside areas prohibit casting, and you need proper paperwork, so the easiest option for angling is going through **Balaton Fishing**, which organises the permissions. The company, located 9km outside of Tihany in Balatonudvari, offers radar-guided trips on dinghies or boats, as well as fishing experiences from shore and jetty.

Scrumptious Seafood

SPOILS OF THE DAY

Fried *hekk* (hake), breaded in flour, pepper and paprika and served with French fries or bread and pickles, is one of Balaton's classic beach snacks. Just ask any of the lake's frequent visitors and they'll often tell you no dish reminds them more of summer swimming sessions and their childhood. The fish is a mainstay of simple stalls, sizzled to a golden crisp, greasing up a paper plate. One of the best stalls for enjoying hake is **Aszófői Halsütő**, a roadside cottage stand between Balatonfüred and Tihany where local fishers chow down when the day's work is done. Hake is the speciality, although pike-perch, carp, bream and trout are in the fryers too. **Fish House** in Siófok is a fish stand with modern flair, beautifully prepared plates and a thoughtfully designed terrace. Both serve not only hake but also other catches of the day fried up.

SOCIALIST STOMPING GROUND

Lake Balaton was once called the 'communist riviera'. In the 1960s and '70s, Balaton became a beach resort catering to high-profile bloc leaders, socialist socialites and trade union workers. Posh Austro-Hungarian villas became the people's accommodation. Siófok, on the southern bank, was beloved for party-hardy discos that drew in young crowds, while northern villages like Tihany were synonymous with spas, vineyards and history. Siófok in particular became a rendezvous point for East and West Germans separated by the Iron Curtain who valued the well-priced spas and the uniquely visitor-friendly border policy, as well as a lack of spy activity, allegedly. Today, Germans continue to make up the biggest number of foreign visitors here, and German is still widely spoken by Balaton locals.

GETTING AROUND

Tihany's ferry to Szántód can be taken on foot, by bicycle or car. A scenic drive looping around the shore back to Tihany takes about two hours in a vehicle without stops.

KESZTHELY

Keszthely is a town of gently crumbling grand houses perched at the western edge of Lake Balaton. It's one of the loveliest places to stay in the area and far removed from the lake's busy hot spots. You can take a dip in the shallow waters from small beaches by day, absorb the lively but relaxed ambience by night, and get a dose of culture by popping into the village's museums and admiring its historical buildings. In the mid-18th century, Keszthely and its surrounds (including neighbouring spa town Hévíz) came into the possession of the Festetics family. Much like the Széchenyis (the Austro-Hungarian Empire's most influential noble family), they were progressives and reformers. In fact, Count György Festetics (1755–1819), who founded the Georgikon, Europe's first agricultural college, here in 1797, was an uncle of István Széchenyi. Don't miss the Festetics Palace, Keszthely's star attraction and a lavish baroque home fit for royalty.

TOP TIP

Every summer, the Keszthely Wine Festival is the village's most bubbly affair. Local winemakers, restaurants and food trucks sell their wares. Bands perform concerts of anything from rock and pop to jazz music, complementing a programme of beach parties and light shows.

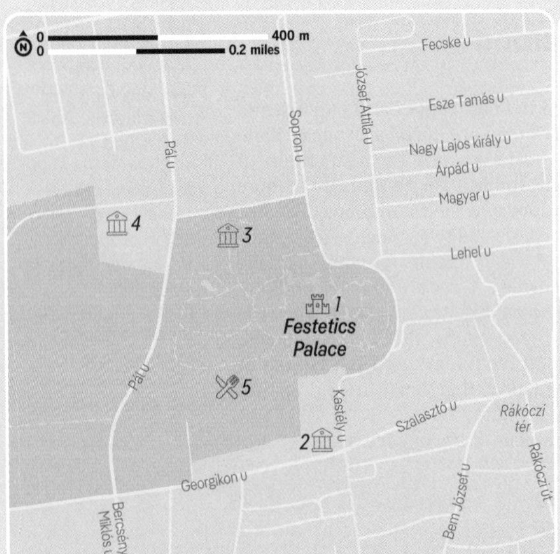

HIGHLIGHTS
1 Festetics Palace

SIGHTS
2 Amazon House
3 Coach Museum
4 Hunting Museum & Model Railway Museum

EATING
5 Palm House

LKONYA/SHUTTERSTOCK ©

Festetics Palace

Baroque Beauty

REFORM-ERA FINERY

The Festetics were one of the most prominent noble families in the Austro-Hungarian Empire. Discover their story and take a fascinating peek into aristocratic life at Keszthely's breathtaking **Festetics Palace**. Construction on the glimmering white 100-room palace began in 1745 on the foundation of another castle's ruins. Two wings in baroque style were extended from the original building 150 years later. Some 18 splendid rooms, including a mirrored dining hall and chapel, are part of the **Helikon Palace Museum**. The palace's greatest treasure, the **Helikon Library**, boasts 90,000 volumes set upon splendid carved furniture, all of which miraculously survived WWII despite great damage nearby. Many decorations in the gilt salons were imported from England in the mid-1800s. The museum's rooms, each in a different colour scheme, are full of portraits, bric-a-brac and furniture, mostly curated by Mary Hamilton, an English duchess who married a Festetic in the 1860s.

If you're up for more eyeballing, the palace can be combined for a lesser price with other on-site attractions: the **Hunting Museum** and **Aquarium**, as well as the **Coach Museum** with more than 50 carriages. The latter combines well with the **Model Railway Museum** and **Amazon House**, a former glam inn turned dive bar, now beautifully renovated into an exhibit on aristocratic travel. Enjoy lunch at the **Palm House** in a gorgeous tropical garden or tastings in the wine cellar.

MORE MUSEUM-HOPPING IN KESZTHELY

Balaton Museum
A thorough introduction to Balaton life from prehistoric times to the present with exhibitions on nature paintings, wildlife and shipping.

Nostalgia Museum
Random objects ranging from antique to retro, including typewriters, communist propaganda, vintage cameras and more.

Toy Museum
Great for kids, possibly even better for adults. Stir up childhood memories with stuffed animals, Barbies and board games, including interesting ones from the Soviet era.

Erotic Panoptikum
Kitschy X-rated museum with fornicating wax figurines and erotic fiction from Voltaire and Rousseau.

GETTING AROUND

Trains to Keszthely run several times daily from Budapest's Keleti station. If you're driving from the capital, take Hwy 71 for a scenic route along Balaton's northern shore, with the chance to stop in Balatonfüred or discover nature on the Tihany Peninsula.

Beyond Keszthely

Has cycling and wandering museums got your dogs barking? Hévíz's thermal waters are sure to soothe any aches and pains.

A stay in Keszthely is most often paired with the neighbouring village Hévíz, 8km away. Hévíz is arguably the most famous Hungarian spa town and home to Europe's largest – and the world's second largest – thermal lake. A soak in this water-lily-laden lake is essential for anyone visiting Balaton. Hévíz is the slowest town in Hungary. The average visitor is aged 60-plus, and frankly, it's impossible to move quickly after unwinding here.

This area is also within striking distance of Croatia, Slovenia and Austria, all within a 1½-hour drive of Keszthely. On the Hungarian side, the remote forests and villages of Őrség National Park are a major highlight.

TOP TIP

Catch some steam during a relaxing canoe ride on Hévíz's warm thermal waters during the wintry months from November to March.

Hévíz

ROBERTHARDING/ALAMY STOCK PHOTO ©

Hévízi-tó

READY, SET, SWIM

Swimming is Hungary's favourite national pastime. This landlocked country has produced its fair share of Olympian divers, many of whom got their feet wet at Balaton's famous cross-swimming race. Started in 1983, Lake Balaton's biggest event is usually held on the last Saturday in July. In 2021, almost 7000 people participated, including children, retirees and even stand-up paddleboarders. On the shore, big crowds of spectators, food trucks and live-music performances create a lively atmosphere. The classic track for professional athletes is 5.2km long. It starts at the pier in Révfülöp, between Balatonfüred and Keszthely, and finishes on the lake's opposite side at Balatonboglár's Platán beach. The current record for crossing the lake is 57 minutes, achieved by Hungarian Olympian Kristóf Rasovszky, in 2020.

Miracle Waters

HOT AND UNBOTHERED

Just outside of Keszthely, the village of **Hévíz** lays claim to Europe's largest thermal lake, which is fed by 80 million litres of thermal water daily. **Hévízi-tó** (Lake Hévíz) is an incredible sight. The temperature averages 33°C and never drops below 22°C, even in winter, allowing you to bathe when there's ice on the fir trees of the surrounding Park Wood. Simply float or indulge in every kind of thermal remedy, massage and scrub imaginable at the on-site indoor spa. A delightful maze of catwalks and piers placed around the lake's fin-de-siècle central pavilion contains platforms for lounging on sun chairs, jumping into the lake or catching shade beneath the pavilions. Piers along the shore allow for sunbathing as well.

Potent Pálinka

ONE-TWO FRUIT PUNCH

Lake Balaton might be famous as a wine region, but while you're here, try another homegrown Hungarian elixir: the fruit spirit *pálinka*. Sometimes referred to as fruit brandy, *pálinka* is known for its high alcohol content (between 37% and 86%), biting taste and pungent aroma. In the village of Cserszegtomaj, about 5km north of Keszthely, you can visit the family-run **Schmitz Distillery** and discover its unique fermentation process. Schmitz *pálinka* is made from local fruits grown around the Southern Transdanubia region including pears, apricots, cherries, raspberries and apples.

GETTING AROUND

If you plan to drive a car you hired in Hungary outside of the country – say to nearby Croatia, Austria or Slovenia – ask the car hire company about *vignettes* (motorway permits) for the countries you want to visit. Not doing so can result in costly penalties.

PÉCS

Blessed with illustrious historic buildings, a number of fine museums and monuments, and a relaxed urban vibe, Pécs (pronounced PEH-ch) could almost be described as the better Budapest. It's certainly a highly welcoming and eye-catching place to visit, a university city with a diversity of international students plus great pubs, culture and gastronomy. It's no wonder many travellers put Pécs second only to Budapest on their Hungarian 'must-see' list (and if they don't, they should!).

Pécs enjoys attractively mild weather. It is sheltered from the northern winds by the Mecsek Hills, and it's equidistant from the Danube to the east and the Dráva River to the south. The microclimate lengthens the summer and is ideal for viticulture and fruit production in the surrounding areas, especially almonds. A fine time to visit is in October when the light takes on a special quality and pink sunsets seem to last forever.

TOP TIP

An afternoon at the Zsolnay Cultural Quarter is perfectly rounded off with a visit to its stylish restaurant, Zsolnay, a contender for Pécs' top dining spot. Creative dishes? Absolutely. The forest-mushroom-infused beef cheeks and raspberry soup stand out. Service is professional and attentive, and the Hungarian wine pairings are lovingly selected.

ARTISAN SHOPPING IN PÉCS

Blázek
Pécs has been known for leatherwork since Ottoman times. Blázek has handbags and wallets.

Monokrom Design Store
Showcases the work of local and Hungarian designers and artists.

Pécsi Műtárgy Galéria
Collect Zsolnay porcelain and other unique items such as grandfather clocks, silver and paintings.

Nostalgic Candy Manufactory
Candies in all shapes, sizes and colours in the Zsolnay Cultural Quarter.

Outstanding Craftsmanship

A HISTORY OF HANDIWORK

In the post-Ottoman era, Pécs flourished as a centre for handicrafts and trade. Manufacturing became the city's bread and butter, and 19th-century factories produced everything from iron to paper, sugar and beer. One of the most important companies was the Zsolnay Porcelain Manufacturer. The **Zsolnay Factory**, founded by the visionary Miklós Zsolnay in 1853, manufactured stoneware and other ceramics that became important decorations for buildings across the country and helped define the Art Nouveau movement. By 1914 Zsolnay was the largest company in Austro-Hungary. After WWI, the factory and its recognition declined because of periods of Serbian occupation and socialism.

Today, it's still possible to see the legendary porcelain being made by hand at the factory located in the sprawling heritage complex, **Zsolnay Cultural Quarter**. The grounds, divided into four quarters (craftsman, family and children's, creative, and university), are a lovely place to stroll, with 15 grand, colourful buildings, 88 statues, parks and promenades. More highlights include a mausoleum dedicated to Miklós Zsolnay, a planetarium and puppet theatre. On the grounds, you can visit the **Zsolnay Porcelain Museum**, displaying 19th-century chinoiserie pieces and Art Nouveau and Art Deco designs in the lustrous eosin glaze. Once the home to the Zsolnay family, several rooms contain many original furnishings and personal effects.

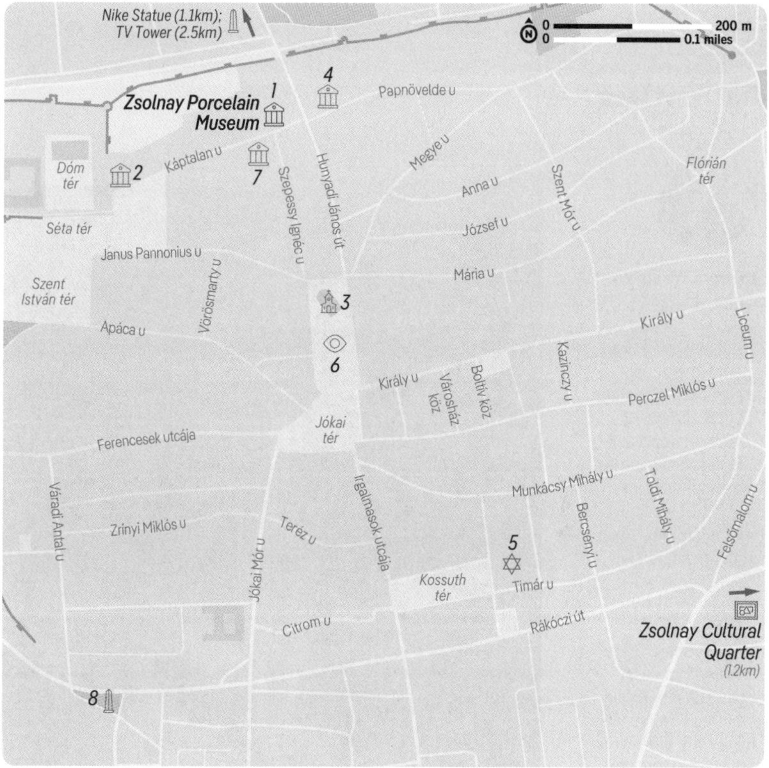

HIGHLIGHTS
1 Zsolnay Porcelain Museum

SIGHTS
2 Ferenc Martyn Museum
3 Inner Town Parish Church
4 Modern Hungarian Gallery
5 Synagogue
6 Széchenyi tér
7 Victor Vasarely Museum
8 Zsolnay Statue

Marvel-Worthy Art Museums

MODERN MAGYAR ART

Pécs' selection of painted works is fabulous. Spend a day at the **Victor Vasarely Museum** admiring the work of the father of op art, Victor Vasarely, with clever 3D illuminations that seem to burst from the walls. Afterwards, check out the **Ferenc Martyn Museum** dedicated to his predecessor,

WHERE TO DRINK IN PÉCS

WunderBar
Delightful *kert* (courtyard) hidden off the main street, with stiff drinks and friendly cats.

Cooltour Café
Retro hangout with ruin bar vibes. Its rear garden feels like a secret spot.

Tüke Borház
Classy wine bar tucked away in a stone house in the hills.

WHY I LOVE PÉCS

Barbara Woolsey, writer

What makes Pécs so great? The people-watching. Throughout history, Hungary's fifth most populous city has also been its most multicultural, and it's a treat to watch this diversity still thriving today. Pécs' cobblestone streets are lively all day: elderly couples share cake, and parents push prams past baroque buildings. Terraces fill up with after-work crowds soaking up peachy sunsets, and doe-eyed university students trudge around seeking comfy barstools. Newcomers enjoy Pécs' spirited yet sentimental blend of old and new, a place where ancient history meets modern joie de vivre.

ISTVAN CSAK/SHUTTERSTOCK ©

TV Tower

a Pécs-born sculptor and painter. The **Modern Hungarian Gallery** exhibits the art of Hungary from 1850 to today across several floors. Works run the gamut from impressionist paintings to visually striking and even menacing contemporary installations.

WHERE TO EAT HUNGARIAN FOOD IN PÉCS

Maci Lángosozó
Hole-in-the-wall *lángos* (deep-friend dough) joint loved by locals for its big portions and endless toppings. €

Bagolyvár Étterem
Terrace restaurant with incredible views. Indoors, live music and delectable *paprikash* and dumplings abound. €€€

Morzsa
New-wave bakery and regional Hungarian products with a modern bistro twist. €€€

Pécs from Above

CLIMB A COMMUNIST RELIC

Get acquainted with Pecs' Iron Curtain history at the **TV Tower**. Despite being Hungary's tallest building, it is a delightfully untouristy attraction with an unsuspecting entrance and little signage. The 200m-tall construct sits atop the 535m summit of Misina Hill. Take the lift up on a clear day, and from the viewing platform you can see Pécs and its historic buildings, the ribbon of the Danube and the Mecsek Hills. Sunset views are the finest.

Footsteps of Faith

RICH RELIGIOUS DIVERSITY

Pécs, the 'Borderless City', is a melting pot of different cultures and beliefs. Hungarians, Croatians and Swabians have historically lived here together, and in 1998 Unesco awarded Pécs for maintaining minority cultures and helping refugees of the Balkan Wars.

Pécs' multicultural fabric is discovered through its religious buildings. The former Pasha Gazi Kassim Mosque, now the **Inner Town Parish Church**, dominates the main square of Széchenyi tér. The Ottomans built the square-based mosque with stones from the ruined Gothic Church of St Bertalan, and Catholics moved back in the early 18th century. Spot prevailing Islamic elements including windows with distinctive ogee arches, faded verses from the Quran and lovely geometric frescoes. Pécs' beautifully preserved 1869 Conservative **synagogue** is south of Széchenyi tér. Built in the Romantic style in 1869, it serves a community of about 100 Jews today. About 2700 of the city's Jews were deported to Nazi death camps in May 1944.

Sitting Pretty

HISTORIC SQUARES AND MONUMENTS

Pécs' mild climate and large population of students and young professionals make it a place where people love to hang out outside, enjoying snacks and sipping coffee. The main square of **Széchenyi tér** with its grand fountain is the city's hub and the ultimate place for people-watching. Students also love to congregate at the **Nike Statue**, a hilltop monument with amazing city views, and at the **Zsolnay Statue**, built in 1907 after citizens and businesses pooled funds together.

PERFECT FAMILY WEEKEND IN PÉCS

Péter Árvai, a University of Pécs student coordinator and president of the Alliance Française de Pécs, is a husband and father to a two-year-old. He shares his favourite spots to visit with his family.

Vásárcsarnok Market
We love to enjoy a traditional breakfast: *lángos*, local sausages and black pudding, and if we're feeling really hardcore, garlicky cooked pork tongue.

Pécsi Kávé
My go-to drink at the cafe is an espresso lemonade.

Tettye Park
We love hiking on the weekends, especially around this park and the medieval bishop's residence on the hillside.

Reggeli
A great lunch spot, with nice local Hungarian options and a great ambience.

GETTING AROUND

Pécs' downtown is easily explored on foot, but for attractions outside of it, such as the TV Tower, having a car makes life easier.

Several daily direct trains connect Pécs with Budapest's Keleti station.

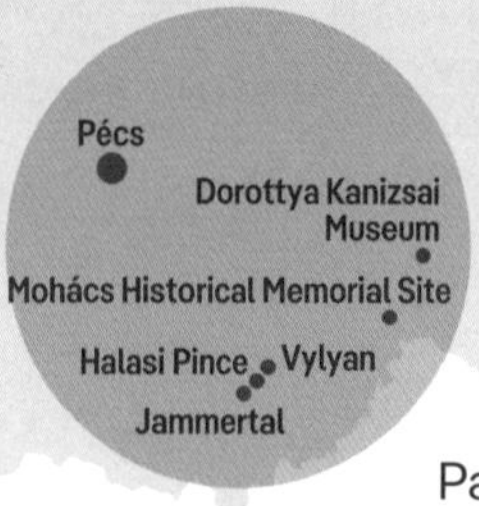

Pécs
Dorottya Kanizsai Museum
Mohács Historical Memorial Site
Halasi Pince
Vylyan
Jammertal

Beyond Pécs

Pass through Pécs' city walls to get in touch with Southern Transdanubia's remote glory, from lush wines to relics of turbulent times.

Once upon a time, the Romans settled in Pécs for its fertile soil and abundant water. Today, nature's splendour still thrives across Southern Transdanubia, and there's nothing like hopping on a train and seeing it for yourself. From the rolling greens of the Mecsek Hills to Villány's wine country, the perfect day trip from Pécs likely includes a show-stopping vantage point and a glass of homegrown cab franc. Keep heading east, and eventually you hit the Danube and the sleepy port town of Mohács. Thirsty history buffs, take note: great museums explore the region's tumultuous past and are a starting point of a white wine route.

TOP TIP

Busójárás, Mohács' pre-Lenten free-for-all carnival celebration, sees locals adorned with freakish horned wooden masks parading through town in late February or March.

Villány vineyards

BERNI0004/SHUTTERSTOCK ©

BERNI0004/SHUTTERSTOCK ©

Wine cellars, Villány

The Battle of Mohács, Explained

REBUILDING AFTER DESOLATION

The two famous battles of Mohács, one in 1526 and one in 1687, marked the beginning and end of Ottoman rule in Hungary. At the **Mohács Historical Memorial Site**, delve into the defeat of the ragtag Hungarian army by the Ottomans on 29 August 1526, a watershed moment in national history. With it came partition and foreign domination lasting almost five centuries. The memorial site's counterpart, the **Dorottya Kanizsai Museum**, tells the 17th-century story of the Ottomans' defeat. A large collection of costumes introduce the Sokác, Slovenes, Serbs, Croats, Bosnians and Swabians who repopulated the devastated area. Significantly, both sites aim to provide a balanced account of history from both the Hungarian and Turkish perspectives.

Move Over, Burgundy

RED RED WINE

While Lake Balaton tends to be more geared towards white wines, Villány is mostly famous for reds. Its most popular grape varieties are cabernet franc and portugieser. Take a train to Villány, about 35km from Pécs, and choose from scenic wineries focused on deep aromatic nectars. The **Jammertal** and **Vylyan** wine estates both boast pretty vineyards and cosy wine cellars. Jammertal's claim to fame is its merlot (the 2015 was awarded the world's best red), while Vylyan is worth a stop for fruity pinot noirs and its Bogyólé blend. **Halasi Pince** in the centre of Villány's village is a lovely estate, guesthouse and restaurant with a fantastic menu that uses modern plating to showcase traditional Hungarian ingredients.

FRIGHTENING FESTIVAL

If you can't make the **Busójárás** festival in late February or March, the **Busóház** museum in Mohács is the place to visit, telling the story of the festival from its origins. Marvel at the scary devils' and rams' head masks on full display – they're less scary when not being worn (just a little).

Legend has it that the ethnic Šokci peoples fled Mohács to nearby swamps and woods away from Ottoman troops. After spending days preparing weapons and the self-carved masks, they eventually attacked Mohács. The Ottomans, believing that they were demons, departed. According to another telling, the festival emerged as a South Slav spring rite with *busós* (masks) used to scare off winter and welcome spring.

GETTING AROUND

Besides travelling by car, taking the train is the fastest, most convenient means of exploring Pécs' countryside. Bus services to Mohács are frequent but take longer.

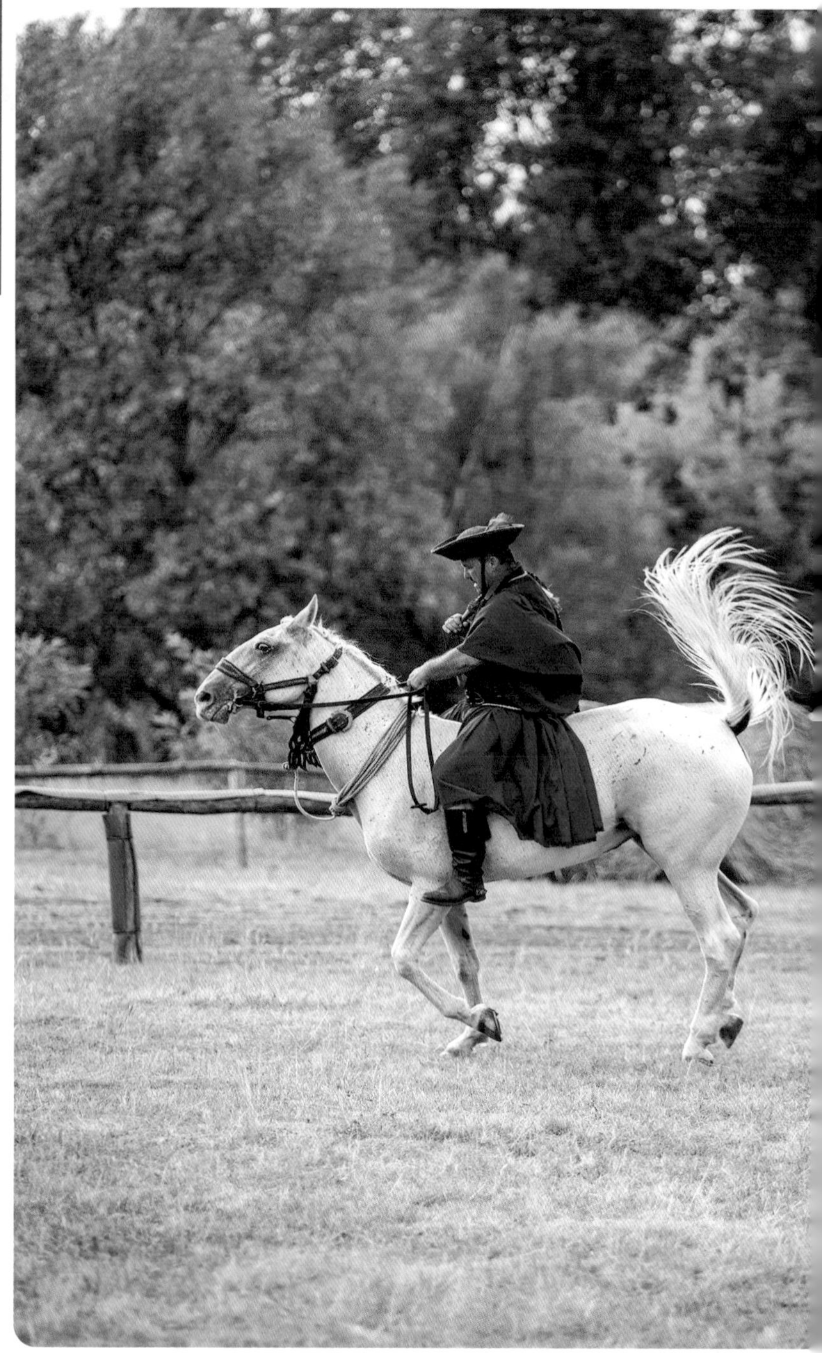

Above: Csikós (cowboy), Hortobágy National Park (p214). Right: Cifrapalota (p219), Kecskemét

THE GREAT PLAIN

BIG SKIES, RURAL ROMANCE AND ART NOUVEAU

Hungary's heartland is an intoxicating cocktail of infinite countryside imbued with moody romance, splendid architecture, and national parks beloved by birds and people.

Like the Outback for Australians or the Wild West for Americans, Hungarians view the Nagyalföld (Great Plain) – also known as the *puszta* – (literally 'deserted') romantically, as a region full of hardy shepherds fighting the wind and snow in winter and trying not to go stir-crazy in summer as the notorious *délibábak* (mirages) rise off the baking soil. Many of these notions come as much from the collective imagination as they do from history, but there's no arguing the spellbinding potential of big-sky country. The horse and herding shows at Hortobágy National Park and at Bugac in Kiskunság National Park recreate this pastoral tradition.

The region is also home to fabulous cities that are anything but 'plain'. In the northeast, dynamic Debrecen holds ample appeal for history lovers, culture vultures and party animals, and it's the launchpad for exploring Hortobágy National Park.

Only an hour south of Budapest, Kecskemét, nicknamed the 'orchard of Hungary', is famous for its apricot brandy *(pálinka)*, Art Nouveau-decorated town centre and clutch of one-of-a-kind museums.

The jewel of the Great Plain is Szeged, a culture-filled city on the Tisza River near the border with Serbia. Besides its own lineup of stunning Art Nouveau buildings, it's also a haven for foodies. Famous for its paprika, salami and fish soup, the city is also gaining a solid reputation for its modern Hungarian cuisine.

THE MAIN AREAS

DEBRECEN
Faith, festivals and forest. **p210**

KECSKEMÉT
Rural charmer oozing culture and character. **p217**

SZEGED
Lively Art Nouveau riverside beauty. **p221**

Find Your Way

Flat as a pancake, the Great Plain is bordered by Serbia and Romania. Many train and bus routes cross the borders. This region is sparsely populated with most residents living in Debrecen, Szeged and Kecskemét.

Kecskemét, p217
This gentle town at the doorstep of Kiskunság National Park brims with whimsical Art Nouveau buildings, pretty pedestrian squares and a handful of quirky museums.

Szeged, p221
Bisected by the Tisza River, Szeged is a treasure chest spilling over with eye-popping Art Nouveau, a packed cultural calendar, outdoor cafes and green spaces.

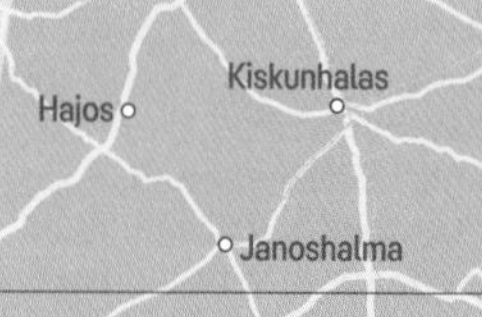

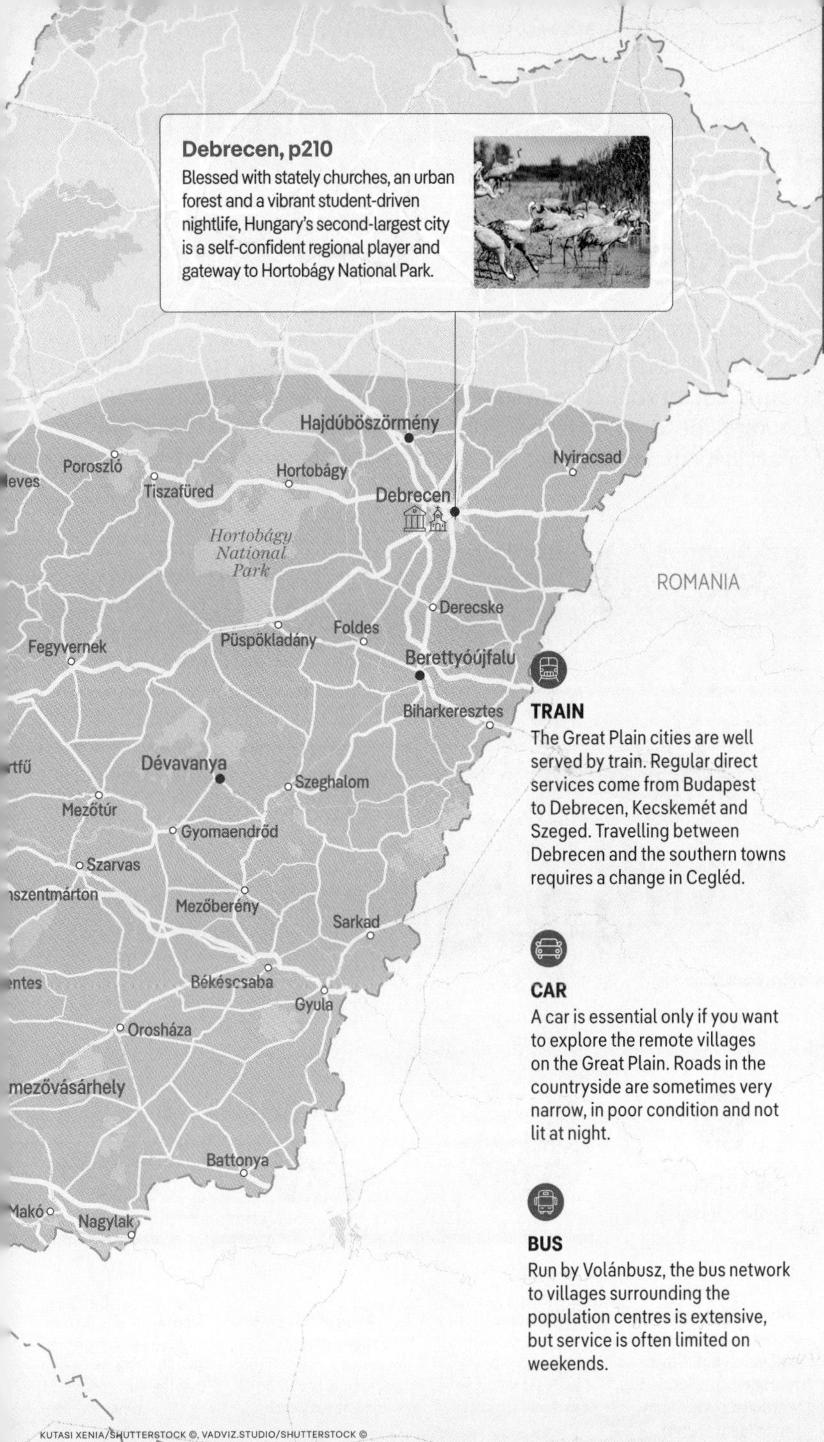

Debrecen, p210

Blessed with stately churches, an urban forest and a vibrant student-driven nightlife, Hungary's second-largest city is a self-confident regional player and gateway to Hortobágy National Park.

Hajdúböszörmény
Poroszló
Tiszafüred
Hortobágy
Debrecen
Nyiracsad
Hortobágy National Park
Derecske
Foldes
Püspökladány
Fegyvernek
Berettyóújfalu
Biharkeresztes
Dévavanya
Szeghalom
Mezőtúr
Gyomaendrőd
Szarvas
Mezőberény
Sarkad
Békéscsaba
Gyula
Orosháza
Battonya
Makó
Nagylak

ROMANIA

TRAIN

The Great Plain cities are well served by train. Regular direct services come from Budapest to Debrecen, Kecskemét and Szeged. Travelling between Debrecen and the southern towns requires a change in Cegléd.

CAR

A car is essential only if you want to explore the remote villages on the Great Plain. Roads in the countryside are sometimes very narrow, in poor condition and not lit at night.

BUS

Run by Volánbusz, the bus network to villages surrounding the population centres is extensive, but service is often limited on weekends.

Plan Your Days

The Great Plain is as much a place as a state of mind. Scratch at its soul in the endless countryside, but find its beating heart in its dynamic cities.

SHEVCHENKO ANDREY/SHUTTERSTOCK ©

Reformed Great Church (p210), Debrecen

If you only have one day

- If you like architecture, museums, good food and a hopping bar scene, focus on **Szeged** (p221). But for a primer on *puszta* life, point your compass to **Hortobágy National Park** (p214) just outside Debrecen. Meet indigenous animals up close, have your photo taken with dashing *csikósok* (cowboys) and observe the extensive bird population.

- Return to **Debrecen** (p210) in the afternoon to tick off its main sights, leaving the climb up the tower of the **Reformed Great Church** (p210) until the shadows grow longer. Indulge in a sublime meal at **IKON** (p213) before capping the day with bar-hopping along Simonffy utca.

SEASONAL HIGHLIGHTS

The grasslands come back to life in spring, while summer is the peak season for outdoor pursuits and festivals. Nightlife in Debrecen and Szeged reawakens in autumn as students return.

MAY

Szeged Wine Festival is a 10-day extravaganza around Dom tér, while the **Apricot & Brandy Festival** takes over Kecskemét's squares.

JUNE

Late June to August, the **Szeged Open-Air Festival** presents top musical acts against the spectacular backdrop of the Votive Church.

JULY

The five-day **Campus Festival** in and around Debrecen's Nagyerdei Stadium has concerts, theatre, films, food and wine.

PARLANTESTE/SHUTTERSTOCK ©, CAROLIN JAHN/SHUTTERSTOCK ©, VISION INVASION/SHUTTERSTOCK ©

Three days in the Great Plain

- Follow the one-day itinerary at a more leisurely pace and stretch your Debrecen sightseeing into day two, spending more time in its fabulous museums and **Nagyerdei Park** (p211). After lunch, for instance at **Next Bistro** (p213), take the train south across the *puszta* to **Szeged** (p221), the Great Plain's most sophisticated city. Book ahead for an unforgettable dinner at **Alkimista** (p224).

- Dedicate the following day to exploring Szeged's marvellous city core, a symphony of Art Nouveau jewels like **Reök Palace** (p222). Take a **boat ride** (p226) on the Tisza and try the hearty local fish soup.

If you have more time

- Get to know Debrecen and Szeged better and fold a day and night in delightful **Kecskemét** (p217) into your itinerary. Besides flaunting its own ensemble of architectural treasures from the Middle Ages to the 20th century, the town is also famous for its produce, especially apricots that find their ultimate destiny in *barackpálinka*, a cockle-warming brandy.

- If you've overindulged, clear the cobwebs on a nature exploration of the **Bugacpuszta** (p218), the most accessible section of nearby Kiskunság National Park. Alternatively, steer east to Makó for a full detox at **Hagymatikum Thermal Bath** (p227), which delivers architectural eye-candy along with healing waters.

AUGUST

Events include Debrecen's **Flower Carnival**, Kecskemét's **Hírös Week Festival** of music, and the folkloric **Hortobágy Bridge Fair**.

SEPTEMBER

Cauldrons of fish soup is the draw of Szeged's **International Tisza Fish Festival**, along with bands and a craft market.

OCTOBER

Peak month for **bird-watching** in the national parks of Hortobágy and Kiskunság.

DECEMBER

Christmas markets brighten towns. Debrecen's Piac utca has lights, tantalising aromas and stalls selling handicrafts.

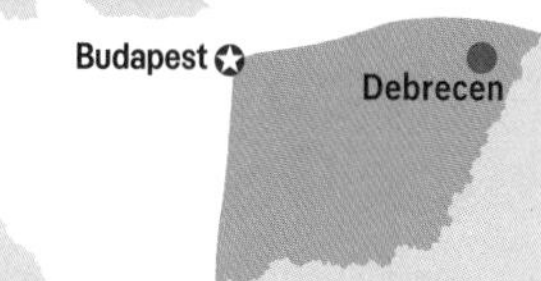

DEBRECEN

Change and renewal are part of Debrecen's DNA. Having survived medieval fires, WWII bombs and the Cold War, Hungary's second-biggest city has been busy positioning itself as the eastern region's dynamic economic, cultural and education hub. This translates into revamped museums, reinvented landmarks, sparkling boutique hotels and an increasingly sophisticated food scene. The airport welcomes flights from around Europe and Israel, and international companies are setting up shop in six new industrial parks ringing the city. All this development is quite a departure for a city that's been historically known as the stronghold of Hungarian Protestantism (it's even been called the 'Calvinist Rome'). In summer, festivals take over the sprawling pedestrian area below the Reformed Great Church and venues like Nagyerdei Stadium and the Water Tower in Debrecen's city park. Thermal baths and a state-of-the-art water oasis are also part of the park, while the nearby university boasts close to 30,000 students from 120 countries.

TOP TIP

Tram 1 is ideal for both transport and sightseeing. From the train station, it runs north along Piac utca to the Reformed Great Church and then carries on to Nagyerdei Park and the university, where it loops around for the same trip southward.

Grand Views & an Empty Chair

INSIDE AND ATOP AN ICONIC CHURCH

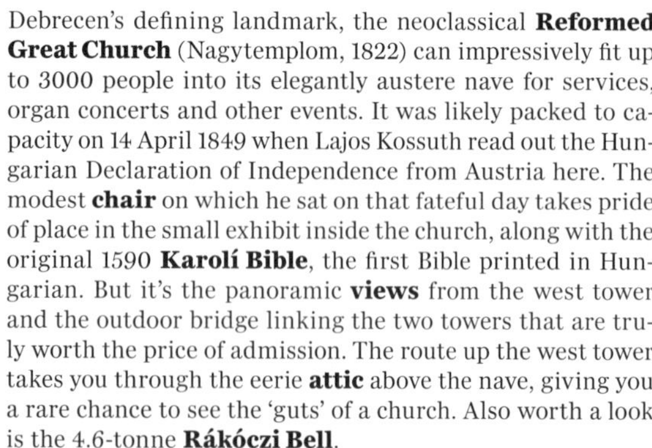

Debrecen's defining landmark, the neoclassical **Reformed Great Church** (Nagytemplom, 1822) can impressively fit up to 3000 people into its elegantly austere nave for services, organ concerts and other events. It was likely packed to capacity on 14 April 1849 when Lajos Kossuth read out the Hungarian Declaration of Independence from Austria here. The modest **chair** on which he sat on that fateful day takes pride of place in the small exhibit inside the church, along with the original 1590 **Karolí Bible**, the first Bible printed in Hungarian. But it's the panoramic **views** from the west tower and the outdoor bridge linking the two towers that are truly worth the price of admission. The route up the west tower takes you through the eerie **attic** above the nave, giving you a rare chance to see the 'guts' of a church. Also worth a look is the 4.6-tonne **Rákóczi Bell**.

BEST BARS IN DEBRECEN

Maszek
Killer cocktails and other libations at this high-octane drinking den on Simonffy utca.

Roncsbár
This maze-like ruin pub is an essential party pen with an old tram car in the garden, cymbals dangling from the bar ceiling, and a hall for concerts and DJ nights.

Window on the World

ECLECTIC TREASURE CHEST

Mummies or folk art, coins or Samurai swords – no matter your interest, the **Déri Museum** is likely to have you covered. The core of the collection comes courtesy of Frigyes Déri, an entrepreneur with a passion for historic weaponry and artefacts from the Japanese Edo period. A few years before his death in 1924, he donated the precious bunch to the city of Debrecen. Pride of place, however, goes to another acquisi-

SIGHTS
1 Déri Museum
2 Nagyerdei Park
3 Reformed Great Church
4 University of Debrecen
5 Water Tower

ACTIVITIES
6 Aquaticum Spa

EATING
7 IKON

tion: the trilogy of monumental canvases depicting the Passion of Christ by Mihály Munkácsy, one of Hungary's most celebrated 19th-century artists. If you're not going inside, at least cast more than a passing glance at the four superb bronzes by local sculptor Ferenc Medgyessy, who merits his own museum nearby.

Debrecen's 'Green Lung'

ESCAPING THE URBAN BUSTLE

Take a break from sightseeing by hopping on Tram 1 for a 10-minute ride north to family-friendly **Nagyerdei Park** (Great Forest Park). Stroll beneath the leafy canopy, chill on

WHERE TO STAY IN DEBRECEN

Malom Hotel
Mod-cons combine with industrial-style decor to reflect the building's steam mill origins. **€€**

Centrum Hotel
Central but quiet landing pad of cosy, elegant rooms with balconies, plus free breakfast and parking. **€€**

Régi Posta Fogadó
Boutique inn in Debrecen's oldest building (1690) features updated rooms oozing historical ambience. **€€**

DEBRECEN'S HISTORIC CENTRE WALKING TOUR

This 2km walk kicks off on **1 Kossuth tér**, Debrecen's central square, where the twin-towered **2 Reformed Great Church** (p210) forms the majestic backdrop to the massive Lajos Kossuth monument. Nearby, a Venetian glass mosaic of the city's coat of arms brightens the pavement. Kossuth tér caps Piac utca, Debrecen's grand boulevard flanked by ornate merchant houses. Hook north past a small park between the Great Church and the neoclassical **3 Calvinist College**, alma mater of numerous Hungarian writers and poets. A frescoed staircase leads to the green-colonnaded Great Library, with 600,000 volumes, as well as the Oratory, where the breakaway National Assembly met in 1849. There's a museum with religious treasures, although these pale in comparison to Mihály Munkácsy's stunning trio of canvases depicting the Passion of Christ, the star exhibit of the eclectic **4 Derí Museum** (p210). For contrast, saunter over to the cutting-edge **5 MODEM Center for Modern and Contemporary Art** for works by Hungarian and international artists. Steer south to the Jewish Quarter where the pink **6 Pastí Street Orthodox Synagogue** does double duty as a house of worship and conference/event centre. Don't miss the remnants of a mikvah (Jewish ritual bath) in the basement and the haunting Holocaust memorial in the courtyard. Debrecen's Jewish community (currently Hungary's largest) gathers for services steps away in the **7 Status Quo Ante Synagogue**. Head back to Piac utca via Simonffy utca, Debrecen's boisterous 'bar mile', and turn right to the **8 Small Reformed Church**, nicknamed 'incomplete church' because of the missing onion dome that fell victim to a storm in 1907.

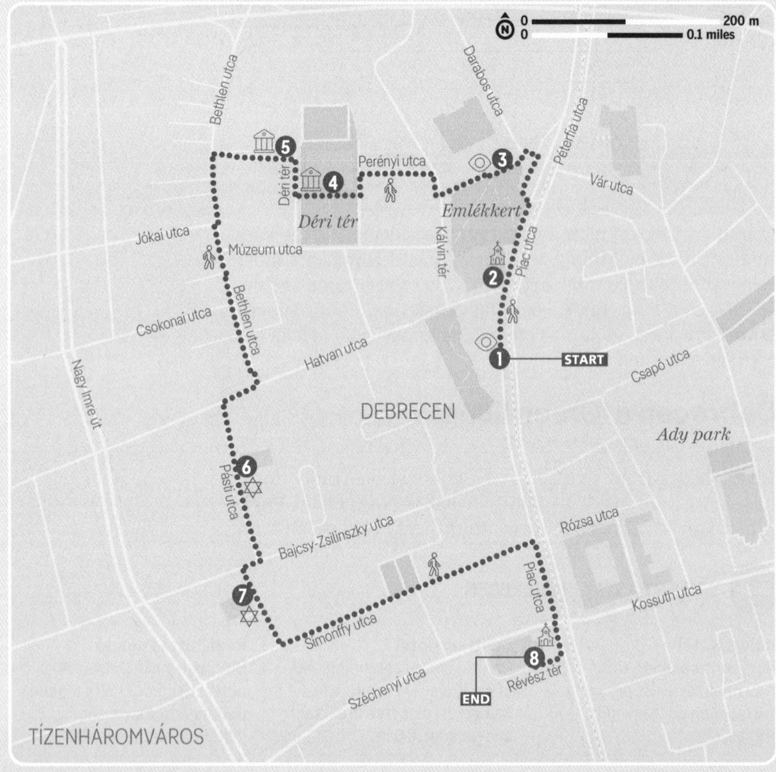

Nagyerdai Park (p211)

a sunbed by Froggy Pond (Békás-tó) or experience Hungary's fabled spa culture during a soak and steam in the thermal mineral spring waters and sauna landscape of the **Aquaticum Spa** complex. Its adjacent alfresco aquapark is tailor-made for tiring out the kids on hot summer days. To see it all from above, hoof it to the top of the historic **Water Tower** (Víztorony) near Debrecen's sparkling football stadium. In summer, the garden around the tower turns into one of the city's most beloved open-air bars and the site of festivals and special events. The park's leafy trails segue smoothly into the campus of the **University of Debrecen**, with an impressive neo-baroque main building overlooking a sculpture-studded fountain. According to local tradition, students must take a dip in the water after graduating.

Star Power on a Plate

CULINARY FLIGHTS OF FANCY

Local top chef Ádám Thür has for years enriched Debrecen's culinary landscape with his organic-produce-driven modern European cuisine. In 2022, his stylish **IKON** restaurant finally got the coveted recommendation in Michelin's Hungary guide. The food may be stellar, but the ambience is deliciously down-to-earth so as not to distract your taste buds from smoothly balanced plates like Mangalica pork schnitzel or veal sweetbread.

BEST RESTAURANTS IN DEBRECEN

Kis Padlizsán Vegan Bistro
The 'Little Eggplant' slings the best in global comfort food, made with love but without meat. **€**

Next Bistro
Design-focused outpost wows discerning palates with next-gen versions of Hungarian and international faves. **€€€**

DG Italiano
Charming joint in a historic building brings la dolce vita to Debrecen with fresh pasta and excellent mains. **€€€**

Pizza, Kávé, Világbéke
Pizza, coffee and world peace are a winning trifecta, but the desserts of this cult cafe are killer too. **€€**

GETTING AROUND

Central Debrecen is compact enough for exploring on foot. Public transport stops running at 11pm, but taxis are cheap. Parking in the centre is free from noon on Friday until 6am Monday. The airport and city centre are linked by bus.

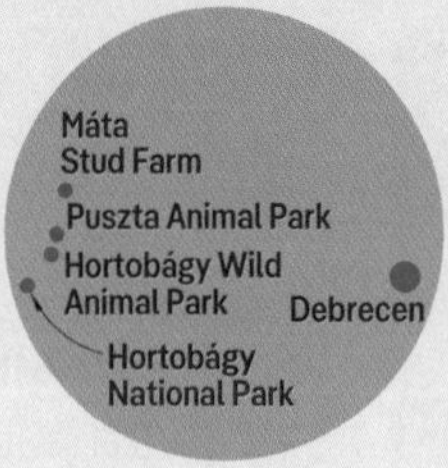

Máta
Stud Farm
Puszta Animal Park
Hortobágy Wild
Animal Park
Debrecen
Hortobágy
National Park

Beyond Debrecen

Immerse yourself in the beautiful, quiet and timeless mystique of the Hungarian *puszta,* an endless expanse lidded by cornflower skies.

Debrecen is the gateway to Hortobágy National Park (Hortobágy Nemzeti Park), the jewel of the Hungarian *puszta.* An 810-sq-km mosaic of alkaline pastures, steppes, meadows and marshes, it was established in 1973, making it Hungary's oldest national park. Its entry point is tiny Hortobágy village, some 40km west of Debrecen, once celebrated for its sturdy cowboys, folksy inns and Gypsy bands. You can see the staged recreation of all this, complete with traditionally costumed *csikósok* (cowboys), at a *puszta* horse show. Venture beyond the village to explore more of this flora- and fauna-rich national park that was added to Unesco's World Heritage list in 1999 in recognition of its harmonious interaction between people and nature.

TOP TIP

Most sights and attractions are closed from November until March and usually in bad weather during the other months.

Hortobágy National Park

Csikósok **(cowboys) at a *puszta* horse show**

Cowboy Culture on Display

A PRIMER ON PASTORAL LIFE

Your first stop in **Hortobágy village** should be the Hortobágy National Park visitor centre to pick up tickets, maps and advice from the helpful staff. They've temporarily set up shop in the Round Theatre until the restoration of the main building (also in the village) is completed. The top attraction in the village is the landmark 167m **Nine-Hole Bridge**, built in 1833 and spanning the marshy Hortobágy River. It has the distinction of being the longest – and certainly the most sketched, painted and photographed – stone bridge in the country. Just in front stands the **Hortobágyi Csárda**, a charmingly kitsch-filled roadside inn. As you'll discover in the small museum inside, it dates to 1781 and is one of the original eating houses used by salt traders on their way from the Tisza River to Debrecen. Inns provided itinerant Roma fiddlers with employment, and Gypsy music and *csárdak* (inns) have been synonymous ever since.

Yee-haw, Hungarian Style

SHOWTIME IN THE PUSZTA

Staged it may be, but the 1½-hour Puszta experience at the 350-year-old **Máta Stud Farm**, 3km north of Hortobágy village, sort of *is* a real slice of Hungary. This is one of the biggest studs for indigenous livestock farming and horse breeding, mostly of the famous Nonius breed. During the programme,

THE PUSZTA: FROM FOREST TO TREELESS PLAIN

Half a millennium ago, the Great Plain was not a treeless steppe but forest land at the constant mercy of the flooding Tisza and Danube Rivers. The Ottomans felled most of the trees, destroying the protective cover and releasing the topsoil to the winds. Villagers fled north or to the market towns. The region had become the *puszta* (meaning 'deserted' or 'abandoned') and home to shepherds, fisher folk, runaway serfs and outlaws. The Great Plain has few fortifications because the Ottomans demanded they be destroyed as part of the agreement of retreat. In the 19th century, regulation of the rivers dried up the marshes and allowed for methodical irrigation, paving the way for intensive agriculture, particularly on the southern plain, but flooding still occurs to this day.

WHERE TO SLEEP & EAT

Sóvirág Vendégház
Chalet-like guesthouse with garden, six rooms with balconies or terraces, plus a sauna-and-Jacuzzi zone. **€€€**

Hortobágyi Csárda
Feast on traditional shepherds' dishes such as *bográcsgulyás* (beef and pepper stew) at this celebrated roadside inn. **€€€**

Pizza Sfera
This place in the village serves Hungarian mains, but most people stick to the pizza. **€**

TOP TRAILS AT HORTOBÁGY NATIONAL PARK

Connect with nature on these paths in Hortobágy National Park. The 5km-long **Egyek-Pusztakócs Nature Trail** meanders through rehabilitated marshland, starting at an inn near Kócsújfalu about 19km west of Hortobágy village. It skirts the Górés Farm, which operates a bird rescue centre, and a kurgan, a Bronze Age burial mound. Keep an eye out for brightly feathered bee-eaters that make their home here. Some 46km west of the village, the 2km out-and-back **Szálkahalom Nature Trail** kicks off at the kurgan for which it was named and offers a great opportunity to see the hardy low-lying flora eking out an existence on these alkaline grasslands. With luck, you might even spot a red-footed falcon. Both of these trails require a park pass available from the visitor centre.

you ride in a horse-drawn wagon across the wide-open prairie past barns and nodding T-shaped draw wells while bumping into grazing grey cattle, herds of galumphing water buffalo and Racka sheep showing off their spiralling horns. For most visitors, the highlight is watching the *csikósok* (cowboys), clad in their traditional cornflower-blue loose-fitting shirts and trousers, cracking their bullwhips and performing tricks with their Nonius horses. The most impressive feat is the 'Puszta Five': standing balanced on the back of two galloping horses, with three more reined in front. After the show, you're free to roam the grounds, visit the horses, look into the main barn, and check out historic carriages and traditional black Nádudvar pottery. Tickets are sold at the **Nyerges Presszó** cafe at the far end of the stud farm.

Wings of Desire

BIRDS OF THE PRAIRIE

Hortobágy National Park has some of the best **bird-watching** in Europe. Its flat expanse is aflutter with nearly 300 species (of the continent's 530), from grebes, herons and egrets to spoonbills, storks, warblers and kestrels. October is a great month to visit, when between 60,000 and 140,000 common cranes stop over on their annual migration. A top spot to pull out your binoculars is the vast network of **fishponds** (Hortobágyi-halastó) about 7km west of Hortobágy village. Walk or cycle along interpretive trails and climb the observation towers. From April to October, a narrow-gauge train shuttles 5km along the central dyke. The fishponds are one of three nature trails that require a park pass available from the visitor centre.

Walk on the Wild Side

MEET LOCAL WILDLIFE

To see wolves, jackals, wild horses, vultures and other animals that roamed the *puszta* before it was farmed, visit **Hortobágy Wild Animal Park**. The only way to get here is by a shuttle that departs from the village. Once at the park, you're free to walk around and explore on your own. For a chance to see the wild horses, however, you need to pay a separate fee for a guided Jeep tour. To observe rare breeds typical of the *puszta* up close, head to the small **Puszta Animal Park**, 2km south of the village. It's a fun place for kids of all ages, and you get to meet heavy-set long-horned grey cattle, the curly-haired Mangalica pig and the Racka sheep, whose corkscrew-like horns are particularly devilish.

GETTING AROUND

Several buses make the trip daily from Debrecen's main bus station on Külsővásártér straight to Hortobágy village. Trains from Debrecen stop about 500m north of the village and at the fishponds. The national park has no other public transport, so you'll need your own wheels (car or bicycle) to get around.

KECSKEMÉT

Lying halfway between the Danube and Tisza Rivers in the southern Great Plain, Kecskemét is ringed with vineyards and orchards that don't seem to stop at the limits of this 'garden city'. Indeed, Kecskemét's agricultural wealth was used wisely, and today it boasts some of the finest architecture of any small city in Hungary. Along with colourful Art Nouveau and Secessionist buildings, its museums and the region's excellent *barackpálinka* (apricot brandy) are major draws as well. Kiskunság National Park is right at the back door. Established in 1975, this disjointed patchwork of nine 'islands' of land protects such habitats as saline meadows, sand dunes, swamps and marshland that are home to a whopping 3100 plant and 8800 animal species, most notably birds. Fun day trips range from hiking in the sandy, juniper-covered hills to a horse show in the park's Bugacpuszta 'island' and a trip to a horse farm.

TOP TIP

Beyond Bugac, Kiskunság National Park can be quite confusing. To plan an approach, study the park's website (knp.hu) or drop into the House of Nature in Kecskemét for information. Staff also organise birding and other outdoor tours. The Tourinform office opposite Cifrapalota is helpful, too.

The Magic of Simplicity

MASTERPIECES OUTSIDE THE MAINSTREAM

One of the few of its kind in Europe, the **Museum of Hungarian Naïve Artists** (Magyar Naiv Művészek Múzeuma) gives the star treatment to an art form that's often dismissed as not being 'real art' but that deserves to be taken more seriously. In fact, many admired artists – Franz Marc, Paul Gauguin and Frida Kahlo among them – found inspiration in the folksy themes, skewed perspectives, childlike compositions and bold colours that characterise the genre. As you explore the galleries of this 18th-century building, pay special attention to the warmth and craft of Rozália Albert Juhászné's work, the druglike visions of Dezső Mokry-Mészáros and the bright and comical paintings of András Süli. Something extra special is the Magritte-like glass painting of János Balázs. Also keep an eye out for weavings by Anna Kiss and woodcarvings by Pál Gyursó.

Watery Fun

KEEPING COOL ON HOT DAYS

Kecskemét's main summer attraction is the **Adventure Spa & Waterslide Park**, a sprawling water park 3km southwest of the centre. It's loaded with fun things to do for kids of all ages – five pools and slides (including one with six lanes), ball courts, lawns and other diversions. A more subdued, grown-up ambiance rules **Kecskemét Baths**, a year-round, rather

BEST RESTAURANTS IN KECSKEMÉT

Bagatell Étterem
Casually stylish restaurant between the town hall and theatre serves inspired modern Hungarian fare. €€€

Vincent Étterem
Fine Hungarian and international food, such as marbled Mangalica pork and duck ragù risotto, justify the trip to the outskirts. €€€

Kisbugaci Csárda
Huge meaty portions paired with folksy charm, wooden benches and plates on the wall. €€

KECSKEMÉT

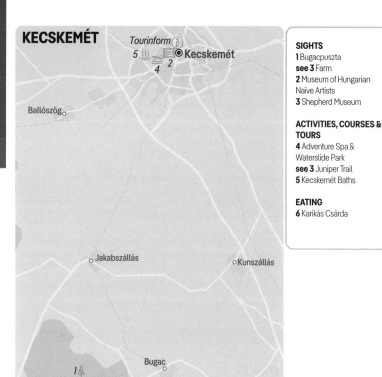

Tourinform
Kecskemét
Ballószög
Jakabszállás
Kunszállás
Bugac
0 5 km
0 2.5 miles

SIGHTS
1 Bugacpuszta
see 3 Farm
2 Museum of Hungarian Naïve Artists
3 Shepherd Museum

ACTIVITIES, COURSES & TOURS
4 Adventure Spa & Waterslide Park
see 3 Juniper Trail
5 Kecskemét Baths

EATING
6 Karikás Csárda

extravagant complex with thermal baths, swimming pools, full spa facilities and every wellness treatment known to humankind.

Horse Tricks & Sand Steppe

TRADITIONAL LIFE ON THE PLAIN

The most easily accessible 'island' of Kiskunság National Park is the **Bugacpuszta**, about 35km south of Kecskemét. The entrance to this park section is located at the **Karikás Csárda**, a traditional inn about 5km west of Bugac. Buses from Kecskemét go only as far as this village. A small booth has information and tickets to the park and the horse show, which for many visitors

WHERE TO STAY IN KECSKEMÉT

Boutique Hotel Center
Slicked up in 2020, this central outpost sports modern designer rooms and a free breakfast buffet. **€€**

Fábián Panzió
Super-friendly and professionally run guesthouse with homemade breakfast and spotless rooms wrapped around a courtyard garden. **€**

Aranyhomok Business City-Wellness Hotel
Full-service property with proper wellness facilities and rooms decorated with photos of city landmarks. **€€€**

OLD TOWN KECSKEMÉT WALKING TOUR

This 1.5km tour checks off the best sights in Kecskemét's centre. A great way to start is with *lángos* (deep-fried dough with toppings) and tea in the **1 market hall** whose stalls fill Tuesday to Sunday with fresh fruit and veg. Get here early to see it at its animated best. Make your way to Rákóczi út, the town's beautiful, tree-shaded central boulevard, where a grand white-columned former cinema now houses the **2 Leskowsky Musical Instrument Collection**. Pop inside to see, hear and play tarogats, tapsurs, tambourines and other weird and wonderful sound makers from around the world. Retrace your steps to have your head turned by the drop-dead gorgeous **3 Cifrapalota**, an exhibit space in an Art Nouveau palace with whimsical majolica inlays. The majestic white structure across the street is the Moorish-style **4 synagogue** turned conference centre. Rákóczi út culminates at leafy Szabadság tér, Kecskemét's park-like central square, where **5 Vincent Bar & Pastry**, a stylish cafe-bar with a tempting cake selection, invites a break. Carry on to the 14th-century **6 St Nicholas Church**, Kecskemét's oldest house of worship, whose lavish baroque interior is accessed via a tranquil courtyard. In front, on the square, stands the monumental bronze **7 statue of Lajos Kossuth** with a strapping male nude wielding a scythe squatting at his feet. It faces the sandy-pink, step-gabled **8 City Hall**, designed by Ödon Lechner in a striking mashup of Art Nouveau and folkloric elements and topped by tiles from the Zsolnay porcelain factory in Pécs. This tour ends at the adjacent **9 Great Catholic Church**, the largest Zopf-style (late baroque) church in the Kiskunság region.

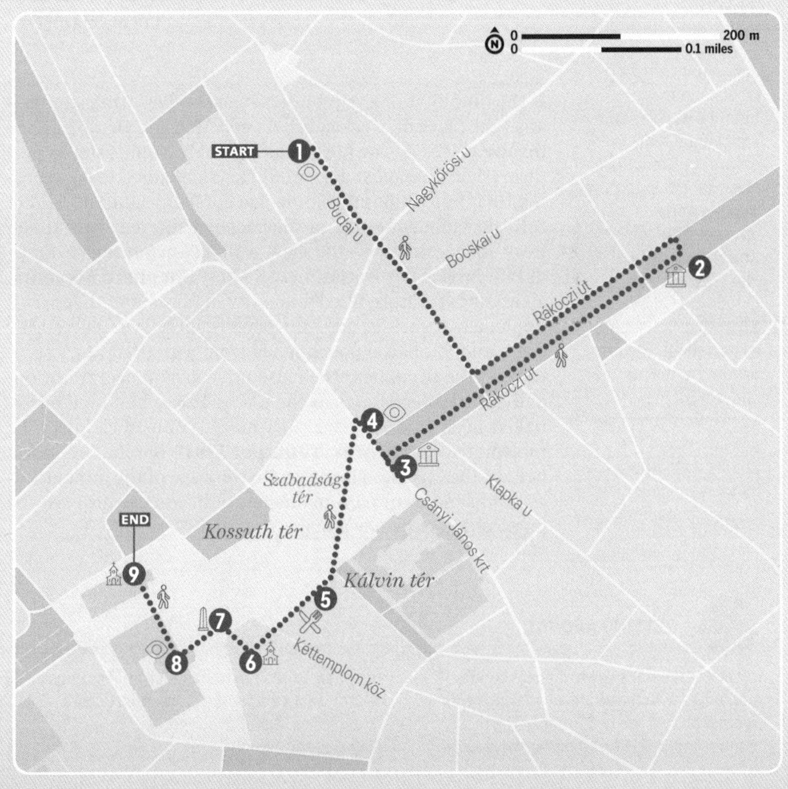

KECSKEMÉT'S ECCENTRIC MUSEUMS

Kecskemét teems with unique private museums. The **Boszó Collection** is an oddly fascinating assortment of period furniture, folk art, religious items and clocks amassed by painter János Bozsó (1922–98) and housed in a pretty 18th-century cottage. The granddaddy of all Kecskemét museums is the amazing **Folk Art Collection**, a dozen rooms in a 200-year-old brewery crammed with embroidery, weaving, woodcarving, furniture, textiles and agricultural tools from across the Great Plain. Music fans shouldn't skip the world-renowned **Zoltán Kodály Institute of Music Education**. Established in 1975 in a baroque monastery, it has a small exhibit devoted to the life and work of the eponymous composer and inventor of the Kodály method of musical education.

SKOVALSKY/SHUTTERSTOCK ©

Cifrapalota (p219)

is the highlight of a trip to Bugacpuszta. Performances usually take place on weekends between May and October. They involve *csikósok* (cowboys) making noble Nonius steeds perform tricks that most dogs would be disinclined to do, cracking their bullwhips and riding five horses around the field at full tilt while standing on the backs of the rear two. If you miss – or are not into – the show, walk 1.5km (or catch a horse-drawn carriage) from the inn to the tiny **Shepherd Museum**, a circular structure filled with stuffed fauna and shepherds' implements, such as carved wooden pipes, embroidered fur coats and a tobacco pouch made from a gnarled ram's scrotum. At the **farm** near the museum, you can meet traditional livestock breeds such as the Kisber Felver half-bred horse, naked neck chickens and curly-haired Mangalica pigs. The interpretive circular 1.1km **Juniper Trail** (Boróka Sáv) starts behind the farm and leads you to the edge of the juniper forest and sand dunes. From an elevation, you can still see the damaged wreaked by a major fire in 2012.

GETTING AROUND

All of Kecskemét's key sights are handily contained with the old town, making getting around on foot the best option. The most central car park is on Lestár tér, next to the city hall. Buses run from Kecskemét to Bugac, the closest stop for the Bugacpuszta. Hire bicycles at Tourinform, diagonally opposite Cifrapalota.

SZEGED

The cultural capital of the Great Plain and Hungary's third-largest city, Szeged is an embracing town that's easy to love. It's filled with eye-popping Art Nouveau masterpieces, grand public squares and ample green spaces straddling the languid Tisza River. A lineup of theatre, opera and music performances reaches its sonorous crescendo during the summertime Szeged Open-Air Festival. A burgeoning student population keeps cafes, bars and clubs bustling year-round. While justly famed for its traditional food (including a paprika-laced fish soup), a small league of next-gen chefs has also been busy sharpening Szeged's progressive cuisine scene profile.

It's hard to imagine that the watery fingers of the Tisza almost choked Szeged off the map in 1879, when the river burst its banks, destroying most houses, killing 600 people and leaving 60,000 homeless. The town bounced back and, as a result, today enjoys an architectural uniformity unknown in most other Hungarian cities.

TOP TIP

See Szeged from a watery perspective on a boat cruise departing down from Roosevelt tér just south of the inner city bridge (Belvárosi híd). Excursions offered by Sétahajó (hajokirandulas.hu) last an hour and take you northward to where the Maros River flows into the Tisza and then southward past the old town.

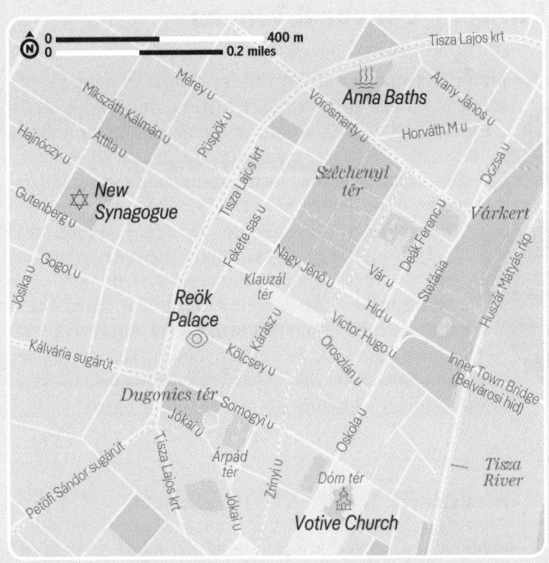

BEST PLACES FOR A CASUAL MEAL IN SZEGED

John Bull Pub
English-pub-style restaurant popular for more than three decades with proper pints and Hungarian pub grub. **€€**

Cirmi
Hipster gastro-pub with craft beer, good wine and the best burgers in town.**€**

Rudi és Fickó
This feel-good lair with mix-and-match furniture is a top spot on emerging Oroszlan utca. **€€**

Lángosgyár
This unassuming hole-in-the-wall in the market hall has plied generations of locals with generously topped *lángos*. **€**

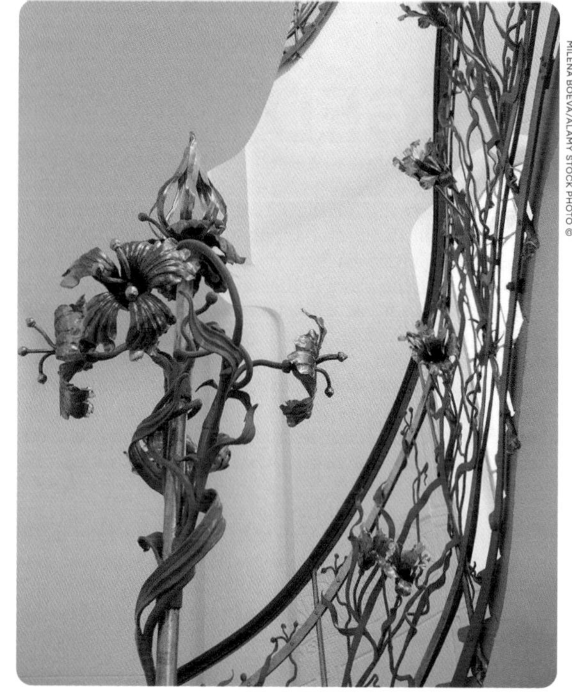

MILENA BOEVA/ALAMY STOCK PHOTO ©

Wrought-iron detail, Reök Palace

Flowers, Leaves & Waves

MARVEL AT ART NOUVEAU PERFECTION

A romantic symphony of lily-and-ivy motifs gracing an undulating facade shaped like a jutting ship's bow, **Reök Palace** (1907) is an architectural showstopper and the pinnacle of Szeged's wealth of wonderful Art Nouveau buildings. Designed as a family residence, it is considered the principal work of Ede Magyar, who kept his architectural studio downstairs. The interior is just as outstanding, especially the frilly wrought-iron staircase, which you can see on its own or in combination with a spin around the latest high-calibre exhibit of the **Regional Art Center**. Pop into the downstairs cafe for artisanal French confectionery by a two-time national cake winner amid eye-candy decor by Hungary's leading designer, Zoltán Varró.

ABUNDANCE OF ART NOUVEAU

Hungary is a treasure trove of gorgeous Art Nouveau buildings. Discover how the country became such an epicentre of the style in the Architecture chapter (p278).

WHERE TO STAY IN SZEGED

Science Hotel
High-tech boutique hotel with award-winning science-inspired design, living-room-style community spaces and comfy beds. **€€€**

Mozart Hotel
Retro-style charmer near sights and top restaurants with 15 rooms drenched in gold and red hues. **€€**

Dóm Hotel
Smart and central hotel with a popular in-house restaurant and relaxing Jacuzzi, sauna and massages. **€€€**

SZEGED'S TOP SIGHTS WALKING TOUR

This 3km walk bags key sites in central Szeged, starting at the neo-baroque **1 city hall** in Széchenyi tér, a square so large it's almost a park. Ogle the quirky, top-heavy tower and then meander north to **2 Gróf Palace**, Szeged's largest Art Nouveau building, decorated with floral mosaics. Stroll along the Tisza and across the park to admire the green-and-orange floral majolica ornamentation adorning the **3 Deutsch Palace**. Nearby, the neo-baroque **4 National Theatre** is easily recognised by its bulging semi-circular facade. Continue to the dignified **5 Móra Ferenc Museum**, a pillared depository of folk art, natural history and paintings by top Hungarian artists like Mihály Munkácsy. Make your way to pedestrian Kárász utca, an elegant shopping street, and turn left for the grand **6 Klauzál Sq** flanked by town palaces of different architectural stripes. Turn right for the **7 Reök Palace** (p222), Szeged's finest Art Nouveau structure that's covered with a mind-blowing green-and-lilac exterior. After a break in the downstairs cafe, retrace your steps to Kárász utca and turn right to marvel at the **8 Unger-Mayer House**, an Art Nouveau jewel by Ede Magyar. In front of you, on Dugonics Sq, loom the palatial main university building and a musical fountain where people like to gather. Follow Somogyi utca past the English-Romantic style **9 Black House** to Dom tér, dominated by the massive red-brick pile of the **10 Votive Church** (p224). The Romanesque St Demetrius Tower in front of it, a remnant of a 12th-century church, looks diminutive in comparison. Finish off with a spin around the arcades flanking Dom tér that shelter the **11 Pantheon**, with more than 100 busts that are a who's who in Hungarian art, literature, science and history.

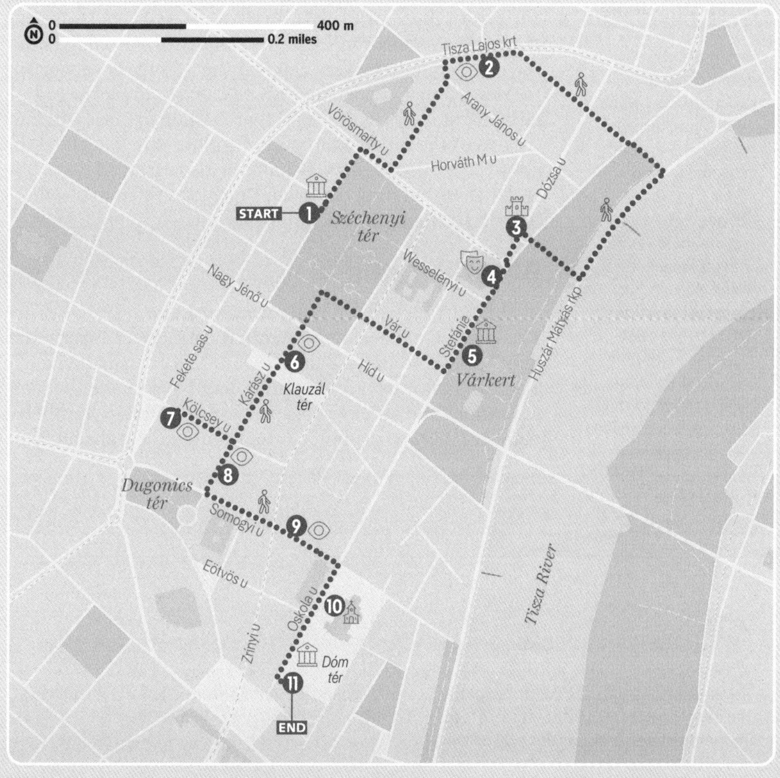

FINE DINING IN SZEGED

Szeged boasts a dynamic culinary scene poised to enter the big leagues. In 2022, two of its restaurants were listed in Michelin's Hungary guide. The most buzzed-about space is **Alkimista Kulináris Mühely**, a 16-seat 'speakeasy' that has foodies in a head spin over its intellectually ambitious Hungarian cuisine. Hit the bell to be beamed into this parallel universe where owner-chef Krisztina Katkó does double duty as a storyteller who guides you through the perfectly paced seasonal tasting menu. Each dish is like poetry on a plate and creatively paired with regional natural wines. Around the corner, **Alabárdos Étterem** has been a Szeged institution since 1967. Both the design and menu have of course been dusted off immensely to deliver bold culinary sorcery fit for 21st-century tastes.

Towering City Church

PANORAMIC CITY VIEWS

Szeged's landmark cathedral, known as **Votive Church**, is almost the church that wasn't. Planning launched right after the Great Flood in 1879, but competing designs, cost overruns, war, revolution and inflation delayed its consecration until 1930. The result is an architectural hodgepodge of Romanesque, Gothic and Byzantine elements with made-to-impress dimensions and a gaudily festive interior swathed in frescoes. Concerts played on the organ, boasting an astonishing 9040 pipes, are an aural delight. To climb one of the twin towers, enter via the subterranean **Votive Church Exhibition Centre**. It also houses vaulted galleries that chronicle the construction saga and showcase church-related objects.

Symphony in Stone

PEARL OF SZEGED'S JEWISH HERITAGE

It's impossible not to be awed by the beauty of the monumental **New Synagogue** (1903) and its dazzling blue-and-gold interior. An Art Nouveau masterpiece by Lipót Baumhorn, it is in use by Szeged's small Jewish congregation and also hosts concerts and other cultural events. Its most striking feature is the cobalt-blue stained-glass dome, which looks like a giant eye. Crane your neck to study the details: stars floating around the cupola represent the infinity of the world, while the pomegranate flowers capping the 24 pillars supporting the dome (one for each hour in the day) stand for the Jewish faith. Light filters in through ethereal stained-glass windows created by the artist Mano Róth. For close-ups, take the stairs up to the 1st-floor gallery. Baumhorn also designed many other gorgeous buildings in town. Download the tourist office's 'Jewish Heritage Szeged' app for details.

Blissful Baths

TAKE THE WATERS IN STYLE

The lovely, cream-coloured **Anna Baths** (Anna Fürdő) were built in 1896 to imitate the tilework and soaring dome of a Turkish bath. Rich architectural detail surrounds the modern saunas and bubbly pools. You can even fill up your bottle with free thermal drinking water from the fountain out front.

GETTING AROUND

If you're driving, park the car and explore the mostly pedestrian city centre on foot. Tourinform hires bikes, as does Bike Szaki, located just outside the historic centre, about 1km southwest of the Votive Church.

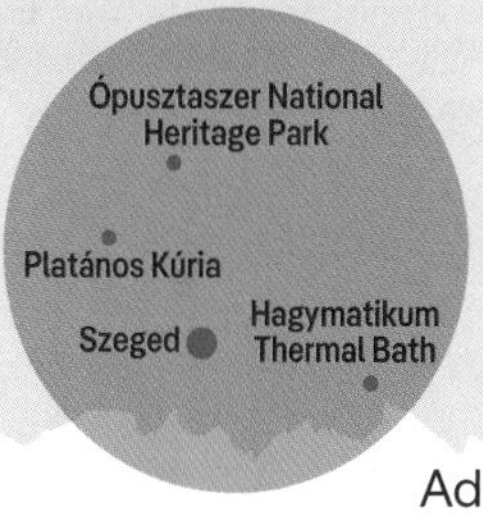

Ópusztaszer National Heritage Park
Platános Kúria
Szeged
Hagymatikum Thermal Bath

Beyond Szeged

Add a dose of nature and intriguing sights to your travels around the Lower Tizsa Valley.

Szeged's allure and abundant attractions easily keep visitors engrossed for a couple of days, but try to tear yourself away to see the other wonderful things on the menu in the southern Great Plain. Right outside the city, the southern reaches of Kiskunság National Park are a feast for outdoor enthusiasts, including the intriguing Lake Fehér, whose rich winged population make birdwatchers' hearts skip a beat. East of here, close to the Romanian border, Makó is home to perhaps the most beautiful modern bathing temple in Hungary, designed by the country's pioneer of organic architecture. History buffs should make a beeline to the Ópusztaszer National Heritage Park, an open-air museum punctuated by a fabulous panoramic painting.

TOP TIP

Be sure to taste the Tisza River fish soup *(halászlé)*, made with four kinds of river fish, onions from Makó and local peppers.

Csikósok **(cowboys) herding steers**

WETLAND WONDERLAND

A paradise for birders, **Lake Fehér** (Fehér-tó, meaning White Lake) was originally Hungary's largest saltwater lake. In the early 20th century, it was transformed into a 14-sq-km system of fishponds to control the flood risk in the Lower Tisza region. Still used for fish farming, the 'lake' is part of Kiskunság National Park, and a Ramsar Convention–recognised wetland where nearly 300 bird species have been spotted. Learn more at the **Tisza Valley Exhibition Centre** (Tisza-völgyi Bemutatóház) in Szatymaz and then head out on the 2km **Gull Study Trail** to scan the muddy, reed-fringed lake system for herons, grebes, swans, reed buntings and various warblers. Black-headed gulls have colonised Korom Island. During the autumn migration, the lake is a popular layover for common cranes, geese and ducks.

TIBOR BOGNAR/ALAMY STOCK PHOTO ©

Hagymatikum Thermal Bath

Giant Panorama & Open-Air Museum

TIME TRAVEL THROUGH HUNGARIAN HISTORY

In 895 CE, fierce Magyar warriors led by Árpád conquered the Carpathian Mountains, marking the beginning of Hungarian settlement in Central Europe. A millennium later, another Árpád, last name Feszty, depicted the country's genesis on a 120m long and 15m high panoramic painting. Called the '*Feszty Panorama*', it brings to life imagined and romanticised scenes from the conquest and is the crowd magnet of the **Ópusztaszer National Heritage Park**, about 30km north of Szeged and served hourly by bus. Roaming around this vast outdoor complex is a deep dive into Hungarian his-

WHERE TO STAY & EAT IN MAKÓ

Grand Hotel Glorius Makó
Hang your hat in this stately hotel with mod rooms and a restaurant; next to the Hagymatikum. **€€€**

Kelemen-Ház Étterem
Warmly decorated casual spot that doles out big portions of Hungarian classics along with pizza and burgers. **€**

Cafe Rocco
Brick walls and beams form a cosy backdrop for beer, pizza and Hungarian belly-fillers; good onion soup. **€€**

tory and the national self-image. To get up to speed on key events between the 9th century and today, watch the short 3D movie in the visitor centre. Your exploration of the expansive grounds could start with a selfie with Árpád crowning a pompous monument. From here, stroll past the ruins of a medieval monastery to the yurts of the Nomad Village, where you can try your hand at archery or dress like a Magyar. Beyond this is the Skanzen, a cluster of traditional rural buildings that illustrate aspects of daily life on the Great Plain at the turn of the 20th century. Some cottages contain shops selling traditional items, herbs and teas.

Make it to Makó

SWIM IN AN ARCHITECTURAL JEWEL

Makó, a small town about 36km east of Szeged, is famous for two things: the delicious Makó onion and the densest cluster of buildings designed by Imre Makovecz, Hungary's meister of the organic school of architecture. The boldest of the 10 sculptural structures dotted around Makó is the **Hagymatikum Thermal Bath**, Makovecz' final masterpiece, completed one year after his death in 2012. *Hagyma* is Hungarian for onion, a shape reflected in the many domes that create its distinctive roofline. The complex boasts a whopping 18 indoor and outdoor pools, nine saunas and the full spectrum of spa treatments. Kids love the slide pool and the Sherwood Pool with its playful surprises. Grown-ups like to marinate in the 37°C thermal pool or kick back in the cave pool with its otherworldly acoustics. Everyone loves splashing among the floral pillars of the Adventure Pool.

From Pig Farm to Puszta Haven

WHISPER-QUIET NATURE RETREAT

In Balástya, about 20km north of Szeged, a former pig farm has been rebooted as an elegant equestrian country getaway thanks to a horse- and nature-loving couple from Szeged. Called **Platános Kúria**, the estate picks up on an emerging trend in Hungarian tourism that caters for upscale rural tourists. The three sycamores *(platános)* that give this place its name front the wooden terrace of the six-room English-style manor house, complete with a common room where Churchill would have felt at home. Diversions include horse rides through the forest, chilling in the spa or sipping cocktails by the outdoor pool.

MORE ICONIC MAKOVECZ BUILDINGS IN MAKÓ

Hagymaház (Onion House)
Makovecz' first commission in Makó, this cultural centre references nature with two leaf-shaped towers flanking the steeply terraced auditorium where tree-shaped pillars hold up a ribcage-shaped roof.

Makói buszpályaudvar (bus station)
With its tree-shaped roof and cathedral-like wooden waiting hall, Makó's central bus station is one of the most beautiful in the country.

Zenepavilon
In Makó's music pavilion next to the thermal bath, a bird-shaped damper hanging above the central dome controls the acoustics.

GETTING AROUND

The Szeged region is well served by buses, including frequent services to Makó, Ópusztaszer, Balástya and Szatymaz from Szeged's main station on Mars tér next to the market hall.

Above: Tokaj (p243). Right: Traditional emboidery

NORTHERN HUNGARY

WINE, FOLKLORE AND FORESTS

Cultured towns, world-famous wine country and toy-town villages that cherish their traditions make Hungary's north tailor-made for travellers wishing to connect deeply with the country's spirit.

Northern Hungary is a tantalising tapestry of sprightly towns, sprawling forests laced by hiking trails, superb wine regions, gracefully ageing castles, thermal springs, traditional folk culture and Unesco World Heritage Sites. The modest mountain ranges of Mátra and Bükk form what is called the Northern Uplands. In a country as flat as a *palacsinta* (pancake), these foothills of the Carpathians soar above most of Hungary.

The main town is light-hearted Eger, characterised by gorgeous baroque buildings and a hilltop castle with a heroic history. From its ramparts, you can zoom in on the surrounding vineyards that produce dry, full-bodied Egri Bikavér, aka Bull's Blood, the region's signature wine. Just 130km east of Eger, petite Tokaj is the heart of an even more illustrious wine region with a pedigree going back to the Middle Ages. Grapes growing on its lush undulating hills make wonderful dry whites, but it's the Tokaji Aszú dessert wines that are the 'drops of pure gold' referenced in the Hungarian national anthem.

Northern Hungary is bookended by two sparsely populated rural areas where folk-art traditions have been preserved through generations. In the west, Hollókő holds fast to the craft of the ethnic Palóc people and some of their ancient customs. For an even greater time warp, visit the Bereg region in the far eastern reaches, replete with horse-drawn carts, dirt roads and tiny wooden churches.

THE MAIN AREAS

EGER
Cultured baroque beauty. p234

TOKAJ
Capital of wine. p243

Find Your Way

Hemmed in by Slovakia to the north and Ukraine in the east, northern Hungary is comparatively hilly and even home to the country's highest mountain (Kékestetö, 1014m).

Tokaj, p243

The hub of Hungary's most celebrated wine region, charismatic Tokaj is cradled by vineyards, two rivers and villages with a long Jewish heritage.

Eger, p234

This small-town beauty, which captivates with a famous castle, an enchanting old town and wine cellars dispensing 'Bull's Blood', is a gateway to Bükk National Park.

CAR

Unless you're sticking to the main towns and their immediate surrounds, having your own wheels makes exploring the remote villages, natural attractions and offbeat sights around northern Hungary a whole lot easier and time-efficient, especially in the

BUS

If you don't have a car, buses are your best bet to reach rural towns and villages, including Hollókő. The Volánbusz bus network comprehensively covers nearly every settlement in northern Hungary.

TRAIN

Budapest-Keleti has many daily direct connections to Eger. Heading to Tokaj may require a change in Miskolc. Travelling between Eger and Tokaj requires a change in Füzesabony. Change in Nyíregyháza if travelling to Vásárosnamény from Tokaj or Budapest.

Young woman in traditional folk costume, Hollókő (p242)

Plan Your Days

Drink Bull's Blood, roam medieval castles and baroque towns, and explore Hungary's folkloric heritage on a trip around this rural region anchored by charming Eger and Tokaj.

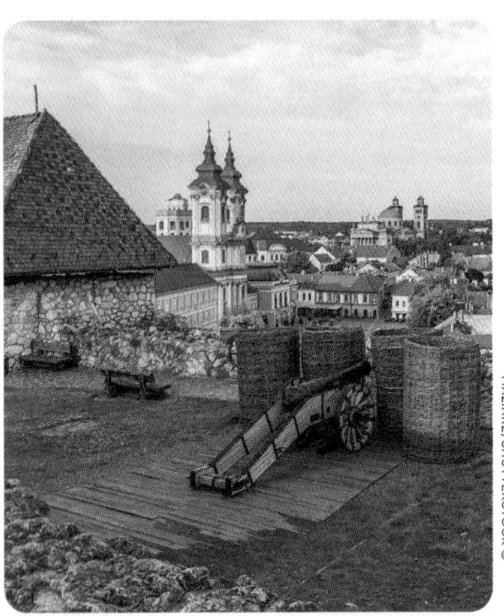

MAZIARZ/SHUTTERSTOCK ©

Eger (p234)

If you have only one day

- With just one day, concentrate on **Eger** (p234). Fuel up by joining locals in the market hall for belly-filling *lángos* (deep-fried dough with toppings) at **Lángos à la Rohlicsek** (p235) and then head to **Eger Castle** (p234) to go low in the underground casements and high on views from Szép Bastion.

- Follow our **Old Town Walking Tour** (p237) before taking a break at a cafe. Relax in the **Turkish Bath** (p236) and then sample Bull's Blood wine at **Bolyki** (p238) or in the **Valley of the Beautiful Women** (p238). Finish up with dinner at **Macok Bistro** (p235).

SEASONAL HIGHLIGHTS

Summer can get crowded, but it's also the peak of the festival season. May to October are best for hiking, birdwatching and other outdoor pursuits, while the grape harvest beckons in autumn.

APRIL

Easter festivals are everywhere, but festivities in the self-proclaimed 'capital of Easter' in Hollókő are the region's most riveting.

JUNE

The three-day **Tokaj Wine Festival** features concerts, crafts, culinary treats and wine from both top producers and smaller cellars.

JULY

Feszt!Eger brings pop, rock, indie and classical music to an outdoor stage set up at Bolyki, a quarry turned winery.

PIOTR GIBOWICZ/SHUTTERSTOCK ©, GTS PRODUCTIONS/SHUTTERSTOCK ©, FERENC SZELEPCSENYI/SHUTTERSTOCK ©

Three days around northern Hungary

- After a day in Eger, it's time to explore the nature of Bükk National Park. Drive or catch the train to **Szilvásvárad** (p240) and enjoy forests, wildlife and a waterfall while hiking the **Szalajka Valley** (p240), stopping for a lunch of local trout at Sáfrány Pisztráng.

- On day three, head east to **Tokaj** (p243), a small town whose world-famous Tokaji Aszú dessert wine has been all the rage since the days of Louis XIV and Voltaire. Sample this and other local varieties, including the excellent dry furmint, at wine cellars like **Rákóczi Cellar** (p244) before relaxing over dinner at **Toldi Fogadó** (p244).

If you have more time

- With more than just a few days, you have time for a deep dive into northern Hungary's remote corners and their distinctive folk art, costumes and traditions. The Matyó people around Mezőkövesd create motif- and colour-rich embroidery, a skill kept alive at **Matyódesign** (p241) in tiny Tard.

- West of Eger, **Hollókő** (p242) is home to the Palóc ethnic group and a 'living village' with a medieval castle and meticulously preserved rural architecture. In the **Bereg region** (p246) in the far northeast, you can admire charmingly naïve church murals and a cemetery with boat-shaped tombstones.

AUGUST

The 10-day **Zemplén Festival** brings the Tokaj wine region alive with a fun and festive lineup of cultural events.

SEPTEMBER

Tokaj-Hegyalja Harvest Days, held since 1932, is a three-day festival that marks the end of the regional grape harvest.

OCTOBER

The **Egri Bikavér Festival Days** celebrate Eger's famous Bull's Blood with special wine dinners, winery tours and gala events.

DECEMBER

Mulled wine and chimney cakes, carolling and concerts for Eger's **Christmas market** turn the main square into a winter wonderland.

Eger
Budapest

EGER

Everyone loves Eger, and it's easy to see why. Cradled by vineyards and brimming with ornate baroque buildings, Eger (pronounced 'egg-air') is a jewellery box of a town with loads to see and do. Soak in its laid-back sophistication and lively esprit on a wander around the cobweb of pedestrianised lanes in the historic town centre. Standing sentinel above Eger is a mighty castle, a symbol of national pride. It was here where brave local soldiers temporarily halted the Ottoman military advance into Europe. The Ottomans eventually conquered the town, which is why you can still climb a minaret and wallow in the warm waters of the Turkish Bath. Despite its charisma, Eger remains remarkably unspoiled by tourism, except perhaps in the famous Valley of the Beautiful Women, where you can traipse from wine cellar to wine cellar tasting the celebrated Eger Bull's Blood (Egri Bikavér) and other local wines.

TOP TIP

Wine aficionados should hop on the Dottika Eger 'mini-trains' at the main square (Dobó István tér) for the 15-minute ride to the Valley of the Beautiful Women. On Saturdays, the hop-on hop-off Egri Bor Busz loops around eight wineries outside the valley. The modest ticket price includes discounts for wine purchases or tastings.

BEST VIEWPOINTS IN EGER

Szép Bastion
Topped by three crosses, this bastion, also called Calvary Hill, marks the highest point of Eger Castle.

Eger Eye
Soar high aboard this 30mFerris wheel that's lovely when illuminated after dark.

Lyceum terrace
Pinpoint the sights after climbing 314 steps to the sweeping terrace on the 9th floor of the Lyceum.

Minaret
Brave a narrow spiral staircase to the top of this 40m-high spindle, a relic from the Ottoman occupation.

Symbol of National Pride

EXPLORE A MEDIEVAL FORTRESS

With its towers, turrets and bastions, **Eger Castle** cuts a commanding figure above the old town and is an essential stop on a visit to Eger. Even a stroll around the grounds and the views from the panoramic walkway are reason enough to come up here. Erected in the 13th century, the fortress had its finest moment in 1552, when vastly outnumbered Hungarian soldiers under the command of István Dobó fended off the Ottoman army's siege. Today, the castle is home to the **István Dobó Castle Museum**, spread across several exhibits. An ongoing restoration project has updated existing areas and opened up others previously closed to visitors. You can learn about castle history in the Gothic **Bishop's Palace** or join a guided visit to István Dobó's tomb in the **Heroes' Hall**. If you only have time for one exhibit, though, head to the **casemates**, fortified gun emplacements hewn into solid rock. Enter via the Dark Gate to arrive in a hall where displays and excellent high-tech videos vividly zero in on the history and construction of the castle. From here, you'll also have access to an underground tunnel system built in 1570 to allow soldiers to move safely between bastions.

Eger's 'Sistine Chapel'

OLD BOOKS AND GRAND ILLUSIONS

The **Lyceum**, Eger's main university building, is a baroque beauty in its own right, but its star attraction is the

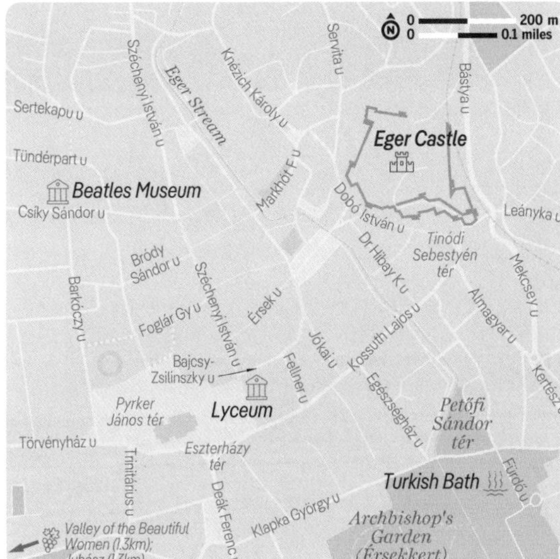

Archdiocesan Library, established in 1793. It holds 170,000 leather-bound tomes (the oldest from 1048), of which only a selection is lined up neatly on floor-to-ceiling oak shelves. Even more mesmerising, though, is the trompe l'oeil ceiling fresco that depicts scenes from the Council of Trent, a key event in the Counter-Reformation that updated Catholic doctrine. Note the lightning bolt setting heretical manuscripts ablaze. Bohemian artist Johann Lucas Kracker created this cunning 3D illusion on a ceiling that's only 1m deep. Ask for a free pamphlet to learn more. Above the library are several floors of science-related exhibits (separate admission), including a small astronomy museum and a hands-on experiment room. At the very top and reachable from the 9th-floor **panorama terrace** is the 18th-century **camera obscura**, an endearingly low-tech device that projects a live picture of the town onto a table with the help of lenses and mirrors.

All You Need is Love

AN ODE TO THE FAB FOUR

The Beatles probably never set foot in Eger, but that didn't stop two local lads from amassing an amazing collection of

TRIUMPHS & TRIALS

Eger has had several fine moments in history, but none greater than the Siege of 1552 when István Dobó and his motley crew fended off the Ottomans for the first time during the 150 years of occupation. The Ottomans came back in 1596, and this time captured the city, turning it into a provincial capital and erecting several mosques and other buildings, until they were driven out at the end of the 17th century. Eger also played a central role in the attempt by Ferenc Rákóczi II to overthrow the Habsburgs early in the 18th century, and it was then that much of Eger Castle was razed by the Austrians. The city flourished again in the 18th and 19th centuries, when it acquired most of its wonderful baroque architecture.

WHERE TO EAT IN EGER

Macok Bistro
Stylish and relaxed; inventive spins on regional classics using local ingredients; among Hungary's top restaurants. **€€€**

1552
Eclectic feel-good decor is the perfect backdrop for Matyás Hegyi's innovative New Hungarian fare. **€€€**

Lángos à la Rohlicsek
Best *lángos* in town; tucked away upstairs in the bustling farmers market hall on Katona tér. **€**

HOW BULL'S BLOOD GOT ITS NAME

The story of the Ottoman attempt to take Eger Castle is the stuff of legend. Eger's wine apparently played a significant role in the Hungarian defenders' success to keep the Ottomans at bay. It's said that national hero István Dobó fortified his troops' morale with a ruby-red local wine. When his soldiers fought on with increased vigour – and stained beards – rumours began to circulate among the Ottomans that the defenders drew their extraordinary strength from drinking the blood of bulls. The invaders retreated – for the time being – and the name Bikavér (Bull's Blood) was born. Read about the siege in thrilling detail in *Eclipse of the Crescent Moon*, a celebrated novel written by Géza Gárdonyi in 1899.

WANDERLUSTER/ALAMY STOCK PHOTO ©

Turkish Bath

memorabilia, now engagingly displayed at the interactive **Beatles Museum** at the Hotel Korona. Ask for a guided tour or head out on your own to follow a timeline of band milestones. Explore two floors crammed with videos, album covers, clothes, posters, photographs, and other flotsam and jetsam – and even pop into a Yellow Submarine.

Pampering Ottoman Style

TIME OUT FOR SPA TIME

Nothing beats a soak and steam at the **Turkish Bath** (Török Fürdő), where people have soothed aches and pains since 1617. Propel yourself into a state of bliss by taking a dip in the golden-domed **Big Mirror Pool**. It's the oldest and most spectacular of the bath's half-dozen pools fed with mineral spring water that derives its healing benefits from radon. Other glow-restoring options include saunas and a steam room along with a long menu of massages and treatments. Locals also like to drink the water – bring a bottle to fill up from the fountain in the small park next to the Turkish Bath.

WHERE TO STAY IN EGER

Imola Udvarház
Six sleek and stylish apartments perfect for self-caterers under the nose of the castle. **€€€**

1552
Superb boutique hotel in a baroque building with themed rooms inspired by milestones in Eger's history. **€€€**

Villa Florencia
Central guesthouse in an old building with modern beamed rooms, a plant-filled courtyard and free breakfast nearby. **€€**

EGER OLD TOWN WALKING TOUR

This 1.5km tour links Eger's castle with Dobó István tér, the main square, checking off key sights and hidden highlights along the way. Start below the castle in Kossuth Lajos utca, one of Eger's prettiest streets, lined with such architectural gems as the former Orthodox synagogue that's been rebooted as the 1 **Sándor Ziffer Gallery**. Crossing the little Eger stream soon takes you to the 2 **County Hall** (Megyeháza), a standout among the street's baroque buildings. Note the wrought-iron grid above the entrance portraying Faith, Hope and Charity before trying to find the stork holding a snake in its beak in the two even more ornate gates down the passageway. All three are the work of Henrik Fazola, who also designed the balcony and window grills of the nearby rococo 3 **Provost's Palace** (Kispréposti palota). Kossuth Lajos utca culminates at Eszterházy tér, dominated by Hungary's second-largest church, the mighty 4 **Eger Basilica** (Egri Bazilika). Although under renovation, you can still admire some of its beautiful altars, ceiling frescoes and chapels. Opposite the church is the 5 **Lyceum** (p234), the main university building with its breathtaking library and superb views from the 9th-floor terrace. Continue north to the baroque 6 **Archbishop's Palace** (Egri Érseki Palota), with an exhibit that lifts the veil on the day-to-day life of bishops. Don't miss the enchanting bird frescoes rediscovered in 2013 under 30 layers of paint. Head east to the heart of Eger, the lively main square anchored by a statue of local hero István Dobó and flanked by the sublime baroque 7 **Minorite Church of St Anthony of Padua** with a famous altarpiece by Johann Lucas Kracker. Finish up with a panoramic spin on the 8 **Eger Eye** Ferris wheel.

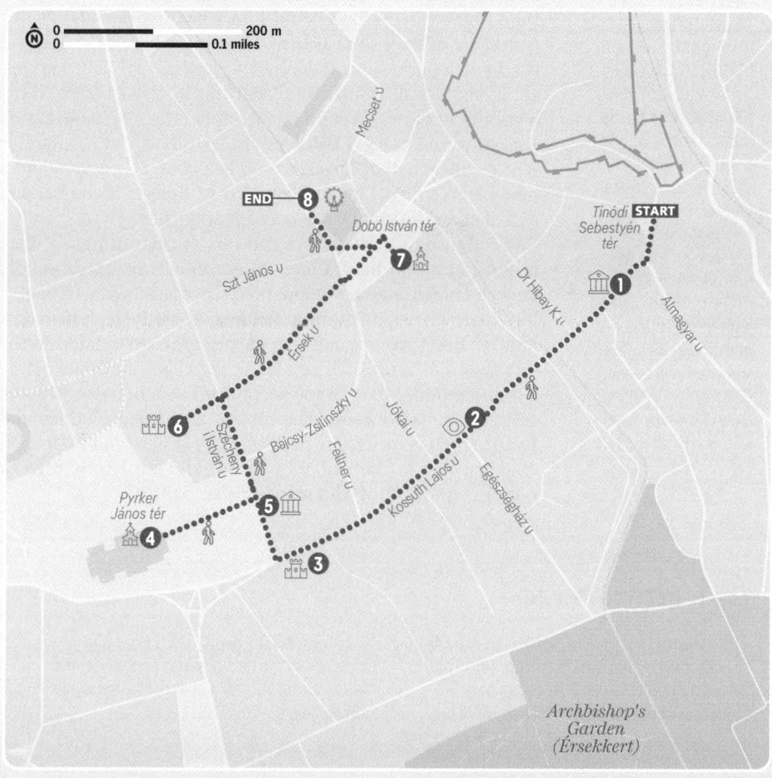

WINE BEYOND THE VALLEY

The antithesis of Eger's traditional wineries, **Bolyki** is set in a massive medieval quarry where the stones that built the city were extracted. Its charmingly eccentric owner, János Bolyki, has poured his heart and cash into creating not only fabulous wines but also a dynamic community space for events, parties and a summer concert series called **Feszt!Eger**.

Bolyki offers wine tastings and tours, but it's fine to just swing by for a glass. Even the whimsical bottle labels reflect Bolyki's unconventional spirit. In case you're wondering: the two giant rocks partly blocking the entranceway broke off in 2007, squashing a giant steel tank and creating a river of red wine in the process. On the city outskirts, Bolyki is a stop on the Egri Bor Busz route.

Wine tasting, Valley of the Beautiful Women

Bulls, Blood & Beauty

THE ULTIMATE WINE CELLAR CRAWL

A wine lover's fantasy come true, the evocatively named **Valley of the Beautiful Women** (Szépasszony-völgy) consists of more than 200 wine cellars carved into volcanic rock about 1km southeast of Eger's city centre. Hugging a horseshoe-shaped road and a park, several dozens of these *pincék* (cellars) welcome visitors to sample the local tipple. If you want to try a variety of wines, order a one-decilitre taste of each. Eger's signature red is **Egri Bikavér** (Bull's Blood), while popular white wines include Olaszrizling, Leányka, Hárslevelű and a new blend called Egri Csillag (Star of Eger). Of course, you can also order full glasses, carafes or bottles.

The choice of wine cellars can be a bit daunting, so walk around first and have a look. Most *pincék* are traditionally decked out (think dark wood, tiled stoves and wine trinkets), but some places, including **Juhász**, sport a sleek next-gen look. In fine weather, most people prefer to sip outside on the terraces. The ambience gets quite jolly, especially on balmy summer nights. To help you keep your brain in balance, some cellars also serve food. The bistros with picnic tables and picture menus lining the path into the valley tend to be a bit cheaper. Get to the valley by walking along Király utca or hopping on the **Dottika mini-train** (p234).

GETTING AROUND

You need only your own two feet to explore Eger's main sights, which are located in and around the Old Town. Drivers can park for free at Hadnagy Utcai Parkoló south of the Archbishop's Garden. Nearby Eger Bike hires bicycles by the half-day, day and week, and offers tours. The main taxi rank is on Fellner Jakab utca east of the Lyceum.

Beyond Eger

Dip into a pool of outdoor activities from hiking trails and waterfalls to a narrow-gauge train and an observatory in Bükk National Park.

At the same latitude as Burgundy in France, Eger is the hub of one of Hungary's most celebrated wine regions. It's most famous for the legendary Egri Bikavér, a dry, full-bodied blend of Kékfrankos (Blaufränkisch) mixed with other reds, usually merlot, cabernet sauvignon and cabernet franc. The wine region hugs the foothills of Bükk National Park, which protects one of northern Hungary's most inviting range of hills. It takes its name from the beech (*bükk*) trees growing here, and provides ample opportunities for hiking and other outdoor excursions. A popular destination is the village of Szilvásvárad, whose attractions include a romantic waterfall and the national Lipizzaner stud farm.

TOP TIP

The Egervár train station, north of Eger Castle, serves Szilvásvárad via Szarvaskő and other villages in the Bükk range.

Narrow-gauge train (p241)

THINGS TO DO IN & AROUND EGER

Barbara Balogh, co-owner of Nomad Hotel & Glamping in Noszvaj, shares her favourite things to do in her downtime. @nomadnoszvaj

Horse riding
When I need some peace, I go horse riding in the Bükk Mountains. There are plenty of ranches you can choose from around Eger, including Karap Lovastanya.

Spas
Some of the numerous spas in the area are open at night, and there is nothing better than soaking in hot water under the stars, for instance at Demjén.

Antique market
The third Sunday of every month is treasure-hunting time for me. One of the biggest antique markets is held behind the Eger Basilica. What you can't buy there doesn't exist!

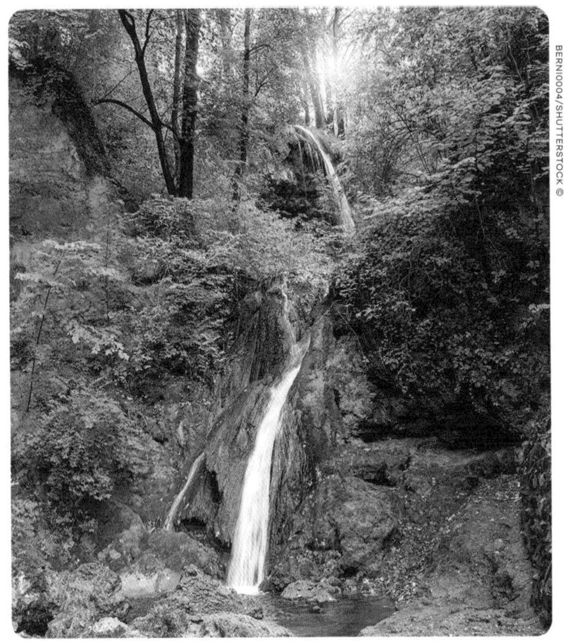

BERNI0004/SHUTTERSTOCK ©

Bükk National Park

Bucolic Bükk

FUN IN THE COUNTRYSIDE

An easily accessible natural escape, the Bükk range of hills is a gentle mosaic of upland plateaus, thick pine forests and abundant wildlife. Most of it is protected as **Bükk National Park**. One of the most beloved destinations among Hungarian families is **Szilvásvárad**, 30km north of Eger and served by train. The hillside village is famous for being home of the national **Lipizzaner stud farm** (Állami Ménesgazdaság) and for the natural charms of the **Szalajka Valley** (Szalajka-völgy). South of town, a 4km-long trail follows a placid alder-flanked stream to the lovely **Fátyol waterfall** that cascades down a dozen or so limestone steps. En route, you'll pass a wildlife park, a forest museum, ponds teeming with trout, and a rock spring filled with turquoise water. If you've worked up an appetite, sample the local speciality – baked or smoked trout, for instance at **Sáfrány Pisztráng** near the waterfall.

WHERE TO EAT IN THE BÜKK RANGE

Iszkor
Book ahead at this excellent six-table farm-to-fork restaurant in Mályinka, about 13km northeast of Szilvásvárad. **€€€**

Nomad Restaurant
Nomad Hotel's modern-rustic country restaurant with an exceptional breakfast buffet, light lunches and multicourse reservation-only dinner. **€€€**

Vadász Étterem
Been-here-forever tavern that serves hearty Hungarian dishes – game is a speciality – in Répáshuta near the observatory. **€€**

The valley is also served by a **narrow-gauge train**, which terminates above the waterfall. Many people hike up and return by train, or vice versa.

Caves, Glamping & Wine

A VILLAGE PACKED WITH SURPRISES

Just 10km northeast of Eger, the village of **Noszvaj** is a gateway to the Bükk range and a handy place to base yourself in nature while staying close to the city. Although it looks unassuming, the village packs in much more than first meets the eye. A well-hidden highlight is **Pocem barlanglakások**, a cluster of ancient cave dwellings turned artist colony. You're free to walk around and explore the caves and whatever art is on display. Many grottoes are themselves works of art, such as the Pentaton obscura, a deep cavity with mystical acoustics. If you fancy playing Flintstones for a night, rent a **cave apartment** at the adjacent Farkaskő Vendégház.

In fact, Noszvaj has become somewhat of a hub when it comes to eccentric accommodation. The artistic family that runs **Nomad Hotel** pioneered glamping in Hungary by adding romantic open-plan forest cabins with *Architectural Digest*-worthy design, as well as comfortable bubble tents, to its cosy country-style rooms in the main house. At nearby **Treehouses Noszvaj**, you can sleep in a sleek multilevel wooden vertical dwelling.

Wine drinkers should not miss **Thummerer**, one of Hungary's top-rated wineries, 2km south of the village. It produces about 25 types of wine, including an elegantly robust Egri Bikavér. Tours of the vast cellar maze carved into volcanic tuff are followed by a wine tasting with food pairing (book ahead).

Out of this World

STARGAZING IN THE FOREST

You need to travel only 30km from Eger to journey into space at the high-tech **Bükk Astronomical Observatory** (Bükki Csillagda) in Répáshuta. Opened in 2022, it's the newest attraction in the region, which was named a stargazing park by the International Dark Sky Association in 2017. At the hilltop facility, you can touch a meteorite, learn about the solar system with the help of augmented reality and holograms, watch a 3D film in the planetarium, peek through state-of-the-art telescopes or travel to Mars in the VR-room. Displays and audio are also in English.

EMBROIDERY OF THE MATYÓ

Mezőkövesd, about 25km southeast of Eger, is the hub of the Matyó, an ethnic group famous for its flat-stitch floral embroidery that originally decorated traditional dresses and is on Unesco's list of Intangible Cultural Heritage. On a mission to keep this age-old skill alive, a hip young woman named Rozi Váczi from the tiny nearby village of Tard founded **Matyódesign**, a fashion company that pulls the traditional craft into the 21st century. She employs several dozen Matyó women, most of them pensioners, who brighten everyday clothes – T-shirts, dresses, coats – with their colourful embroideries. You can see the magic happen at Matyódesign's sewing studio/showroom/shop in Tard (call ahead). For a full immersion in Matyó culture, including a hands-on embroidery session, ask Rozi about her day-long workshops.

WHERE TO STAY IN THE COUNTRYSIDE

Faluhely Major
Four season-themed rooms furnished with upcycled materials in converted sheepfold in Mátranovák. The host cooks soulful meals. €€€

Pénzpataki Vadászház
Near the observatory in Répáshuta, this quaint country inn also has a restaurant and guest kitchen. €

Villa Szilva Vendégház
Szilvásvárad guesthouse where wood-panelled rooms come with private patios overlooking a garden with barbecue equipment. €

Where the Past is Present

BASTION OF TRADITIONAL HUNGARIAN CULTURE

Every Easter, a gentle twist on the Ice Bucket Challenge takes place in **Hollókő** (Ravenstone in English), about 90km west of Eger. Unmarried men wearing traditional costume douse local 'maidens' clad in folkloric dresses with water in a time-honoured (if somewhat out of time) ritual meant to ensure their – yes – fertility. In return, the young women reward their 'tormentors' with beautifully decorated Easter eggs. It's the culmination of the famous **Hollókő Easter Festival** that takes over this fairy-tale village in the Cserhát Hills for three days of singing, dancing and eating. Cloaked in the rich folk-culture tapestry belonging to the Palóc people, Hollókő's main attraction is the quaint folk architecture of the **Old Village** (Ófalu). The whitewashed wattle-and-daub houses with carved balconies and overhanging porch roofs have held Unesco World Heritage status since 1987.

Although tourist-geared, it feels more like a living village than an open-air museum. Some cottages harbour shops selling local products; others house printing or weaving workshops, small museums (of dolls, dresses and local history) and restaurants. Cheese lovers should drop by **Gazdura** to sample the handmade gomolya, a fresh sheep cheese flavoured with spices from pepper to paprika. During the week, it's best to arrive in Hollókő by mid-morning at the latest since many places close early in the afternoon. There's parking just outside Ófalu, next to the tourist office.

BEST PLACES TO EAT IN HOLLÓKŐ

Muskátli Vendéglő
Top-rated cottage restaurant serving mouth-watering local dishes, best enjoyed in the flower-bedecked courtyard. Try the Palóc soup with green beans. €€

Mikszáth Étterem
Modern dining room at the Castellum Hotel offers the gamut of local and international dishes, including a wicked marzipan poppy seed crème brûlée. €€€

Kalácsos
Sweet little bakery that sells bread and baked goods, including *hókifli*, crescent-shaped pastries filled with nuts, plum or apricot. €

History, Hikes & Views

TRAIPSING THROUGH PALÓC COUNTRY

The nature protection area surrounding Hollókő is laced with gentle walks into hills and valleys. Nearly every visitor tackles the 1km stroll from the tourist office through the woods to **Hollókő Castle** (Hollókői Vár). Built in the 13th century, the imposing pile looks as if it was plucked from a fairy tale. Its exhibits on weaponry and heraldry are ho-hum, but the view from the keep across fields and forested hills without a trace of human occupation is giddying. For another fabulous view, follow trail signs to the quirky **Palm of God** (Isten Tenyere), a lookout point in the shape of a wooden hand, created by artist Benjámin Csíkszentmihályi in 2020. It's part of the Farkaskútvölgy horse park and riding school, and about a 2.5km walk from Hollókő's tourist office.

GETTING AROUND

Buses and trains serve villages in Bükk National Park, including Szilvásvárad. Noszvaj is served by bus. For Tokaj, change in Miskolc.

Travelling from Eger to Hollókő by public transport requires multiple changes – forget about it.

TOKAJ

Curled into the confluence of the Bodrog and Tisza Rivers, the town of Tokaj practically eats, sleeps and breathes wine. It's the hub of the Tokaj-Hegyalja wine region, the rock star among Hungary's wine-producing areas thanks to the world-renowned sweet Aszú dessert wine that has been produced here since the 15th century.

Built on the slopes of a volcanic hill, Tokaj is an intimate, picturesque jumble of historic buildings, nesting storks and wine cellars, and best explored on a leisurely ramble. The focal point of the pedestrianised Old Town is Kossuth tér, a square guarded by a church and framed by grand townhouses built by merchants during Tokaj's heyday in the 18th and 19th centuries. Cellars and restaurants along here and in the flower-filled lanes of the upper village provide plenty of opportunities to sample the tasty local tipple, while the rivers provide ample options for recreation on and off the water.

TOP TIP

Tokaj is one of 27 villages in the Tokaj-Hegyalja region that's sprinkled with hundreds of mostly small wineries. The Tourinform office at Serház utca 1 offers customised 'Wine Bus' tours that give you a behind-the-scenes look, plus a tasting session at three wineries (minimum two people, book four to five days in advance).

Grape Immersion

TOKAJ'S WINE MUSEUMS

For a deep dive into regional wine culture, pop into Tokaj's twin museums dedicated to all things grape. The somewhat old-school **Tokaj Museum**, in an 18th-century mansion built by Greek wine traders, leaves nothing unsaid about the history of Tokaj and the Hegyalja region. Aside from winemaking tools and an Aszú sorting table, you can also admire fine icons, medieval crucifixes, Judaica and exhibits on nature. Modern and interactive curation makes the **World Heritage Wine Museum**, a five-minute walk away behind Tokaj's old synagogue turned convention centre, considerably more engaging. Learn about 'wine diplomacy', the story of the 1811 Aszú and how to pair Tokaj wines with food before hopping on a stationary bicycle or behind the steering wheel of a fire-engine-red Fiat 500 for virtual tours of the wine country. Reduced combination tickets are available.

ASZÚ

Volcanic soil, sunny climate, two rivers and a mountain barrier combine to make Tokaj-Hegyalja Hungary's top-rated wine region, most famous for its Aszú. The sweet golden nectar is made from ripe grapes infected with *Botrytis cinerea* mould that almost turns them into raisins on the vine. Aszú can be blended from any of the six grape varieties grown in the Tokaj region, the most important being the indigenous furmint. Wines are rated per the number – from four to six – of *puttony* (baskets for picking) of grapes added to the base wines.

Made with Passion

TASTING TOKAJ'S LIQUID GOLD

Private cellars (*pincék*) and restaurants for wine tastings are scattered throughout town. Start with 100mL glasses – you may swallow more than you think! If you're serious, the correct order is to move from dry to sweet: furmint, dry Szamorodni, sweet Szamorodni and then the Aszú wines. The last, dessert-like wines have a rating of four to six *puttony* (a measure of how much of the sweet essence of noble rot grapes has been used). The granddaddy of tasting

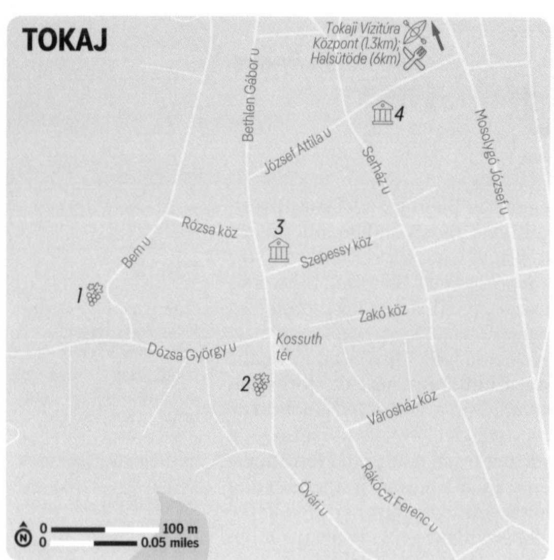

SIGHTS
1 Hímesudvar
2 Rákóczi Cellar
3 Tokaj Museum
4 World Heritage Wine Museum

BEST RESTAURANTS IN TOKAJ

LaBor Bistro
Trendy restaurant with a contemporary vibe serving pizza and updated spins on Hungarian cuisine. €€€

Toldi Fogadó
This upmarket outpost excels at duck and fish dishes (try the catfish) along with tasty meat-free mains. €€€

places is the 600-year-old **Rákóczi Cellar** on the main square (Kossuth tér), where bottles of wine mature in long corridors (one measures 28m by 10m). Uphill behind the church, **Hímesudvar** is a homier option with an atmospheric 16th-century cellar, shop and garden.

Boats, Birds & Fried Fish

WATER TOURING ON BODROG AND TISZA

From May through October, hour-long sightseeing boat tours ply the Tisza and Bodrog waters from docks just south of the Tisza Bridge. It's a calm and relaxing experience, but unless you speak Hungarian, the commentary will be lost on you. Better to paddle the calm waters under your own steam. Hire a kayak or canoe, for instance from **Tokaji Vízitúra Központ**, a water centre on the Bodrog, about 2km north of Tokaj. A popular destination is **Halsütöde**, a famous outdoor fish fryer in Timár with a terrace overlooking the Tisza, about 6km from the rivers' confluence in Tokaj. The water centre also hires stand-up paddleboards, organises birdwatching and other tours, and has camping facilities.

GETTING AROUND

No car is needed to explore compact Tokaj, so park it on the street or in any car park. Most of the car parks are free.

Sauska
Holdvölgy
Demetervin
Szent Tamás
Mád Winery
Tokaj

Beyond Tokaj

Lift your spirits by tooling along undulating country roads through a mosaic of bucolic villages and hills robed in lush vineyards.

Tokaj is an ideal launchpad for touring the 27 villages in the surrounding Tokaj-Hegyalja wine country, which was declared a Unesco World Heritage Site in 2002. Some of Hungary's finest vineyards blanket the hills around Mád, a placid town that is closely connected to the region's pre-WWII Jewish history. Its baroque synagogue is a shutterbug's delight and the starting point of a 150km-long Jewish heritage route.

Tokaj wine is so famous that it's even mentioned in the Hungarian national anthem. Its author, Ferenc Kölcsey, is the celebrity occupant of the cemetery in Szatmárcseke, famous for its boat-shaped tombstones and a highlight of the Bereg, an off-grid region near the Ukrainian border that's still deeply steeped in tradition.

TOP TIP

Book ahead for cellar tours and wine tastings, either directly at the wineries or through a site like winetourism.com.

Tokaj-Hegyalja wine country

RIPKA GERGELY/SHUTTERSTOCK ©

REUTERS/ALAMY STOCK PHOTO ©

Rabbis lead a pilgrimage group in Mád

BEST PLACES TO STAY IN THE BEREG REGION

Baráth Vendégház
Delightful Tákos guesthouse with four large, bright bedrooms and a sweet host who's an awesome cook. €

Kuruc Vendégház
Tradition meets mod-cons, including a pool and a communal kitchen, at this five-room charmer in Tivadar. €€

Hunor Hotel
Modern hotel in Vásárosnamény with retro-style rooms, a spa (Jacuzzi, sauna, indoor pool) and an excellent restaurant. €€

Grape Escape

WINE COUNTRY ON TWO WHEELS

Cycling is an excellent and increasingly popular way to experience the beauty and serenity the vineyard-blanketed rolling hills of Tokaj. Ask at your accommodation or a Tourinform office to arrange bike hire or go to **Zenit Vízibázis**, a riverside holiday complex across the bridge from Tokaj that rents bicycles and boats. Ambitious riders can tackle the full 70km loop from Tokaj via Bodrogkeresztúr, Szegi, Szegilong, Erdőbénye, Abaújszántó, Tállya, Mád, Tarcal and back to Tokaj. But even a shorter ride has its rewards.

A popular destination is Mád, some 18km northwest of Tokaj, where a top pick is **Holdvölgy**, a high-tech winery in an edgy building where tastings are set up like treasure hunts through the labyrinthine 600-year-old cellar network. Other

WHERE TO STAY & EAT BEYOND TOKAJ

Gróf Degenfeld Castle Hotel
Chateau-like outpost in Tarcal with elegant old-world decor, heated outdoor pool and superb wine cellar. **€€€**

Hotel Botrytis
Stylish, service-oriented boutique hotel in Mád with spacious rooms and a hot tub with garden views. **€€**

Első Madi Bistro
Charming roadside restaurant in Mád with a huge terrace and Hungarian dishes with international influences. **€€**

options include **Mád Winery**, where you'll feel like an ant standing next to rocket-sized steel tanks; **Demetervin**, which has a strict focus on organic wines grown in harmony with nature; and **Sauska**, which specialises in sparkling wine. Call ahead for cellar or vineyard tours and wine tastings.

Vineyard Pastorale

DRINKING IN DREAMY VIEWS

To feel like a ship stranded in a sea of vines, follow the path winding through the **Szent Tamás vineyards** (incidentally among the most prized in the Tokaj region) to the **viewpoint** at the top. Max out on the spirit-lifting 360-degree views of hills robed in rows of lush vineyards by coming up here just before sunset with a blanket, a bottle of wine and some snacks.

In Search of Miracles

TOKAJ'S JEWISH HERITAGE

Until WWII, the Tokaj region was home to a thriving community of Hasidic Jews, who first arrived in the 16th and 17th centuries from other parts of Eastern Europe and gradually took over the wine trade from Greek merchants. The few who survived the Holocaust emigrated, especially to Brooklyn, New York. These days, thousands of their descendants flock to Tokaj every year to follow a 150km-long pilgrimage route called **Footsteps of the Wonder Rabbis**, which links 10 villages and their synagogues, cemeteries and other sites related to their ancestors' history. The route starts in Mád at the **Jewish Cultural and Information Centre** in the former rabbi residence, where an exhibit fills you in on the history of Jewish communities in the region and Hungary in general. It sits right below the beautifully renovated baroque synagogue that's a genuine gem for architecture lovers.

A key stop is **Bodrogkeresztúr**, where Rabbi Yeshaya Steiner, the most legendary of the five 'wonder rabbis', lived in the early 20th century. Back then, Jews and gentiles alike came to him in times of need, seeking his wisdom, blessing or supernatural intervention. These days, the faithful visit his former home at Kossuth utca 65 and pray at his grave in the Jewish cemetery atop Derezla Hill.

SECRETS OF THE BEREG REGION

Márti Szegedi, a licensed tour guide in Tokaj, shares her tips for the Bereg region, where her grandparents lived. (tokajiseta.hu)

This region is full of hidden treasures, especially if you're interested in spiritual places, folk art, gastronomy and active tourism. It's a bit at the 'end of the world' but so worth discovering!

Route of Medieval Churches
The Hungarian part of this route, which also goes to Ukraine and Romania, has 37 churches.

Plum Road
Plum is the key fruit in the Bereg region. People use it for jam, dried plums and *pálinka* (fruit brandy).

Baktalórántháza Forest Nature Conservation Area
Keep an eye out for mushrooms, birds and badgers on a walk around this oak forest.

GETTING AROUND

A car is by far the easiest way to explore the Tokaj-Hegyalja region, but zero tolerance for drinking and driving is making the bicycle an increasingly popular mode of transport for those on a wine-tasting mission. Bus travel is limited and requires careful timing.

DRIVING TOUR OF THE BEREG REGION

To get off the beaten path, make a beeline to the Bereg region, a major hub of Hungarian folk art. This isolated pocket of quaintness is about 100km east of Tokaj and hemmed in by the Tisza and Szamos Rivers and the Ukrainian border. Hire a car and bring a sense of adventure for this 45km tour connecting five folksy villages whose ways of life are pickled in time and tradition. English is rarely spoken, and you may need to ask around to find the keeper of the church key. Start in 1 **Vásárosnamény**, the region's only sizable town and once an important trading post on the Salt Road. Swing by the Bereg Museum to acquaint yourself with regional cross-stitch, textiles, pottery and painted Easter eggs before heading to 2 **Tákos**. The main attraction here is the 18th-century wattle-and-daub Calvinist church with a coffered ceiling painted with blue and red flowers and an ornately carved 'folk baroque' pulpit sitting on a millstone. Nearby 3 **Csaroda** is home to a lovely 13th-century Romanesque church with frescoes, endearingly crude folk murals and pews decorated with birds. Somewhat livelier, with actual shops, 4 **Tarpa** lies 13km southeast of Csaroda. It's known for its plum products and has one of Hungary's last examples of a working 19th-century horse-driven dry mill. The final stop is 5 **Szatmárcseke**, famous for its intriguing cemetery with 1200 prow-shaped grave markers unique in Hungary. The notches and grooves detail information like marital status and social position. Native son and Hungarian national anthem writer, Ferenc Kölcsey, is also buried here. To get there from Tarpa, cross at the Tivadar, turn left (east) and carry on another 7km.

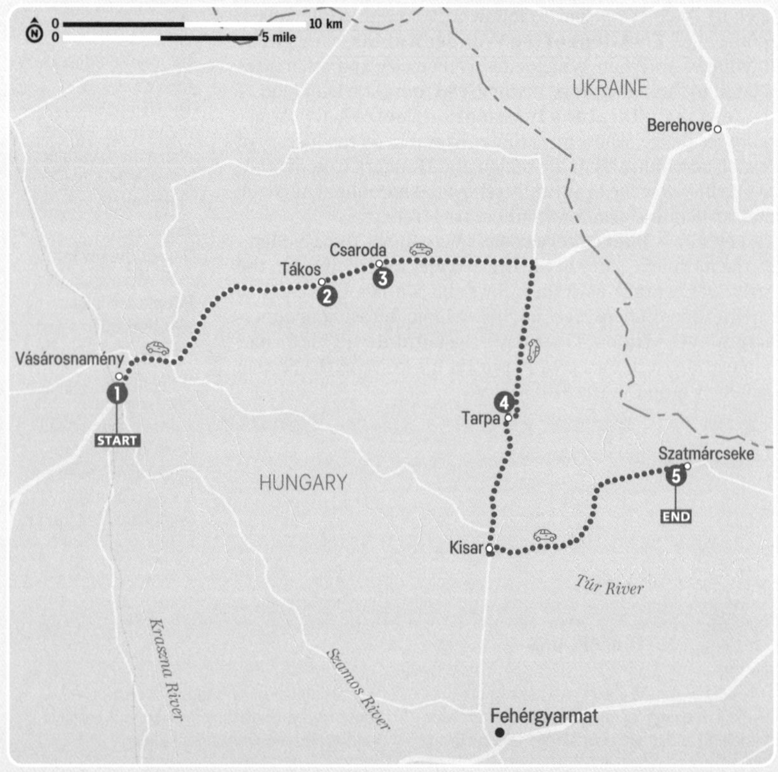

Church murals, Csaroda

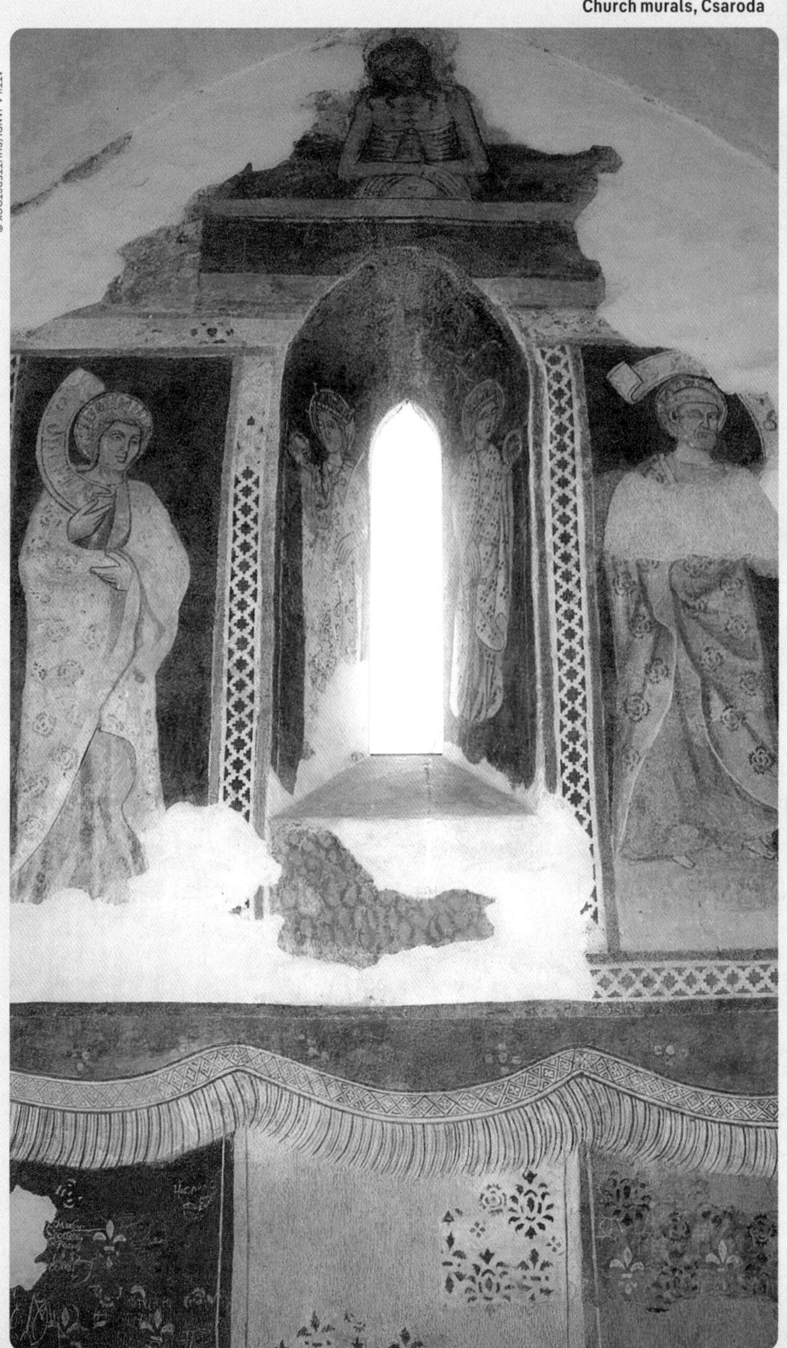

ATTILA JANDI/SHUTTERSTOCK ©

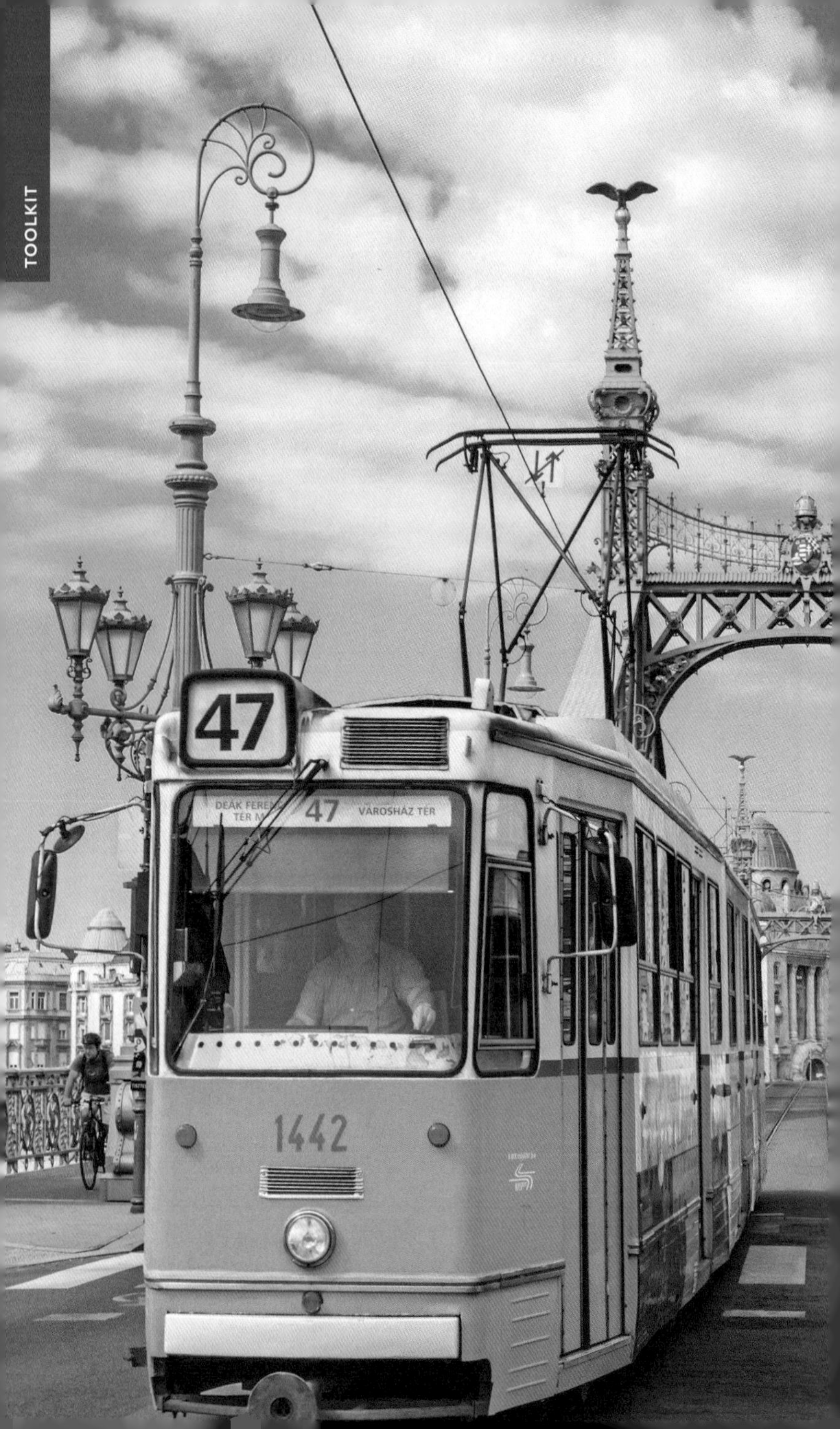
47
DEÁK FERENC
TÉR M
47
VÁROSHÁZ TÉR
1442

TOOLKIT

The chapters in this section cover the most important topics you'll need to know about in Hungary. They're full of nuts-and-bolts information and valuable insights to help you understand and navigate Hungary and get the most out of your trip.

Tram on Liberty Bridge (p68), Budapest

Arriving

For most travellers visiting Hungary, Budapest is the main point of entry. Liszt Ferenc International Airport is about 16km southeast of the city centre. Restaurants, cafes and duty-free shops can be found at the SkyCourt that connects the two terminals, as well as at Pier 1 at Terminal 2A. The main international train station in Budapest is Keleti train station.

Visas

EU citizens don't need a visa for any length of stay. Those arriving from outside the Schengen Area can stay for up to 90 days in any six months without a visa.

Currency

For various economic reasons, Hungary has not yet adopted the euro. While euros are sometimes accepted, it's better to pay in forint to get a favourable exchange rate.

Wi-fi & Mobile

Free wi-fi is widely available and mostly reliable, especially at the airport, hotels and cafes. Mobile coverage is widely available, and there are no roaming charges for EU citizens.

Tourist Tax

Most cities and towns levy a tourist tax on accommodation of around a few hundred forints (about €1 to €1.50) per night per adult. Under-18s aren't charged.

From Budapest's Liszt Ferenc International Airport

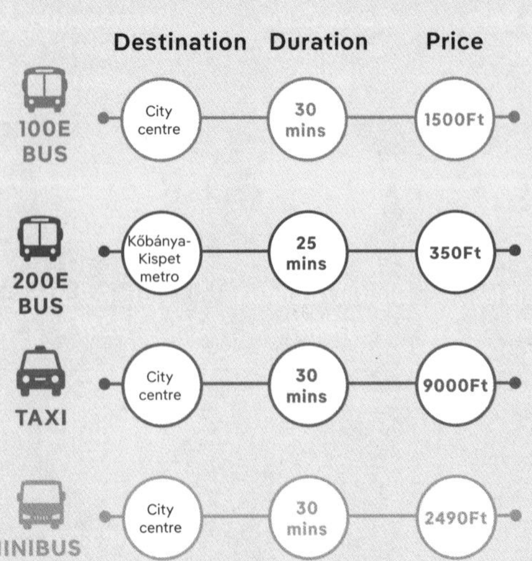

	Destination	Duration	Price
100E BUS	City centre	30 mins	1500Ft
200E BUS	Kőbánya-Kispet metro	25 mins	350Ft
TAXI	City centre	30 mins	9000Ft
MINIBUS SHUTTLE	City centre	30 mins	2490Ft

DON'T FORGET YOUR SWIMSUIT

Hungary is a landlocked country, but getting into the water is a must any time of the year. In summer, Hungarians flock to Lake Balaton, Central Europe's largest lake, reachable in two hours from Budapest by train. Balaton isn't Hungary's only impressive body of water: the world's biggest swimmable thermal lake is in Hévíz, where the healing water is 22°C in winter and 32°C to 38°C in summer. If you don't have time to travel far beyond Budapest, head to Lake Lupa for a quick dip in summer or relax in the capital's many thermal baths and pools year-round.

Getting Around

Hungary has no domestic flights; it's small enough to get around by train or bus. Public transport is reliable, and the roads are in good condition.

TRAVEL COSTS

Rental
From 15,000Ft a day

Petrol
Approx. 800Ft/litre

Train ticket from Budapest to Lake Balaton
From 4500Ft return

Bus

Volánbusz runs an extensive bus network. Buses can sometimes be quicker than trains for long distances and can also take you to some places trains can't. Buy tickets online (volanbusz.hu) or from the main bus station at Népliget in Budapest.

Car

A car is necessary only in rural corners of Hungary. International car-hire firms have offices in Budapest. Motorways marked with an M are tolled, and all vehicles must pay. There are no toll gates, so buy a permit online to avoid a fine (hungary-vignette.eu).

TIP

On public transport, EU citizens with student cards get discounts, and seniors over 65 from the EU ride free.

TICKET INSPECTION

Hungary has an old-fashioned way of ensuring everyone travels fairly on public transport. In Budapest, tickets have to be purchased and then validated. Machines are at all stations and on buses, and electronic tickets have QR codes. Armband-wearing inspectors can appear anywhere, even before you exit the metro. Conductors validate your ticket on board domestic trains. On buses, your ticket must be shown to the driver when boarding.

DRIVING ESSENTIALS

Drive on the right.

Speed limits are strictly enforced: 50km/h in built-up areas; 90km/h on secondary and tertiary roads; 110km/h on most highways and dual carriageways; 130km/h on motorways.

.00

The blood alcohol limit is 0.0 g/L.

Train

MÁV operates reliable services to major towns in Hungary. Budapest has three main stations: Keleti serves northern and part of northeastern Hungary, trains from Nyugati head to the Great Plain and the Danube Bend, and Déli serves Transdanubia and Lake Balaton. Tickets are available online (jegy.mav.hu) or from machines at stations.

Boat

Mahart PassNave (mahartpassnave.hu) runs excursion boats and hydrofoils on the Danube River from Budapest to popular destinations like Szentendre, Visegrád and Esztergom from spring to autumn (usually April to September). Balaton Shipping Company's passenger ferries serve about 20 ports on Lake Balaton.

Bicycle

Hungary offers endless opportunities for cyclists: challenging slopes in the north, much gentler terrain in Transdanubia, and flat though windy and hot (in summer) cycling on the Great Plain. Riding from Budapest to Lake Balaton is a particular highlight. Cycle hire is possible in all major towns.

Money

CURRENCY: **HUNGARIAN FORINT (FT)**

Credit Cards

Most restaurants, hotels, shops, car-hire companies and petrol stations across Hungary accept credit cards, especially Visa and MasterCard. American Express isn't always accepted. When travelling outside Budapest, it's wise to have another payment option on you just in case it's not possible to pay by card.

Digital Payment

In Hungary, all shops, restaurants, cafes and bars with a till connected to the internet are required by law to provide a cashless payment option for customers. Therefore, making payments by card or using a digital wallet on your phone is widely accepted across the country.

Tipping

Add 10% for table service at restaurants. Instead of leaving money on the table, tell the server how much you want to pay in total, including the tip. Many restaurants automatically add a service fee of about 12% – check the receipt or ask before paying – in this case, a tip isn't expected.

HOW MUCH FOR A...

Public transport ticket
350Ft

Museum ticket
3000Ft to 4000Ft

Pint of beer
700Ft

Ticket to Széchenyi Baths
6800Ft to 8200Ft

HOW TO... save money

Budapest Cards (budapestinfo.hu/budapest-card) are available for 24, 48, 72, 96 and 120 hours and can save you money, depending on your itinerary. They offer access to free and discounted activities, and some include extras like airport transfers or cruises on the Danube. If you're planning to travel extensively in the country, consider buying a Hungary Card that offers discounts countrywide. The card costs from 15,400Ft (24 hours) to 29,500Ft (120 hours; five days).

EXCHANGING MONEY

Money exchange booths at airports and train stations don't usually offer the best rates. Private booths and banks can be better – always check the 'buy' and 'sell' rates displayed. The bigger the difference, the less convenient the exchange will be for you. It's easy to find ATMs in major cities and towns, but some, such as Euronet, charge high conversion rates. The value of the forint can fluctuate frequently. Many hotels and guesthouses give their rates in euros. In such cases, you can usually pay in either euros or forint.

LOCAL TIP

Carry a little cash and some coins on you – smaller shops and ice-cream parlours appreciate it and might struggle to break larger banknotes.

Accommodation

Sleep Like the Stars

Budapest boasts all the big international hotel chains: Ritz-Carlton, Hilton, Kempinski, Corinthia, Four Seasons and many other five-star hotels housed in gorgeous buildings. The Four Seasons, for instance, has taken over the Gresham Palace, a true Art Nouveau masterpiece. A-list stars who've temporarily relocated to Hungary to work on a film often stay in these luxury hotels.

Stay at a Real Mansion

If you're a romantic at heart, love historic architecture or want to stay in accommodation with Downton Abbey vibes, search online for a castle hotel *(kastélyszálló)* in Hungary. These hotels are housed in impressive, elegant mansions that are reminiscent of castles or palaces. Northern Hungary has a good selection set in bucolic hillside scenery.

Overnight on the Cheap

If all you're looking for is a bed, Budapest has cheap hostels galore, but there are fewer in the countryside. Mingle with an international crowd on hostel-organised pub crawls, karaoke nights and themed dinner parties. In Budapest's party district (inner District VII), the quality can sometimes be lower. In the countryside, look for cheap guesthouses instead.

HOW MUCH FOR A NIGHT IN...

a *kastélyszálló*
From 25,000Ft

a hostel
From 4000Ft

a high-end hotel
From 100,000Ft

In the Boondocks

Wild camping is prohibited in Hungary, so you can't just set up a tent anywhere and sleep under the stars, but the country does have dedicated campsites. Some campsites have few facilities, while others are large and fully equipped and can accommodate camper vans. Some even have restaurants on their premises. Check camping.info/en/country/hungary for sites.

KOSMOSIII/SHUTTERSTOCK ©

Airbnb with Fin-de-Siècle Splendour

These days, Airbnb needs no introduction, but what makes it special in Hungary, especially in Budapest, is that you get to stay in historic buildings that have seen decades of urban life unfold. Some still hide bullet holes on their facades from the 1956 Uprising, while others are just so gorgeous that they regularly host film crews of big Hollywood productions.

BUDAPEST PARTY TOURISM

Nicknamed the 'party district' in recent years, Budapest's inner District VII attracts hordes of party animals and night owls every summer. Because party tourism is concentrated in this relatively small space, the constant noise, an increase in drug trafficking and public urinating have made the area unlivable for residents. But change is on the horizon. Nightlife spots in the district can stay open after midnight only if they adhere to strict rules set by the local municipality, which control noise and toilet use. Subsequent years are expected to see Inner District VII transformed into a cultural hub.

Family Travel

Hungary is a family-friendly country, with loads of attractions for the young, the old and everyone in between. Little ones get discounts on public transport and entry to museums and attractions, with some museums specifically geared towards kids. Many thermal spas across the country have slides, wave pools and designated kiddie pools, and most restaurants offer children's menus.

Enjoying Hungary's Waters

While children under 14 are not allowed to use the thermal water pools at baths – some like Rudas will not even let them enter – there are still ways to enjoy Hungary's abundance of water with the family. In Budapest, Római Baths is a family-friendly bath with fun pools and slides, while in the countryside, most major towns have spa complexes.

Facilities for Families

Breastfeeding in public isn't common in Hungary, and nappy-changing facilities aren't always easy to find. Major towns have playgrounds, and prams are widely used, so many restaurants and sights are accessible – more so in Budapest than in the countryside.

Getting Around

Children under six travel for free on Hungary's public transport network. Older kids with an EU student card get a discount. Families with small children or people who are pregnant will almost always be offered a seat or help with prams. If you rent a car, inform the company if you need a child seat.

Dining Out

Most restaurants have high chairs and a menu for kids that includes crowd-pleasers like chicken nuggets, fries and spaghetti. If you don't see a kids' menu, you can ask for a half-portion serving or a simple dish made especially for them.

KID-FRIENDLY PICKS

Budapest Zoo and Botanical Garden (p151)

Home to about 1000 species, the zoo is a great place for families to spend the afternoon.

Lake Balaton (p181)

The shallow waters of Lake Balaton, especially on the southern shore, and plentiful cycle lanes are great for active families.

Szamos Marzipan Museum, Szentendre (p162)

Imagine Madame Tussauds but with marzipan.

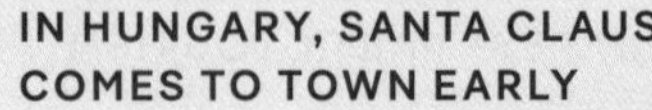

IN HUNGARY, SANTA CLAUS COMES TO TOWN EARLY

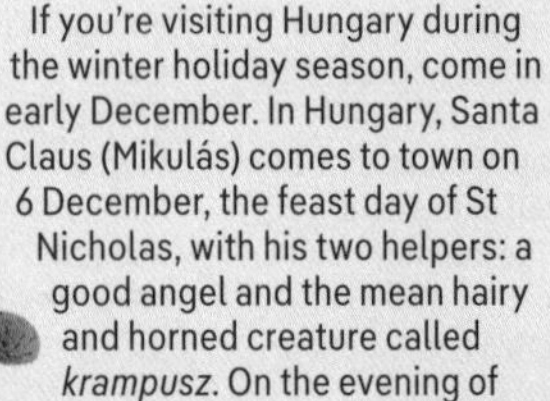

If you're visiting Hungary during the winter holiday season, come in early December. In Hungary, Santa Claus (Mikulás) comes to town on 6 December, the feast day of St Nicholas, with his two helpers: a good angel and the mean hairy and horned creature called *krampusz*. On the evening of 5 December, children shine their boots and place them on the windowsill, and Mikulás fills them with chocolate and small gifts by sunrise. At this time of the year, family-friendly events take place across the country and often even the real Finnish Joulupukki pays a visit from Lapland.

Health & Safe Travel

INSURANCE

Hungary doesn't have any serious health risks, but it's still wise to make predeparture preparations. The European Health Insurance Card (EHIC) allows EU citizens to receive emergency state-provided healthcare. Foreigners are entitled to first-aid and ambulance services only when they have suffered an accident and require immediate medical attention; follow-up treatment and medicine must be paid for.

Drugs

Hungary has some of the harshest drug laws in the EU, and all drugs are of the same 'class', meaning the same rules that apply for heroin also apply for cannabis. Purchasing, consuming and possessing illegal drugs are all criminal offences, and foreigners caught are held accountable to the same standards as locals. Avoid people selling questionable substances in Budapest's party district (inner District VII).

Petty Crime

Theft and other types of petty crime aren't that common in Hungary but can happen anywhere. Be mindful of your belongings in crowded areas and on public transport. Don't leave your bike unlocked and avoid people aggressively selling stuff on the street. Thefts from hire cars are not uncommon. Don't leave anything of value, including luggage, inside the car.

TAP WATER

Hungary has heaps of clean water, and tap water is safe to drink anywhere in the country and is high quality according to EU standards.

USEFUL NUMBERS

Ambulance	Police	Fire service	Central help
☎104	☎107	☎105	☎112

Scams to Avoid

Dodgy restaurants and clubs in Budapest's party district (inner District VII) may overcharge foreigners, so check prices before you order. Don't hail taxis off the street and avoid the seemingly friendly touts waiting outside popular party destinations – call a reputable company instead. If a public transport ticket machine is not giving back coins, check if the coin slot has tape over it.

SOLO TRAVEL & WOMEN TRAVELLERS

Hungary is a popular and generally safe destination for solo travellers. Solo travellers in Budapest have a massive array of budget-friendly and social accommodation options, including hostels that organise pub crawls and other outings. Women travelling alone should not encounter any particular problems besides some mild local machismo.

Food, Drink & Nightlife

When to Eat

Reggeli (breakfast, 8am to 10am) is traditionally hearty. Sweet and savoury options fill the table.

Ebéd (lunch, noon to 2pm) is a three-course meal consisting of soup, a main dish and dessert. Many restaurants offer cheap lunch specials.

Vacsora (dinner, 7pm to 9pm) can be a larger meal if the family sits together or simply leftovers from lunch or a light meal.

MENU DECODER

Allergének Allergens
Bárány Lamb
Bor Wine (*fehér* means white; *vörös* is red)
Borjú Veal
Csirke Chicken
Desszert Sweets such as ice cream, cakes or *palacsinta* (pancakes)
Disznó Pork
Ebédmenü Lunch special
Előétel Entrée, often cold and a small serving
Fél adag Half portion
Főétel Mains, generally meaty
Főzelék Vegetable roux served with meatballs, sausages or fried eggs
Gyerekmenü Kids' menu
Hal Fish
Kacsa Duck
Köret Side dish
Leves Soup; traditionally consumed as a first course
Marha Beef
Pörkölt Stew made of beef, veal, chicken or game
Pulyka Turkey
Sör Beer (small beer is *pohár*; a pint is *korsó*)
Szervízdíj Service fee; sometimes it is automatically added to restaurant bills
Üdítő Soft drinks
Vegetáriánus Vegetarian

Where to Eat

Cukrászda Cake shop or confectioner with cake and other sweet treats.

Csárda A rustic countryside inn that serves hearty portions of home-style cooking, often accompanied by live music.

Étterem Restaurant, ranging from inexpensive to Michelin-starred establishments.

Étkezde Canteen offering simple and inexpensive Hungarian dishes.

Kávéház Coffee house. Great for coffee and cake or a more filling meal.

Pékség Bakery offering fresh local pastries.

Vendéglő Restaurant that serves inexpensive regional dishes or home-style cooking.

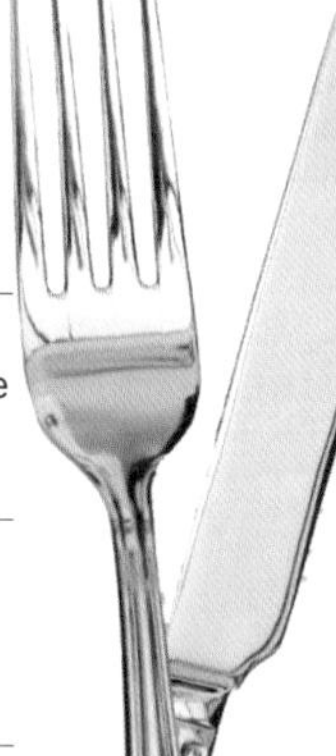

HOW TO... mix fröccs

Hungarians are serious about their wine, perhaps no surprise when the country makes so much of it. But when you see locals buying a bottle, you'll probably also spot fizzy mineral water in their shopping basket, which is used for making *fröccs* (wine spritzer). One of the ways to a Hungarian's heart is knowing how to mix a good *fröccs*. *Fröccs* is most often made with white or rosé wine. A *kisfröccs* (small spritzer) is 100mL of wine and the same amount of sparkling water. A *nagyfröccs* (big spritzer) is double the wine and 100mL of water. A *hosszúlépés* ('long step') is 100mL of wine and 200mL of water, while a *házmester* ('janitor') is 300mL of wine and 200mL of water. Knowing these four combinations will make you an honorary Hungarian.

HOW MUCH FOR A...

Lunch special
2500 to 3500Ft

Cup of coffee
550Ft

Dinner at a Michelin-starred restaurant
50,000 to 80,000Ft

Restaurant breakfast
2000 to 4000Ft

Kürtőskalács (chimney cake)
1000 to 1500Ft

Craft beer
2000 to 4000Ft

Small glass of wine
1000 to 1500Ft

HOW TO... drink pálinka

If you mingle with Hungarians, it won't be long before the country's most revered beverage, *pálinka*, makes an appearance and you're offered a glass, often from a homemade bottle. Be it a celebration, a funeral or just a regular Tuesday, Hungarians need no excuse to neck a shot of it. They religiously believe in *pálinka*'s healing powers and maintain that it can cure anything from toothaches to upset stomachs and sore throats.

Pálinka is a fruit brandy with an alcohol content ranging from 37.5% to 86%. The most common fruits used are plums, cherries, grapes, pears, apples and peaches, but others can be used too. The only unbreakable rules are that *pálinka* must be fermented exclusively from fruit grown in Hungary, not from concentrates, and must be distilled and bottled in the country.

There are several different types of *pálinka*, distinguished by the fruity base ingredient, the production method and the ageing process: *kisüsti* ('small pot') is double-distilled *pálinka* made in a small copper pot; *érlelt* ('aged') is kept for a minimum of three months in an oak or mulberry barrel; *ágyas* ('bedded') rests for a minimum of three months on a layer of ripe or dried fruit; and *törköly* ('grape') is made from grape pomace.

Eight localities have been granted their own Protected Designation of Origin (PDO), including plum from Szatmár, apricot from Kecskemét and apple from Szabolcs.

The Hungarian Spirit

Pálinka should be served at room temperature in a tulip-shaped glass – round at the bottom, narrow at the rim. Full glasses should be clinked, sipped and savoured, although locals will likely challenge you to gulp it in one go.

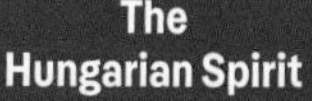

PAPRIKA, HUNGARY'S BELOVED INGREDIENT

Paprika, an essential ingredient in Hungarian cuisine, is a spice made from drying and then grinding the pods of different types of *capsicum annuum* peppers. It's cultivated primarily around the cities of Szeged and Kalocsa on Hungary's Great Plain. Between 8000 and 10,000 tonnes of the spice are produced annually, more than half of which is exported. Hungarians each consume about 500g of the red stuff annually – it is richer in vitamin C than citrus fruits (and it was a Hungarian who discovered the existence of vitamin C from paprika!). Not only is paprika used when preparing dishes, but it also appears on restaurant tables as a condiment beside the salt and pepper shakers at any respectable establishment.

Paprika is that secret ingredient that gives Hungarian dishes their characteristic taste and colour. Almost all Hungarian recipes call for paprika – not just a sprinkle but several tablespoons – including *gulyás* (goulash), *pörkölt* (stew), *lecsó* (ratatouille) and *halászlé* (fish soup). Should you need an extra dose of it when your restaurant dish arrives, you can sprinkle on even more. You can add paprika to pretty much anything from soups to sauces, while some cold dishes can also do with a touch. If you want to take some paprika home with you from a Hungarian market, you'll usually find it sold in half-kilo unlabelled plastic bags. Choose between *édes* (sweet) or *csipős* (hot).

Responsible Travel

Climate Change & Travel

It's impossible to ignore the impact we have when travelling, and the importance of making changes where we can. Lonely Planet urges all travellers to engage with their travel carbon footprint. There are many carbon calculators online that allow travellers to estimate the carbon emissions generated by their journey; try resurgence.org/resources/carbon-calculator.html. Many airlines and booking sites offer travellers the option of offsetting the impact of greenhouse gas emissions by contributing to climate-friendly initiatives around the world. We continue to offset the carbon footprint of all Lonely Planet staff travel, while recognising this is a mitigation more than a solution.

Spread Out Your Visit

Budapest bears the brunt of tourism to Hungary, with Lake Balaton in second place. Plan your trip outside July, August and Christmas, and spend some time outside the capital to experience Hungarian hospitality in the countryside.

Get Around on Two Wheels

Hungary has great cycling routes, including the Danube Cycle Path, which follows the river from its source in Germany through Budapest to Romania and beyond. In all major Hungarian towns, you can hire bikes to get around.

Ditch the Plane

Budapest is connected to major cities in nearby countries by train, including Vienna, Bratislava, Munich, Berlin and Prague. Local trains can also take you around the country to explore Hungary beyond Budapest.

Budapest has market halls full of fresh produce, and in the countryside, farmers markets take over towns' main squares on weekends. Pick up honey, Hungarian sausages and more for a picnic or to take home.

On Sundays, WAMP Design Centre sets up shop at Bálna Budapest, a striking glass shopping centre in Southern Pest, where Hungarian designers sell tote bags, jewellery, clothes, stationery, art and more.

Cut down on paper waste by purchasing tickets on the Budapest Go app – where you can also plan your journeys – the MÁV site (mavcsoport.hu) for trains and the Volánbusz site (volanbusz.hu) for buses.

SERGIY ZAVGORODNY/SHUTTERSTOCK ©, GSDESIGN/SHUTTERSTOCK ©. OPPOSITE PAGE: JACZIA/SHUTTERSTOCK ©

Hungarian is a wonderfully unique language. Learning just a few words goes a long way, especially in the countryside. For some useful words and phrases, see the Language section of the Toolkit (p268).

Get to Know All of Hungary in One Place

Visit Szentendre's Hungarian Open-Air Ethnographic Museum (p160) to see folk architecture and traditional ways of life from 11 regions of Hungary in one place. Walk or hire a bike on-site to explore the reconstructed buildings and villages.

Visit National Parks

Hungary's landscape is gentle rather than dramatic, but its flora and fauna are outstandingly diverse. See this biodiversity at the country's 10 large national parks, many of which are also Unesco World Heritage Sites.

Drool over freshly baked local pastries at a friendly neighbourhood bakery.

Grab a drink at Premier Kultcafé in Budapest, which hires staff with disabilities.

40%

Hungary passed a law in 2020 that requires reducing carbon emissions by at least 40% by 2030 compared with 1990 levels. The country aims to be carbon neutral by 2050.

Stay Sustainably

Choose locally run accommodation options across the country and ask about their environmental practices. Support businesses that are cutting down on single-use plastic and water waste, as well as those that have sustainability certifications from recognised organisations.

RESOURCES

bikemaffia.com
Philanthropic organisation on wheels.

worldpackers.com
International website for volunteering opportunities.

aiesec.org
Runs volunteer programmes in Hungary of varying lengths.

Use local guides to get to know Hungary, whether that's a walking tour of Budapest or an excursion in a national park. Hearing stories from local people brings Hungary to life, and supports small businesses and entrepreneurs.

LGBTIQ+ Travellers

Compared with Western European countries, Hungary's LGBTIQ+ scene has a long way to go. The government enacts anti-LGBTIQ+ laws, and negative attitudes in older generations linger, but young people are generally open and accepting. In the countryside, the LGBTIQ+ community keeps a low profile, but the capital has a lively and diverse gay scene with bars, events and parties.

Budapest Pride

Budapest Pride, Hungary's biggest LGBTIQ+ event, usually takes place in July, filling the capital with events, workshops, talks and parties for the whole month. The festivities close with a well-attended colourful parade that brightens up the city's streets and squares, leading to a rave Rainbow Party at Budapest Park. Recent Pride events have passed without incident, but some counter-events in the past have led to confrontation. Budapest Pride organisers work closely with the police to ensure safety, and security volunteers are present at the events.

GAY-FRIENDLY BARS

While Budapest doesn't have a 'rainbow district' like other European capitals, bars welcome all, and some are specifically gay-friendly. Local favourite **Alterego** stages drag shows, while **Why Not Café** is a more intimate venue with a riverfront terrace. The welcoming atmosphere of **Polyglon** is always conducive for a party.

PARTY!

Even without a huge range of LGBTIQ-specific spots, Budapest bars host regular themed parties. **Garçons** is the biggest of the bunch, held at well-known Budapest venues monthly. **Hello** is a gay pop party, **Ludus** is LGBTIQ-themed, and **WOW** (Women on Women) offers a wild night to the hippest queers.

Cultural Events

Humen Fesztivál (humenfesztival.hu) is a cultural festival with theatrical and contemporary dance performances, art exhibitions and other events focusing on social acceptance. It usually takes place in September.

Labrisz (labrisz.hu) is an association that provides a safe space for LGBTIQ+ women with the aim of building community. They organise regular events, including talks, film screenings and game nights.

AN OUTDATED MINDSET

While Budapest has a solid gay scene and gay visitors generally have a good time in Hungary, the country's stance on LGBTIQ+ issues is out of step with many other parts of Europe. The Hungarian government strongly promotes a conservative Christian agenda and imposes laws against the local LGBTIQ+ community. While travellers aren't generally affected, be aware that PDA may attract unwanted attention, especially outside of Budapest.

Did you know?

A Hungarian coined the term 'homosexuality'. Historians say the word was first used by Karl-Maria Kertbeny, a Hungarian journalist, in secret correspondence with fellow queer activist Karl Heinrich Ulrichs.

Accessible Travel

Hungary has been making strides to make public areas and facilities more accessible for travellers with disabilities. Wheelchair ramps, accessible toilets and audible traffic signals are becoming commonplace in the cities, but more improvements are needed to make the country truly accessible for all.

Accessible Sightseeing in Budapest

Most major sights in Budapest are fully accessible. Cobblestone streets in the Castle District might be problematic, but Fisherman's Bastion, Matthias Church and the Hungarian National Gallery are accessible.

Airport

Request assistance at least 48 hours before departure on the airport's website (bud.hu). Assistance call points in the terminals are equipped with cameras, microphones, and buttons for hearing- and visually impaired passengers.

Accommodation

Budget hotels are not always accessible, but newer and larger ones usually are. Many Budapest apartment buildings have lifts and ramps, so Airbnbs might be accessible. Ask in advance if you require accessibility features.

Getting Around Budapest

Almost all of Budapest's sights can be reached by public transport. Some bus and tram routes in the city centre have low-floor vehicles. Only metro line M4 offers a lift at every stop.

Taking the Waters

In Budapest, Gellért, Széchenyi, Lukács and Rudas baths are accessible. At Lake Balaton, the most popular beaches have barrier-free access to the water.

FREE TRAVEL

EU nationals over 65 can use public transport in Budapest and around the whole country for free with valid ID.

DINING OUT

Many restaurants, cafes and bars around the country are accessible, including their toilets, but these features aren't always advertised on their websites. Budapest has plenty of restaurants and cafes with streetside tables.

RESOURCES

Hungary4All *(hungary4all.hu)* A great resource for wheelchair-friendly activities in the city – especially if travelling with children who have limited mobility – with a comprehensive list of accessible attractions.

BKK *(bkk.hu/en/travel-information/public-transport/accessibility)* Has thorough information on getting around the capital. The Budapest Go app is an online journey planner that shows the quickest routes, timetables and the availability of low-floor vehicles.

The city of **Kaposvár** won an award in 2013 from the European Commission for its work on accessible tourism. It has more than 100 accessible pedestrian crossings, and the city tourist information centre offers braille maps and audio guides.

Digital Nomads

Nomadic Magyar tribes settled in the Carpathian Basin more than 1000 years ago, but these days, it's laptop-toting digital nomads flocking to this ancient land and its dynamic capital.

Why Budapest?

Easily satisfying the most important nomad necessities, Budapest's blisteringly fast wi-fi, abundance of remote-worker-friendly cafes, excellent coworking spaces and low cost of living grant digital nomads and location-independent professionals a high quality of life in a Central European location at roughly half the cost of other popular nomad hubs like Lisbon and Berlin. Budapest is safe too, with one of the lowest crime rates in Europe. Combine all that with a cosmopolitan student and expat community, stunning architectural gems, and tons of things to do and see, and it isn't hard to see why Budapest is becoming a popular hub for digital nomads and remote workers looking for a European base to call home.

GETTING SOCIAL

Rocking up to a new city without knowing anyone is of course a little daunting, but Budapest has an active English-speaking social scene of expats, international students and other long-term visitors. Meet people by joining the Budapest Digital Nomads Facebook group (facebook.com/groups/648464231947085) or by browsing local events on Facebook.

Costs

While you can expect to pay more for rent, utilities and dining out in the capital than elsewhere in Hungary, Budapest is considerably less expensive than other European cities. Although accommodation prices have increased in recent years, you can still snag a one-bedroom apartment in the city centre for less than €500 per month depending on the length of your stay. According to Nomad List, a helpful online resource for digital nomads, you can expect to pay around €2000 a month to live in Budapest as a digital nomad, making it one of the cheapest capital cities in Europe for remote workers.

Benefits

Budapest's famous nightlife, thermal baths and gastronomic offerings make for excellent after-work evenings out and weekend activities. Staying fit and active after a hard day's work is easy too, thanks to the city's well-equipped gyms, yoga centres and parks, such as Margit Island with its dedicated padded running track along the Danube. But be warned: you'll need to pack a fair degree of self-discipline to stay at your laptop instead of enjoying the city's cultural events throughout the year. You'll never be bored in Budapest, and many digital nomads stick around much longer than they'd originally planned.

Nomads shouldn't have any issue paying for their lattes and *lángos* with their foreign bank cards in this increasingly cashless capital. Google Pay and other mobile payment systems are widely accepted, and plenty of phone apps, like Foodpanda and Bolt, can take care of your food and transportation needs.

HOW MUCH FOR...

Monthly coworking membership
50,000Ft

Coffee
600Ft

Monthly public transport pass
9500Ft

Beer
500Ft

Lunch
1200Ft

Gym membership per month
13,000Ft

Monthly SIM card and data plan
4000Ft

Socialising

Often reserved and reticent, Hungarians are friendly folk underneath, and many, especially those under 40, speak excellent English. That being said, be prepared for a level of directness and honesty in interactions with locals that you may not be used to. But it's exactly this forthrightness that makes these connections genuine. You might need to try a little harder to make friends here, but once you do, you've generally made a friend for life.

As with any country, learning a little of the local lingo goes a long way, and it opens doors for social connection and community. As a non-Hungarian speaker, the easiest way to meet other nomads and English-speaking locals is through coworking spaces, Facebook and WhatsApp groups, and traveller- and expat-targeted events.

White Card

In 2022, the Hungarian government introduced a digital nomad visa called the White Card, giving non-EU nomads, freelancers and entrepreneurs the right to work and live in Hungary for a maximum of two years. The White Card has a strict income requirement (applicants must earn at least €2000 per month), as well as other criteria. Check official government websites for the latest information. For shorter visits, Hungary is in the Schengen Area, which allows stays of up to 90 days for some non-EU citizens.

RESPONSIBLE TRAVEL: NOMAD EDITION

The ability to work remotely and travel the world is a privilege not yet available to most people around the world. As responsible digital nomads and remote workers, we should work to mitigate the potential negative effects of our presence in local communities.

While we certainly stimulate local economies, our impact on housing markets can drive up prices to unaffordable levels for locals, effectively displacing them from their homes. At the same time, as more and more businesses cater towards the needs of nomads, locals end up getting the short end of the stick – like having their local fruit and veg shop turned into a trendy, air-conditioned cafe they can hardly afford.

We should also be aware of the impact we have on the environment through our travels, especially when we travel by plane. To minimise these adverse effects, choose lesser-known hubs to visit, spend your money at locally owned businesses and spread it around: don't just go to the same place every other nomad goes to. If possible, elect to travel overland by train, and get around by bicycle or foot once you're there.

All this being said, digital nomadism, on the whole, is a net good to the communities we visit, but we should always think a little harder and deeper about the effects we have on those less able to move around the world with ease.

Shaun Busuttil

HOW TO... be a digital nomad in Budapest

1. Find a Place to Stay

Compared with other European capitals, the rental market in Budapest is comparatively affordable, and Airbnb remains the most popular platform to find short-term accommodation. Longer stays, which generally have better rates, can be snatched up in Facebook groups. Visit Budapest, Hungary Apartment Rentals (facebook.com/groups/budapestrentals) and Budapest Flats and Apartments For Rent (facebook.com/groups/249052758449086) for listings. Many flats are specifically geared towards remote workers and location-independent nomads, and come with dedicated workspaces and fast and reliable internet connectivity. The 6th, 7th or 8th districts are the heart of the city, with plenty of cafes, coworking spaces, bars, restaurants and gyms within easy walking distance. For a more local, quiet and less-touristy slice of Budapest life, stay in Buda (and play in Pest) instead.

2. Pick a Cafe

Skip Starbucks. Budapest has plenty of remote-worker-friendly cafes with speedy wi-fi and ubiquitous power outlets with much better coffee. In fact, combining work with cafe-hopping is one of the best ways to discover the city. In Pest, top coffee spots include Flow (flowcoffee.hu), Fabrik (facebook.com/fabrikbudapest) and Madal Cafe (madalcafe.hu) near Ferenciek tere. Other cafes popular with digital nomads and remote workers are Magvetö Café (facebook.com/MagvetoCafe) and Massolit Books & Café (facebook.com/MassolitBudapest), both in the 7th District. On the other side of the Danube, Kelet Cafe & Gallery (keletkavezo.hu) serves great coffee and tasty treats and offers a cosy space to get work done in Buda.

3. Choose a Coworking Space

Remote workers seeking more structure and stability in their 'office' won't be disappointed with the range of coworking spaces in Budapest. KAPTÁR Coworking (kaptarbudapest.hu) and Impact Hub Budapest (budapest.impacthub.net) offer comfortable hot and fixed desks, as well as everything else you need to stay productive. These coworking spaces organise workshops and social events for learning and networking with other nomads and freelancers. If you prefer working from cafes but still want the social side that comes with a coworking membership, KAPTÁR has a membership package that grants you access to its community and professional events.

TRANSPORT FOR NOMADS

Getting around the compact metropolis on your own is easy. Budapest has an extensive and efficient public transport system, plus Lime electric scooters and the MOL Bubi bike-share network. Hungary's geographical position also makes it the perfect base for travel around Europe. Several capital cities are within quick and easy reach of Budapest by train, bus and plane: Vienna in under three hours by train; Bratislava in two and a half hours by bus; and Berlin, Prague and Warsaw just over an hour's flight. Within Hungary's borders, Szeged, Pécs and Lake Balaton are easily accessible by train and worth exploring.

Nuts & Bolts

OPENING HOURS

Normal business hours are 8am to 5pm. Businesses and government offices often close early on Friday afternoons.

Banks 8am–5pm Monday to Thursday, to 4pm Friday

Bars 5pm to late

Museums 10am–6pm Tuesday to Sunday

Restaurants 11am–11pm; breakfast places open by 8am

Shopping centres 8am–10pm

Supermarkets 7am–7pm Monday to Friday, to 3pm Saturday; some also 7am to noon Sunday, but others are closed Sundays.

Smoking

Smoking is prohibited in public indoor areas, public transport stations and around playgrounds.

Weights & measures

Hungary uses the metric system. Decimals are indicated by commas.

Toilets

Public toilets are rare and often unclean. In restaurants, paying guests may use the toilets.

GOOD TO KNOW

Time Zone
Central European Time (GMT/UTC +1) in winter, GMT/UTC plus two hours in summer

Country Code
36

Emergency Number
112

Population
10 million

PUBLIC HOLIDAYS

New Year's Day
1 January

Memorial Day of the 1848 Revolution
15 March

Easter March/April

Labour Day 1 May

Whit Monday May/June

Foundation of the State 20 August

Memorial Day of the 1956 Revolution
23 October

All Saints' Day
1 November

Christmas
25 December

Electricity 230V/50Hz

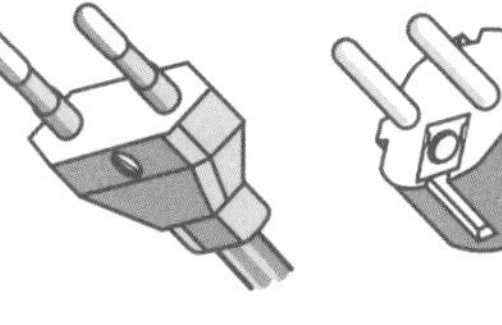

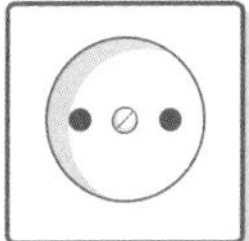

Type C
220V/50Hz

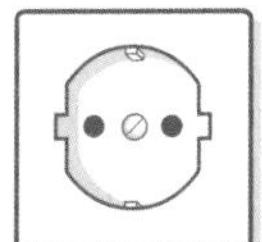

Type F
230V/50Hz

Language

Hungarian is a unique language. Though distantly related to Finnish, it has no significant similarities to any other language in the world. If you have some background in European languages, you'll be surprised at just how different Hungarian is.

Basics

Hello. Szervusz (singular). *ser·vus*
Szervusztok (plural). *ser·vus·tawk*

Goodbye. Viszlát. *vis·laat*

Yes. Igen. *i·gen*

No. Nem. *nem*

Please. Kérem. *kay·rem*

Thank you. Köszönöm. *keu·seu·neum*

Excuse me (to get attention). Elnézést kérek. *el·nay·zaysht kay·rek*

Excuse me (to get past). Bocsánat. *baw·chaa·not*

Sorry. Sajnálom. *shoy·naa·lawm*

Do you speak English? Beszél angolul? *pol be·sayl on·gaw·lul*

I (don't) understand. (Nem) Értem. *(nem) ayr·tem*

Directions

Where's (the market)? Hol van (a piac)? *hawl von (o pi·ots)*

What's the address? Mi a cím? *mi o tseem*

How do I get there? Hogyan jutok oda? *haw·dyon yu·tawk aw·do*

Can you show me (on the map)? Meg tudja mutatni nekem (a térképen)? *meg tud·yo mu·tot·ni ne·kem (o tayr·kay·pen)*

Signs

Bejárat Entrance

Férfiak Men

Nők Women

Nyitva Open

Zárva Closed

Információ Information

WC Toilets

Time

What time is it? Hány óra? *haan' āw·ra*

It's (one) o'clock. (Egy) óra van. *(ej) āw·ra von*

morning reggel *reg·gel*

afternoon délután *dayl·u·taan*

yesterday tegnap *teg·nop*

today ma *mo*

tomorrow holnap *hawl·nop*

Emergencies

Help! Segítség! *she·geet·shayg*

Stop! Álljon meg! *aall·yawn meg*

Go away! Menjen innen! *men·yen in·nen*

Call a doctor! Hívjon orvost! *heev·yawn awr·vawsht*

Call an ambulance! Hívja a mentőket! *heev·yo o men·tēū·ket*

Eating & drinking

What would you recommend? Mit ajánlana? *mit o·yaan·lo·no*

That was delicious! Ez nagyon finom volt! *ez no·dyawn fi·nawm vawlt*

Cheers! (to one person)
Egészségére! (polite) *e·gays·shay·gay·re*
Egészségedre! (informal) *e·gays·shay·ged·re*

Cheers! (to more than one person)
Egészségükre! (polite) *e·gays·shay·gewk·re*
Egészségetekre! (informal) *e·gays·shay·ge·tek·re*

NUMBERS

1 **egy** *ej*

2 **kettő** *ket·tēū*

3 **három** *haa·rawm*

4 **négy** *nayj*

5 **öt** *eut*

6 **hat** *hot*

7 **hét** *hayt*

8 **nyolc** *nyawlts*

9 **kilenc** *ki·lents*

10 **tíz** *teez*

DONATIONS TO ENGLISH

goulash, paprika, vampire

DISTINCTIVE SOUNDS

The Hungarian language may look daunting with its long words and unusual-looking accents, but it is surprisingly easy to pronounce.

Kissy Kissy

When two female friends or a man and a woman meet, they may give each other a kiss on both cheeks. Relatives also frequently kiss upon meeting one another. Men, however, normally shake hands. If your hosts or friends go to kiss you, remember to present your left cheek first. A polite greeting from children to adults, or men to women, is:

I kiss your hand – Kezét csókolom

While this is common to hear, you're not actually expected to kiss the person's hand as you say this.

False Friends

These words are not sexual invitations, so don't think you've got lucky if someone says them to you. *Ifjúság*, pronounced like 'if-you-shag', actually means 'young people', and *mi újság*, which sounds a bit like the caveman's invitation 'me-you-shag', is really 'What's up?'.

Must-Know Grammar

In Hungarian, the order of words in a sentence is more flexible than in English, but it's not entirely arbitrary. Hungarian emphasises words by bringing them forward to the beginning of the sentence.

WHO SPEAKS HUNGARIAN?

Hungarian is also spoken as a minority language in certain parts of Eastern Europe, such as Slovakia and much of Croatia, the region of Serbia and Montenegro known as Voivodina, and parts of Austria, Romania and Ukraine. This is a legacy of WWI. After their victory, the Allies redivided parts of Europe and formed new nations, with Hungary losing a third of its territory.

STORYBOOK

Our writers delve deep into different aspects of Hungarian life

Liszt Music Academy (p121)

A HISTORY OF HUNGARY IN 15 PLACES

From their nomadic origins in the Ural Mountains to their settlement in the Carpathian Basin more than 1000 years ago, the Hungarian people have a tumultuous history of tragedy, resilience and hope – universal themes that speak to the trials and tribulations of asserting nationhood and independence amidst a sea of oppositional actors.

HUNGARY IS ONE of the oldest countries in Europe, and its rural regions and urban centres bear testament to historical dramas that swept through these lands. This country has seen the rise and fall of empire and waves of foreign conquest while maintaining its declarations of a unique national identity. Hungary's influence on European history cannot be overstated, despite its relatively small size and population. A proud people with an indefatigable spirit and enviable record of achievement – in the sciences, the arts and scholarship – Hungarians have cultivated a rich cultural landscape over the centuries, a legacy born out of its strategic positioning at the crossroads of Central Europe. Yet Hungary and its people exude an unmistakable distinctiveness that sets them apart from their European neighbours, which extends far beyond their linguistic exceptionality. A journey through Hungarian history hints at these collective qualities, moulded through twists of fate and the roll of the historical dice.

1. Parliament

BIRTH OF BUDAPEST

Despite the country's ancient origins, the Hungarian capital is only 150 years old, created on 17 November 1873 after the merger of three cities (Pest, Buda and Óbuda). Designed by renowned Hungarian architect Imre Steindl, the palatial Parliament building features baroque, Renaissance and neo-Gothic elements, and was commissioned shortly after the capital's unification in an act of national celebration. Although officially completed in 1904, this symbol of Hungarian sovereignty and pride on the banks of the Danube was inaugurated in 1896 to mark Hungary's 1000th anniversary. Tragically, Steindl went blind before the completion of his masterpiece, dying in 1902.

For more on Parliament, see page 96

2. Aquincum

ROMAN ORIGINS

Like in much of Europe, the ancient Romans left their mark on Hungary. This open-air archaeological site in today's Óbuda bears testament to this period of history. Founded as a military and commercial outpost at the end of the 1st century CE, Aquincum was the capital of the Roman frontier province of Pannonia Inferior before succumbing to destructive ruin by marauding nomadic tribes from the east in 350 CE. Excavated remains of the town, once home to 30,000 inhabitants, include temples, an amphitheatre and thermal bathhouses. Legend has it that the Roman Emperor Marcus Aurelius wrote part of his *Meditations* here.

For more on Aquincum, see page 78

3. Basilica of St Stephen

A ROYAL HAND

Canonised in 1083, St Stephen, Hungary's first king, played a crucial hand in the creation of the country, and this mummified appendage of his is now on display inside this neoclassical cathedral in the heart of Budapest. Completed in 1905, Hungary's most sacred Catholic church was built to honour the patron saint who founded the Hungarian nation more than 1000 years ago. Besides housing ecclesiastical and symbolic treasures, such as the royal crown, the top of the basilica dome offers some of the best views of the city.

For more on the basilica, see page 98

4. Hollókő

LIVING CULTURE

Preserved as a living example of rural life and Hungarian folkloric traditions, this ethnographic village is an open-air museum and a Unesco World Heritage Site. The native Palóc community here speak a distinct dialect of Hungarian, prompting scholars to debate its origins, either as a Hungarian ethnic group made unique through separation and isolation or a distinct people who later mixed with Magyar tribes. As with much of early Hungarian history, it remains a mystery. Visit Hollókő in Easter when traditional costumes and folk traditions are on full, joyous display.

For more on Hollókő, see page 242

DIEGO GRAND / SHUTTERSTOCK ©

5. Great Synagogue

HUNGARY'S HOLOCAUST

For centuries, Jews enjoyed relative peace and protection in Hungary under strongman Miklós Horthy, and Budapest was home to a sizeable Jewish population. Tragically, the Holocaust decimated this community, with more than half a million men, women and children – 60% of Hungarian Jewry – sent to their deaths in Nazi concentration camps across Europe. Budapest's Great Synagogue (pictured) stands as a tribute to Hungary's Jewish heritage. Seating more than 3000 worshippers, it is the second-largest synagogue in the world. Next door, the Budapest Jewish Museum is the former home of the father of Zionism, Theodor Herzl.

For more on the synagogue, see page 116

6. Heroes' Square

A MILLENNIUM OF MAGYAR

In the closing decades of the 9th century, Prince Árpád and six Magyar chieftains lay claim to the Carpathian Basin. Shortly after, the first incarnation of the Hungarian state was born, making Hungary one of the oldest countries in the world. Construction of this square, the largest in Budapest, began in 1886 to commemorate 1000 years of Hungarian nationhood. This spatial symbol of Magyar longevity is populated with cast-iron statues of key figures of Hungarian history as well as the archangel Gabriel, who stands atop a 36m pillar brandishing the Hungarian national crown as an enduring testament to Hungary's Christian roots.

For more on the square, see page 138

7. Ipolytarnóc Fossils

PREHISTORIC PRESERVATION

Millions of years before Magyar tribes settled the Carpathian Basin, Hungary was submerged under a sea and later a jungle canopy. Around 17 million years ago, a huge volcano erupted, launching ash into the air and preserving a slice of Hungary's ancient geological past. Known as 'prehistoric Pompeii' and located inside the Novohrad-Nógrád Geopark straddling the Hungary–Slovakia border, the Ipolytarnóc Fossils Nature Conservation Area is a magnet for natural history buffs, with 17- to 23-million-year-old fossilised animal footprints, leaf impressions and petrified trees on display, as well as the ancient remains of sharks, dolphins and crocodiles.

8. Vörösmarty tér

WRITING A NATION

Named after a prominent figure in Hungarian literature, Vörösmarty tér in the centre of Budapest pays homage to a national hero. Born in 1800, Mihály Vörösmarty was a soft-spoken poet, playwright and patriot, and a fierce champion of Hungarian national identity. Using the pen as a weapon against Habsburg oppression that sought to suppress the use of the Hungarian language, his poetry explored Hungary's turbulent history as well as its contemporary political woes in beautiful Hungarian verse that was unmatched at the time. Today, Vörösmarty is most famous for penning *The Flight of Zalán*, considered the greatest epic in Hungarian literature.

For more on Vörösmarty, see page 95

9. House of Terror

BUILDING BRUTALITY

If these walls could talk, they'd scream. Hungary's subjugation under fascist and communist occupation is on brutal display inside this museum and memorial (pictured right), a former Nazi prison and secret police headquarters. Through multisensory and interactive exhibits and walls adorned with photographs of perpetrators and victims, this dark chapter of modern Hungarian history is brought to tragic light. In the basement, reconstructed prison cells once used to interrogate, torture and kill prisoners are a stark reminder of the cruelty of these successive murderous regimes.

For more on the House of Terror, see page 118

10. Pannonhalma Abbey

BENEDICTINE BEGINNINGS

This spectacular hilltop abbey in western Hungary played a pivotal role in the diffusion of Christianity through Hungary and medieval Central Europe. Not only did the Benedictine monks who founded the monastery in 996 convert the pagan Magyars into Christians, thereby nudging the nascent nation westward, but they opened the first school in the country, too. One of the oldest historical buildings in the country, Pannonhalma Abbey safeguards the oldest surviving document containing the Hungarian language, dating to 1055. Today, about 50 monks call the abbey home.

For more on the abbey, see page 176

11. New York Café

A MEETING OF MINDS

Built in 1894 during the height of Budapest's artistic and cultural renaissance, this opulent, neo-Renaissance-style cafe features marble columns, sparkling chandeliers and gilded features, prompting many to call it the most beautiful cafe in the world. But don't let its pretty face fool you. Like the coffee houses in nearby Vienna, New York Café was a meeting place for the city's writers, artists and intellectuals, making it an important urban institution and a place of political and social critique. Celebrated Hungarian novelist Ferenc Molnár wrote his most famous work, *The Paul Street Boys*, within these caffeinated walls.

For more on the cafe, see page 289

12. Mosque of Pasha Gazi Kassim

OTTOMAN OCCUPATION

Hungary's defeat at the Battle of Mohács in the 16th century by the Ottomans not only resulted in the death of King Louis II and approximately 20,000 of his soldiers, but it also sparked the beginning of 150 years of foreign occupation. Nowhere is this more visible than in the southwestern city of Pécs, which was transformed from a hub of ecclesiastical power into a western outpost of the Ottoman Empire. The Mosque of Pasha Gazi Kassim (pictured above) in Széchenyi tér is one of the finest surviving examples of Ottoman architecture in the country, bearing testament to this period of foreign rule.

For more on the mosque, see page 201

13. Kispipa Bar & Food

SOUNDS OF SORROW

Kispipa restaurant on Akácfa utca in Budapest once reverberated with the sombre sounds of Hungary's most melancholic songwriter. Famous for writing the international hit 'Gloomy Sunday' – blamed for a string of suicides across Europe in the 1930s – Rezső Seress was a Hungarian pianist and composer who performed nightly here in the 1950s and '60s to a motley audience of bohemians and the Jewish working class. Tragically, Seress ended his own life in 1968 after a lifelong battle with depression. The legendary restaurant has since been transformed into a chic cocktail bar that still pays homage to this iconic Hungarian musician.

14. Corvin Cinema

BATTLE SCARS

This 100-year-old cinema played a leading role in one of the most dramatic moments of recent Hungarian history. During the Revolution of 1956, freedom fighters László Iván Kovács and Gergely Pongrátz used the cinema as a rebellion stronghold against Soviet Occupation in the Battle of the Corvin Passage. Beginning as a protest against a faltering Hungarian economy, diminishing quality of life and mass unemployment, the uprising had a revolutionary zeal that was ultimately crushed 18 days after fighting began, despite significant military victories. Imre Nagy, the revolution's appointed leader, was executed two years later for his role in the rebellion.

15. Memento Park

DEMOCRATIC TRANSFORMATIONS

The collapse of the Berlin Wall and the removal of the electric fence between Hungary and Austria – both in 1989 – sent structural shockwaves throughout the Soviet Bloc. In Hungary, the political vacuum left by the collapse of the Soviet Union cleared the path for democracy, and for the third time in the nation's 1000-year history, Hungary became a republic. Memento Park serves as a memorial of Hungary's 40 years under Soviet rule. Statues of influential communist figures, such as Marx, Lenin and Béla Kun, were rounded up and laid to rest at this outdoor museum and socialist graveyard in southwest Budapest.

For more on the park, see page 70

MEET THE HUNGARIANS

Get to know a Hungarian and you'll soon find out that those notoriously not-so-smiley faces hide kind-hearted, funny and generous personalities. KATA FÁRI introduces her people.

INSTEAD OF DESCRIBING what my people are like, I'll show you. Let's imagine we're heading to the Hungarian countryside to visit friends.

Even the most die-hard urbanites want to keep a connection with the countryside, especially Lake Balaton, and nothing bad should ever be said about the 'Hungarian Sea'. We pick up a bouquet of flowers and a bottle of wine on the way because a Hungarian never shows up empty-handed. We're polite and punctual – being late is frowned upon. The friends we visit are welcoming, but they may initially keep you at a distance. Hungarians can be reserved, but they value and invest in long-term relationships. We make introductions, and you bet there's a Zoli, Peti or András in the group – Hungarian names get recycled a lot. They're also backwards, so Hungary has no 'John Smiths', only 'Smith Johns'. Women give each other two air kisses, and men shake hands. Say a loud *csókolom* to Grandma in the corner, which means 'kiss it' (their hand, of course!). We're family oriented, and it's not uncommon for multiple generations to live together. You may be asked personal questions – Hungarians are direct and tell it like it is.

Out come shots of *pálinka* (fruit brandy). Hungarian households are hardly ever without a bottle, usually homemade. The *pálinka* certainly makes it easier to learn those difficult Hungarian words as you're proudly told that it's one of the hardest languages in the world. You'll probably be taught some cuss words because we can curse eloquently. We're a clever nation – a Hungarian always finds the *kis kapu* (little gate), meaning the exception to a rule.

As the afternoon unfolds, we eat food that feeds the soul as much as the stomach, and we drink wine and beer. Drinking is an important part of social life but also a problem – alcoholism is prevalent. Witty jokes fly because Hungarians have a good sense of humour, but come nightfall, more mellow and serious topics may surface. It's a stereotype that Hungarians are always negative, but we do have a certain penchant for the blues and are prone to doom and gloom. To understand this sentiment, remember that Hungarians have been oppressed for centuries by the Ottomans, Germans, Austrians and Soviets, and we lost two world wars, two revolutions, and a big and prosperous chunk of our country. Even today, Hungary's future feels uncertain. We're not pessimistic; I'd rather call it cautious. We're resilient, too – we lived through the worst of times but managed to keep our customs, traditions and language alive despite great efforts to destroy them.

When it's time to go, you'll take some food with you because Hungarians are generous. I hope that one day you make this fictional gathering a reality because if you make a Hungarian friend, you're friends for life.

Budapest & the Rest

Hungary has a population of about 10 million, of which more than 1.7 million live in Budapest. The next most populous town is Debrecen, with only about 200,000 residents – quite a gap!

I'M HUNGARIAN, BUT WE'RE A MIXED NATION

I was born in Kecskemét on the Great Plain – but surprisingly I can't ride a horse – to Hungarian parents, but I have mixed roots. Most Hungarians do because the country has been invaded numerous times throughout the centuries, including by the Ottomans, Austrians, Germans and Soviets, so we're a mixed nation by default. I moved to Budapest to go to university, as many young people looking for opportunities do. Similarly to others in my generation, I've travelled extensively abroad. Many young Hungarians never come back, but foreigners often fall in love with Hungary and relocate here. Perhaps that's why I always come back, no matter how far away my sense of adventure takes me: Hungary is a wonderful country, and Budapest's beauty can truly steal your heart.

ARCHITECTURE IN HUNGARY

Hungary is an architectural treasure trove, with hundreds of beautiful baroque, neoclassical, Eclectic and Art Nouveau buildings across the country. By Steve Fallon

ARCHITECTURE IS INEXTRICABLY tied to Hungary's history, reflecting the good times, the spare times, the struggle for independence, wars fought on its soil and reconstruction.

Roman Foundations

The ancient Romans were Hungary's first master builders. By the end of the 1st century CE, they had introduced everything from writing to viniculture to their new province of Pannonia, but most importantly they brought stone architecture, establishing garrison towns and settlements to the west and south of the Danube River. Today, in cities like Pécs (called Sopianae by the Romans), Sopron (Scarbantia) and Szombathely (Savaria), you'll find Roman tomb sites, walls, forums and temples dedicated to the Egyptian goddess Isis by legionnaires. But no place in Hungary from this period is as complete as the Roman civilian town of Aquincum in the Óbuda district of Budapest, with amphitheatres, houses with fountains, and paved streets. The site has a wonderful exhibition on brickmaking and the use of *opus caementicium* (concrete), a Roman invention that allowed giant pillars to support heavy weights.

Remnants of Romanesque & Gothic

You won't find as much Romanesque and Gothic architecture in Hungary as you will in neighbouring countries – the Mongols, Ottomans and Habsburgs destroyed most of it here. When Stephen ascended the throne in 1000 CE, he ordered that a church be built in every 10 villages. Most were in Romanesque style, with a single nave, round arches and heavy column-like piers. Few survive, but the 13th-century Benedictine Abbey Church at Ják near Szombathely is a fine example of Romanesque architecture, with its showstopper *porta speciosa*, a stepped portal carved in geometric patterns 12 layers deep and featuring carved stone statues of Christ and the Apostles. The splendid abbey at Pannonhalma in Western Transdanubia is another Romanesque gem. In Budapest, check out the remains of the 13th-century Dominican convent on Margaret Island.

The first building erected in Hungary (in fact in all of Central Europe) in the new-fangled French Gothic style was the castle at Esztergom, started under Béla III (1173–96). Budapest's Royal Palace incorporates many Gothic features, including the sedile (niches with seats) along the Castle District's narrow streets and some carvings at the southern entrance of Matthias Church. The chapels in Pest's Inner Town Parish Church have some fine Gothic tabernacles. Sopron, Eger and Nyírbátor in the northeast also have important Gothic churches. For applied Gothic art, have a look at the 15th-century altarpieces at the Christian Museum in Esztergom and in the Hungarian National Gallery in Budapest.

Renaissance & then Ottoman Occupation

Renaissance architecture found royal favour from King Matthias Corvinus and his Italian wife Queen Beatrix in the late 15th century. They had Italian craftsmen rebuild the Gothic palace at Visegrád in the Renaissance style. The sheer size of the residence and its stonework, fountains and gardens were the talk of medieval Europe. The Corpus Christi Chapel in the Basilica of St Peter in Pécs and the Royal Palace at Visegrád both contain valuable Renaissance artworks. But the Hungarian Renaissance ended in the early 16th century with the arrival of the Ottomans, who destroyed some of its greatest achievements.

The Ottomans themselves left behind a small but often stunning architectural legacy of new and transformed buildings, such as the mosque in Pécs rebuilt from the ruined Gothic Church of St Bertalan and now known as the Mosque Church, the 40m-high minaret in Eger and several hammams (Turkish-style baths) in Budapest, including the Rudas and Veli Bej baths. One of the finest examples of sacral architecture is Gül Baba's Tomb in Buda's Rózsadomb district.

Bountiful Baroque

A large part of Western Transdanubia remained in the hands of the Habsburgs during the Ottoman occupation and was spared the ruination suffered in the south and on the Great Plain. After the Ottomans were expelled a century and a half later, the influence of Vienna only increased, and Western Transdanubia received Hungary's first baroque churches, extremely ornate structures that were the Roman Catholic church's response to the austere houses of worship of the reformed Protestant sects. They built many secular buildings in the baroque style as well, and the medium-light shade of brown that in the late 18th century became the signature colour for all Habsburg administrative offices – as well as many churches – became known as 'Maria Theresa yellow'.

You'll find examples of ecclesiastical baroque architecture in virtually every town and city in Hungary. For baroque on a grander scale, visit Esterházy Palace at Fertőd in Western Transdanubia or Eger's Minorite Church and nearby Archbishop's Palace. The ornately carved altars in the Minorite Church at Nyírbátor and the Abbey Church in Tihany are baroque masterpieces. In Budapest, visit the 18th-century monastery housing the Kiscelli Museum in Óbuda or the Nagytétény Castle Museum in the huge Száraz-Rudnyánszky baroque mansion in south Buda.

A Mix & Match of Revived Styles

In the early to mid-19th century, Eclectic style came into vogue. It has become the catchword for a style in which a single piece of work incorporates a mixture of elements from previous historical styles to create something new and original. The styles are typically revivalist – Renaissance, Romanticist, Classicist – and each building might be entirely consistent within the style chosen or an eclectic mixture. It can be argued that distinctly Hungarian architecture didn't come into its own until the mid-19th century, when Mihály Pollack, József Hild and Miklós Ybl were changing the face of Budapest or racing around the country building cathedrals, including the ones in Esztergom and Eger. In Budapest, Pollack was responsible for the neoclassical Hungarian National Museum. The neoclassical movement was a statement of intent, showing that Hungary was a heroic nation worthy of statehood. Indeed, less than a year after the museum opened, the poet Sándor Petőfi recited his 'Nemzeti Dal' (National Song) from the front steps, sparking the 1848 Revolution.

Hild designed St Stephen's Basilica, Hungary's largest cathedral, around the same time, but when the dome collapsed during a storm, it wasn't completed for another half-century and in Ybl's Renaissance revivalist design. Hild was also asked to design the Vigadó building, but money ran out, and it eventually went to Romanticist architect Frigyes Feszl. Both Hild and Feszl also submitted designs for the ambitious Great Synagogue – Hild's was neoclassical, Feszl's Byzantine – but Ludwig Förster's distinctive Moorish Revival plan won the contract. Two other Eclectic buildings that have become Budapest landmarks are Imre Steindl's Hungarian Parliament, which stretches along the Danube, and Ybl's sublime Opera House, with near-perfect acoustics. Hild also designed the 1836 neoclassical cathedral at Eger and later worked on the cathedral at Esztergom on the Danube Bend. The Esztergom Basilica was consecrated in 1856 with a sung Mass composed by Franz Liszt.

NADEZHDA BOLOTINA/SHUTTERSTOCK ©

NAME/CREDIT ©

THE 40-YEAR 'BIG SLEEP' AFTER WWII LEFT MANY ART NOUVEAU BUILDINGS BEATEN BUT STANDING – A LOT MORE, IN FACT, THAN REMAIN IN IMPORTANT ART NOUVEAU CENTRES SUCH AS PARIS, BRUSSELS, NANCY AND VIENNA.

Art Nouveau: Hungary's Signature Style

The art form and architectural style known in English by its French term Art Nouveau ('New Art') flourished in Europe and the United States from 1890 to around 1910. It began in Britain as the Arts and Crafts Movement founded by William Morris (1834–96), which stressed the importance of manual processes and attempted to create a new organic style in opposition to the imitative banalities spawned by the Industrial Revolution. The style soon spread to Europe, where it took on distinctly local and national characteristics. In Vienna, a group of artists called the Secessionists lent its name to the more geometric local style of Art Nouveau architecture: Sezessionstil (Szecesszió in Hungarian). In Budapest, the use of traditional facades with allegorical and historical figures and scenes, folk motifs, Zsolnay ceramics and other local materials led to a varied style. Though working within an Art Nouveau/Secessionist framework, this style emerged as something uniquely Hungarian.

Fashion and styles changed as whimsically and rapidly at the start of the 20th century as they do today, and by the end of the first decade, Art Nouveau and its variants were considered limited, passé and even tacky. Fortunately for the good citizens of Budapest and us, the economic and political torpor of the interwar period and the 40-year 'big sleep' after WWII left many Art Nouveau/Secessionist buildings beaten but standing – a lot more, in fact, than remain in important Art Nouveau centres such as Paris, Brussels, Nancy and Vienna.

The foremost architect associated with this style in Hungary is Ödön Lechner. Among his greatest masterpieces in Budapest are the Museum of Applied Arts, the Royal Postal Savings Bank and the Institute of Geology. Other fine examples of Art Nouveau include the Liszt Music Academy,

P279: Pannonhalma Abbey (p176); Above: Museum of Applied Arts (p133)

the Gresham Palace (now a Four Seasons Hotel) and the Párisi Udvar, a shopping arcade transformed into a Hyatt hotel. Art Nouveau doesn't just decorate grand buildings: walk around central Pest and an Art Nouveau surprise awaits around just about every corner, such as Lindenbaum House, the city's first Art Nouveau block with a front facade entirely covered in suns, stars, peacocks, flowers, snakes, foxes and long-haired nudes.

Beyond the capital, you'll find excellent examples of this style in Szeged (Reök Palace, 1907), Kecskemét (Cifrapalota/Ornamental Palace, 1902) and Debrecen (County Hall, 1912). In Pécs, visit the Zsolnay Porcelain Museum. Founded in 1853, the factory produced many of the majolica tiles used to decorate Art Nouveau buildings throughout the country.

Utilitarianism & Contemporary Architecture

Post-WWII architecture in Hungary is largely unexceptional. After the war, the new communist regime pushed art aside in favour of building hundreds of thousands of new homes in *lakótelepek*, housing estates of identical high-rise blocks. By no means luxurious or even attractive, they provided much-needed housing for those left homeless after the war, and many are still in good condition.

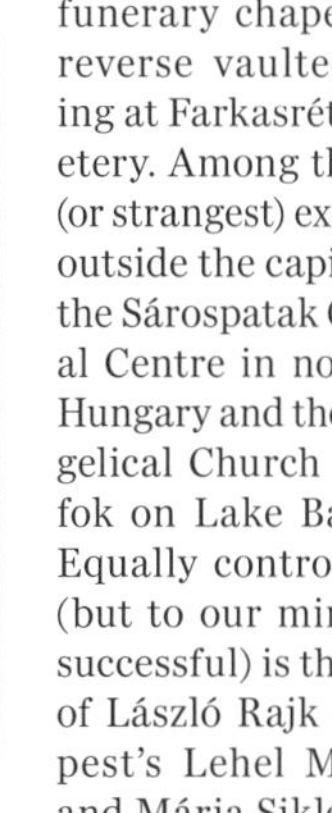

A TRIO OF RECENT BUILDINGS IN AND AROUND BUDAPEST'S CITY PARK WORTH A CLOSER LOOK INCLUDE THE JAPANESE-DESIGNED UFO-LIKE HOUSE OF MUSIC

One exception to all the post-war mediocrity is the work of Imre Makovecz, who developed his own 'organic' style using unusual materials like tree trunks and turf. In Budapest, take a look at his office building at Szentkirályi utca 18 and the spectacular funerary chapel with reverse vaulted ceiling at Farkasréti Cemetery. Among the best (or strangest) examples outside the capital are the Sárospatak Cultural Centre in northern Hungary and the Evangelical Church at Siófok on Lake Balaton. Equally controversial (but to our mind less successful) is the work of László Rajk (Budapest's Lehel Market) and Mária Siklós (National Theatre).

A trio of recent buildings in and around Budapest's City Park worth a closer look include the Japanese-designed UFO-like House of Music, the relocated Museum of Ethnography that rises high at both ends and has a rooftop green space, and the ING office building, with glass-and-limestone boxes bound by metallic 'ribbon'. Also noteworthy are the Bálna building, a whale-shaped shopping and cultural centre on the Danube; the M4 metro stations; and the László Papp Budapest Sports Arena.

Left: Evangelical Church, Siófok (p192); Above: House of Music, Budapest (p146)

FOLK ART:

EXUBERANT EXPRESSIONS OF HUNGARY'S SOUL

Hungary is rich in preserved and living folk traditions that express and cherish the bonds shared among people through time.
By Andrea Schulte-Peevers

FROM THE BEGINNING of the 18th century, as segments of the Hungarian peasantry became more prosperous, regular people sought to make the world around them more beautiful by painting and decorating everyday objects and clothing. The best place for a primer on the range and depth of their creativity is the Museum of Hungarian Applied Folk Art in Budapest, but several smaller collections are scattered around the country, including the Derí Museum in Debrecen, the Folk Art Collection in Kecskemét and the Bereg Museum in Vásárosnamény. The Budapest Festival of Folk Arts in mid-August is a huge showcase featuring the work of artisans from all over Hungary.

Embroidery: Traditional to Trendy

Embroidery is the pinnacle of Hungarian folk art, with three groups standing out for their acumen: the Palóc people of the Northern Uplands, especially around the village of Hollókő west of Eger; the Matyó from Mezőkövesd east of Eger; and the women of Kalocsa on the Danube south of

Tiszafüred ceramics

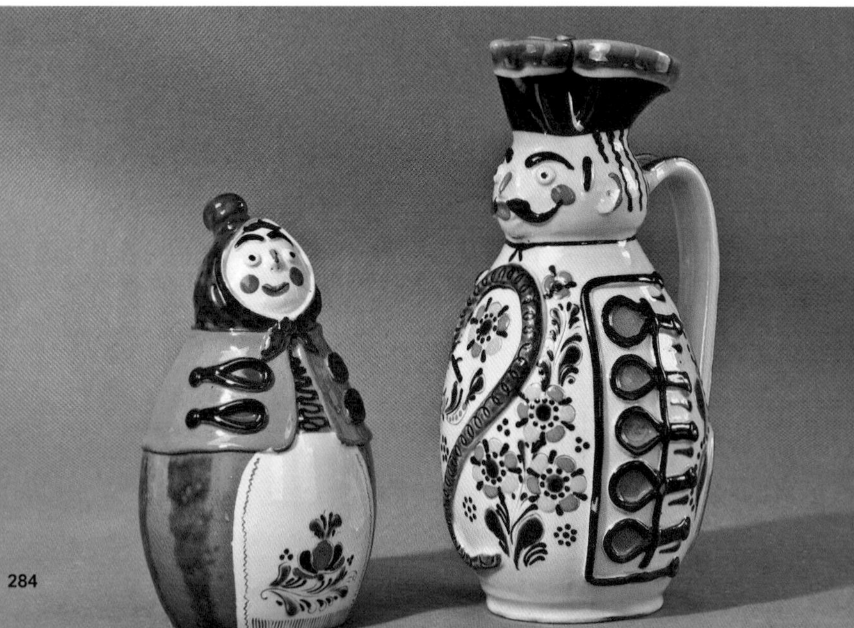

Budapest. The needlework of Matyó seamstresses is especially intricate and even made it onto Unesco's List of Intangible Cultural Heritage. In the village of Tard, it's possible to visit the workshop of Matyódesign, a company that has breathed new life into classic local patterns by applying them to chic styles worn by fashion-conscious folk in the streets of Budapest.

Power of Pottery

Hungarian folk pottery is world-class, and no local kitchen would be complete without a couple of pairs of matched plates or shallow bowls decorating the walls. The centre of this industry is the Great Plain – Hódmezővásárhely, Karcag and Tiszafüred in particular – though fine examples can also be found in Transdanubia, especially the Őrség region. Potters make jugs, pitchers, plates, bowls and cups; the rarest and most attractive pieces are the inscribed pots *(írókázás fazekak)* usually made to celebrate a wedding day. Vessels in the form of people or animals like the Miska jugs from the Tisza River region are endearing as well.

Another standout is the striking black pottery from Nádudvar near Hajdúszoboszló. The characteristic charcoal colour comes from the high content of red ferric oxide in the area's clay soil, which during the firing process yields high-quality black iron oxides. The whimsical floral designs are then etched into the clay with pebbles.

The most famous ceramicist was Margit Kovács, who combined Hungarian folk, religious and modern themes to create Gothic figures. The best place to admire her work is at the Margit Kovács Ceramic Collection in her hometown of Szentendre.

Kalocsa emboidery and lacework

LEFT: IGNIS FATUUS 99/SHUTTERSTOCK ©, RIGHT: VITFOTO/SHUTTERSTOCK ©

Tactile Textiles

The main centre of cottage weaving has always been the Sárköz region in Southern Transdanubia, and its distinctive black and red fabric is copied everywhere. Simpler homespun versions can be found in the northeast, especially around the Tiszahát. Because of the abundance of reeds in these once marshy areas, the people here became skilled at cane weaving as well.

Carvings, Furniture & Folk Painting

Objects carved from wood or bone – mangling boards, honey-cake moulds, mirror cases, tobacco holders, salt cellars – were usually the work of herders or farmers in winter. The shepherds and swineherds of Somogy County south of Lake Balaton and the cowherds of the Hortobágy excelled at this work.

Most people made and decorated their own furniture in the old days, especially cupboards for the *tiszta szoba* (parlour) and trousseau chests with tulips painted on them, the *tulipán láda*. Some of the finest examples around are the tables and chairs made of golden spotted poplar from the Gemenc Forest near Tolna.

Folk art spills over into fine art in the form of ceiling and wall paintings. Among the best and most charming examples of the former can be found in churches, especially in the Bereg region, as well as in Füzér in the Northern Uplands and the Ormánság. Outstanding folk art paintings, for instance by János Balázs and András Süli, can be admired in the Museum of Hungarian Naïve Artists in Kecskemét.

LANDLOCKED HUNGARY: CRAZY ABOUT WATER

Perhaps because Hungary is without a coast, water means much more to Hungarians than just a splash. By Anthony Haywood

HUNGARIANS LOVE THE water and water activities, but it's also an element of the country that unites and divides. The Danube, Europe's second-longest river, winds its way through three countries before it reaches Budapest, splicing the capital into two parts that were linked permanently by a bridge only from 1849. Beloved as it is, 95% of Hungary's surface water originates from the country's neighbours, making cordial relationships a necessity.

Roman Foundations

In the northwest, Hungary shares a reedy wetland and a large lake with Austria (Fertő in Hungarian, Neusiedler See in German). Fertő is the largest endorheic lake in Central Europe, meaning no water flows out of it. Despite this, the lake has a long history of shrinking and drying up, most recently in the mid-19th century. Today, parts of it are a transnational park, called Fertő-Hanság National Park on the Hungarian side. A bike path runs around its perimeter, but the part in Austria is the most accessible. The Hungarian section consists mostly of inaccessible wetlands of dense reeds that offer a habitat for birdlife.

No body of water in Hungary is more important than the Danube. After flowing through the heart of the capital, the river heads into the Danube-Dráva National Park on the Croatian border. It exits sublimely, flowing through a further six countries, before splitting into channels that drain into a Black Sea delta. It was from this delta that Greek sailors began edging their way upstream from the 7th century BCE. They called the river the 'Ister' and used stretches of it for trade. For the Romans, the river was named the 'Danuvius', and its waters formed the dividing line not only between north and south, but also symbolically as the border between civilisation and the barbarism they saw beyond.

The Danube is sprinkled with fortresses built to fend off invaders or to protect the spoils of victory. The Romans built defensive walls – the limes – along parts of its banks in the 1st century, and the civil settlement of Aquincum was protected by a military camp in the Óbuda district of

Budapest. The Huns and Magyars came, and then the Mongols, who raged through in the 13th century. In the 1500s, the Ottomans took over until the Habsburg armies routed them 150 years later. Today, these castles and fortresses towering over the Danube are spectacular vantage points for great views and historical explorations.

Against these impressive backdrops, cargo barges ply the Danube's waters, while hydrofoils and excursion boats set off from piers in the capital and elsewhere. Hungarians push off from the green banks of the Danube in kayaks and canoes to explore its backwaters. Swimming beaches and beach bars dot the river's shore. One of the Danube's most picturesque sections is where it makes an abrupt turn south, called the Danube Bend, and flows towards Budapest.

More than a Lake

Lake Balaton is Hungary's largest lake and the biggest in Central Europe, but it's relatively shallow and modest in size: just over 70km long, 14km wide at its broadest point and just 11m deep. But Balaton is larger than life for landlocked Hungarians, who travel to its shores to bathe in warm summer waters, cycle around its perimeter on the 210km Balaton Cycling Route, walk the hills, drink wine from local vineyards, or get together with friends in bars and clubs.

Balaton has always been a relaxing retreat, especially in summer. Much has changed since communist-era escapism, when party apparatchiks hung out in villas and dangled their legs in the water while trying to stave off an encroaching loss of power. The villas in the town of Balatonvilágos, on the northeastern shore just 70km from Budapest, once housed the highest and mightiest in Hungary. But families also enjoyed cheap 'trade union' holidays on Lake Balaton. Thanks to the lake's proximity to Budapest, it remains a popular place for carefree summers and splashy relaxation for all.

HUNGARIANS PUSH AND THROW A BALL AROUND THE POOL WITH GUSTO, BUT THEIR SPECIAL RELATIONSHIP WITH WATER GOES FAR BEYOND THAT.

Taking the Waters

Budapest is bubbling over with baths. Warm to scalding water, ranging from 21°C to 76°C, gushes from some 123 thermal and more than 400 mineral springs. A few kilometres west of Lake Balaton, Lake Hévíz is known for its curative powers and for being the world's largest swimmable active thermal lake. One far-fetched myth claims that Roman Emperor Flavius Theodosius was cured here as a child, which led to the creation of the lake.

Playing with Water

Hungarians are an Olympic powerhouse in water polo. When Hungary played the Soviet Union at the 1956 Melbourne Olympic Games shortly after the USSR crushed the Hungarian Uprising (known as the 'blood in the water match'), water, politics and blood flowed together in a sport Hungarians follow with pride and enthusiasm. Hungarians push and throw a ball around the pool with gusto, but their special relationship with water goes far beyond that. Water means many things to Hungarians: sport, dubious mythology, healing, politics, but above all, a leisurely escape into a different element despite living hundreds of kilometres from the sea.

P287: Lake Heviz (p197); Above: Water polo match, Alfréd Hajós National Sports Pool (p113)

COFFEE MEETS CULTURE IN BUDAPEST

Once the haunts of intellectual greats, Budapest's coffee houses were the birthplaces of important cultural moments, movements and works of literature. By Kata Fári

A TRIP TO Budapest isn't complete without visiting one of the city's historic coffee houses, many of which still safeguard their fin-de-siècle splendour. Grab a seat at a marble table to enjoy a cup of java and a decadent slice of cake, and take a moment to reminisce about all that's happened within these hallowed walls.

In the late 19th and early 20th centuries, Budapest's coffee houses were the centre of social activity, and they buzzed with life. Hungary's intellectual greats filled these spaces not only with cigarette smoke but also with bright ideas and enlightened thinking. The greatest men of the time gathered to discuss politics, gamble, relax and work. Women visited coffee houses less often because it was considered inappropriate to frequent these places on their own until decades later. Writers would linger for entire afternoons over a single cup of coffee, which already cost more than most of them could afford. Sometimes they paid with poems or a chapter from a novel, and one inventive cafe owner came up with the *javító kávé* ('enhanced coffee') that allowed patrons to add a little more coffee or water to their cup without being charged more. There was cheerful bonhomie among these men. Their intellectual exchanges inspired new architectural and literary movements, and contributed to the birth of many significant novels and poems.

So much transpired at Budapest's coffee houses that listing every significant event that took place and shaped Hungarian history, literature and culture would be no easy task. It was at a coffee house that young Hungarians gathered their grievances against the Habsburgs, which led to the 1848 Revolution, and that the editorial teams of two of the most influential newspapers at the time, *Nyugat* and *Hét*, were formed. The Hungarian Society of Impressionists and Naturalists (MIÉNK) was also born in a coffee house thanks to painters extraordinaire Pál Szinyei Merse, József Rippl-Rónai and Károly Ferenczy. Great writers put pen to paper in coffee houses, drafting the most significant novels and poems in Hungarian literature. These were the places to think and speak freely, away from the eyes of Big Brother. Perhaps this is why the post-WWII communist government closed most of them, but let's not rush that far ahead.

The Ottomans introduced coffee to Hungary in the 16th century, but the locals, being big wine drinkers, didn't care for it much at the start. According to local lore, the Ottomans invited a Hungarian lord for dinner, and when he was about to leave after the meal, the host said, 'Not so fast – the black soup is yet to come', referring to the cup of coffee taken at the end of a meal. But this sentence was also a secret signal to his

janissaries to capture the Hungarian. While it's questionable whether this happened – there are no historic records of it – the saying lives on. If a Hungarian says, *'Hátra van még a fekete leves'*, it means the worst or something significant is still yet to come.

Hungarians took a shine to java, and coffee houses started popping up in the 18th century. By the final decades of the Austro-Hungarian Empire, Budapest counted some 550 cafes, and all groups found their favourite. Actors preferred the Pannónia, painters the Műcsarnok and architects the Japán Kávéház. The Japán Kávéház was where Ödön Lechner, 'the Hungarian Gaudí' and master of Art Nouveau, taught his students, often drawing his designs on the marble tables. But the most important coffee houses of the time were Centrál, the New York Café and Hadik, all of which are still open and serving coffee.

Started in 1887, Centrál is the oldest of the trio, and the many literary luminaries who worked tirelessly on the *Nyugat* are memorialised in portraits decorating the walls. After thorough renovations, Centrál reopened in 2022, safeguarding its prominent past but with a progressive mindset. Though the dark wood panelling was removed from the walls and tan leather booths were installed, the stucco ceiling and marble tables still remind visitors of Centrál's glorious past. Besides coffee, it offers everything from breakfast to cocktails. As a nod to the cafe's olden days, you can select a poem from Centrál's collection for staff to read aloud at your table.

The New York Café opened in 1894, and rumour has it that on opening night, author Ferenc Molnár and his journalist friends threw the keys of the coffee house into the Danube so that it could never close. This might have actually happened in 1927 when the cafe reopened after WWI (as Ferenc Molnár was only 16 in 1894), but it is a significant event that since has been symbolically repeated more than once with a fake key. Regardless, the New York Café did stay open 365 days a year for many decades, and Molnár was a regular. He wrote one of the greatest Hungarian novels of all time, *A Pál utcai fiúk* (The Paul Street Boys), here. The New York wasn't just a cafe, but the starting point of modern Hungarian literature. It hosted virtually every writer of note and treated them kindly, offering a discounted *írótál* (writer's plate) with cold cuts, cheese and meat – even available on credit – plus free paper and ink. In the 1910s, filmmakers also made the New York their spot, and Mihály Kertész (Michael Curtiz), director of *Casablanca*, was a regular before Hollywood beckoned. Though the New York Café's interior still looks more or less the same as it once did, today's clientele is slightly different, with more tourists than Hungarian writers. But visitors are drawn for the same reason those Hungarian intellectuals were back in the 19th century. Decorated in gold, marble and red velvet, the New York Café is called 'the most beautiful cafe in the world'. Besides coffee and cake, you can try more nourishing traditional Hungarian dishes amid an aristocratic atmosphere, often while live Hungarian music is played.

Hadik opened in 1906, and while not nearly as ornate as the New York or Centrál, it became a literary haunt for writers in Buda. Ridiculing its less impressive interior, author Frigyes Karinthy – whose portrait you can still spot on the mural behind Hadik's staircase – compared this cafe to a shopping bag, which is why the ruin bar adjacent to Hadik today is named Szatyor Bár ('shopping bag'). Hadik is once again an established hangout for local creatives. Hungarian director László Nemes wrote the script for his Oscar-winning film *Son of Saul* (2015) here and donated two pages of the original work to the cafe. Hadik offers tasty Hungarian dishes, coffee and beer, and while the interior is now more modern and dominated by exposed brick, it has a few nods to the past, such as a classic chandelier, Thonet chairs and the Karinthy slice on the menu – the namesake author's favourite chocolate cake.

Budapest's other noteworthy historic coffee houses with impressive interiors are the Művész, Gerbeaud and Gerlóczy. While today the capital has more cafes than you can shake a stick at, and locals tend to frequent new-wave places instead of historic haunts, Budapest's classic coffee houses still stand strong as reminders of a piece of the past that Hungary will cherish forever.

New York Café, Budapest

BUDAPEST: THE HOLLYWOOD OF EUROPE

Hollywood heads to Hungary to make some of its biggest blockbuster films – here's why. By Kata Fári

EVEN IF YOU haven't been to Budapest yet, chances are you've seen its gorgeous Art Nouveau buildings, winding river and busy streets on the silver screen. Hungary is a hub for filmmaking and has attracted scene scouts for major Hollywood productions, including *Evita* (1996), *The Martian* (2015), *Inferno* (2016), *Blade Runner 2049* (2017), *Red Sparrow* (2017), *Midsommar* (2019) and *Dune* (2020). Why is it that Hollywood so often heads to Hungary to make its big films?

First off, it's cheaper. Production and employment costs are significantly lower in Hungary than in countries like the United States, and films made in Hungary also get great tax breaks. Productions that spend a big part of their budget in Hungary are eligible to receive some of the production costs back from the Hungarian government, an incentive that is proving fruitful for both sides.

Next, we can set the scene. With stunning spas, historic streets, belle-époque buildings and other architectural delights around every corner, Budapest is downright beautiful. The city's colourful and versatile architectural landscape – partly a result of the county's turbulent history and partly thanks to creative architects

Hungarian State Opera House (p105)

like Ödön Lechner, Miklós Ybl and Imre Steindl – gives Budapest a chameleon-like ability to stand in for cities from Paris to Moscow, Rome and even Buenos Aires.

If filmmakers require more far-fetched locations, Budapest still delivers. When *The Martian* needed a futuristic headquarters for NASA, Budapest gave the production team the Bálna building, a shopping and cultural centre in southern Pest. When *The Spy* demanded a glamorous casino, the Hungarian State Opera House stepped in, and when *Midsommar* wanted the serene beauty of the Swedish countryside, the capital offered its outskirts that are filled with lush forests and greenery. The contrasts of Budapest provide filmmakers with a catalogue of options: crumbling buildings next to cutting-edge glass structures, cobblestone streets next to fabulous modern avenues, and a busy metropolitan feel below hills and forests that are still within city limits.

EVEN IF YOU HAVEN'T BEEN TO BUDAPEST YET, CHANCES ARE YOU'VE SEEN IT ON THE SILVER SCREEN.

Bumping into a celeb on the street or at a local restaurant isn't uncommon. Because so many movies are made here, A-list stars often make Hungary their temporary home and end up falling in love with the country. Tom Hanks called Budapest one of the most beautiful cities in the world. Jennifer Lawrence praised the city's people and culture, even though she almost got into a bar fight. Kate McKinnon bravely rapped a Hungarian song in front of millions on the *Tonight Show*.

Bálna building

LEFT: MITZO/SHUTTERSTOCK ©, RIGHT: ARCHITECT: KAS OOSTERHUIS. BOTOND HORVATH/SHUTTERSTOCK ©

Filmmakers flock to Hungary for reasons besides low costs and Budapest's architectural diversity. The country also has skilled film crews and cutting-edge studios, such as Korda Studio in Etyek, which houses one of the largest sound stages in the world. NFI Studios in Fót boasts one of the biggest water tanks in the world, built for *Blade Runner 2049*. The studios also have backlots for scenes set in medieval or Renaissance times, as well as Wild West towns, New York City and American suburbia.

While blockbuster Hollywood films are being shot in Hungary, the country is also building its own industry. Hungary had something of a golden age of filmmaking in the 1980s, and director István Szabó won an Academy Award for *Mephisto* in 1982. Sadly, decades of creative drought followed, and Hungarian films were often considered low-quality and unprofessional. But ever since László Nemes' *Son of Saul* won an Academy Award in 2016, Hungarian film production has had a renaissance. Many noteworthy Hungarian films have been made since then, including the Academy Award–winning short *Sing* (2016), Academy Award nominee *On Body and Soul* (2017), *1945* (2017), *Aurora Borealis* (2017), *Bad Poems* (2018), *Sunset* (2018), *Ruben Brandt, Collector* (2018) and *Those Who Remained* (2019). Many Hungarian films are available with English subtitles on streaming platforms.

Next time you're watching a film, look out for beautiful Budapest locations on the big screen – and perhaps make a list of the spots to visit in person on your trip to Hungary.

HUNGARY'S GIFTS TO THE WORLD: 10 REMARKABLE INVENTIONS AND DISCOVERIES YOU DIDN'T KNOW WERE HUNGARIAN

Hungarians are well-educated people who have given the world groundbreaking inventions and discoveries. By Kata Fári

FOR A COUNTRY of its size, Hungary has a high proportion of Nobel Prize laureates, and its people are responsible for several creations and ideas you're likely familiar with but probably didn't know came from Hungary.

Hand-Washing Regimen, Ignác Semmelweis (1818–65)

Semmelweis is widely considered the first person to discover the medical benefits of handwashing. He found that childbed fever – a common and deadly illness in the 19th century – was spread by doctors who did not wash their hands between dissections and seeing patients, which transmitted infectious material from autopsies to susceptible mothers. However, Semmelweis' peers viewed his ideas with scepticism. He was ridiculed and committed to an insane asylum, where he died at just 47 years old after being beaten by the guards. Decades later, his hygienic recommendations were validated, and Semmelweis came to be known globally as the 'saviour of mothers'.

Pulitzer Prize, Joseph Pulitzer (1847–1911)

Born József in Hungary, Pulitzer was a publisher who left money in his will to create a prestigious prize for journalists, as well as a journalism school at Columbia University in New York City. Today, the Pulitzer Prize is synonymous with excellence in the fields of journalism, literature and musical composition, and it's an award many writers dream of achieving.

Kodály Concept, Zoltán Kodály (1882–1967)

If you've ever learned music, you've likely sung the scales and learned the solfege hand signs for do, re, mi, fa, so, la, ti, do. This teaching tool was developed by Hungarian composer Zoltán Kodály. He created the Kodály Concept, an experience-based approach to teaching basic musical skills and learning to read and write music.

Atomic Bomb

Five Hungarian scientists – Tódor Kármán, János Neumann, Leó Szilárd, Ede Teller

Left: Rubik's Cube; Right: Teqball match

and Jenő Wigner – were part of the United States' Manhattan Project, which developed the first nuclear weapons. Born and educated in Budapest, the scientists fled Hungary for political reasons and eventually emigrated to the USA. Because of the Hungarian scientists' heavy accents and peculiar native language, their American colleagues joked they might as well be from Mars and nicknamed them 'the Martians'. The Hungarians played up the joke, and when asked about the Fermi paradox ('Is there extraterrestrial life?'), Szilárd wittily replied, 'They are among us, but they call themselves Hungarians'. Teller was particularly proud of his initials (ET), and Kármán has a crater on Mars named after him.

Tódor Kármán (1881–1963) was an expert in aerodynamics and designed an early version of the helicopter, called Petróczy-Kármán-Zurovecz. He also led the development of the first helicopter that was able to hover while tethered to the ground.

János Neumann (1903–57) was one of the best mathematicians of his time. His most famous invention is the Von Neumann machine, the predecessor of modern computers.

Leó Szilárd (1898–1964) developed the idea of the nuclear chain reaction and designed the CP-1, the first atomic reactor, with Enrico Fermi.

Ede Teller (1908–2003) developed the world's first hydrogen bomb with Stanislaw Ulam, which was successfully tested in the Pacific Ocean. Teller and Ulam's hydrogen bomb design remains classified.

Jenő Wigner (1902–95) laid the foundation for the theory of symmetries in quantum mechanics and received the Nobel Prize in Physics.

Discovery of Vitamin C, Albert Szent-Györgyi (1893–1986)

Hungarian scientist Albert Szent-Györgyi won the Nobel Prize for discovery of the vitamin in 1937, and the story is particularly Hungarian. Albert's wife gave him paprika for dinner, but he didn't like it and took it to the laboratory instead and found that it contained large amounts of vitamin C. He came up with the name ascorbic acid, reflecting its antiscorbutic (scurvy-fighting) properties.

Ballpoint Pen, László Bíró (1899–1985)

A journalist by trade, Bíró was frustrated by smudges and leaks common in the pens of his time and noticed how quickly newspaper ink dried compared with his fountain pen. He teamed up with his brother György, a chemist, to develop a new type of pen made of a ball that turned in a socket filled with fast-drying ink. As the ball turned, it picked up ink from a cartridge and rolled to deposit it on paper. Today, the ballpoint pen is commonly called a 'biro' in many countries.

Hologram, Dénes Gábor (1900–79)

Electrical engineer and physicist Dénes Gábor invented holography, for which he received the 1972 Nobel Prize in Physics. Unlike photography, which only reproduces shapes and colours, a hologram also records volume in three dimensions.

Rubik's Cube, Ernő Rubik (1944–)

Hungarian architecture professor Ernő Rubik invented one of the most beloved toys of all time, the Rubik's Cube, in 1974. Rubik originally used the cube as a learning exercise to teach his students about 3D spaces. Millions are still sold and solved each year.

Microsoft Word & Excel, Károly Simonyi (1948–)

An early employee at Microsoft, Budapest-born software engineer Károly Simonyi was the man behind some of the company's most successful software, including Word and Excel. He's currently the only person who has been to space twice as a tourist and is only the second Hungarian in space.

Teqball, Gábor Borsányi (1977–) & Viktor Huszár (1985–)

Invented in 2012 by two football enthusiasts, teqball is a relatively new sport, best described as table tennis played with a soccer ball and players' bodies instead of paddles. Football clubs including Manchester United, Arsenal and Real Madrid have their own custom tables, and famous players include David Beckham, Ronaldinho and Lionel Messi. Teqball might soon even make an appearance as a sport played at the Olympics.

INDEX

Map Pages **000**

Map Pages **000**

"Vines have been growing on Lake Balaton's hilltops since the 1st century BCE, cultivated by the ancient Romans and medieval monastic orders."

Barbara Woolsey

"Standing majestically atop Castle Hill, the Royal Palace is one of Budapest's most emblematic and recognisable attractions."

Kata Fári

THIS BOOK

Design development Marc Backwell

Content development Mark Jones, Sandie Kestell, Anne Mason, Joana Taborda

Cartography development Katerina Pavkova

Production development Sandie Kestell, Fergal Condon

Series development leadership Darren O'Connell, Piers Pickard, Chris Zeiher

Commissioning Editor Angela Tinson

Product Editor Kate James

Book Designer Virginia Moreno

Cartographer Julie Dodkins

Assisting Editors Janet Austin, Lauren Keith, Charlotte Orr, Christopher Pitts, Saralinda Turner, Fionnuala Twomey

Cover Researcher Hannah Blackie

Thanks Esteban Fernandez, Gwen Cotter

Paper in this book is certified against the Forest Stewardship Council™ standards. FSC™ promotes environmentally responsible, socially beneficial and economically viable management of the world's forests.

Published by Lonely Planet Global Limited
CRN 554153
9th edition - July 2023
ISBN 978 1 78701 666 8

10 9 8 7 6 5 4 3 2 1
Printed in Malaysia